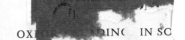

OXFORD READINGS IN SO...

Criminal Justice

D0264584

Criminal Justice

EDITED BY

Nicola Lacey

OXFORD UNIVERSITY PRESS

1994

Oxford University Press, Walton Street, Oxford OX2 6DP

Oxford New York
Athens Auckland Bangkok Bombay
Calcutta Cape Town Dar es Salaam Delhi
Florence Hong Kong Istanbul Karachi
Kuala Lumpur Madras Madrid Melbourne
Mexico City Nairobi Paris Singapore
Taipei Tokyo Toronto

and associated companies in
Berlin Ibadan

Oxford is a trade mark of Oxford University Press

Published in the United States
by Oxford University Press Inc., New York

British Library Cataloguing in Publication Data
Data available

Library of Congress Cataloging in Publication Data
Data available
ISBN 0–19–876362–X
ISBN 0–19–876361–1 (pbk.)

Typeset by Hope Services (Abingdon) Ltd.
Printed in Great Britain
on acid-free paper by
Biddles Ltd.
Guildford & King's Lynn

Acknowledgements

I am grateful to the Series Editors of Oxford Readings in Socio-Legal Studies for their invitation to prepare this collection, and to Richard Hart and John Whelan of OUP for their encouragement and assistance in, respectively, the earlier and later stages of the process. Lucia Zedner was, as always, extraordinarily generous in her perceptive remarks on an early draft of the Introduction, in her patient response to numerous telephone calls when I was agonizing over the choice of readings, and in sending photocopies whilst I was working on the collection further away from a library than any sensible academic would have been. Philip Drinkall did an excellent job of impersonating a criminal justice student whilst trying to have a holiday, and gave me some very useful comments on the Introduction.

I also have several long-term debts of gratitude which I am happy to have the chance to acknowledge here. First, I should like to thank the students on the Criminal Justice and Penology course at Oxford University whom I have taught during the last ten years. Their interest and enthusiasm has made teaching criminal justice one of the most stimulating parts of my job, and the discussions which I have had with many of them have been influential in forming my views about criminal justice and, hence, the shape of this collection. Similarly, my thanks are due to my criminal justice colleagues—in particular, Andrew Ashworth, David Faulkner, Roger Hood, Andrew Sanders, and Matthew Weait— whose energy and commitment to the subject have meant that criminal justice seminars and informal discussions have constituted a regular forum for the exchange of ideas in an otherwise fragmented working environment. I have also been lucky to have the intellectual companionship of and shared commitments with fellow members of the editorial board of *Social and Legal Studies*, in particular Paddy Hillyard, Joe Sim, and Carol Smart, discussions with whom are a source of both support and inspiration in my work in this field.

Most importantly of all, David Soskice has been accommodating my intellectual (and other) enthusiasms and allergies for the past decade with a degree of cheerfulness and generosity which contradicts all the assumptions of rational choice theory. I have discussed many of the ideas in the

Introduction with him and, as always, his critical acuteness and appetite for debate have been invaluable in helping me to develop my arguments. My deepest thanks go to him for the warmth and consistency of his support.

N.L.

New College, Oxford
January 1994

Contents

Note on the Readings

The readings which follow do not aim to cover anything like the full range of practices and agencies which are relevant to criminal justice: nor do they include contributions representing all the relevant disciplinary approaches. This would have been impossible within a collection of this size. Rather, the aim has been to include pieces which deal with some of the most important stages of the criminal process and which treat their subject-matter in such a way as to suggest ideas and critical approaches which may be pursued in turn in other areas.

The readings are organized in roughly chronological sequence, moving from those primarily concerned with the construction of crime to pre-trial processes, trial, and the articulation and execution of sentence. But many of the papers address several stages of the process or focus upon issues of general relevance and upon agents involved, formally or informally, throughout. A notable example in this respect is Shapland's piece on victims of crime.

Three main preoccupations characterize the readings in this collection. First, several are concerned with what might be called the 'big picture' of criminal justice—its significance as a source and symbol of social order, and its place and modes of operation within specific forms of political society. This is particularly true of the pieces by Box, Carlen, Cohen, and Hillyard, but it is an important sub-theme in those by McBarnet, Nelken, and Rutherford.

Secondly, many of the readings are concerned to advance our understanding of the nature of the discretionary powers wielded by agents at particular stages of the criminal process, and to illuminate our view of how those agents understand their own roles and responsibilities. These include the pieces by Ashworth, Box, Carlen, Eaton, Galligan, McBarnet, and Sanders.

Thirdly, many of the readings are concerned with normative and practical questions about specific reforms: with the politics underlying developments in criminal justice practices; with the general values and ideals in terms of which reforms may be framed; and with the institutional processes by means of which they may be realized. This is an explicit focus of the arguments by Ashworth, Daly, Galligan, Rutherford, and

Shapland, but it is arguably an implicit concern of every piece in the collection.

Many of the readings engage the reader's sympathy and imagination at the same time as appealing to his or her intellect, in a practical demonstration of the inseparable roles of the affective and the rational in the study of criminal justice (as indeed of all human practices).

The limited set of recommendations for further reading at the end of the collection is intended to fill some of the institutional and disciplinary gaps which inevitably remain, and to allow the reader to pursue some of the general theoretical ideas suggested in the Introduction in greater depth.

Introduction: Making Sense of Criminal Justice

Over the last twenty years there has been an explosion of interest in 'criminal justice'. This interest has spread beyond criminology departments to generate a wide array of courses and an extraordinary wealth of research incorporating law, politics, sociology, and other disciplines. Undoubtedly, the fascination of criminal justice flows, at least in part, from the cultural prominence of criminalization as a form of social control. One has only to open a newspaper or watch the television news in, for example, Britain or the United States to witness the extent to which crime, fear of crime, government criminal justice policy, and the activities of the more visible enforcement agencies such as the police preoccupy many contemporary western societies. Given its social and political prominence, the status of criminal justice as a particularly coercive and costly governmental repertoire claims our attention. Furthermore, the diversity of social practices encompassed within the notion of 'criminal justice', and the variety of practical, interpretive, and political questions which they raise, contribute to its interest.

Yet this variety can also pose difficulties for criminal justice students, who sometimes feel that they are presented with a fascinating landscape but little in the way of a map—or at least of a map which is of any interpretive use. All too often, the general 'theories of criminal justice' which purport to help us make sense of the concrete practices illuminated by empirical research turn out to be too abstract and/or too narrow in focus to fulfil that promise. The purpose of this Introduction is to make some suggestions about the sorts of theoretical framework which might enable us to make sense of criminal justice studies without imposing an unrealistically rigid or unduly circumscribed model on the complicated processes with which we are concerned. In developing these suggestions, I shall also be constructing an argument about the kinds of research that are illuminating and, in particular, about the relationship between 'theoretical' and 'empirical' work.

What is criminal justice?

At first sight, it seems relatively easy to define 'criminal justice': it is simply a convenient shorthand expression for the study of the various social institutions and practices concerned with identifying and responding to actual or suspected breaches of criminal law. However, this very simple definition immediately raises a number of important questions.

Crime and criminal justice

First, there is a cluster of questions about what, if anything, unifies the category 'crime', about what is encompassed within criminal law, and about how 'breaches' of criminal law are interpreted. As a starting-point, we could say that criminal law proscribes behaviour which is regarded by lawmakers as wrong, harmful, or otherwise socially undesirable. But this tells us little about what distinguishes wrongs for which lawmakers resort to criminal prohibition as opposed to, say, civil regulation. Nor does it give any hint of the complex factors which influence both the initial definition of something as a crime and its modification in enforcement practice. One of the main temptations which has to be resisted in studying criminal justice is that of thinking of the crime to which criminal justice agencies purport to respond as an unproblematic 'given', rather than as the product of a series of interpretive decisions.[1] These decisions, which, as we shall see, are made as much by unofficial as by official individuals and agencies, construct as criminal such a wide variety of kinds of behaviour that it is difficult to find any thread unifying them.

The focus of this volume is on the criminal process rather than on criminology or criminal law. In other words, it concentrates on the various practices which deal with those suspected to be or identified as offenders—policing, plea-bargaining, prosecution, trial, sentencing—rather than on the sources and interpretation of what is regarded as crime. None the less, we need to keep in mind that crime is the product of many layers of interpretation, and that this 'social construction' of crime is of constant relevance to both the practical operation and the social significance of all aspects of the criminal process. To take a few obvious examples, consider the attitudes of both ordinary citizens and the police to what makes people commit offences and to what count as 'real' or important crimes, or citizens' beliefs about the kinds of reported

---

[1] For examples of criminological analysis of these questions, see Steven Box, *Power, Crime and Mystification* (Tavistock, 1983), chs. 1–2; Carol Smart, *Women, Crime and Criminology* (Routledge, 1976), ch. 4.

crime (domestic violence as compared with burglary), and the kinds of reporter (a white middle-class householder as compared with a young black person living in temporary accommodation), that the police will take seriously. These attitudes have direct effects on citizens' reporting and on police investigative and recording practices. These practices in turn shape the partial enforcement reflected in the official crime statistics; the statistics feed back into the dominant social conception of the shape and extent of the 'crime problem' with which criminal justice is concerned, and, in a self-reinforcing cycle, the dominant conception flows on into reporting and recording practices. These are merely some of the ways in which the articulated legal definitions of crimes are modified in interpretive enforcement practice.[2]

Criminal justice as discrete?

Secondly, our initial definition raises the question of what, if anything, holds criminal justice together as a discrete area of study. This question arises at two levels. First, it arises in terms of the *approach* of criminal justice courses. Some texts on criminal justice proceed as if it were a distinctive or coherent discipline in its own right, as criminology has sometimes been taken to be. However, it seems more plausible to think of criminal justice as held together rather in terms of its subject-matter, in relation to which a variety of descriptive and normative intellectual projects are carried forward, employing the tools of a wide set of disciplines within the humanities and social sciences.

Hence, the question of discreteness arises, secondly, in terms of the *subject-matter* of criminal justice courses. Given the open-ended nature of crime, which encompasses a vast array of different activities, and given the variety of different agencies and practices involved in 'identifying and responding to actual or suspected breaches of criminal law', is it appropriate to start from the assumption that all are involved in the same enterprise? The paradigm 'response' to identified offenders is punishment. But practices of punishment are themselves very varied, and the

---

[2] For a more detailed account of this process, see Ch. 1 below; see also Paddy Hillyard, *Suspect Community: People's Experience of the Prevention of Terrorism Acts in England* (Pluto Press, 1993), ch. 12; Kathryn McCann, 'Battered Women and the Law: The Limits of the Legislation', in Julia Brophy and Carol Smart (eds.), *Women in Law* (Routledge and Kegan Paul, 1985), 71; Mike McConville, Andrew Sanders, and Roger Leng, *The Case for the Prosecution* (Routledge, 1991), ch. 2. The British Crime Surveys, which collect data based on victimization surveys, have helped to shed light on general patterns of non-enforcement: Pat Mayhew, Natalie Aye Maung, and Catriona Mirrlees-Black, *The 1992 British Crime Survey* (HMSO, 1993).

ideas informing them include not only distinctively punitive principles such as that of giving the offender his or her 'just deserts' but also quasi-medical or welfare-oriented notions of 'treatment' or 'rehabilitation'. We need to ask ourselves whether cautioning, conditional discharges, probation orders, intermediate treatment, and imprisonment can all be regarded as part of a coherent category of punishment—as penal in the same sense.

According to one view, it is possible to conceive of criminal justice as a 'system' or at least as an integrated set of processes all forming part of one overarching, coherent social practice identified in something like the general terms of our initial definition. Viewed in another way, however, it looks more like a diverse array of agencies and activities, all operating with their own discrete values and goals and employing different kinds of discretionary power, in an essentially fragmented set of practices. For example, even a single agency such as the police has various different sorts of responsibility, ranging from quasi-military functions of keeping order, at one extreme, to mundane administrative tasks and social-welfare work, at the other. These differentiated tasks are mapped onto a particular professional culture and a hierarchical command structure which are also important for understanding how priorities among the various tasks are determined and how those undertaking those tasks view their roles. We cannot assume, for example, that the goals and values of rank-and-file police officers are the same as those of officers in higher positions, and this makes a difference to how policies determined at one level of the hierarchy are understood and implemented at another.[3]

Criminal 'justice'?

Finally, our initial definition prompts reflection on the significance of the word 'justice' in this context. It could be argued that the inhumanities perpetrated within the criminal processes of most societies render the idea of criminal 'justice', or talk of the criminal 'justice' system, inappropriate. None the less, the word 'justice' is highly significant, for it marks the fact that the practices which form the subject-matter of criminal justice aspire to moral and political legitimacy, and do so in terms of certain values. Their conceptualization in terms of criminal 'justice' therefore has both sociological and normative significance. Sociologically, it signifies that the power wielded within the criminal process always has to be concerned with its own legitimation. Particularly in a society marked by persistent, patterned inequalities which are reproduced and exaggerated by

---

[3] See Peter K. Manning, *Police Work* (MIT Press, 1977); Robert Reiner, *The Politics of the Police* (Wheatsheaf, 1985; 2nd edn., 1992), pt. II.

state punishment, criminal justice is constantly at risk of being seen as cruel or oppressive, with consequent risks to the background support and compliance on which its stability and effectiveness depend.[4] Whilst criminal justice power is ultimately coercive, its exercise depends at almost every level on many forms of cooperation and consensus. Without these, the resort to coercion is liable to become both more repressive and less effective, because it serves to reinforce lines of social division and disintegration which are themselves implicated in the production of certain kinds of crime.[5] For example, it is widely accepted that the collapse of police–community relations in many urban areas of Britain at the time of the inner city disorders of the early and mid-1980s was both a product and a cause of police resort to 'hard' methods of law enforcement such as patrol by armoured vans and strategies of mass arrest; for the use of these methods reinforced the very mistrust of and sense of alienation from the criminal justice process which had made them appear necessary. They were therefore, even from the point of view of the police themselves, largely counter-productive.[6]

Normatively, the reference to 'justice' signifies the substantive ideals in terms of which criminal justice processes might be regarded as legitimate. Here again, however, we are met with a bewildering diversity of relevant questions. Is 'criminal justice' concerned with justice to offenders and suspected offenders, or to victims of crime, or to society as a whole? If it is concerned with all of these, how do these ideas of justice relate to one another and what happens when they come into conflict? We need to ask whether there is anything distinctive about 'criminal justice' as opposed, for example, to 'social' or 'distributive' justice in relation to goods such as wealth and political power. This raises general questions about the nature of social justice, and in particular about whether it is appropriate to regard justice as essentially a question of the fair distribution of rights or other entitlements, or whether justice is concerned equally or alternatively with fostering relations of reciprocity and an ethic of care.[7]

---

[4] In what terms criminal justice power may be judged to be effective is one of the central questions to be raised in this Introduction; the reference to 'effectiveness' here is not intended to evoke only 'hard' criteria of 'success' such as trends in officially recorded levels of crime or recidivism rates.

[5] For a more detailed argument about the relationship between punishment and social integration, see John Braithwaite, *Crime, Shame and Reintegration* (Cambridge University Press, 1989).

[6] See R. Kinsey, J. Lea, and J. Young, *Losing the Fight against Crime* (Blackwell, 1986).

[7] See Carol Gilligan, *In a Different Voice* (Harvard University Press, 1982); for a discussion of the specific relevance of competing ideas of justice to criminal justice and to gender issues, see Ch. 8 below.

If we regard 'criminal justice' as to some extent discrete, this suggests that there can be 'criminal justice' even in an otherwise unjust society: criminal justice practices may contribute to the overall balance of justice in society even if they also inevitably perpetrate injustices. Yet the inter-action of criminal justice and wider social justice is clear. In a society in which people are very differently situated in relation to the proscriptions of criminal law, and in which factors such as race, ethnicity, nationality, class, gender, and age widely affect not only life chances in general but also official and unofficial beliefs about people's predispositions to break criminal laws, the impact of criminal justice is virtually certain to be very unequal. Most people would agree that persistent patterns of unequal impact raise, at the very least, important prima-facie questions of social justice. Here we touch on questions which have preoccupied scholars seeking to produce general 'theories of criminal justice' or 'penal philosophies'. We shall return in due course to consider what such theories have to offer at either a normative or an explanatory level.

The diversity of criminal justice

The issues raised by each of these questions need to be borne in mind as we move on to think about the range of agents, institutions, and processes which are comprehended within 'criminal justice' as character-ized by our preliminary definition. Once we have assessed the extent of the practical diversity of criminal justice, we shall be better equipped to reconsider how the definition needs to be modified. For the moment, we need to attend to three main dimensions of criminal justice: two having to do with criminal justice practices, and the third with disciplinary approaches to criminal justice. In the following discussion, I shall be tak-ing the criminal process in England and Wales as my model. However, most of the general points to which I shall be drawing attention are of direct relevance to many other systems.

Criminal justice agents and their social identities

The first thing to consider is the range of people involved in decision-making and action relevant to criminal justice. I shall speak of them as 'agents' so as to mark their important influence. But we should bear in mind that the social identities of these agents—the roles they are play-ing, the professional groupings within which they are acting, and the cul-tures, incentive structures, and values which these encompass—are always relevant in trying to understand agents' behaviour; for, inevitably, they provide the context in which decisions are made and actions taken.

When we think about criminal justice, the agents who immediately come to mind are the official groups directly involved in the administration of the criminal process: the *police*, the *Attorney-General*, the *Director of Public Prosecutions*, the *Crown Prosecution Service and other official prosecuting authorities*, *defence lawyers*, the *magistrature*, the *judiciary*, the *probation service*, the *prison service*, the *Parole Board*, the *relevant sections of the Home Office*. Each of these groups has a wide range of discretionary powers relevant to the enforcement of criminal laws. Many of these powers flow from primary legislation, delegated legislation, and other official sources such as common law or Home Office circulars. But significant discretionary powers are simply what we might call 'situational': that is, they are implicit within a particular operational or administrative context. For example, a police officer patrolling his or her beat is equipped with certain explicit powers, notably under the Police and Criminal Evidence Act 1984. However, he or she is also vested with considerable discretion as to how those formal powers are to be exercised: which among many possible candidates should be stopped and questioned; which parts of the beat should be most intensively patrolled. Similarly, magistrates and judges hearing a case are vested with formal powers under legislation, but they also have discretionary powers which are implicit within the trial situation: the choice of demeanour towards witnesses, the terms in which a sentence is expressed, and so on. It is therefore important to be acquainted not only with the formal scope of official agencies' powers but also with information about how they are exercised and the practical contexts in which that exercise takes place.

Yet a full picture cannot be gained merely by learning the legal status of these official groups or by considering evidence about their activities and institutional context, important though these things are. To get a real sense of how their discretionary powers are exercised, we also need to know a great deal about the cultural context in which these agents are operating, and about how they themselves see their task. For example, legal and quantitative empirical work on the police has increasingly been supplemented by ethnographic and other agent-centred research which tries to shed light on how police officers see their role and how the values and culture of the police service affect the nature and priorities of policing.[8] This kind of research is more advanced in relation to the police and

---

[8] See n. 3.

the prison service than to the other groups we have mentioned.[9] In the case of the police, research has thrown light not only on qualifications, training, and day-to-day activities but also on factors such as police attitudes to their various responsibilities and the people with and for whom they work, their political views, the central roles of racism and sexism in police culture, their sense of their own social status, the strength of their identification with their professional role, and the impact this has on who they associate with, where they live, and so on. This sort of research would be equally illuminating in the case of other agents such as the magistrature and the judiciary, defence lawyers, the Crown Prosecution Service, and probation officers. It could help us to attain a fuller understanding not only of their behaviour but also of how their powers might be structured and their activities rendered more accountable.

The agents mentioned so far all operate within some clear professional or official context, and most of them hold public office and wield coercive and/or interpretive powers which have been explicitly delegated to them by state authority. But it would be a great mistake to assume that criminal justice has only to do with the state or state-sponsored agencies, or indeed that only the decisions and actions of those with an explicit official role are relevant to the administration of the criminal process. It is one of the most neglected features of that process that its whole operation depends on the decisions and actions of *ordinary citizens*.[10]

The roles played by citizens are themselves very varied. *First*, they have a role as electors and, hence, as the group to whom the public law-making and law-enforcing agencies are ultimately accountable. This is important because of its connection with the sociological question of legitimation already mentioned. *Secondly*, citizens report suspected offences, give information to the police and other official agencies, act as witnesses in trials, and so forth. Since the vast majority of recorded offences come to the notice of the police by citizen report rather than by detection,[11] and since cases cannot be constructed by the police and prosecution, or administered by the court, without the input of those with relevant evidence to give, this role of citizens is of central importance to

[9] *Staff Attitudes in the Prison Service* (HMSO, 1985); Vivien Stern, *Bricks of Shame* (Penguin, 1987; 2nd edn. 1993), ch. 5; see also Andrew Rutherford, *Criminal Justice and the Pursuit of Decency* (Oxford University Press, 1993).

[10] I use the term 'citizen' as a convenient shorthand, but I do not mean to obscure the significance of formal citizenship status in the application of criminal justice power to particular people.

[11] The figure has been estimated at between 77% and 96% of crimes recorded by the police: see Keith Bottomley and Ken Pease, *Crime and Punishment: Interpreting the Data* (Open University Press, 1986), 34.

the administration of the criminal process. Furthermore, it entails that, where citizens regard official criminal justice power as illegitimate, or mistrust criminal justice agencies, large segments of potentially criminal behaviour will go unadministered. *Thirdly*, citizens may be called to serve on juries in Crown Court trials—a function whose literal role in fact-finding is at least matched by its ideological importance in legitimating the imposition of coercive criminal justice power. *Fourthly*, citizens become involved in criminal justice as victims of crime. This will often involve reporting or giving evidence; in some systems it may also involve more direct participation in the administration of the process, through mediation schemes, through schemes requiring victims to be consulted at various decision-making junctures, and even through their delivering statements about the impact of crimes upon them immediately prior to sentence.[12]

Fifthly, citizens become involved in criminal justice as offenders or suspected offenders. This role is often ignored in considering how criminal justice is administered, because the position of the defendant is generally regarded as a powerless and relatively passive one. Whilst there is a truth in this, it is also important to realize that defendants—and particularly certain kinds of defendant—sometimes play a more proactive role than the conventional picture assumes. They do so, typically, by using what power they have outside the criminal process to negotiate or manipulate the ways in which and the extent to which criminalizing norms are applied to them. The obvious example is that of powerful corporations, but wealthy or otherwise influential individuals may also be involved in what have been called strategies of 'creative compliance'.[13] *Sixthly*, lay volunteers have an important place in the administration of the criminal process. In assisting victims, helping to run community-based penalties, developing crime-prevention initiatives such as neighbourhood watch schemes, and in many other ways, volunteers play an important role in criminal justice.[14] The separation between 'lay' and 'official' input into criminal justice practice should not be exaggerated, however. State officials and norms are still influential in lay practice, and the volunteer role is often realized in terms of particular, relatively formalized institutions.

[12] See Ch. 13 below.

[13] See Doreen J. McBarnet and Christopher Whelan, 'The Elusive Spirit of the Law: Formalism and the Struggle for Legal Control' (1991) 54 *Modern Law Review*; Doreen J. McBarnet, 'It's Not What You Do but the Way that You Do It', in D. Downes (ed.), *Unravelling Criminal Justice* (Macmillan, 1992), 247.

[14] R. I. Mawby, 'The Voluntary Sector's Role in a Mixed Economy of Criminal Justice', in R. Matthews (ed.), *Privatizing Criminal Justice* (Sage, 1989), 135.

Good examples would be Prison Boards of Visitors and, within the police, Police Consultative Committees and Special Constables, each of which has both important practical functions and a crucial role in adding legitimizing to the process. Lay magistrates might also be looked at in this way. *Finally*, private commercial enterprises are increasingly involved in the administration of criminal justice. Business is involved in a range of what might be seen as criminal justice functions, such as running privatized prisons, undertaking security, policing, and law-enforcement arrangements in a vast number of public and private spaces, and administering electronic surveillance systems.[15]

Two further sets of agents call for special mention. First, *politicians*—notably the government, but also the opposition front bench—have a distinctive role in criminal justice. Their importance lies not only in the fact that the government has direct control of legislative and other policy-making responsibilities with respect to the administration of criminal justice.[16] It lies also in the fact that the terms in which political debate about criminal justice takes place can have a strong influence on the relevant attitudes and dispositions of citizens and other agents. It can, moreover, do so in ways which render politicians' concern with the legitimation of criminal justice power and of government's role as an effective 'manager' of the criminal process very difficult to realize.[17] For example, consider a politics which places intense emphasis on 'law and order' problems, accompanied by increased investment in aspects of the criminal process such as policing and prisons—a combination found in Britain since the late 1970s. Such a politics is likely to generate both a greater awareness and fear of crime (and hence willingness to report it) and a greater capacity in enforcement agencies to process and record complaints. Given the gap between the levels of crime which might be reported and recorded and that which actually is, a greater emphasis on law and order in fact tends to lead to an apparent worsening of the problem.

Furthermore, general governmental economic and social policy clearly has material implications for criminal justice. To take some examples, the sale of council housing in the 1980s in Britain vastly increased the number of home owners and, consequently, of those with home insurance. It is widely thought that this was an important factor in producing a rise in

---

[15] See Les Johnston, *The Rebirth of Private Policing* (Routledge, 1992), chs. 4–5.

[16] See Ch. 12 below.

[17] For further discussion of the discourse of government managerialism in criminal justice, see Nicola Lacey, 'Government as Manager, Citizen as Consumer', Vol. 57 *Modern Law Review* (1994).

the recorded rate of property crime, as a greater proportion of victims of theft and burglary had the direct incentive of insurance requirements to report their loss. More broadly, a government's economic and social policies may reinforce existing social divisions, particularly in terms of the distribution of long-term unemployment. Where this is the case, it creates conditions in which certain kinds of offending are likely to arise and in which the prospects for criminal justice power being exercised in a positive and reintegrative way, as opposed to acting as a stigmatizing and disintegrative social force, are correspondingly reduced.[18]

The second set of agents deserving special mention is the news *media* and, indeed, the media of popular culture, whose importance in propagating images of the 'crime problem' and of law-enforcement activities should not be overlooked. These images may have very important effects on factors such as the level and intensity of fear of crime, disposition to report offences, satisfaction with the administration of the criminal process, and perceptions of legitimacy. The conduct of the media therefore has direct implications for how the relevant roles and activities of the agents concerned are perceived and practised.[19]

We have considerably broadened our horizons relative to those of the original identification of official criminal justice agents and agencies. The list of relevant agents could be almost endlessly extended. To give just a few examples, there are the public and private forensic science services, whose work can produce crucial evidence in the construction of cases; public bodies such as the Serious Fraud Office and the Factories and Health and Safety Inspectorates; the medical and, particularly, psychiatric professions; and social workers. In the case of each set of agents, questions relevant to criminal justice include not only their observable actions but also their goals, concerns, values—what they think criminal justice is all about, and their role within it. Also relevant are their resources and capacities for coordinated action (both within their own agencies and with other institutions). To some extent these will be relative to their particular professional or institutional context: that is, to their specific social identity. But equally relevant are broader aspects of social organization which have a pervasive influence within both individual consciousness and social institutions. In particular, assumptions based on significant social divisions organized

[18] See Braithwaite, *Crime, Shame, and Reintegration*, and Ch. 1 below.

[19] See Stuart Hall, Chas Critcher, Tony Jefferson, John Clarke, and Brian Roberts, *Policing the Crisis: Mugging, the State and Law and Order* (Macmillan, 1978), ch. 3; Steve Chibnall, *Law-and-Order News* (Tavistock, 1977); Stanley Cohen, *Folk Devils and Moral Panics* (St Martin's Press, 1972).

around socio-economic class, ethnicity, race, gender, and age are likely to be important in influencing how these various agents wield the discretionary power their role in criminal justice accords them.

Practices within the criminal process

Cutting across the divisions among the relevant agents mentioned above, the second thing to consider is the diversity of practices and decisions encompassed within criminal justice, each of which is characterized by its own practical imperatives and normative preoccupations. At first sight, the idea that criminal justice is concerned with identifying and punishing offenders seems rather straightforward. But a moment's thought about the various stages involved in the administration of even the relatively rare case which does run through from initial suspicion to formal punishment, and about the myriad institutions which may be involved in this process, displaces the initial impression of simplicity. Taken as a whole, only a small proportion even of recorded offences results in a conviction.[20] Furthermore, even among cases resulting in formal conviction, only a very small number attract the full panoply of a trial as opposed to a plea of guilty followed by sentence. Many other recorded offences involve someone's being cautioned, bound over to keep the peace, or otherwise diverted from the full criminal process. Naturally, the proportion of cases formally followed through is strongly related to the type of offence in question.[21] A person suspected of homicide will almost certainly be proceeded against, even in the face of medical evidence which suggests that they were mentally incapacitated at the time of the offence, whereas a person suspected of theft has a far higher likelihood of being cautioned or even ignored. But, as we shall see, the type of offence is far from being the only important factor in determining whether or not a potential criminal case becomes an actual one.

[20] The *1988 British Crime Survey* estimated that only 3% of all offences committed result in a conviction; this figure rises to 4% if cautions are included. The survey estimated that 41% of all offences are reported, 26% are recorded, and a mere 7% are cleared up. See *A Digest of Information on the Criminal Justice System*, ed. Gordon C. Barclay (Home Office Research and Statistics Dept., 1991), 31. The *1992 British Crime Survey* estimated the proportion of offences committed resulting in a conviction as 2%; it is estimated that 3% result in a caution, with 7% being cleared up, 30% recorded, and 50% reported: *Digest 2: Information on the Criminal Justice System in England and Wales*, ed. Gordon C. Barclay (Home Office Research and Statistics Dept., 1993), 29.

[21] The *1992 British Crime Survey* estimates that, in the case of wounding, 48% of all offences are reported, 25% are recorded, 19% are cleared up, 14% result in a conviction or caution, and 10% result in a conviction. The relevant figures for burglary are 73%, 46%, 11%, 3%, and 3%; and, for vandalism, 27%, 15%, 3%, 1%, and 1.5%.

In this section, I shall look at the administration of criminal justice, organized, for the purposes of the exposition, as a roughly chronological series of practices. Each of these stages can be regarded as a kind of filter, drawing in and filtering out certain possible cases according to a more or less distinctive, conscious or unconscious, determinate or open-ended decision-making process.[22] First, there is the construction of a particular action or event as criminal. This, as we have already seen, is itself a complex process, involving not only formal law-making but also, crucially, a number of interpretive decisions on the part of witnesses and/or the police. The relevant context therefore includes media interpretations of crime, the activities of pressure groups, and social practices aimed at 'crime prevention'—neighbourhood-watch schemes and vigilante organizations, for example—all of which are likely to influence official and unofficial attitudes about what kinds of behaviour constitute the 'real' or most important crime problems confronted by society.

At least as soon as a suspected offence is reported to the police, a process of official yet largely invisible interpretive construction begins. In deciding whether or not to take a particular kind of crime seriously— indeed, whether to take a particular *reporter* seriously or not—the police, who have the major investigatory resources in most cases, begin a process which transforms the case. Cases do not simply come into the world 'weak' or 'strong'; to a significant extent, they are made so by the commitment or non-commitment of investigatory resources.[23] In making the relevant decisions, the police will be preoccupied by a number of different concerns: available resources; the need to present themselves as efficient to both the public and central government; values about what constitutes 'real' crime; specific policies such as Home Office guidelines on cautioning and general predispositions to caution or otherwise divert certain kinds of offender (the young, the mentally ill, the 'respectable' first offender) from the formal criminal process; perceptions of local or national 'crime problems' and special powers related to these (such as the Prevention of Terrorism Acts); prejudices about groups seen as likely to be involved in crime; concerns about relations with the local community. Thus, the whole conduct of police investigations—distribution of resources and operational priorities, proportion and patterns of cases taken up, styles and thoroughness of questioning—is central to how the cases which get further into the system are selected and presented.[24]

[22] For persuasive use of the metaphors of filters and nets, see Ch. 10 below.
[23] For further discussion of these ideas, see Chs. 1 and 3 below, and Bottomley and Pease, *Crime and Punishment*, chs. 1–2.   [24] See n. 2.

These practices ultimately result in *a decision that no crime has taken place ('no-criming'); to take no further action; to caution the offender; or to refer to the Crown Prosecution Service (CPS)*. The police therefore send only a selection of cases to the CPS. This body, which is formally independent of the police, is entrusted with the *decision whether to prosecute* within a delegated statutory framework which directs it to consider whether or not there is a reasonable prospect of conviction and, if so, whether a prosecution is in the public interest. Clearly, this framework for the structuring of prosecution discretion leaves a significant margin for the operation of other concerns—local resources and priorities among offences, for example. Whilst the CPS is independent in the sense that it can refuse to proceed with a case referred to it by the police, it cannot be aware of cases never referred to it in the first place, and is more-over heavily dependent on the quality of the case already constructed by the police. Therefore the decision to prosecute is a product of discretionary decision-making not only by the CPS but also by the police. Apart from the decision to prosecute, the CPS also has responsibility for *preparing the prosecution case for trial* and, therefore, for further building up its strengths and removing its weaknesses. Whilst the police and the CPS have some claim to count as the paradigm investigatory and prosecution agencies, many other official bodies, such as the Health and Safety Inspectorate and the Serious Fraud Office, are also involved, as are private agencies such as store detectives (occasionally even to the extent of taking private prosecutions). At this stage defendants charged with offences which are triable either summarily (before magistrates) or on indictment (before judge and jury) currently have the right to elect for trial by jury.[25] (Magistrates may also direct that the case be heard in the Crown Court.)

Another important moment in the earlier stages of the criminal process is the *bail decision*. In less serious cases the decision to grant bail will generally be made by the police, but they have the power to remand

---

[25] The Royal Commission on Criminal Justice, which reported in 1992, recommended the abolition of this right of election, primarily on the basis that about 70% of those choosing jury trial in fact go on to plead guilty. The Commission argued that this meant that the costs incurred in putting such cases before the Crown Court are unjustified (*The Royal Commission on Criminal Justice* (HMSO, 1993), Cm. 2263, ch. 6, paras. 4–19). This recommendation has given rise to strong criticism because of its erosion of the right to jury trial. For critical discussion of the Royal Commission's analysis of the criminal justice system and its recommendations for reform, see Mike McConville and Lee Bridges (eds.), *Criminal Justice in Crisis* (Edward Elgar, 1994); Andrew Ashworth, 'Plea Venue and Discontinuance' (1993) *Criminal Law Review* 830.

for short periods pending bail applications to magistrates' courts.[26] Like the decision to prosecute, the discretionary bail decision is structured in terms of statutory criteria which embody a presumption in favour of bail which has to be displaced by considerations crucial to the administration of justice—considerations such as the likelihood of the defendant's absconding or using bail to pervert the course of justice or the need to protect the public or the defendant him- or herself.[27] However, the statutory criteria themselves point in a number of directions, and it is widely recognized that the apparent presumption in favour of bail translates in practice into just the opposite, at least in cases regarded as relatively serious. Bail decisions, including the imposition of bail conditions and decisions about how to respond to their breach, raise important questions from a civil libertarian point of view. On the face of it, pre-trial remand (which is all too often served in overcrowded and squalid conditions) is at odds with the presumption of innocence. These civil libertarian concerns are accentuated by the fact that significant numbers of defendants remanded in custody are either acquitted at trial or sentenced to noncustodial penalties even where convicted. Furthermore, questions arise about the adverse impact which remand may have on a defendant's ability to assist in the preparation of the defence, and the possible impact on the court of a defendant's arriving in handcuffs accompanied by police or prison officers. Also relevant at this stage is magistrates' power to bind a person over to keep the peace or be of good behaviour and to require sureties for that undertaking—a power widely used in cases of public disorder.[28]

Next, we need to consider *plea-bargaining*. The precise extent of bargaining between judge, prosecution service, defence lawyer, and defendant over both charge and sentence in relation to a guilty plea is highly contested due to the difficulty which subsists in conducting

[26] See Ch. 4 below; also Bottomley and Pease, *Crime and Punishment*, 68–71; Nicola Padfield, 'The Right to Bail' (1993) *Criminal Law Review* 510.

[27] See Bail Act 1976, s. 4, schedule 1. Under s. 66 (6) of the Criminal Justice Act 1993 courts are directed to regard the commission of an offence whilst on bail as an aggravating factor at the sentencing stage. The Criminal Justice and Public Order Bill currently before Parliament proposes substantial inroads on the presumptive right to bail, notably in the case of suspects charged with serious offences against the person who have previous convictions or where the alleged offence appears to have been committed whilst the suspect was on bail. It also provides for police powers to attach conditions to bail, a police power of arrest for failure to answer police bail, and the possibility of a court's reconsideration of a grant of bail on the basis of fresh information. See Criminal Justice and Public Order Bill (HMSO, 1993), clauses 20–4.

[28] See Nicola Lacey, Celia Wells, and Dirk Meure, *Reconstructing Criminal Law* (Weidenfeld and Nicolson, 1990), 103–5.

research, particularly into judicial involvement in the process.[29] However, it is quite clear that defendants are regularly offered concessions in terms of charge levelled and of sentence to be imposed in return for a plea of guilty, and that the extent of the practice is such that the entire system would grind to a halt if it were to be abandoned. Clearly, plea-bargaining raises a number of difficult questions within the criminal process. How does it fit with the presumption of innocence, and, if it is a product of purely managerial concerns, can it be justified? It is impossible to be confident that the defendant's bargaining position is always sufficiently strong to ensure that he or she pleads guilty only when genuinely so. The question is also problematic because, given that guilt is a question of legal *interpretation*, it cannot in principle be determined conclusively in advance of a trial. It is difficult to ensure that the criteria on which bargaining proceeds are clear to all concerned, and are consistently applied. Another relevant question concerns the extent to which the hope of a bargained plea of guilty may affect the resources that the defence devotes to the preparation of the case.

Plea-bargaining is just one of the aspects of criminal justice of which *defence lawyering* is an important component. The usual stereotype of the criminal defence lawyer is that of the barrister defending his or her client's case in court, but this, of course, is a relatively esoteric aspect of the practice. Of much greater day-to-day significance is the representation of clients at police stations during questioning, advice on pleas, the preparation of the case, and the plea in mitigation at the sentencing stage. Given the vast preponderance of proceedings in magistrates' courts, most of this work is done by solicitors rather than by barristers, and often indeed by para-legal workers, articled clerks, or even secretarial staff in solicitors' firms.

Next, in a small proportion of cases, there is *the trial*. The vast majority of criminal proceedings in England and Wales take place before lay magistrates advised by a legally qualified clerk. The rest are before stipendiary magistrates or before Crown Court judges sitting with lay juries of twelve citizens, with whom decisions of guilt or innocence ultimately rest. In either case, the contested trial is a highly ritualized affair, not least in terms of the spatial organization of the court itself, with its fixed posi-

---

[29] See John Baldwin and Michael McConville, *Negotiated Justice* (Martin Robertson, 1977); Mike McConville and Chester Mirsky, 'Looking through the Guilty Plea Glass' (1993) 2 *Social and Legal Studies* 173; *Royal Commission on Criminal Justice*, paras. 41–58. Easier to assess is the actual frequency of guilty pleas, which currently stands at 91% in proceedings in magistrates' courts.

tions for all the major participants.[30] In Crown Court trials, the judge in principle decides all the relevant questions of law, whilst the decision as to whether the facts justify a conviction on the basis of that law is determined by the jury. Since the prosecution has a legal burden of proving its case beyond reasonable doubt, the jury's finding of guilty must be supported by a majority of at least 10–2.

Like other important stages in the criminal process, the trial comprehends a large number of kinds of discretionary power. Leaving aside the most obvious powers—interpreting the relevant criminal law and finding the facts—there are several less often remarked upon but equally influential factors. These include the magistrates' or judge's demeanour towards advocates and witnesses; how discretionary rules about the admission of evidence or objections to particular lines of questioning are interpreted; defence and prosecution lawyers' constructions of the case and their tactics in cross-examination; and the way in which the judge sums up the legal issues to the jury—a process which gives judges and clerks in magistrates' courts an influence over the determination of the facts, albeit not a definitive one.[31] Legal constraints on research into the operation of juries have made it difficult to assess the nature of jury decision-making—an extraordinary gap in our understanding of trials. Research on the trial process has shown that one of its dominant characteristics is the constraint which it imposes on the ability of witnesses (including the defendant) to articulate their own understanding of the events and actions which are at issue.[32] It has revealed the ways in which even unusually articulate and confident defendants can be represented in a particular light by a combination of legal definitions of relevance and clever cross-examination. Such research calls into question the effectiveness of the presumption of innocence even for the few defendants whose cases reach a full trial. This implication must be of particular concern in a system which has recently acknowledged a number of appalling miscarriages of justice,[33] and in which procedural safeguards such as the right to silence are under imminent threat of abolition.[34]

[30] See Paul Rock, 'Witnesses and Space in a Crown Court' (1991) 31 *British Journal of Criminology* 226.

[31] See Rosemary Pattenden, *Judicial Discretion and Criminal Litigation* (Clarendon Press, 1989).

[32] See Pat Carlen, *Magistrates' Justice* (Martin Robertson, 1976); Doreen J. McBarnet, *Conviction: Law, the State and the Construction of Justice* (Macmillan, 1981) (see Ch. 6 below).

[33] For an account of one of these miscarriages, including an acute analysis of the judicial role, see Chris Mullin, *Error of Judgment* (Poolberg Press, 1987).

[34] See Criminal Justice and Public Order Bill, clauses 27–31. These proposals have been made notwithstanding the Royal Commission's recommendation that the right to silence

At the close of a trial in which a conviction has been recorded, or following a plea of guilty, there is the *sentencing process*.[35] In the case of defendants who have pleaded guilty (in other words, the large majority), their lawyer's plea in mitigation at the sentencing stage will be his or her main contribution to their defence. In England and Wales, sentencing proceeds within a statutory framework consisting of maximum sentences for most offences and the general injunction to impose sentences commensurate with the seriousness of the offence, in the light of information given in a pre-sentence report. The preparation of pre-sentence reports, in which probation officers give general information about the offender's background and the broader circumstances in which the offence came to be committed—including aspects such as psychiatric health, employment status, family circumstances—therefore constitutes another important criminal justice practice. Notwithstanding the statutory sentencing framework, there subsists a substantial margin of discretionary power within which sentencers' own views about what constitutes relevant factors, and their own penal philosophies—retributive, rehabilitative, deterrent—can come into play.[36] The open-endedness of sentencing decision-making is increased by the wide array of potential sentences available to the court—financial, community-based, or custodial—with further variations and refined statutory conditions for special categories of offender such as juveniles, young adults, and those regarded as suffering from mental disorders. Furthermore, a number of related discre-

be retained (ibid., paras. 4–30). The Royal Commission's main recommendations relevant to the avoidance of future miscarriages of justice are to be found in chs. 9–11 of its report, with other important recommendations appearing in chs. 3 and 4. To the dismay of many commentators, in spite of the fact that the Royal Commission was appointed as a direct result of the cases of the Guildford Four, Maguire Seven, and Birmingham Six, both its terms of reference and the thrust of its analysis are much concerned with the question of the efficient use of resources, with reforms geared to ensuring the conviction of the guilty often appearing to occupy as important a place as those concerned to ensure the acquittal of the innocent. For critical discussion, see Nicola Lacey, 'Missing the Wood . . . Pragmatism versus Theory in the Royal Commission', in McConville and Lee Bridges (eds.), *Criminal Justice in Crisis*; Robert Reiner, 'Investigative Powers and Safeguards for Suspects' (1993) *Criminal Law Review* 808; John Jackson, 'The Evidence Recommendations', ibid. 817; Andrew Ashworth, 'Plea Venue and Discontinuance', ibid. 830; Joanna Glynn, 'Disclosure', ibid. 841; Peter Thornton, QC, 'Miscarriages of Justice: A Lost Opportunity', ibid. 926. Even the modest proposals made by the Royal Commission for the organization of forensic science facilities, some modification of the Court of Appeal's role, and the creation of an independent Authority to consider allegations of miscarriages of justice have failed to find their way into the 1993 Bill.

[35] For an excellent and detailed account, see Andrew Ashworth, *Sentencing and Criminal Justice* (Weidenfeld and Nicolson, 1992).

[36] See Criminal Justice Act 1991, pt. I, as amended by Criminal Justice Act 1993, ss. 65–6; and Chs. 4, 7, 8 below.

tionary decisions may be taken by sentencers. These include decisions on the appropriate response to breaches of conditional sentences such as certain probation orders, suspended sentences, or the non-payment of financial penalties; decisions on victim compensation and/or reparation; and recommendations on release from indeterminate sentences at a later date.

Once past the sentencing stage, we move on to the vast and fragmented penal apparatus which characterizes most modern societies. A number of the most important bureaucratic and coercive processes need to be considered. Of particular cultural salience (and ethical complexity) is *the practice of imprisonment* and the administration of the prison system. The practice of incarcerating offenders (and suspected offenders) is one in which the essential deprivation of personal liberty can be given a large number of different twists and refinements according to prison regime. The contemporary orthodoxy about imprisonment is that it is meant to be 'as' and not 'for' punishment. Yet, within the inevitably punitive parameters of the deprivation of liberty, prison can be designed to (further) punish, to attempt to 'cure' or 'train', merely to 'incapacitate', or some combination of these. The extent to which prisoners are invited or required to participate in education, therapy, work, and leisure activities, or are subjected to further punitive treatment or brutality, the groups by whom these practices are administered (uniformed officers, educational and other staff from outside the prison, volunteers), and the aims with which they are administered have a decisive impact upon the kind of social practice that imprisonment turns out to be.[37] This wide variation in actual and possible prison regimes calls into question whether there is one prison system or many: the experiences, powers, training, and priorities of prison staff, prison governors, and prisoners vary within any one institution, just as the regimes in different institutions (particularly the low and high security, the more and less crowded, and those for men as compared with those for women) are vastly divergent.[38] Also of particular importance are the processes through which prisoners' complaints are dealt with, the prison disciplinary system, and the *early release system*, through which medium-term prisoners are automatically released half-way through their articulated sentence, subject to recall up to the three-quarter point, and long-term prisoners are eligible for discretionary early release at the half-way point, the decision being made by the Parole Board.[39]

[37] See Ch. 11 below.

[38] Compare, for example, the experiences recounted by Jimmy Boyle before and after his transfer to the Barlinnie Special Unit (*A Sense of Freedom* (Pan, 1977)), and these experiences with those of the women in Cornton Vale (Ch. 11 below).

[39] See Criminal Justice Act 1991, pt. II.

In spite of the paradigm place which the prison tends to occupy in contemporary images of penality, the vast majority of sentenced offenders are in fact given non-custodial penalties.[40] A large number of bureaucratic and regulatory practices are involved in the *administration of financial and community penalties*. Fines—the most common sentence in England and Wales—are administered by courts. The amount of a fine is supposed to be related to the offender's ability to pay, and fine defaults may lead to the imposition of a custodial sentence.[41] Perhaps more interesting are the social processes whereby the 'community penalties' such as community-service orders or probation orders are executed.[42] Like imprisonment, these penalties are inherently open-textured within their coercive parameters. Thus, the frequency and nature of the interactions between offender and probation officer or community worker, the nature of the work involved and its geographical and social location, and the variety both of professional groups (social workers, psychiatrists, teacher) and of volunteer groups involved are all influential in determining what it means to serve a probation or a community-service order. Precisely because of their number, because of the fact that their practice is decentralized, and because they tend to operate only within relatively broadly drawn guidelines (such as those of the Probation Service), it is often in fact difficult to come by the relevant information about these practices except by way of detailed research. Whilst central government does on occasion make specific policy prescriptions (for example, the recent attempt to render probation a more punitive sentence),[43] it is unclear just how these central directions translate into day-to-day practice.

Once again, I have selected only the most significant decision-making processes and social practices within the umbrella of criminal justice: much more could have been said, for example, about victim-support schemes, provision for mentally disordered offenders, and special

[40] In 1991 (1989), 14% (16%) of offenders sentenced for *indictable* offences received immediate custodial sentences, 20% (16%) were discharged, 35% (40%) were fined, 22% (25%) received community-based penalties, 6% received a suspended custodial sentence, and the remaining 2% (4%) were the subject of other forms of sentence. 5% (1%) of those convicted of summary offences received immediate custodial sentences (*Digest 2* and *A Digest of Information*, ch. 5). (The figures for 1991 add up to only 99% in the Digest, and in 1989 to 101%: in the Digest for 1989 the community-based figure includes fully suspended sentences, and attendance-centre orders are included as 'other', whereas in 1991 they are classified as community-based.)

[41] See Anthony E. Bottoms, 'Neglected Features of Contemporary Penal Systems', in D. Garland and P. Young (eds.), *The Power to Punish* (Heinemann, 1983), 166.

[42] See Chs. 9 and 10 below.

[43] Criminal Justice Act 1991, ss. 8–9.

processes for children and young people. But even from this selection it is apparent that these processes and decisions differ in terms of the nature and urgency of their practical imperatives, the clarity of their goals and of the values which inform their practice, and the breadth of discretion which characterizes their operation. And once again broader features of social and political organization and of history and culture—in particular, the social axes of class, ethnicity, and gender—affect the meaning which penal practices can have and their capacity to have positive as well as repressive effects.

Disciplinary approaches

Thirdly, we need to consider the variety of disciplinary approaches which might be brought to bear on these diverse agencies and practices comprehended within criminal justice. Most obviously, *criminology* is relevant to criminal justice: as we have already seen, the interpretation and social construction of crime is fundamental to any proper understanding of the criminal process. The dominant contemporary view is that crime is indeed a social construct in at least two senses: first, particular criminal laws and their interpretations are developed within and are contingent upon their social contexts; second, social conditions are relevant to levels of offending behaviour, which is not simply the product of human 'wickedness' or individual pathology. This contemporary understanding implies that criminology itself does not constitute a discrete discipline, but rather draws on a cluster of disciplinary discourses to shed light on its subject-matter—a view reflected in the preference for some in this area to speak of 'the sociology of deviance'.[44] As this label suggests, *sociology* is one of the main disciplines which contribute to our understanding of criminal justice: since criminal justice's subject-matter consists of a number of social practices, both empirical and theoretical sociology (the latter may be called 'social theory') promise to illuminate the place which criminal justice has in holding societies together—or, indeed, in pulling them apart.

Staying at the level of social analysis, the insights of *political science* are also of relevance to criminal justice. For example, political science can help to shed light on how particular political institutions within and relevant to criminal justice practice work. Comparative political science and political sociology can further sharpen our awareness by revealing how apparently

[44] See Box, *Crime, Power and Mystification*; Stanley Cohen, *Against Criminology* (Transaction Books, 1988), ch. 13.

similar institutional structures can have a very different impact and meaning in different societies, and how, conversely, rather similar social functions may be fulfilled, albeit in different ways, by apparently very different institutional arrangements.[45] To take just one example, 'community-based' penalties or crime-prevention strategies will clearly have a very different meaning in a society in which locally based, informal networks of social ordering and consensus about criminal justice norms are strong and can be drawn on in the realization of criminal justice practice as compared with their meaning in a society in which local communities are fragmented and values are contested.[46] At a yet more concrete level, these general insights may be fleshed out with the analyses of organization theory or public administration. Again, one could debate whether these are discrete disciplines distinct from interpretive sociology, rational choice theory, psychology, and other techniques applied to specific questions. Their particular contribution, however, lies in their potential to help to link the question of individual motivation and values to institutional structure and context.[47]

The potential of *social history* to shed light on the significance of different aspects of criminal justice in the context of their gradual chronological development is clear—as is its own connection with sociology, political science, and other disciplines.[48] For example, Pearson's work on the history of public anxieties about crime casts doubt on contemporary perceptions of an inexorable rise in the level of public danger and disorder.[49] Similarly, Ignatieff's work on the history of imprisonment illustrates the contingency of carceral institutions as a central part of the penal repertoire—a contingency which is at odds with the assumption, pervasive within current public debate, that imprisonment is an absolutely necessary penal institution.[50]

The insights of *political economy* would also be relevant at a number of levels: in explaining the predominance of certain kinds of offending

[45] See M. Damaska, *The Faces of Justice and State Authority* (Yale University Press, 1986).

[46] See Michael King, 'Social Crime Prevention à la Thatcher' (1989) *Howard Journal of Criminal Justice* 291.

[47] For work which draws on the insights of these disciplines, see e.g. Chs. 5 and 10 below; Stuart Asquith, *Children and Justice* (Edinburgh University Press, 1983); Manning, *Police Work*; Hall *et al.*, *Policing the Crisis*, ch. 3.

[48] Important recent contributions to the social history of crime and punishment include Michel Foucault, *Discipline and Punish* (Penguin, 1977); David Garland, *Punishment and Welfare* (Gower, 1985); D. Hay, P. Linebaugh, E. P. Thompson, and C. Winslow (eds.), *Albion's Fatal Tree* (Penguin, 1977); L. Radzinowicz and R. Hood, *The Emergence of Penal Policy* (Oxford University Press, 1991); Lucia Zedner, *Women, Crime and Custody in Victorian England* (Oxford University Press, 1991).

[49] Geoffrey Pearson, *Hooligan: A History of Respectable Fears* (Macmillan, 1983).

[50] Michael Ignatieff, *A Just Measure of Pain* (Penguin, 1989); see also Ch. 12 below.

behaviour and the political salience of crime, law, and order at particular moments. More generally, economic concerns are important in constraining the development and administration of particular criminal processes in the light of broad fiscal concerns.[51] The relevance of *law* is evident, in helping us to understand the authority and force of the offence definitions which are the official starting-point for the social conception of crime, as well as the distinctive power of legal discourse to depoliticize and represent as 'objective' determinations of guilt.[52] Furthermore, in providing frameworks for the constitution of ongoing regulation of criminal justice practices, legal studies may illuminate not only our understanding of how they work but also of how they might be made to work differently.[53] Finally, this suggests the contributions of *ethics* and of *political philosophy* to developing the evaluative frameworks on the basis of which existing criminal justice practices may be criticized and reconceived.[54]

Which of these various approaches are regarded as of most significance is an important index of how a particular society and its relevant agencies conceive of crime and punishment. To give some crude examples, a society which regards crime as a form of individual pathology based on biological difference will be likely to be preoccupied by a quasi-scientific criminology and a psychiatric or segregating penality. Conversely, one which regards crime as socially produced will tend to think in terms of the sociology of deviance, with penality understood in terms of political science, political economy, and social history.

Two general differences of approach within scholarly work on criminal justice need to be noted. First, we could distinguish between intellectual projects which are primarily descriptive or explanatory and those which are primarily evaluative or normative. The social history and sociology of punishment, which seek to explain the development and operation of particular practices, speak in a voice which is different from that of normative penal philosophy, which develops and analyses principles and ideals against which those practices may be evaluated or in terms of

---

[51] For work which draws on the insights of political economy, see e.g. Ch. 1 below; Nils Christie, *Crime Control as Industry* (Routledge, 1993); Leslie T. Wilkins, *Punishment, Crime and Market Forces* (Dartmouth, 1991).

[52] See Lacey *et al.*, *Reconstructing Criminal Law*; Alan Norrie, *Law, Ideology and Punishment* (Kluwer, 1991); Norrie, *Crime, Reason and History* (Weidenfeld and Nicolson, 1993).

[53] See Chs. 5 and 7 below.

[54] See e.g. John Braithwaite and Philip Pettit, *Not Just Deserts* (Oxford University Press, 1990); H. L. A. Hart, *Punishment and Responsibility* (Clarendon Press, 1968); Nicola Lacey, *State Punishment* (Routledge, 1988).

which reforms might be framed. Secondly, we might distinguish approaches which are primarily concerned with the individual agent (rational choice theory, psychology, psychiatry, and some forms of criminology) from those which are primarily concerned with the institutional framework or social context (such as the sociology of deviance, institutional political science, social history).

Yet on closer inspection neither of these distinctions is as clear as it might seem. The first raises interesting and important questions about how distinct normative and descriptive projects really are, and about how they relate to one another. Is it possible to make prescriptions about a practice unless we understand how it works? Are our explanatory interpretations of criminal justice practices really untainted by our normative commitments? The second distinction should prompt us to question whether it makes sense, in constructing either the individual agent or the institution as the primary unit of analysis, to assume that there is any sharp discontinuity between the two. Since individual agents act within institutional and social contexts, and in the light of particular values and goals, as well as acting upon the development of these broader contexts, the idea of a primary focus on one or the other begins to look problematic. Each of these distinctions, and the doubts we have raised about them, need to be borne in mind as we move on to consider how we might reach some understanding of this bewildering disciplinary diversity and of the practical diversity of the subject-matter on which it has a bearing.

A general theory of criminal justice?

One common suggestion is that we can only make sense of criminal justice if we are equipped with a 'general theory'—an account which organizes the diversity which we have encountered in a systematic way. Whilst such theories differ in the extent to which they purport to be explanatory or normative, even the primarily explanatory theories are informed by implicit ideas of the values which criminal justice processes seek to promote and which constrain the exercise of criminal justice power. Conversely, the normative theories are informed by an implicit descriptive understanding of what criminal justice is all about. Among these theories, two sets of ideas stand out and call for specific consideration.

According to the first kind of view, criminal justice is indeed all about *doing justice*, and 'justice' in a distinctive sense.[55] The background idea is

---

[55] See A. von Hirsch, *Doing Justice* (Hill and Wang, 1976).

that members of a society owe one another reciprocal obligations to for-
bear from breaking criminal laws—laws which are assumed to be in the
antecedent interest of all, because they protect some of the most important, widely recognized interests of individuals and of the polity itself.
According to this view, the practice of attempting to identify and punish
offenders is integral to the pursuit of just social relations, for only
through the punishment of those who have taken an unfair advantage by
breaking the law can the just relations of the pre-existing moral equilib-
rium be restored and the interests of both victim and society given due
recognition. This sort of argument is associated with theories of punishment which emphasize its symbolic or expressive features, and with
those which explain the value of punishment in terms of desert or reparation. As far as the criminal process is concerned, it tends to be associated
with a commitment to the importance of 'due process': that is, procedural safeguards such as the presumption of innocence and the requirement that offenders have some substantial element of responsibility for
their breaches of criminal law, which can thus be meaningfully conceived
as 'unfair' advantages.[56]

While the 'justice' approach does conceive of criminal justice as a relatively discrete sphere, it also contains seeds which undermine this separateness; for the idea that the justice of punishment is independent of
broader social justice is called into question by the obvious fact that the
weight of the burden of complying with criminal law is directly related to
the social situation of the offender. To take an obvious example, the starv-
ing person who steals a loaf of bread cannot meaningfully be said to have
taken the same kind of unfair advantage as the wealthy fraudster. This
account therefore raises in an acute form the question of how penal practice in an unjust society can contribute to social justice in a broader sense.

The continuity between criminal justice and broader social justice is
more explicit in the other main approach to theorizing about criminal justice. According to this view, criminal justice power is legitimated in terms
of its capacity to secure beneficial consequences. The most influential version of this view is the utilitarian theory, according to which the sole
motivation and good of human beings is the pursuit of pleasure, or prefer-
ence-satisfaction, and the avoidance of pain, or preference-frustration.[57]

---

[56] On the distinction between 'due process' and 'crime control' models of the criminal
process, see Herbert Packer, *The Limits of the Criminal Sanction* (Stanford University Press,
1968), pt. II.

[57] See Jeremy Bentham, *An Introduction to the Principles of Morals and Legislation* (1789), ed.
H. L. A. Hart and J. H. Burns (Methuen, 1982).

Whilst both punishment itself and the costs of the criminal process are, according to this view, prima-facie evils, criminalization and punishment may be justified wherever they counterbalance those evils and serve to maximize overall human happiness. This is typically effected by reducing the level of pain-producing offending, whether by individual or general deterrence, incapacitation, reform of offenders, prevention of resort to less utility-maximizing methods such as private vengeance, the assuagement of victims' grievances, or general education.

According to this view, the pursuit of social justice is essentially an instrumental enterprise, in which the effects of various means of dealing with social disutilities and promoting social utilities are weighed up. Whilst 'criminal justice' may be seen as a distinctive *means* of pursuing social good, the terms in which the good which it pursues is to be measured are just the same as those to be applied to, say, the education system or the handling of the economy. Notably, as regards the criminal process, the commitment of such consequence-oriented approaches to procedural safeguards such as the right to silence or the presumption of innocence will be entirely contingent upon their contribution to the effectiveness of the process as a whole. This does not mean that utilitarian approaches eschew procedural safeguards, for procedural safeguards sometimes contribute to utility. Furthermore, as we have seen, efficacy is dependent on a baseline of legitimacy, and the latter is in turn dependent on certain procedural principles which may have an important place in the social conscience. Thus, while a hard-nosed utilitarian might dream of educating the citizenry out of such 'prejudices', utilitarian systems must learn to accommodate them as long as they exist.

This is not the place to evaluate the normative recommendations of these theories or of the various syntheses of them which have been offered by philosophers of punishment.[58] Two things only need to be noted at this stage. First, when read as explanatory theories about the criminal process, each of these general approaches clearly has a place. The notion that criminal processes are geared to 'doing justice' in something like the former sense is one which helps to account for both a number of actual features of criminal processes and the social meaning—the symbolic and practical significance for members of the society—of having a criminal justice system. In the case of many kinds of offence (murder, assault, theft, driving while intoxicated) and many penal practices (imprisonment, fining), it does seem plausible to say that what might be called a

---

[58] For a fuller discussion, see Lacey, *State Punishment*, ch. 2.

'moral analogy' holds. In other words, criminalization and punishment reflect a collective *judgement* about what is not acceptable, and enunciate a general standard of social behaviour which is assumed at some level to be shared and which constitutes a significant expression of the projected identity of the social order. Conversely, the utilitarian view helps to account for the important sense in which criminal justice both is and is seen as a set of practices which responds to—which 'manages'—a certain set of social 'problems', and whose success or failure is to be judged (at least in principle) in primarily instrumental terms such as relative costs and impact on levels of offending and re-offending.

Equally obviously, however, even some combination of these two approaches fails to give a complete account of what 'criminal justice' is all about. In order to fill the gaps, we need to know a great deal more about how the 'wrongs' or 'harms' associated with 'crime' are defined in a society—how the 'crime problem' is constructed. We need to know about the social, political, and economic conditions which obtain, and about the more detailed practices and the values, goals, and occupational culture—what might be called the 'operative ideologies'—of those who administer social practices relevant to criminal justice. We need, too, to know about the social distribution of offending behaviour which meets with official response, for this is likely to have an impact on the meaning which punishment can have. If penal power is consistently invoked in relation to certain groups within the population—for example, young men from certain ethnic groups[59]—in ways which systematically benefit other groups to a far greater extent, this will have clear implications for both the legitimacy and the efficacy of criminal justice. In particular, it will affect whether punishment can have any socially reintegrative effects, drawing offenders back into the group of those who regard criminal justice power as legitimate rather than marking and reinforcing their exclusion.[60] It is the challenging project of discovering how to link our very general theoretical understandings with these and other chaotic realities of social practice which has so often eluded those committed to theorizing criminal justice.[61]

---

[59] See Marion Fitzgerald, *Ethnic Minorities in the Criminal Justice System* (Royal Commission on Criminal Justice Research Study no. 20, HMSO, 1993).

[60] See Braithwaite, *Crime, Shame and Reintegration*.

[61] For a rare exception, see Michael King, *The Framework of Criminal Justice* (Croom Helm, 1981).

Criminal justice and social order

The social construction of crime and consequent relevance of criminological issues to criminal justice, the questionable disciplinary and practical discreteness of criminal justice, and the difficulty of identifying the reference of its appeal to 'justice' all make it hard to fix on an appropriate starting-point for thinking about criminal justice. In the light of reflection on the different aspects of criminal justice as a set of practices and as a subject, is it possible to improve on our original formulation of criminal justice as the study of the various social institutions and practices concerned with identifying and responding to actual or suspected breaches of criminal law? Could a different formulation suggest a more productive approach to the development of an adequate theoretical framework which would not exclude potentially relevant issues?

One attractive possibility is to shift our perspective slightly and reconceive criminal justice, in the sense of the practices of identifying and responding to offenders, as a related but not entirely coordinated set of practices geared to the construction and maintenance of social order. At the most general level, criminal justice could be seen as an instrumental and expressive regulatory practice which is legitimated, in a broadly liberal society, by its avowed commitment to the protection of certain interests which are regarded as of fundamental importance to all members of society, and which operates by means of a relatively distinctive but in important respects porous set of procedures and publicly endorsed coercive apparatuses. This is not to say, of course, that criminal justice practices actually do fulfil these liberal-egalitarian functions, or even that they are intended to do so by those with most influence over their development and exercise. It is rather to identify this conception as the core of criminal justice's capacity to *present itself* as legitimate: in other words, as its basic *ideology*. Criminal justice, that is, is concerned with social order not exclusively or even primarily in an instrumental, straightforwardly empirical sense, but rather with social order in a symbolic sense: with a society's sense of itself as a cohesive, viable, and ethical entity.

For brevity, I shall refer to criminal justice conceived of in this way as a *social ordering practice*.[62] The notion of 'social ordering' has advantages over the more usual 'regulation' or 'social control' because both regulation and control suggest a narrow instrumentalism which marginalizes

---

[62] Cf. the approach taken by David Garland, *Punishment and Modern Society* (Oxford University Press, 1990), ch. 12; see also E. Durkheim, *The Division of Labour in Society* (Free Press, 1964).

the emotive, symbolic aspects of punishment.[63] Furthermore, social control conjures up an image of repression, whereas, although criminal justice undoubtedly has repressive aspects, we need to leave room for the recognition that parts of criminal justice practice can be positive and productive in certain respects.[64] That is, we may need to recognize that, notwithstanding the inevitable injustice perpetrated and reinforced by penal practice in an unjust society, a certain core of criminal justice practice may none the less be justified in that it fulfils positive purposes which would otherwise be either left unfulfilled (for example, the recognition of victims' legitimate grievances) or fulfilled by even less attractive means (for example, by recourse to private vengeance).

This shift in perspective has several advantages. First, it serves to emphasize the continuity between criminal justice and other practices and institutions such as education, religion, child-rearing, conventional morality, and civil law. Secondly, by being explicit about what connects diverse criminal justice practices, it provides a substantive basis for criminal justice studies and an analytic framework which can help to identify and explain the way in which changes or attempted reforms in one part of the process can have (often unintended) implications and effects in other parts. Thirdly, it connects up the normative and the explanatory: criminal justice, within this conception, simply *is* a practice which is informed by certain evaluative ideals (not necessarily in themselves coherent, let alone consistently recognized) and which is therefore susceptible of critique on the basis of its own legitimating ideas as well as on the basis of values external to it. Furthermore, the impulse to attempt to justify criminal justice ordering is underpinned by what we understand about the nature of the practice—its coerciveness, its connection with state power, its brutalizing and socially divisive effects, its economic costs. This starting-point reveals the philosophical and sociological enterprises to be inextricably linked: without an understanding of what criminal justice is about, in the sense of how criminal justice practices work, 'theories of criminal justice' are bound to be misdirected. Yet the converse is equally true: everything we see as a problem, an abuse, or a dysfunction in criminal justice is only so relative to an evaluative framework. So, normative discourses constructed in terms of equality, oppression, the limits of state action, human rights, and so on are integrally related to sociological analyses of criminal justice.

[63] Cf. the idea of criminal justice as 'social censure': see Colin Sumner (ed.), *Censure, Politics and Criminal Justice* (Open University Press, 1990).

[64] Cf. Pat Carlen, 'Crime, Inequality and Sentencing', in Pat Carlen and Dee Cook (eds.), *Paying for Crime* (Open University Press, 1989), 8.

Finally, the suggested focus makes a rather specific assumption about what might broadly be called the social functions of criminal justice. It shifts the critical spotlight from specific offences, offenders, and penalties to the broader question of how societies generate the conditions for their own continued existence—what serves to maintain them, and the role of criminal justice practices within that framework. It thus locates the general project of studying criminal justice within the umbrella of social theory, and constructs criminal justice as having to do with societies and their members generally rather than with offenders and officials in particular. In particular, this location brings with it a potentially powerful set of conceptual tools which, I shall suggest, can help us to develop the kinds of middle-order theoretical frameworks which we need if we are to arrive at understandings which are reasonably systematic yet not blinkered by the precepts of a too-constraining normative or explanatory model.

Three factors are of particular importance. *First*, approaching criminal justice as a social ordering practice dictates that we pay equal attention to its instrumental and its symbolic features. In other words, it suggests that we must attend not only to criminal justice practices themselves but also to the meanings they have for their participants, their subjects, and their observers, including their appeal to emotional and effective attitudes. This entails, of course, that, while quantitative empirical research and official statistics are of importance, they always need to be supplemented by qualitative, agent-centred, and institutionally focused studies. Indeed, this approach implies that the significance of statistical work is more complex than is sometimes noted. For example, changes in crime or reporting rates cannot be taken at face value, but have precisely to be *interpreted* in the light of the broader factors which I have been concerned to emphasize here.[65] Needless to say, qualitative, like quantitative, research has its methodological complexities: agents' own accounts cannot necessarily be taken at face value, and themselves have to be appraised critically in the light of our understanding of the institutional and cultural context. The essential point, however, is that the study of criminal justice, like that of all human practices, is an enterprise which seeks to interpret a set of social processes which are themselves engaged in interpretive construction. This entails that we should not be misled into thinking that we are engaged in straightforward 'description' of the kind which is suggested by the word 'empirical'.

---

[65] See Bottomley and Pease, *Crime and Punishment*. This is an obvious enough point, yet one which is astoundingly little acknowledged in public debate about criminal justice in England and Wales.

Furthermore, this approach suggests that the instrumental and the symbolic cannot be separated neatly: the material effects of particular practices will depend on their meaning for those subject to or observing them. Only by being aware of these assumptions, stories, and ideologies can we begin to make sense of criminal justice practices and see what role they play in the construction of social order. For example, the idea of criminal justice as enunciating quasi-moral judgements in fact constrains which policies can be instrumentally effective. A too blatantly managerial use of criminal justice power may turn out to be ineffective if it fails to command the support of a critical mass of citizens or officials who see the relevant norms as expressing quasi-moral judgements. Similarly, a certain kind of instrumentalism—for instance, the image of the government as an 'efficient manager of the criminal process'—itself constitutes (contrary to its value-free, technocratic self-conception) an *ideology* of what criminal justice is all about, and one which, over a period of time, can feed into and alter the attitudes and practices of those involved in the process.

Secondly, this social theory framework dictates that we think constantly about the contributions both of individuals and groups of agents and of broader institutions and social structures to criminal justice. Clearly, the actions and decisions of individuals and groups of individuals are of major relevance to every level of the criminal process. Yet if we are to understand them we need to attend to factors beyond the decision-maker him- or herself, albeit without going so far as to assume that these actions or decisions are completely determined by those broader factors. For decisions are made in the context of underlying features of the social order: relatively concrete institutions (such as courts); powerful discourses (such as law); patterns of social organization and prejudice (such as class, gender, or racial or ethnic division); locally dominant ideologies (such as aspects of professional culture within the police). These underlying factors, which are sometimes called 'structures', both constrain and facilitate human choices, just as our choices and decisions in turn feed back into the constitution of the underlying institutional constraints. There is thus a constant movement back and forth between 'agency' and 'structure'—a movement which belies the idea that the two are dichotomous. The interconnection of the individual and the institutional levels, which can be obscured by the rather static and monolithic resonance of the term 'structure', is well captured by the term 'practice': a relatively structured field of action of agents or groups of agents, which can only be understood in terms of the assumptions, values, goals, and interpretive frames which inform the agents' actions and infuse the surrounding context in which those actions take place.

A *third* methodological advantage of this framework is that it allows us to see that coercive power such as that associated with criminalization and punishment is not only held and exercised by criminal justice agents and agencies, but needs additionally to be understood as inhering, less tangibly but no less influentially, in the ideologies or value-systems which inform criminal justice practices, and in the discourses in which those ideologies are expressed. This is particularly important because it helps to explain the limited success and unintended effects which often characterize instrumental efforts at penal reform. It can also help us to understand the real complexity of urgent political projects such as the rendering of criminal justice power more transparent and accountable. If power inheres in, for example, the discursive construction of 'real' offenders, of suspect populations, and of 'real crime' in police culture or judicial ideology, the imposition of regulatory legal frameworks geared to the structuring of policing or sentencing discretion in order to achieve a more even-handed practice is likely to be ineffective or even counter-productive; for it fails to engage with the deeper factors which underpin policing, prosecution, or sentencing practice.

This broad view of power also helps to displace the simplistic assumption that criminal justice is all about *punishment*; for the constellation of powerful practices associated with criminal justice is not merely engaged in a crude and distinctive kind of instrumental coercion via the threat of punishment, but rather connects with a multifarious set of disciplinary techniques—social work, psychiatry, education, sexuality—which subtly propagate and 'enforce' a wide variety of social norms.[66] This suggests that the precise shape of criminal processes is of intrinsic importance. The details of criminal justice power, as increasingly revealed in research, have an ordering significance far beyond the impact of the obviously normative and coercive aspects of the process. Particularly at the 'edges' of the paradigm view of what count as criminal justice practices—in the 'intermediate treatment' of juveniles, in therapeutic regimes in prisons and for probationers, in the construction of pre-sentence reports—these subtler forms of discipline and ordering are firmly in operation. We need to reread the significance of the practices closer to the instrumental-coercive paradigm in the light of this recognition.[67]

---

[66] See Foucault, *Discipline and Punish*; Carol Smart, *Feminism and the Power of Law* (Routledge, 1989), ch. 1.

[67] For an outstanding example of this kind of enterprise, see Ch. 11 below.

A sensitivity to the diversity of modes and sites of power involved in criminal justice seen as a social ordering practice is crucial if we are to look beneath the surface of criminal justice developments. Current penal practice in Britain is supposedly based on an essentially 'just deserts' approach which has grown out of both instrumental loss of faith in the rehabilitative ideal and civil libertarian concerns about its repressive implications.[68] At a number of institutional levels, therefore, criminal justice practices such as sentencing have been reconstructed by legal and other means better to reflect just deserts or the non-rehabilitative instrumental concerns, such as managerial efficiency and economy, which are central to governmental ideology. One important aspect of these reforms has been a general concern with consistency, uniformity, and coherence, and hence with what are generally thought of as 'due process' values.[69] On one level this is a plausible account of recent developments. But many other normative frameworks have also been productive in maintaining both the perceived legitimacy and the operative feasibility of criminal justice practices during this period. For example, in prisons and community-based sentences, attempts at reform have never been abandoned:[70] in policy on young offenders, rehabilitation and deterrence have continued to inform penal practice; indeterminate prison sentences, characterized by discretionary parole, continued until 1991 and still exist for long-term prisoners; sentence levels for some offenders have increased markedly, in a political quid pro quo which facilitates the diversion of other offenders from the process for straightforwardly managerial reasons.

If we are to make sense of this chaotic picture, we will have to look beyond official criminal justice rhetoric to the reality of criminal justice practice—whilst also recognizing the sense in which the rhetoric is a part of the reality. The stories that the government and official agencies tell us (and which we tell one another) about criminal justice values are central to how the legitimacy of the criminal process is maintained. To develop any understanding of this process, we need to keep an eye on larger issues about the justification of criminal justice power and the politics of its construction and exercise in a society in which the background conditions of inequality and injustice, along with unavoidably repressive

[68] See Chs. 7 and 10 below.

[69] For example, in the instantiation of a duty on sentencers to give reasons for their decisions: Criminal Justice Act 1991, pt. I.

[70] See Barbara Hudson, *Justice Through Punishment* (London: Macmillan 1987); *Penal Policy and Social Justice* (Macmillan 1993).

features of criminal justice, constantly threaten to undermine the legitimacy and, hence, the stability of the criminal process.

Concluding thoughts

I have argued that our starting-point in approaching the study of criminal justice should be the assumption that the various practices geared to the identification of and response to suspected offences and offenders have significance in terms of how social order is conceived and reproduced. Societies do in some meaningful sense process and punish people because it is thought that they deserve it or because their actions are seen as posing certain social problems which need to be managed. But these frameworks themselves need to be understood within a yet broader one, which may help to explain the significance of ideas of retributive justice or of why certain things are constructed as social problems (moreover as social problems calling for a criminal justice response), and to explain how the tensions between instrumental and expressive features of criminal justice are managed.

In terms of study and research, my argument has emphasized the interdependence of theoretical and practical, of descriptive and normative projects, and the multi-disciplinary approach of criminal justice studies. We need to avoid the twin extremes of being drowned in the quagmire of chaotic (if fascinating) detail and of being committed to a rigid theoretical model which blinds us to whole tracts of significant social practice. We can do no better than to embrace a self-consciously eclectic approach which entails moving back and forth between general conceptions and hypotheses, on the one hand, and the specificity of social practices, on the other.

In this Introduction, I have been particularly concerned to emphasize the importance of locating criminal justice studies within the broad umbrella of social theory, and of attending to the values, ideologies, and interpretive frameworks which explicitly and implicitly inform criminal justice practices. This approach entails that criminal justice studies can contribute to our more general understanding of societies. It draws our attention to criminal justice as an index of how civilized a society is, and to general questions such as how negative, repressive, or socially disintegrative criminal justice power has to be, and to what degree (if any) it can have positive, socially integrative functions. What I hope to have provided is a large-scale map which will help in maintaining a balance between the institutional and the individual, the evaluative and the analytical, the general and the particular. Equipped with such a map, we have a reasonable hope of being able to make sense of the varied terrain of criminal justice and to formulate and reformulate independent and critical judgements in the course of studying criminal justice.

The Criminal Justice System and 'Problem Populations'

STEVEN BOX

Although there are numerous state officials in the criminal justice system, three groups will be analysed in this chapter. These will be: magistrates and judges; probation officers; and police. It will be shown that the unintended and unwitting contribution each makes to reducing anxieties created by the existence of a population surplus to the requirements of the productive system, flows from these officers making decisions guided by the 'logic' of their situation as they *perceive* it.

 ## The courts and changing sentencing practices

Over the last decade or so, the criminal justice system has been faced with what it *believes* to be a growing problem of crime and a growing number of persons who need prison both to deter and incapacitate them. The belief in the 'crime problem' comes from an awareness that the number of crimes recorded by the police is increasing, and also from the increased numbers of persons being processed through the courts. However, the judicial response is not purely mechanical. It does not simply respond passively to an increased 'work-load' by maintaining the same sentencing practices. Instead, the judiciary responds actively, changing its practices to fit what it perceives to be a changed situation. Not only is it more receptive to the idea that Britain has been experiencing a massive crime wave over the last decade, but it is also more in touch with those social groups who clamour for more prisons, police, and punishment. It therefore responds actively by *increasing* the use of prison sentences and *reducing* the use of non-supervisory sentences, such as fines or unconditional discharges. The outcome is the imposition of more sentences at the higher end of the punishment tariff *over and above* the changes in the volume and pattern of crime. This effect is not a mechanical response to the increased numbers being processed, but is essentially mediated by judicial attitudes and ideological positions which prepare a sufficiently large proportion of judges and magistrates to respond to deteriorating economic conditions by resorting more frequently to severe penal sanctions.

It is as though the judiciary were a barometer of anxiety levels felt by the superordinate class whenever class antagonisms deepen during times of economic crisis and recession. This effect would not be unexpected given *who* constitute the judiciary. After reviewing numerous surveys and reports on the social and educational backgrounds of members of the higher level judiciary, Griffiths (1977) concludes that:

four out of five full-time professional judges are products of public schools, and of Oxford and Cambridge. Very occasionally a brilliant lower-middle-class boy has won his place in this distinguished gathering. With very few exceptions judges are required to be selected from amongst practising barristers and until recently no one without a private income could survive the first years of practice. To become a successful barrister therefore it was necessary to have financial support and so the background had to be that of the reasonably well-to-do family which, as a matter of course, sent its sons to public schools and then either straight to the bar or first to Oxford or Cambridge. (pp. 28–9)

Is it any wonder, given their pedigree background, that those fine gentlemen who comprise the higher echelons of British justice, the Law Lords, Judges of the Queen's Bench, High Court Judges, Circuit Judges, and Recorders, are inclined to make decisions consistent with the beliefs and prejudices of a narrow political spectrum. 'These judges have by their education and training and the pursuit of their profession as barristers, acquired a strikingly homogeneous collection of attitudes, beliefs and principles, which to them represent the public interest' (ibid., p. 193). But on reflection, *their* interpretation of public interests means preserving what they perceive to be the interests of the state and maintaining law and order as they perceive the state to have defined it; boiled down to its sticky essence, this amounts to protecting private property rights, which, given the enormous inequalities in property ownership, means protecting the privileged property sections of the community, and 'the promotion of certain political views normally associated with the Conservative Party' (ibid.).

At the other end of the British judiciary are stipendiary magistrates (of whom there are nearly 100) and lay magistrates (of whom there are over 25,000). These are the cart-horses of the criminal justice system. They lack the class and educational pedigree of the stable traditional upper/middle classes, but the bulk of them are culturally, socially, and politically set apart from the vast majority of defendants who stand uneasily before them on the wrong side of the tipped scales of justice. Magistrates' natural constituency is those concerned with the preservation of property. The knowledge that there are millions of idle hands on the streets, doubtless provokes anxiety in them. For many magistrates (and judges) believe that the unemployed are likely to help themselves to other people's property. They also believe that a major part of their judicial function is to be seen protecting private property. When to these beliefs is added the 'knowledge' that 'crime is getting worse' and the 'fear of crime' is becoming a major social problem—messages that politicians, via the media, communicate—then the judiciary are bound to become more sensitized to the dangers that lurk in high levels of unemployment. Consequently, it is very likely that their decisions, both in terms of verdicts (in magistrates courts where the vast bulk of cases are heard) and sentences, will be tinged with hostility and anxiety whenever they sense a deterioration in class relationships and a slackening of discipline-through-work (or school, or family) among the subordinate classes.

This is not to argue that the judiciary are given explicit instructions, or are part of a gigantic conspiracy, but merely that there is a class 'logic' not only *in their situation*, but *in the perception* of their situation. This 'logic' leads them to make decisions which *in the aggregate* may look like the result of a carefully orchestrated effort but is in fact nothing more than thousands of unrelated, but similar individual decisions. Furthermore, given the 'Constitutional Independence' (but 'political reliability') of the judiciary, there will be no concerted effort to prevent or curtail the steady drift towards more frequent use of severe penal sanctions as judges and magistrates react to what they perceive as growing or potential disruption resulting from the upsurge in the volume of unemployment in particular and an intensification of class conflict in general. In other words, those who do not benefit from these decisions are in no position to change them, and those who do benefit have no interest in changing them.

American criminologist Jeffrey Reiman (1984: 114) argues that the superordinate class allows the judiciary to operate independently for two major reasons. First, by criminalizing mainly working-class people, among whom the unemployed and ethnic minorities are over-represented, the judiciary both creates and sustains the idea that the 'crime problem' which threatens our middle-class civilized way of life, comes essentially from the 'lower orders'. This is a useful ideological fiction because it masks the enormous physical, economic and social costs caused by 'crimes of the powerful', such as corporate crime, commercial fraud, and illegal industrial pollution. Second, by 'punishing' offenders, the courts render them morally defective and thereby help to preserve the social structure and particularly the differences in income and wealth from being implicated in the causation of 'conventional crimes'. Because of these two benefits—its crimes are ignored relatively, and its contribution to working-class crime is concealed—the superordinate class has no interest in changing the criminal justice system or preventing the judiciary from 'disciplining and deterring' the economically marginalized.

This does not necessarily mean that during times of rising unemployment the judiciary increases the severity of penal sanctions only against the unemployed; they may well extend imprisonment across the spectrum of persons found guilty, particularly as the majority of these are bound to be working class and/or ethnically oppressed. None the less, when passing sentences, the judiciary are likely to make fine distinctions even within these subordinate groups. If there is judicial anxiety during times of deteriorating economic conditions, then it would be those convicted persons from groups perceived to be actually or potentially disruptive who would feel the harsher side of judicial discretion. It is possible that even within the unemployed population the judiciary would see crucial distinctions.

For example, unemployed males are more likely to be perceived as problematic because in Western culture, work is not only believed to be the typical way in which males are disciplined but it is also their major source of identity and thus the process by which they build up a stake in conformity. Consequently when males are removed from or denied access to work, it is widely believed that they will have various anarchistic responses among which criminal behaviour is likely to figure quite strongly. These cultural meanings of work attributed to males are likely to have adverse effects on the way in which unemployed males are processed in the criminal justice system.

This is not to argue that when it comes to sentencing, magistrates and judges allow the offender's employment status to override the seriousness of his present offence and previous convictions (if they exist). But when they consider sentences for offenders whose offences and previous convictions are similar, they are still forced, because of prison accommodation and court welfare officers' reports, to take other factors into account. One of the most likely extra factors affecting the sentence imposed on a male offender will be whether or not he is employed. If he is not, the judiciary are more likely to view him as potentially more likely to commit other, particularly economic, offences, and consequently pass an immediate prison sentence. This severe sentence is imposed partly because the judiciary believe it will *incapacitate* him, and thus marginally reduce the crime rate, but also because this sentence may *deter* other unemployed males tempted by the possible economic gains of crime. That there is no such simple relationship between incarceration and crime rates (Biles 1979, 1982; Bowker 1981; Greenwood 1983; McGuire and Sheehen 1983; Nagel 1977) is either unknown to the judiciary or fails to dissuade them from using their common-sense notions of crime-causation to guide them in sentencing unemployed males.

In contrast, and again because of institutionalized sexism, unemployed females can, and for the most part do, slip back into or take up the wife/mother social role and hence become subject to all the informal controls of *being* in the family, thus making criminalization and imprisonment, as forms of social control, unlikely resources to be utilized by the judiciary. Furthermore, given the view held by a large proportion of the population that female employment leads to delinquent 'latch-key' children, it is unlikely that judges and magistrates will favour imprisoning unemployed mothers, for they will be seen as fulfilling their stereotypic gender-role and hence playing their informal part in delinquency control. Removing them to prison would interfere with this vital social service. Indeed, the gender-role of keeping the family together becomes all the more important during times of economic crisis and high unemployment; rapidly increasing the rate of imprisonment for unemployed mothers during such times would jeopardize the 'social reproductive' process, and thus further impair the chances of longer-term economic recovery (Braithwaite 1980: 204). Whilst it is unlikely that the judiciary will necessarily be aware of this macro-functional relationship, the aggregation of their individual decisions not to imprison unemployed females unwittingly brings it about.

In addition to making a distinction between gender, the judiciary will also be affected by the offender's age. Thus young unemployed males will be perceived as potentially or actually more dangerous than older males simply because their resistance to adversity will have been less worn away by barren years of accommodative strategies to inequalities in the distribution of income and life chances (Parkin 1971). They will have experienced less discipline at the work place, and their physical prowess and energy, attributes often considered prerequisites for 'conventional' crime, will still be in prime condition. There is a further reason why the judiciary might be affected by the suspect's age. It is 'common knowledge', no doubt shared by the judiciary, that youth and conventional crime are linked; the peak for these crimes tends to be in the mid-teens. This is also an age-group suffering from much higher than national average rates of unemployment. Consequently it can be expected that the association between unemployment and imprisonment will be greater for a population of younger compared with older males.

Finally, there are reasons why ethnic minorities, particularly young males, would be treated more harshly by the judiciary. Not only is the unemployment rate among this group two to three times higher than its white counterpart, but their demographic characteristics—they are disproportionately aged between 15 and 25 years old—also signal potentially high levels of criminal behaviour. So, as a group, the British black population are doubly vulnerable, first to higher levels of unemployment and second to higher levels of criminality because that is 'youth's speciality'. In addition, black youth is politically marginalized and therefore unwilling and incapable of attempting to struggle for change of the system from the inside.

When racial discrimination is added to these factors, and when there have already been urban riots in which unemployed British blacks figures prominently (Southgate and Field 1982)—a fact blown up out of proportion in highly sensationalized media presentation—there are a whole bundle of reasons why the judiciary would view ethnic minorities as needing discipline. Indeed, in a recent Home Office publication, Stevens (1979: 16) appeared to predict and justify this when he wrote 'representation among those arrested and convicted is also likely to increase, and that the absolute numbers of blacks arrested and convicted will increase rapidly, in the 1980s and perhaps beyond'.

The judiciary would not necessarily have to be aware of these demographic characteristics and social changes, or their likely effects on delinquent behaviour. Individual judges and magistrates merely have to view many young offenders, particularly if they are also black and unemployed, as likely to commit further serious criminal acts, and that would justify imposing, in their 'learned opinion', a sentence of imprisonment.

In dispensing 'justice', magistrates and judges have to make fine distinctions between those convicted even for similar offences. They could not commit to prison all those found guilty of property offences. How are they to make these distinctions? I have argued above that the judiciary operates largely in terms of its theories of crime—what types of person are *really* criminal and therefore likely to re-offend. Since these theories, in one way or another, render the poor morally defective because they make 'wicked' decisions when others living in similar circumstances have the moral fibre to resist, then the courts feel justified in imposing harsher sentences. The process is not sinister. Indeed, when magistrates and judges experience not only a total increase in the 'workload' but also a disproportionate *increase* in those perceived as being criminal and likely to re-offend—namely unemployed and unemployable males—then they are acting out of the best possible motives—to protect the public. Of course some magistrates may use this account cynically, being aware that behind it a certain amount of class warfare is being strategically waged. But there is no need to assume this is true of the majority; they are simply doing their job as they see it ought to be done and how the 'public' demand it. The economic élite, not being harmed by this, simply have no reason to stop it, and consequently the judiciary goes on making the poor criminals and ignoring the alternative possibility that poverty is a crime (Reiman 1984: 116–28). On the other hand, since the élite benefit from the criminal justice system, they are not without sufficient acumen to give it a boost in resources and power occasionally and a nudge in the Right direction.

Although this section has relied exclusively on data relating to England and Wales, the processes it describes also apply to the USA. Thus although judges in America are openly political appointees, that does not depart significantly from Britain where a not dissimilar process goes on behind closed doors. And just as British judges share a common set of cultural assumptions, so do the Florida judges studied by Frazier and Bock (1982). These researchers were impressed with the 'subculture of sentencing', based around 'law and order' views, to which these judges subscribed. Furthermore, there is little reason to consider that American judges do not have views on age, gender, and race similar to those outlined above. Most of the research studies reviewed later reveal that these three social characteristics intrude into US court proceedings because judges consider them to be relevant. In addition, the predicted population growth for black males at risk of committing crime mirrors the British situation. Thus the 20–28 black male population is predicted to grow between 1980 and 1990 by 18 per cent, whereas the comparable white population is expected to grow by only 1 per cent (Austin and Krisberg, 1985: 25). Given the longstanding acceptance of the black = crime equation to the American white mind, these demographic predictions, like their British counterparts, are bound to percolate through to the criminal justice system.

The 'latent' contribution of probation officers to the expansion of social control

The importance of the Probation and After-Care Service, both in North America and Britain, has increased substantially over the last two decades. Murrah (1963) reports a prominent American judge commenting that 'of all the administrative aids available to the judge an adequate, comprehensive and complete presentence investigation is the best guide to intelligent sentencing' (p. 67). A similar enthusiastic evaluation can be found in Hogarth (1971) who reported a Canadian judge's view that 'the presentence report is one of the most important developments in Canadian criminal law during the twentieth century' (p. 246).

Although it is complicated to explain the Probation Service's lurch into prominence, two reasons, also relevant to evaluating the Service's contribution to controlling 'problem populations', stand out as deserving special consideration. These occurred in both North America and Britain, but for illustrative purposes the situation in England and Wales will be examined in detail.

Two changes in the criminal justice system over the last twenty years help to account for the rising importance of the Probation Service. First, the ascendancy of 'individualized justice', particularly for adolescents, which occurred during the late 1960s and early 1970s and was embodied in the 1969 Childrens and Young Persons Act, required courts to obtain much more detailed background information on suspects awaiting trial and offenders awaiting sentence. The Probation Service became the conduit along which this information flowed. Second, the proliferation of 'alternatives to prison', which accelerated with the introduction of parole in 1968 and the spread of community service orders from 1973 onwards, required the Probation Service to prepare many more social inquiry reports to assess whether probation or another 'alternative to prison' could be recommended. The Service thus became a centrally important agency shaping and influencing decisions affecting sentence and parole. It also became more involved with supervisory work beyond straightforward probation orders.

These changes resulted in a rapid numerical expansion of clients being supervised by probation officers. Thus the number of offenders received annually on a Probation Order increased from just under 24,000 in 1973 to 34,000 by 1983. The number of prisoners released on parole under licence to the Probation Service rose from 751 in 1968 to over 6,000 by the mid-1980s. Community Service Orders, many of which are supervised by the

Service, increased to over 30,000 ten years after being made available to the courts. Finally, a proportion of the annual number of 30,000 offenders given a suspended prison sentence over recent years has been taken on as additional statutory work for the Service.

The path of increasing importance has not been smooth, or without 'unintended consequences', for the increased clientele and the deepening involvement in courts and prisons created a constant 'dilemma' for probation officers. It was the typical way in which this dilemma was solved that brought about the Probation Service's contribution to the expansion of social control and, unwittingly or not, contributed to the increasing number of persons, particularly the unemployed, being imprisoned. But first, the nature of the dilemma.

The Probation Service has a vested professional and occupational interest in advocating and demonstrating the relative effectiveness and cost-efficiency of 'alternatives to prison', particularly those with which it is intimately involved. In order to justify the allocation of state resources and secure their occupational existence, they need to prove that the services offered will, at worst (and hopefully results will be better than this), produce a rate of re-offending no higher than that among persons released from prison. Furthermore, they need to demonstrate that this superior comparative effectiveness can be achieved at a much lower cost per offender. Of course, this latter objective is easy to achieve—the daily cost of a British prisoner is at least twenty times higher than that of a probationer. The relative costs in America are not that dissimilar. Funke (1985) has estimated that the average cost of paying for a 500-bed prison is roughly $11.5 million per year. This would pay for nearly 20,000 probationers on a one-year order.

The former goal—effectiveness—is like 'hunting the snark'. Despite a wide variety of ingenious schemes for reforming, educating, helping assisting, training, treating, supervising, befriending, and counselling offenders, 'nothing seems to work'. At least that is the dismal conclusion arrived at by Martinson (1974) in his classic evaluation study of numerous attempts to measure the effectiveness of various methods to reduce recidivism. It would not be unreasonable to conclude from this that the Service, like other correctional/control agencies, lacks a proven technology or demonstrated professional expertise. None the less, the illusive goal of effectiveness has to be pursued. Consequently, probation officers have to aim, through their 'recommendations' to courts and prison Parole Boards, to secure not only sufficient clients, but also ones who are *suitable*. Numbers are clearly important because these can be welded as a bargaining lever to wrench more funds from central and local governments. The suitability of clients is essential if results flattering to the service and therefore enhancing their demands for more resources are to stand any chance of being achieved.

These professional and occupational interests do not fit easily with another feature of the Probation Service. As an integral part of the criminal justice system, it constantly has to secure its *credibility* with the courts and prisons. According to Walker and Beaumont (1981), there is a simple reason for this. They argued that 'Although official accounts concede probation officers' flexibility and discretion in the methods they use there is *an expectation that they will always act as agents of the court* (my emphasis) (p. 26). Being aware of this expectation, individual probation officers feel a strain towards appearing reasonable, fair, and just to magistrates, judges, and prison higher officials. Clearly a reputation for being soft, sentimental, and 'out of touch with reality', will render a probation officer's recommendations impotent. To avoid this, officers need to develop a sensitivity to local courts and prison officials and, particularly with the former, a sixth sense in predicting what kind of sentence will be imposed, or at least the narrow range of possibilities under consideration. They also have to gauge whether the sentence will be imposed irrespective of any skilled written advocacy of an alternative. If they assess this to be likely, it would be prudent to write a report which flatters the court rather than waste time and effort pointlessly opposing it. Any probation officer who is seen to prioritize occupational interests by recommending probation orders, community orders or some other sentence with which they might become involved in a supervisory capacity, and is considered blinkered to the courts' sentencing practices, will not only incur its displeasure, but will lose personal credibility and cast a shadow on the whole local Probation Service.

'Second-guessing' the sentence is difficult because within the judiciary two 'systems of justice' reside as uneasy bedfellows. The first, *individualized justice*, presumes that offenders are more deprived than depraved, and that with skilful, professional insight, each individual offender's personal problems can be identified and, to some extent, ameliorated. Under this system, 'what' the offender did becomes relegated to 'what' kind of problems the offender confronted both at the time of the offence and prior to it. In the determination of sentence, guilt becomes less important than the offender's 'needs' and suitability for professional intervention. This requires fairly extensive interviewing to gather sufficient information to form a recommendation.

The second system, sometimes called the *justice* or *tariff* model, is based on the classical idea that the offence should determine sanction. The more serious the offence, the more severe should be the sanction. The offender is punished not because of personal qualities, or the conditions surrounding the offence, but because the offence itself deserves, indeed demands, a particular sanction. There is no need to delve into the suspect's past or present circumstances, or psychological characteristics. The primary and overriding issue is the establishment of guilt. Once this is settled, the sanction, in principle at least, should be determined automatically. Since, under this system, judicial discretion is minimized, a robot, properly programmed, could dispense justice!

Although these two systems of justice are distinct theoretically, they are rarely realized in practice in a way that resembles their pure form. Indeed, in the USA, and in the UK particularly, both systems operate simultaneously. This creates a second strand in the dilemma facing Probation Officers. Is the court likely to see a particular case more in terms of the 'justice' or the 'individualized' model?

With some cases this is no problem. At the most serious end of the offence spectrum, the 'tariff'/'justice' system is likely to dominate; at the trivial, first-offender, adolescent end, the 'individualized' model is likely to weigh more heavily in the minds of magistrates. However, these are extremities. The majority of cases are in between. In these, there is likely to be a fine balance between elements incorporated from both models. The officer's dilemma is how to guess this balance correctly so as not to lose credibility with the courts (Roberts and Roberts 1982; Rosecrance 1985).

As in medicine, and other service-professions, dilemmas and ambiguities are resolved by applying the same defensive principle, 'when in doubt, it is better to be safe than sorry'. When making recommendations to the court, officers' discretion has to be tempered by an awareness that they are its agents. As Walker and Beaumont (1981) argue:

the dominant influence in reports [by officers] is that they are written for an *audience*—the court. This determines the approach taken, the content and the style. It also acts as a constraint, determining the limit of material considered relevant. (p. 21)

In attempting to 'gauge' the court's mood, and in particular predict whether it will lean towards the 'tariff' or 'individualized' system of justice, and which type of sentence it might impose when it has made this decision, probation officers will tend to be *cautious*. Their 'faces', and beyond that, their professional credibility, depend upon it. Consequently, where there is ambiguity, and there often is, they will tend towards making sentence recommendations which favour applying the 'tariff' model, and where, on a prima-facie basis, this indicates imprisonment, recommend that sentence.

This creeping conservatism, understandable in terms of preserving professional standing, has an 'unintended' effect, or as sociologists call it, a 'latent function'. It might lead to more prison sentences being recommended than the courts would have imposed otherwise, and in this way unwittingly contribute towards increasing the control of 'surplus populations'.

This possibility is reinforced by a second consideration. In attempting to select suitable clients, probation officers may move slightly from the principled position of recommending an 'alternative to custody', particularly where the client is estimated by them to be a poor risk and unlikely to respond well to their professional services. In this circumstance, they might push the offender up the 'tariff' and recommend custody. In other words, some offenders, who from another more 'individualized' perspective might look like suitable cases for not being imprisoned, become, through the process of officers protecting their professional and the Service's interests, transformed into just the opposite.

Thus the increased involvement of the Probation Service in the criminal justice system over the last two decades, an involvement premised on the basis of developing more genuine alternatives to imprisonment, has probably made a contribution, no doubt unintended and unwitting, to pushing up the number of persons sent to prison. It has done this by being too cautious, and *over-predicting* the number of cases for which courts would have handed down a prison sentence. The courts, having little reason not to accept these recommendations, go ahead and imprison the offender. If the interests of the courts, as perceived by magistrates, were threatened by these recommendations, they would lean heavily on the Service to change its practices, and maybe even lose a practitioner or two. But since the courts' interests are not harmed (just as the national interest, as perceived by the government, is not harmed by the courts' sentencing practices), they are, on the whole, willing 'to be influenced' by officers' correctly anticipated recommendations. It is harmlessness of probation officers' sentence recommendations that explains the very high agreement between these and the actual sentence reported in research conducted in Britain (White 1972), Canada (Hagan 1975), and the USA (Carter and Wilkins 1967; Neubauer 1974; Myers

1979), and not that the courts are unduly influenced against their judgement to accept them. Indeed, according to American criminologist John Rosecrance (1985):

officers exert a minimal influence upon the sentencing process . . . [because] . . . when decision making is actually required, it is done by correlating a recommendation with informal but existing sentencing parameters. Knowledge of current sentencing concepts and policies allows the probation officer to select satisfactory or 'ball park' recommendations. Through a process of bureaucratic winnowing, only probation officers who are willing to provide such recommendations consistently are assigned to the presentence investigation unit. These officers are rewarded for their compliance and come to accept the prevailing sentencing parameters as 'natural'. (pp. 549–50)

By pushing more offenders into custody than they need have, the Service creates a problem for itself. It still has to secure sufficient numbers of clients to justify its own demands for financial resources. Officers find themselves filling this gap by recommending probation and/or community service orders to some offenders who would never previously have been given a supervisory sentence in the first place. These are offenders whom officers predict would be treated more in terms of the 'individualized' model of justice by the courts, and who, by virtue of their personal qualities, offer the service a strong possibility of not being 'failures'. Some at least of these would previously have been either fined, or given a conditional/unconditional discharge.

The results, doubtless unintended, of probation officers resolving the dilemma between securing occupational interests and gaining credibility in the courts, is that they contribute not only to widening the net of social control, but also to the increasing number of persons being sent to prison. They trawl into the net of social control persons who would not have been caught previously, and they shunt a proportion from the *soft* end, where they probably deserve to be, to the *hard* end, and thus contribute to the problem of prison overcrowding.

It would be wrong to exaggerate this contribution and thus distort reality too much. Nor would it be justifiable to argue that this contribution is greater than that made by magistrates and judges themselves, or by the next group of control agents to be examined, the police. But none the less it would be naive to assume that the Probation Service and its practitioners, although operating no doubt from benevolent motives, do not bring about consequences they never intended. Social life is too replete with ironies ('latent consequences') for any professional group to be exempt from this 'social fact'.

The police and the control of 'problem populations'

The contribution of the courts, with the Probation Service's assistance, to the problem of prison overcrowding, widening the net of social control, and damping down the potential threat, real or imagined, posed by 'problem populations', is only possible with 'a little help from their friends'. Through their deployment, arrest and prosecution practices, the police supply the judiciary with an increasing number of persons to process, and among these proportionately more are young, unemployed, and/or black. How and why do the police bring this result about?

The police have a particular image of themselves. First, they are the thin 'blue line' protecting upright respectable citizens from the tidal wave of criminality which, as they believe, occurred within the last twenty years and has become a major source of anxiety and worry in the community causing far too many people to stay at home behind bolted doors and locked windows. Second, they view themselves as the 'guardians of public morality'. Although the police realize that over many moral issues, particularly prostitution, homosexuality, abortion, pornography, alcohol, and other drug consumption, there exist heated, volatile disagreements, none the less they tend to identify more with the conservative sides of these debates. Finally, they experience themselves as 'front-line troops' in a war against certain types of dissidents—marginalized, alienated and alien youth, terrorists, football hooligans, industrial agitators, and militant trade-unionists—all of whom, so it appears to those suffering from cultural amnesia, have crawled out of the woodwork only recently. A close reading of either Stan Cohen's *Folk Devils and Moral Panics* (1972) or Geoff Pearson's *Hooligan* (1983) would soon cure this amnesia, but these studies, like other 'demystifying' sociological texts, are doomed to the fate of co-optation, parody or rude dismissal.

From the officers' perspective, these three images—'protector', 'guardian' and 'defender'—coalesce to produce a view of police work as dangerous, socially isolating, and containing problems of authority, which not only undermine efficiency, but frequently poison police–public relationships. Despite these lurking dangers, the police perceive themselves as having a mandate to solve the 'problem of crime', reduce the 'fear of crime' and eliminate the 'enemy within'. To achieve these Herculean tasks, the police cannot be too hindered by procedural niceties to protect the civil and legal rights of citizens. The warnings of politicians and journalists that social order, as we have known it, is under real threat, the demands of frightened citizens for more police and policing, and the legal system turning a permissive 'blind eye' to irregularities, all combine to give the police a secure sense of certainty that it is important, almost at any costs, to get the villains.

The three types of police work outlined above, and which in reality often overlap, require the police to develop routine methods for recognizing certain types of persons as being 'typical criminals', 'symbolic assailants', 'purveyors of immorality', and 'political extremists'. For a number of reasons this rogues' gallery will be lined with portraits drawn from a pastiche of class, sex, and racial ingredients. In the first two 'typifications' particularly, the economically marginalized and ethnic minority males will figure prominently in the foreground.

There are two reasons for these 'stereotypic villains' being portrayed in this way. The first consists of external influences, and the second refers to occupational experiences and organizational needs.

By virtue of their training and general involvement in the acquisition of 'cultural common sense', the police come into contact with versions of criminological theories posing as explanations of criminal activity. The majority of these are 'types of person' accounts, which describe offenders as a pathological, almost subhuman species. They have brain, chromosome, glandular, psychological, or personality disorders; they are, in a word, *flawed*. Sociological theories, such as differential association, anomie, cultural transmission, and control, will definitely play 'second fiddle' to pathology theories, even though all propose some flawed environmental factors, such as bad friends, irresponsible parents, libertarian schools, disorganized neighbourhoods, or some combination of these. Both types of theories suppose that there exists a major 'set of facts to be explained'. These 'facts' are that crime is primarily a lower-class young male activity. Hence each theory is shaped to fit snugly around these 'facts', thus elevating the class/youth/male–crime relationships into *the* touchstones of criminology.

These theories have trickled down, in loosely translated form, from the academe to the minds of laypersons, including the police. Through the acquisition of this 'conventional wisdom', the police 'know' where to find criminals; they live in poor, inner-city areas where the lower-class, economically marginalized and ethnic minorities live semi-ghettoized existences. The police also 'know' how to recognize them: they are pathological or abnormal, or have corrupting friends, inadequate parents, weak teachers, or live in neighbourhoods lacking a sense of community; and above all they have been 'identified' previously either by expulsion from school, caught playing truant, involved with social work departments, or by past dealings with the police. This non-representative sample of citizens becomes the front-line suspects methodically selected by the police as being 'up to no good'.

Politicians and journalists scoop up deposits left by the popularization of academic criminology and give them a reconstructed interpretation to suit their own particular interests. Consider one example—'the scrounger'. The floodlights of engineered opinion picked out the distinguishing features of this 'folk devil' as the unemployed total broke through the barrier of post-war Keynesian consensus welfarism in the late 1970s and early 1980s. An event on 2 September 1982 encapsulates the whole process. On that day, '283 people who walked into an unemployment benefit office in Oxford found themselves arrested by the police on suspicion of fraud' (CHAR 1983: 7). Newspapers used all the imagery of the 'scrounger' to mediate this mass arrest to the public. Who were these fiddlers? They were, according to the London's *Standard*, 'bands of highly organized claimants . . . roving round the country conning "our" money out of the Department of Health and Social Security'. Among them were such moral disreputables as 'seven Irishmen', 'a gipsy couple', 'a top class stripper', 'an unmarried mum' and, of course, 'blacks'. This last 'stereotype', a particularly unpleasant racist slur, was depicted in a *Sun* cartoon. It showed twelve accused claimants riding on a conveyor belt past a magistrates' bench. Four of the claimants were black. This proportion of one-third totally misrepresented the actual ratio. According to CHAR (1983), 'In reality, only 4 out of 283 people arrested . . . were black; two were released without charge, one had his case dismissed, and one was convicted' (p. 49).

Yet the damage was done. Readers of the *Sun* were led to believe that blacks form a significantly large proportion of 'scroungers'. This further reinforced the black = crime equation, which began with the mugging panic of the early 1970s (Hall, *et al.*, 1978) and climaxed with the *Daily Mail*'s screaming headline: BLACK CRIME: THE ALARMING FIGURES. In this classic scare story, policemen's leader Jim Jardine was reported to be calling for at least another 5,000 officers to deal with the problem. Readers were warned that things were deteriorating just like 'across the water in America'. Somehow guns were thrown in, even though guns appear in a minute number of muggings. And Mrs Jill Knight, Tory MP, claimed that the Home Secretary had assured her that 'where serious criminals could be deported back to their countries of origin they would be'. Of course, it was all misinformation. The data on which the story was based referred to only 3 per cent of serious crimes. The race of the vast majority of offenders was simply unknown. But this point was nicely concealed beneath the alarming headlines.

Furthermore, these 'scroungers'—'lazy', 'idle', 'aliens' in our midst—were not the deserving poor. They were not poor at all! They were described as making a fortune. One was reported to have claimed £13,000 illegally even while driving round in an £8,000 sports car. Others had the nerve to insult respectable sensibilities by turning up to collect their dole money in taxis they could afford from the vast hoardings of their fraud or earnings from 'moonlighting' (the contradiction between 'idle' and 'moonlighting' not being apparent to either tabloid journalists or their readers!).

It was alleged to be an enormous fiddle. The *Daily Telegraph*, who claimed that 'one in 12 dole claims are fraudulent', could not put a precise monetary value on it. The *Express*, however, was able to ask whether it was '£100m.? £200m.? or £300m.?' and thus alert readers to its possible size. The *Sun* went further. One of its headlines revealed that 'Dole swindles cost £400m.' And the *Mail* put the cream on the claimants' fraudulent cake by asserting that £500 millions was involved!

The courts were quick to 'legitimate' police action against these deeply wicked scroungers. They heard the cases almost instantly, and handed down severe sentences. Of 139 guilty pleas, all were given a custodial sentence, only two of which were suspended, even though many were appearing in court for the first time and had not been advised by solicitors. Of nineteen pleading 'not guilty', four were finally convicted and given custodial sentences.

The Big Culprits, the Landlords who made a lot more money out of supplying bogus addresses for claimants in return for a 'fee', were ignored by the police, and no one in authority complained. But when claimants and/or their solicitors complained about police irregularities and violation of civil and legal rights, these were either dismissed or condemned to the rubbish tip of 'complaints through the proper channels'.

The lesson police learnt from this one incident—and it is merely a highly publicized example of daily confrontations between some members of the public and the police—is that certain social groups are stigmatized and scapegoated by politicians and the media. As such, they are condemned groups the police are permitted to arrest and criminalize. This segment, by coincidence, as Vonnegut would have it, happens to come from the inner-city lower-class areas, where the economically marginalized and disadvantaged ethnic minorities live. They are, in other words, the *same* people whose crimes form the 'facts to be explained' in mainstream criminological theories.

Selective deployment patterns adopted by the police result in officers, and especially new recruits 'on the beat', coming into direct and personal contact with a limited slice of 'deviant/criminal' life. These deployment policies, determined by higher management, interact with and reinforce media images of the typical criminal and politicians' warnings of our escalating crime problem. They focus on certain parts of urban areas, particularly those 'known' to contain criminal elements or where it is believed that violence is likely to break out. They also concentrate on 'public' places, where 'idle' hands spend most of the unoccupied days and nights. The outcome is that young unemployed males are frequently 'in the sights' of the police. Of course, the institution of 'privacy' which determines that police dwell mainly in public places is not constantly observed. The police frequently penetrate the 'privacy' of those persons living mainly in lower-class areas where the unemployed and ethnic minorities are concentrated.

As a consequence of these deployment patterns, directed as they are by theories of criminality, as well as organizational pragmatism and political cynicism, the police tend to concentrate on 'street' crimes, such as robbery, burglary, theft and assault. These crimes are undoubtedly committed more frequently by lower-class young males, and the unemployed and ethnic minorities are also over-represented in this group. The police will hardly ever meet upper-class criminals deeply involved in corporate violations of state regulations, government malfeasance, professional malpractice, embezzlement, or security/insurance fraud. Only when respectable citizens untypically commit 'street' offences, are the police likely to become involved.

When it is realized the crime on which the police concentrate is only a slice of the total, the 'war against crime' takes on a slightly different colour. In this new light, it can be seen also as a 'war' against those populations surplus to the requirements of the productive process and who are perceived by the state as being willing, at least potentially, to resist. Indeed, if 'street' crime is a form of resistance, albeit a totally 'irrational' form because it victimizes people in a similar predicament, then the state feels some justification for this 'war' against the 'enemy within'.

The population on whom the police concentrate their attention is likely to view itself as 'picked on', 'pushed around', 'unfairly treated' and 'occupied by a police force increasingly resembling the army'. These feelings constitute a massive 'sense of injustice' and this undoubtedly colours police–public relations in parts of the urban landscape. In these encounters, civilian behaviour is likely to be perceived by the police as hostile, uncivil, unpleasant, and above all, as threatening their authority and physical safety. No wonder they are receptive to the media's portraits of 'thugs', 'bully-boys', 'granny bashers', 'louts', and 'hooligans'. These reflect, at least in a distorted form, their interpretation of experiences with young inner-city males, and thus reinforce and 'legitimate' police behaviour (and 'misbehaviour') towards them.

These deployment patterns have another effect which facilitates the police adopting a 'tougher' stance towards certain social groups. They are likely to come into contact with those sections of the community amongst whom the 'fear of crime' is higher than elsewhere. In the USA (Balkin 1979; Braungart *et al.*, 1980; Gordon *et al.*, 1980) and the UK (Clarke and Lewis 1982; Maxfield 1984) the old, women, and particularly old women living in inner-city areas, report higher rates of being afraid to go out after dark, and believe they can protect themselves less easily in a neighbourhood they perceive as being unsafe and growing worse all the time.

These respectable citizens—the old, women, and particularly old women, who contribute little to serious crime and do not threaten police authority—bring out the 'guardian' side of police work. Fortified with this paternalistic, protective mission, the police feel perfectly justified in taking a hard stance towards people they perceive to be threatening the lives of these vulnerable members of the population and destroying the fabric of the community they inhabit. Also, by drawing this cloak of 'protecting the public' over their professional conscience, the police feel able to practise a little 'vigilante' justice, or fall into the habit of charging certain people with offences for which there is no real defence, such as being disorderly, resisting arrest, using threatening behaviour towards an officer, and obstructing the highway (Cain and Sadigh 1982; McBarnet 1982). These tactics are very valuable when the law is seen to be too soft and in need of a little help 'from its friends' to get more right results.

Finally, the police, like any other organization, needs to project an image of itself as efficient, but hard-pressed. It needs the former to mute criticism; it needs the latter to justify the allocation of more financial resources and legal powers. To achieve these objects, it has to 'clear up' a sufficient number of crimes to satisfy the public that the police are doing what they can. But at the same time, the police have to appeal for more resources on the grounds that they could do much better with modern equipment, improved technology, and extended legal powers. In this careful balancing act, it is essential to keep organizational costs down by arresting and prosecuting suspects who are seen by the public to be acceptable targets for police intervention, and who, in addition, present little trouble to bureaucratic routines and procedures. As Chambliss (1969) saw it, the principles governing the administration of justice are simple. He suggested that:

Those persons are arrested, tried and sentenced who can offer the fewest rewards for non-enforcement of the laws and who can be processed without creating undue strain of the organisations which comprise the legal system. (pp. 84–5)

Young, poor, unemployed, ethnic-minority males are the most vulnerable to apprehension, arrest and prosecution, not because they commit more crimes, although they certainly commit more 'street' crimes, but because *in addition* they are in no position to protect themselves, present little trouble to the legal process, and coincide with the media's image of 'villains', an image widely accepted by the public. Thus, although the police have considerable discretion, they feel a strong need to employ it in a selective manner. They do not want to upset their organizational superiors and the work norms they formulate. They do not want to be seen disregarding the fears of respectable old women in inner-city neighbourhoods. They do not want to be seen in dereliction of their mission to defend all that is good from the 'enemy within'. Finally, they do not want to jeopardize their careers by getting on badly with peers. For this host of reasons, police discretionary powers, wide in theory, take on a practical substance around a select group of routinely suspected citizens.

As the number of unemployed has grown over the last decade, it would be expected that unemployed suspects increase disproportionately in those arrested and prosecuted by the police. This is not because the police are the government's poodle and simply respond obediently to commands. The 'logic' of police work is such that it would lead to this result. Media representations, politicians' warnings, citizen complaints, occupational experiences, peer-group socialization, and organizational norms for 'results', all dovetail to produce considerable pressure on constables to behave in highly predictable ways, despite their discretionary powers. At the receiving end of this predictable behaviour will be those conforming to 'folk devil' images, who pose problems for authority by their lack of respect and deference, and who are unable to offer much trouble to the smooth bureaucratic process of being criminalized. By sheer coincidence, as Vonnegut would have it, these just happen to be young, working-class males, amongst whom the unemployed and ethnic minorities will be over-represented. This is not to imply that most of these are 'angels' who have not committed any crime. But crimes, maybe different ones, are also committed by other types of persons from more 'respectable' backgrounds. However, the very nature of police discretion precludes full enforcement of the criminal law. The net police cast to trawl in suspects is so designed not to catch all offenders, but only some. Those caught may be presented as the worst, and most dangerous offenders, but that is more ideological than descriptive. Compared with corporate violations, government offences, and crimes committed by numerous respectable professional groups, these 'street' criminals are small fish. However, ideological messages have real consequences. 'Street' criminals are viewed as *the* criminals, and so the police feel justified in arresting and prosecuting them. This is reinforced by large sections of the public who believe this will do something about the 'crime problem'. It is also supported by politicians who see electoral advantage in waging a war against 'street' crime, as well as cynically seeing it as yet another weapon for controlling the 'social dynamite' part of the 'surplus population' and hence reducing the likelihood of resistance or rebellion.

Furthermore, ethnic minorities form a large part of this 'surplus population', and 'racial prejudice' both in the community and the police gives an unpleasant twist to economic marginalization. As Reiner (1985) sees it:

> The young 'street' population has always been the prime focus of police order maintenance and law enforcement work. The processes of racial disadvantage in housing, employment and education lead young blacks to be disproportionately involved in street culture. They may also become engaged in specific kinds of street crime . . . At the same time, the relative powerlessness of ethnic minorities and lower working-class youth means that the police may be less constrained and inhibited in dealing with them. In times of economic crisis and competition for jobs and other resources, the majority group (especially the white working class) might indeed benefit from the effects of over-policing the blacks, because black stigmatisation as criminal, the acquisition of criminal records, reduces their competitiveness. For all these reasons, the economically marginal ethnic minorities, and especially their youth, are prone to become 'police property'. (p. 136)

Once a group has been identified as 'police property', encounters between them and the police become tense and fraught; each approaches the other in terms of 'stereotypes' which although at first misleading, come, through a kind of self-fulfilling prophecy, to resemble the real thing. The police come to see the economically marginalized as 'criminal' and threatening; the economically marginalized come to see the police as prejudiced oppressors. The outcome is more economically marginalized persons being apprehended, arrested and prosecuted, a process which has intensified during the recent recession.

Conclusion: what this 'radical' view opposes and predicts

The ghost haunting this chapter is an alternative, more orthodox, and doubtlessly more appealing to common-sense explanation of the link between unemployment and imprisonment. According to this orthodox perspective, there is a very mechanistic relationship between unemployment and imprisonment. It proposes that rising unemployment pushes up the crime rate as more individuals are tempted to break the law, a temptation many of them are unable to resist because they lack sufficient moral fibre. (This personal failing is also a major convenient explanation for their being unemployed.) As the rate of crime increases, and assuming a constant rate of reporting crime by the public, and arrest and prosecution by the police, so there is an *automatic* increase in the work-load of the judiciary. As this work-load increases and as more people are convicted of crime, so naturally the judiciary send more people to prison.

While there is obviously some truth in this, particularly the expected increase in the number of prison sentences following more convictions, it has at least two serious flaws. First, the rates of reporting, arrest, conviction, and imprisonment are unlikely to remain constant over time; indeed, they are likely to vary as economic circumstances change. During a time of increasing unemployment, it is reasonable to expect that:

1 reporting of crimes increases, partly because the 'fear of crime' intensifies—this occurs because people *believe* that 'unemployment causes crime', but also because more reporting pushes up the level of 'recorded crime' thereby fuelling the 'fear of crime'!

2 the number of police increases, partly because it attracts some of the unemployed, and partly because the government also *believe* that 'unemployment causes crime', or at least considers it should be prudent enough to increase the police force just in case;

3 the police are likely to adopt a tougher policy towards people in high areas of unemployment because they too *believe* that 'unemployment causes crime' and that these areas might become unmanageable;

4 the judiciary will increase the use of imprisonment and other supervisory sentences, although not simply as a mechanical response to any increase in the numbers convicted, but because they believe this to be a rational means of helping to reduce a crime problem which they perceive is increasing because they too *believe* that the level of unemployment affects the level of criminal activity;

5 the government, despite whatever public pronouncements it makes,

quietly colludes in all these responses, thus significantly influencing the relationship between unemployment and imprisonment.

The 'radical' view developed in this chapter considers that unemployment and imprisonment are linked, but instead of looking at crime and conviction rates as the mediating factors, it has focused on the *belief* that 'unemployment causes crime' and how this belief directly or subtly affects judicial sentencing practice, probation officers' sentence recommendations, and police deployment, apprehension, arrest, and prosecution policies.

The second related flaw in the orthodox perspective is that the relationship between unemployment and crime is nowhere near as simple as is commonly claimed. The response to unemployment depends very much on what it *means* to those experiencing it. This varies across age, gender, class, and ethnic divisions. It is also affected by the actual and perceived *duration* of unemployment, and what is believed to have *caused* it. Crime is only likely to be a response among those unemployed who blame the economic system rather than themselves, who perceive that they will be unemployed for a long time, or become unemployable, who fail to see an institutional way of changing the situation, and who are willing to resist rather than acquiesce, even if that means breaking the law. Even then, whether crime occurs or not would depend upon many other factors, which is why numerous attempts to demonstrate an empirical relationship between unemployment and crime have produced ambiguous and inconsistent results.

Nevertheless, it is clear that many people *believe* that 'unemployment causes crime'. This belief is important for understanding the increasing prison population, because magistrates and judges deliberating over a sentence, probation officers considering which sentence to recommend, and police considering whether to arrest and prosecute, may well be influenced by their *belief*, or by their belief that others *believe*, that 'unemployment causes crime'. This of course is not to argue that unemployment becomes the major determinant of police, probation or judicial decisions. That would be an absurd position to propose. None the less, each of these state agents has to use discretionary power. They cannot simply proceed on the basis of whether or not a crime was committed. They need to make decisions on its seriousness, mitigating circumstances, plausible defence, and take into account a host of other organizational and occupational considerations. In this matrix of extra-legal factors, the suspects' personal characteristics, including age, sex, race, and employment status are taken into account. As unemployment increases, more unemployed persons get caught up in the network of legal control. Their employment status will play a part, maybe only marginal, in affecting the decisions control agents have to make about eventual disposition. None the less, the marginal contribution to many individual cases adds up. When aggregated these individual cases show that the proportion of the imprisoned population who were previously unemployed increases, a proportion in excess of that predictable from simple increases in the number of persons convicted.

It is important to stress once again that this is not a conspiracy theory. The important minor figures in this drama—the judges, magistrates, probation officers and the police—all act in 'logic of their situation'. Each have beliefs—although these are not dissimilar—experiences, occupational, and organization needs, and these combine to make behaviour patterned and predictable. It is the 'unintended consequences' of these individual decisions which, when aggregated, mount up to an increasing prison population, a widening of the net of social control, and a damping-down of the potential threat of 'social dynamite'. The government rests content with these 'unintended consequences' because their 'latent function' does not harm them or the interests they protect. Indeed, they tend to benefit from this 'latent function' and that is why they occasionally give the criminal justice system, broadly conceived, more personnel and resources to get the job done.

Figure 1 represents both the orthodox and 'radical' perspectives on the relationships between unemployment, crime, and punishment.

As the recession deepened over the last decade, so the government felt the need to become more 'coercive'. As part of this 'coerciveness' it allowed, and occasionally nudged, the judiciary to make more custodial or supervisory sentences. For its part, the judiciary were sufficiently anxious about the growing crime problem to respond by stiffening its sentencing policies. Thus the following hypothesis could be deduced:

1 *The rate of imprisonment has increased in recent years over and above that predictable from increases in the numbers convicted.*

The Probation Service, being primarily an agent of the court and wanting to maintain its credibility, found itself anticipating the court's drift towards more custodial sentences and hence sought to align sentence recommendations to this. A second hypothesis can therefore be deduced:

2 *If the person for whom the probation officer is writing a social inquiry report is unemployed, and other things, such as offence and prior record, being equal, this fact will result in a recommended sentence higher up the 'tariff'.*

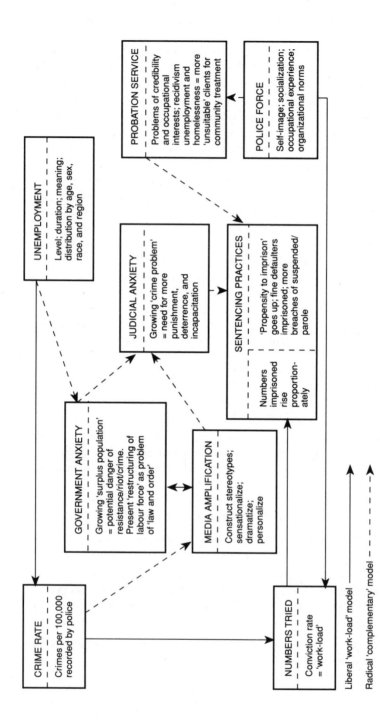

FIGURE 1 *Two models of unemployment–crime–punishment*

UNEMPLOYMENT
Level; duration; meaning; distribution by age, sex, race, and region

CRIME RATE
Crimes per 100,000 recorded by police

GOVERNMENT ANXIETY
Growing 'surplus population' = potential danger of resistance/riot/crime. Present 'restructuring of labour force' as problem of 'law and order'

JUDICIAL ANXIETY
Growing 'crime problem' = need for more punishment, deterrence, and incapacitation

PROBATION SERVICE
Problems of credibility and occupational interests; recidivism unemployment and homelessness = more 'unsuitable' clients for community treatment

POLICE FORCE
Self-image; socialization; occupational experience; organizational norms

MEDIA AMPLIFICATION
Construct stereotypes; sensationalize; dramatize; personalize

SENTENCING PRACTICES
'Propensity to imprison' goes up; fine defaulters imprisoned; more breaches of suspended/parole
Numbers imprisoned rise proportionately

NUMBERS TRIED
Conviction rate = 'work-load'

Liberal 'work-load' model ⟶

Radical 'complementary' model ⇢

Finally, the police, being sensitive to politicians, respectable citizens, the media portraits of 'villains', and organizational norms, will be influenced by the suspect's employment status. Thus, the third hypothesis is:

3 *When deciding what to do with a suspect, the police will be influenced by employment status and impose a harsher disposition. Other things being equal, the unemployed are more likely to be apprehended, arrested, and prosecuted.*

Bibliography

Austin, J and Krisberg, B. (1985), 'Incarceration in the US: the extent and future of the prison', *Annals Amer. Acad. Political and Social Sci.*, 478: 15–30.

Balkin, S. (1979), 'Victimization rates, safety and fear of crime', *Social Problems*, 26: 343–58.

Biles, D. (1982), 'Crime and imprisonment', *Aust. & New Zealand J. Criminology*, 23: 166–72.

Bowker, L. H. (1981), 'Crime and the use of prisons in the US: a time series analysis', *Crime and Delinq.*, 27: 206–12.

Braithwaite, J. and Braithwaite, V. (1980), 'Effects of income inequality and social democracy on homicide', *Brit. J. Criminology*, 20: 45–53.

Braungart, M. M., Braungart, R. G. and Hoyer, W. J. (1980), 'Age, sex and social factors in the fear of crime', *Sociological Focus*, 13: 55–66.

Cain, M. and Sadigh, S. (1982), 'Racism, the police and community policing', *J. Law and Society*, 9: 87–102.

Carter, R. and Wilkins, L. (1967), 'Some factors in sentencing policy', *J. Criminal Law, Criminology and Police Sci.*, 58: 503–14.

Chambliss, W. J. (1969), *Crime and the Legal Process*, (New York: McGraw-Hill).

CHAR (1983), *Poor Law*, (London: Campaign For Single Homeless People).

Clarke, A. H. and Lewis, M. (1982), 'Fear of crime among the elderly', *Brit. J. Criminology*, 22: 49–62.

Cohen, S. (1972), *Folk Devils and Moral Panics*, (London: MacGibbon & Kee).

Frazier, C. E. and Bock, E. W. (1982), 'Effects of court officials on sentencing severity', *Criminology*, 20: 257–72.

Gordon, M. T., Riger, S., LeBailey, R. K. and Heath, L. (1980), 'Crime, women and the quality of urban life', *Signs*, 5: S144–S160.

Greenwood, P. W. (1983), 'Controlling the crime rate through imprisonment', in J. Q. Wilson (ed.), *Crime and Public Policy*, (San Francisco: Institute of Contemporary Studies).

Griffiths, J. S. (1977), *The Political of the Judiciary*, (London: Fontana).

Hagan, J. (1975), 'The social and legal construction of criminal justice', *Social Problems*, 22: 620–37.

Hall, S., Critcher, C., Jefferson, T., Clarke, J. and Roberts, B. (1978), *Policing the Crisis*, (London: Macmillan).

Hogarth, J. (1971), *Sentencing is a Human Process*, (University Toronto Press).

Martinson, R. (1974), 'What works?'—questions and answers about prison reform', *Public Interest*, 35: 22–54.

Maxfield, M. (1984), *Fear of crime in England and Wales*, (London: HMSO).

McBarnet, D. (1982), *Conviction*, (London: Macmillan).

McGuire, W. J. and Sheehen, R. G. (1983), 'Relationships between crime rates and incarceration rates', *J. Research Crime and Delinq.*, 20: 73–85.

Murrah, A. (1963), 'Prison or probation—which and why?', in Kay, B. and Vedder, C. (eds), *Probation and Parole* (Springfield: C. C. Thomas).

Myers, M. (1979), 'Offended parties and official reactions: victims and the sentencing of criminal defendants', *Sociol. Qrtly.*, 20: 529–40.

Nagel, W. (1977), 'On behalf of a moratorium on prison construction', *Crime and Delinq.*, 23: 154–72.

Neubauer, D. (1974), *Criminal Justice in Middle America*, (Morristown, NJ.: General Learning Press).

Parkin, F. (1971), *Class, Inequality and Political Order*, (London: MacGibbon & Kee).

Pearson, G. (1983), *Hooligan: A History of Respectable Fears*, (London: Macmillan).

Reiman, J. H. (1984), *The Rich Get Richer and the Poor Get Prison*, 2nd edn (New York: Wiley).

Reiner, R. (1985), *The Politics of the Police*, (Brighton: Wheatsheaf).

Roberts, J. and Roberts, C. (1982), 'Social Enquiry Reports and sentencing', *Howard Journal*, 21: 76–93.

Rosecrance, J. (1985), 'The probation officer's search for credibility', *Crime and Delinq.*, 31: 539–54.

Southgate, P. and Field, S. (1982), *Public Disorder*, (London: Home Office).

Stevens, P. (1979), 'Predicting black crime', *Research Bulletin* (London: Home Office) 8: 14–18.

Walker, H. and Beaumont, B. (1981), *Probation Work*, (Oxford: Blackwell).

White, S. (1972), 'The effect of social inquiry reports on sentencing decisions', *Brit. J. Criminology*, 12: 230–49.

The Normalization of Special Powers: from Northern Ireland to Britain

PADDY HILLYARD

The aim of this chapter is to describe the different strategies which the authorities have used to deal with political violence in Northern Ireland since 1969. The analysis will attempt to draw out some of the more important features which have tended to be overlooked in those accounts which have been more concerned to highlight the sectarian aspects of the strategies. The principal conclusion of the analysis is that the form of the repressive strategy adopted since 1975, far from being exceptional and a product of the unique circumstances of the political violence in Northern Ireland is, on the contrary, the form which many modern capitalist states are evolving.

No understanding of the various strategies adopted since 1969 is possible without a discussion of law and order in the period from the setting up of the regional government and parliament in the six counties by the Government of Ireland Act 1920.

1920–69: Special powers extraordinary

By mid-summer 1920 the British government had to contend with two law and order problems in the six counties. Both were to remain a feature until the present day. On the one hand, it had to deal with attacks by the IRA and on the other it had to cope with the sectarian attacks, which were mainly carried out on Catholics. It had two forces at its disposal: the Royal Irish Constabulary (RIC), which was controlled by a divisional commissioner outside Belfast and a city commissioner within the city; and various military units stationed in the North.[1] At the time the British government was hard-pressed in the south and west of Ireland and no more troops could be sent north. Indeed, there was in fact pressure for

This is an updated and extended version of a paper published in Darby, J. Northern Ireland. The Background to Conflict, Appletree Press, 1982. My thanks to John Darby for permission to reproduce parts of the original chapter.

troops from the North to be sent south.[2] In October 1920, the British government announced the establishment of the Ulster Special Constabulary (USC).[3] It was based upon the Ulster Volunteer Force (UVF)—a totally Protestant paramilitary force—which had been recognized a few months earlier with the tacit approval of the British government. Hence, the USC was from the outset exclusively Protestant. It was divided into three classes. Class 'A' was for those willing to do full-time duty and be posted anywhere within Northern Ireland; Class 'B' was for those willing to do part-time duty in their own locality; and Class 'C' was for those willing to go on reserve and who could be called upon in an emergency. This last class was vaguely defined and became little more than a device to give gun licences to loyalists and refuse them to Catholics.[4] By August 1922 there were 7,000 'A' Specials, 20,000 'B' Specials, and 17,000 in a reconstituted 'C' Class. There were also 1,200 full-time members of the newly formed Royal Ulster Constabulary (RUC) which had replaced the RIC in May of the same year.

The Specials played the central role in the establishment of the authority of the new government in Northern Ireland. From the outset their activities were controversial. They were undisciplined and partisan and were regarded by Catholics with a bitterness exceeding that which the Black and Tans inspired in the south.

Their sectarian conduct, as Farrell points out,[5] contributed to the peculiarly intense hatred with which the RUC has been regarded ever since by the Catholic population in the North. Not only were the two forces linked together in the public mind, but also half the initial recruits for the RUC came from the 'A' Specials.

While Farrell emphasizes the role of the British government in the creation of the USC, Bew, Gibbon, and Patterson draw attention to the changes which were taking place within the Protestant class bloc.[6] They argue that, in order to challenge Republicanism independently of the British, the Unionist leadership had to give up some of its power to the Orange section of the Protestant working class. The form of the Unionist state apparatus can therefore be seen as a product of the class relations within the Unionist bloc coupled with British approval and support. In other words, they argue that the form of the Unionist state apparatus was not exclusively a product of external politics.

Another central element of the Unionist repressive state apparatus was the Civil Authorities (Special Powers) Act. This was passed in 1922 and gave the Minister of Home Affairs power 'to take all such steps . . . as may be necessary for preserving peace and maintaining order'. It con-

ferred wide powers of arrest, questioning, search, detention, and internment on the police and other agents of the Ministry of Home Affairs. It
constituted an effective abrogation of the rule of law in the sense that the
forces of law and order had the power to arrest and detain anyone they
pleased without having to give any justification and without fear of being
called to account in respect of any decisions later shown to be unjustified.
Northern Ireland from the outset was therefore a state with extraordinary powers.

The Civil Authorities (Special Powers) Act was renewed annually until
1928 when it was extended for five years. At the end of 1933 it was made
permanent. It was extensively criticized in the late 1930's by NCCL.

The law and order strategy of successive Unionist governments was
unequivocal. A constant watch was maintained on Catholic communities
and, whenever the state appeared to be under threat—for example, during the IRA campaigns of 1921–2, 1938–9, and 1956–62—the government
introduced internment under the Civil Authorities (Special Powers) Act.
It was also used on other occasions, as for instance when Republican
politicians were interned for a week during a royal visit in 1951. The
main point to emphasize about internment was its wholly executive
nature. The formal power provided for in the Civil Authorities (Special
Powers) Act permitted the arrest and detention of anyone who was acting, had acted or was about to act 'in a manner prejudicial to the preservation of the peace and maintenance of order'. The responsibility for
making the internment order after arrest lay with the minister who was
also personally responsible for ordering the release of internees. While
there was provision for the appointment of an advisory committee to
review the cases, the minister was not bound to accept the recommendations. Internment was therefore a wholly executive measure. Its use highlighted the executive's direct involvement in suppressing political
opposition. It was not surprising that the Cameron Commission found
that its presence on the statute book, and the continuance in force of regulations made under it, had caused widespread resentment among
Catholics.[7] It had after all been used almost exclusively against them to
suppress all political opposition to the Northern Ireland regime.

As well as the lack of confidence in the forces of law and order and the
festering grievance of the Civil Authorities (Special Powers) Act,
Catholics also had little confidence in the courts in Northern Ireland. This
stemmed principally from the composition of both the judiciary and
juries. The Northern Ireland judiciary throughout its history had been
mainly composed of people who had been openly associated with the

Unionist Party. Of the 20 high court judges appointed since 1922, 15 had been openly associated with the Unionist Party and 14 of the county court appointments had similar associations. Resident magistrates had also been drawn from the same source. While it does not follow that the decisions of judges and magistrates would be partisan, the composition of both the magistracy and the judiciary did little to inspire the confidence of Catholics in the administration of justice.

The composition of juries further exacerbated the problem of confidence in the administration of justice. Partly as a result of property qualification and partly as a result of the rules concerning the right to stand by or challenge jurors, the composition of juries was mainly Protestant. The qualification for jury service was based upon the ownership of property and as Catholics owned less property, this ensured that the majority on the jury list were Protestants. At this stage, the prosecution was entitled to stand by any number of jurors and the defence might challenge up to twelve without giving any reason, and might object to others for good cause. The end result was that most juries, particularly in Belfast, were Protestant. The risk of bias against Catholics was therefore always present.

It can be seen from this brief analysis of the law and order strategy adopted by successive Unionist governments that it was highly repressive, sectarian and centralized. Moreover, throughout the period, no attempt was made to disguise the political nature of the struggle nor of the response. It was successful in so far as it maintained the regime in power for fifty years. But from the outset it continually alienated the minority community from both the law and the state.

1969–71: Reform and repression

The response of the British government, after deploying troops in Northern Ireland in August 1969, was to pressurize the government at Stormont to introduce a series of reforms which, in essence, were aimed to establish a series of institutions to guarantee equality of treatment and freedom from discrimination for the Catholic community.

The principal reforms in the area of policing followed closely the recommendations of the Hunt Committee.[8] The object of the reform was to neutralize the political control of the police and to establish a wholly civilian and non-armed police force. Consequently, the 'B' Specials were disbanded and a new force, the Ulster Defence Regiment, was established under the control of the British army. In addition, the RUC was disarmed and made accountable to a police authority. The continuing violence, however, soon led to the rearming of the police.

The Hunt Committee also recommended the introduction of an independent prosecutor on the Scottish model. But the Unionist government delayed in the implementation of this reform by establishing a committee to consider the proposals.[9]

It was not until after Direct Rule in 1972 that a new office of a Director of Public Prosecutions was set up with full responsibility for the selection and prosecution of all serious criminal charges.

At the same time as the police were being reformed the Unionist government brought in tougher legislation under the Criminal Justice (Temporary Provision) Act 1970 to deal with rioters.[10] The Act provided a six months minimum mandatory gaol sentence for anyone convicted of 'riotous behaviour', 'disorderly behaviour', or 'behaviour likely to cause a breach of the peace'. The new law immediately gave rise to numerous allegations of the partisan way in which the legislation was being enforced.

Outside the area of the administration of justice, other reforms were taking place. The discriminatory practices of local government were dealt with by extending local government franchise but at the same time denuding local authorities of considerable powers. A new centralized housing authority was established and administrative units were set up to manage education, planning, and health and social services.[11]

While all these legislative changes were taking place, the situation on the streets was deteriorating. The relations between the army and the Catholic community were rapidly declining as the army took a tougher line against rioters. In 1970, a routine house search precipitated a large-scale riot and the army introduced a curfew.[12]

The conflict was slowly escalating into a guerrilla war between the army and the IRA.

In summary, in this period the strategy of the British government was not to define the problem in terms of law and order but to deal with it at a number of different levels. On the one hand, there was a very real attempt to correct the arbitrary and inequitable administration of criminal laws and to establish institutions which would deal with the widespread problem of discrimination. Liberal notions such as the separation of powers, the rule of law, the impartiality and objectivity of judges, and democratic institutions to check the exercise of power were mobilized in support of the reforms but no attempt was made to ensure that the notions were realized in practice. The creation of new institutions and the dispersal of power has meant that the various bodies, which are relatively autonomous, have established their own *modus operandi*; they have structured their own targets and objectives. The dominant feature has been their tendency to reconstitute practical and legal problems as technical matters. On the other hand, the increasing violence on the streets, coupled with the demands of the Protestant community for tougher measures, led to the development of a more coercive strategy to deal with the problem of violence.

1971–5: Internment and military security

The strategy in this period was dominated by the use of internment and the development by the army either through encouragement or by default of its own military security policy. This involved the introduction of a series of techniques which have been used in colonial emergencies in the past and developed by Brigadier Kitson.[13] The combined aim of these techniques was to collect as much information on the IRA in particular and the Catholic community in general. I will deal with each component in turn.

Internment and detention

Internment was introduced with the agreement of the British government on 9 August 1971. The army and police arrested 342 men on the initial sweep. Within six months 2,357 persons had been arrested and 1,600 released after interrogation. The introduction, impact, and subsequent use of internment has been extensively documented and the details need not concern us here.[14] The main point to emphasize is that its use provided an example of unfettered ministerial discretion and highlighted the political nature of the struggle. The state's involvement in suppressing political opposition was clear and unequivocal.

After internment, the level of violence increased rapidly. Many Catholics holding public appointments withdrew from these offices and a rent and rates strike was begun. In January 1972 the army killed thirteen civilians during a civil rights march in Derry. An official inquiry by the Lord Chief Justice only inflamed the situation as his report exonerated those responsible.[15]

After Direct Rule was imposed in March 1972, a slight shift took place in the internment strategy. Following the breakdown of discussions between the IRA and the government, a new system of detention without trial was introduced. The principal development was to replace the executive authority of the minister under the Special Powers Act by a new system of judicial determination. All cases now came before an independent judicial Commissioner.[16] The aim was to distance the executive from the day-to-day administration of the emergency powers in an attempt to depoliticize the nature of the response in order to gain the confidence of the minority community in the system. It represented the beginning of a strategy which was to find its ultimate and most sustained and strongest expression in the criminalization policies which were introduced in 1975. The operation of these new procedures received widespread criticisms.[17] The whole system of detention appeared to be dominated by the policies of the security forces and the quasi-judicial hearings were farcical. The new scheme did little to gain the confidence of Catholics. When the government began detaining Protestants in February 1973 the opposition to detention became more widespread.

The last point to note about detention is that those who were detained were not treated like other convicted persons. They were placed in compounds and accommodated in huts rather than cells and were permitted considerable autonomy within the compounds. They were also granted the same rights as prisoners on remand. This meant that they could wear their own clothes and have more visits, letters, and parcels than convicted persons. Similar rights were also extended in June 1972 to those who had been convicted in the courts and who claimed to have been politically motivated. These concessions amounted to what was called 'Special Category Status'.

Further changes were made to the detention procedures after the review of measures to deal with terrorism by a committee chaired by Lord Gardiner.[18] These changes were incorporated in the Northern Ireland (Emergency Provisions) Act of 1975 and involved a slight move back towards a system of executive detention. But they were of little importance as the use of detention without trial was suspended in February 1975 and a totally new strategy for dealing with those involved in political violence was introduced. During the period in which internment and detention had been in operation a total of 2,158 orders were issued.

Diplock commission

At this point it is useful to consider the Diplock Commission[19] because it strongly influenced the way in which the police and army operated in this period. It was also responsible for the form of the strategy adopted in the period 1975 onwards, which will be dealt with later.

The first point concerns the composition of the commission. The members of the commission were Lord Diplock, Sir Rupert Cross, Sir Kenneth Younger, a former Intelligence Corps major, and George Woodcock, a former General Secretary of the TUC. The late Sir Rupert Cross was a Professor of Criminal Law and had been a member of the Criminal Law Revision Committee which recommended the abolition of the right to silence.[20]

The second point concerns the type of evidence the commission collected. The commission did not go to Northern Ireland. Only Lord Diplock visited the Province and then only on two occasions. The bulk of the evidence was oral and was taken from people with responsibility for the administration of justice in Northern Ireland, and from representatives of the civil and armed services.

The third and most important point is that the report was produced for the authorities responsible for law and order and not for the people of Northern Ireland as a whole. The underlying problem of the political struggle between opposing groups of very different aspirations was totally ignored and the sole focus was upon the maintenance of public order. In this context, civil rights in general and the rights of suspects in particular, appear as exceptional, anachronistic, and even subversive. Long-established common law principles were reconstituted as 'technical rules'. For example, the principle concerning the admissibility of statements, which is fundamental in an adversarial system of criminal justice, was described in a number of places as a 'technical rule'. Burton and Carlin appear to make a similar point, regrettably in jargon-laden and absurdly complex language, when they describe the Diplock report in the following way:

Its intra-discursive logic is as incoherent as its epistemological justification. Though argued in terms of essentialized justice, relocated within legal evolution, the changes in the technical guarantees of objectivity remain but a part of the syntagmatic strategy which orders the paradigms of the common law mode towards a unity of its discursive object: the discursive appropriation of an official word whose otherness is beyond recognition.[21]

Most of the commission's recommendations were included in the Northern Ireland (Emergency Provisions) Act which came into force in August 1973. The army was provided with the power to stop and detain a suspect for up to 4 hours, and both the army and police were also given the further power to stop and question any person as to his or her identity and knowledge of terrorist incidents. In addition, the police were given the power to arrest anyone they suspected of being a terrorist and detain them for up to 72 hours. No grounds of reasonableness were required. This particular provision, it should be noted, was introduced to enable the administrative procedures required by the Detention of Terrorists Order to be carried out. The Act also provided extensive powers of search. Finally, the Act abolished juries and introduced far-reaching changes in the rules of evidence.

The Northern Ireland (Emergency Provisions) Act, like the Special Powers Act, constituted an effective abrogation of the rule of law.

Military security

The Act provided ample opportunities for the army to extend its military security policy, which it had been developing throughout 1970. This involved among other things the creation and maintenance of as complete a dossier as was practicable on all inhabitants in Republican areas. The military strategists referred to this as 'contact information'.[22] The principal methods involved interrogation in depth, frequent arrest for screening, regular house searches, and head counts.

Internment provided the first opportunity for interrogation in depth to be used by the army. A group of internees were selected and interrogated in depth using a selection of techniques based upon the psychology of sensory deprivation.[23] The impact and effect of these techniques were considerable.[24] While subsequently there was a committee of inquiry set up under the chairpersonship of Sir Edmund Compton to consider the allegations of torture and brutality during interrogation, the principal issue as to who authorized the techniques was never investigated.[25] As it was, the Compton Committee produced a most unsatisfactory conclusion that while the techniques used did constitute physical ill-treatment they did not amount to brutality. A further inquiry was later established under the chairpersonship of Lord Parker to consider whether interrogation in depth should be permitted to be continued.[26]

In the meantime, the Irish Republic filed an application before the European Commission of Human Rights. The case eventually went to the European Court where it was held that the techniques, contrary to the findings of the European Commission, did not constitute a practice of torture but of inhuman and degrading treatment.[27] The British government undertook that the techniques would never be reintroduced. The government subsequently paid out £188,250 in damages to the persons involved.

The other methods of army intelligence-gathering included the use of foot patrols to build up a detailed picture of the area and its inhabitants, house searches, and frequent arrests for questioning. While these methods were used extensively under the Special Powers Act, their use was increased after the introduction of the recommendations of the Diplock Commission in the Northern Ireland (Emergency Provisions) Act.

No figures are available on the number of people stopped and questioned on the street. Nor are any figures available on the number of persons arrested and detained up to 4 hours. But it is known that these methods were used very widely. On occasion large-scale arrest operations were initiated and people arrested at random for apparently no other reason other than to collect more information on the local community.[28]

Figures are, however, available for the number of house searches and these provide some indication of the extent of the army's intelligence-gathering operations and how they expanded over the period after the introduction of the Northern Ireland (Emergency Provisions) Act. In 1971 there were 17,262 house searches. By 1973 this had risen to 75,000, one-fifth of all houses in Northern Ireland.[29]

Many of the intelligence-gathering activities carried out by the army were of dubious legality. It is very doubtful whether large-scale house searches or the extensive screening was justified under the Act.

In 1974, the powers of arrest and detention were extended still further under the Prevention of Terrorism Act. This was introduced for the whole of the United Kingdom in the wake of the Birmingham bombings. It provided the power of arrest upon reasonable suspicion and 48 hours' detention in the first instance, which could be extended by up to a further five days by the Secretary of State. In practice, this was another form of executive detention, admittedly for only a three-day period.[30]

As the conflict between the army and the IRA intensified the army resorted to a variety of other techniques in order to attempt to defeat the IRA. There is considerable evidence to suggest that the army used *agents provocateurs*, a variety of undercover techniques and assassination squads.[31] In addition, it developed new technologies. These included new methods of crowd control, new surveillance apparatus and the computerization of all its intelligence information.[32]

The RUC during this period took a subordinate role. It was largely excluded from policing the main Catholic areas. There was thus a very clear difference in the deployment patterns of the security forces, with the police mainly controlling Protestant areas where they used an approach closer to the traditional police approach and the army operating principally in Republican areas where it used the methods described above. This differential deployment served only to alienate further the Catholic community.

One response of the RUC to the crisis of confidence within the Catholic community was to concentrate on developing community relations work. A community relations branch was established in October 1970 and the chief inspector in charge of the branch was dispatched to London to study the methods used by the Metropolitan Police in both youth and community relations. The branch worked mainly with young people organizing discos, rambles, adventure holidays, and football matches. In addition, the RUC has made strenuous efforts to establish working relationships with all the local politicians.

From a broader perspective, it can be seen that the strategy in this period had three dominant features. In the first place, the strategy openly acknowledged the political dimensions of the struggle. Detainees were treated like 'prisoners of war' and the politics of those convicted in the courts was recognized in the granting of 'special category status'. Secondly the strategy gave the army considerable autonomy. There was little attempt to control its operations and practices, many of which were of dubious legality. The third feature of the strategy was the extensive use which was made of judges. They were not only used to provide a veneer of respectability to detention, but were also used to chair inquiries. Up to the end of 1975 seven inquiries had been chaired by judges. These were of two types. On the one hand, there were those which investigated some controversial incident or event, such as a Bloody Sunday. On the other, there were those which reviewed the appropriateness of particular policies, for example the Diplock Commission's review of the 'legal procedures to deal with terrorist activities'. The role of judges in part stemmed from the nature of the investigations, but it also reflected the extent to which the authorities hoped to diffuse a difficult political situation or to distance themselves from recommendations which were likely to be controversial. As Harvey has pointed out:

The fiction of the doctrine of the constitutional separation of powers has never been more clearly exposed than by these attempts to assure the public that British judges can provide solutions to the political problems of Northern Ireland.[33]

1975–82: Reconstituting the problem of political violence

Following the Labour government's victory in 1974, it began to reconsider the strategy of dealing with violence in Northern Ireland. It subsequently initiated a totally different strategy. The central aim was to deny totally the political dimensions of the conflict and to reconstitute the problem in terms of law and order. To this end, the government initiated three related policies. First, it began to restore full responsibility for law and order to the RUC. This policy has since been described as Ulsterization. Second, it stopped the use of internment in February 1975 and began to rely upon the courts as the sole method of dealing with those suspected of violence. Third, it announced that special category status would be withdrawn for any prisoner sentenced for crimes committed after 1 March 1976. The latter two policies have been widely referred to as a policy of criminalization.

Ulsterization

The first indication of the Ulsterization policy came in April 1974 when the new Secretary of State for Northern Ireland, Merlyn Rees, announced that he intended to restore 'the full responsibility of law and order to the police'. Later in the year he announced a five-point plan for the further extension of policing. The plan consisted of setting up a series of new local police centres in selected communities to act as focal points for policing. They were to be mainly staffed by RUC reserves working in their own areas.

The impact of the policy of Ulsterization can be best illustrated by considering the numbers in the security forces. In 1973 there were 31,000 security personnel of whom 14,500 were in the UDR, RUC, and RUC Reserve. In 1986 the total numbers were roughly similar, but the numbers in the UDR, RUC and RUC Reserve had expanded to 19,500. As the vast majority of personnel in these forces are Protestant, one effect of the policy of Ulsterization has been to replace British security personnel by Ulster Protestants. The policy of Ulsterization has also been characterized by an expansion in the weaponry for the force. The RUC is now armed with pistols and Sterling sub-machine-guns, MI carbines, and SLRs. In this respect, the RUC has therefore returned to being a military force rather than the civilian force which the Hunt Committee had recommended.

Perhaps the most important development since the start of the Ulsterization policy has been the strengthening of the intelligence capacity of the RUC. This has taken a number of different forms: an expansion in the number of confidential telephones, the use of police informers and various surveillance techniques and the use of arrest and detention powers to interrogate at length all those whom the police consider may provide them with information. The use of these powers for interrogation has been a major feature of the strategy and it appears that the wide-spread screening and trawling which the army carried out in the previous period is now being carried out by the RUC.

The police, as has been noted, have very extensive powers of arrest and detention under the Northern Ireland (Emergency Provisions) Act and the Prevention of Terrorism Act. In addition, they have ordinary powers of arrest under the criminal law. The most frequently used power is Section 11 of the Northern Ireland (Emergency Provisions) Act which allows the police to arrest anyone they suspect of being a terrorist. The use of this power is not surprising as this power is broadest in scope in terms of the degree of suspicion required and allows detention for a longer period than all the other provisions except the seven-day power under the Prevention of Terrorism Act. The almost exclusive use of Section 11 rather than ordinary powers of arrest illustrates very clearly the way in which emergency powers become the norm. More importantly, the effect of mainly using this particular power has been to shift the basis of arrest from suspicion of a particular act to suspicion of the status of the individual.[34]

No figures are regularly published for the number of arrests and prosecutions under the Northern Ireland (Emergency Provisions) Act in contrast to the practice for arrests under the Prevention of Terrorism Act. However, two sets of arrest figures have been published which illustrate not only the extent to which arrest and detention powers are used only for intelligence-gathering, but also how the practice is on the increase.

The Bennett Committee[35] noted that 2,970 persons were arrested under the Northern Ireland (Emergency Provisions) Act and Prevention of Terrorism Act and detained for more than 4 hours between 1 September 1977 and 31 August 1978. But only 35 per cent were subsequently charged with an offence. In other words, over 1,900 people were arrested, interrogated, and subsequently released. The other set of arrest figures was published in reply to a parliamentary question in Hansard on 7 December.[36] These figures show that between 1 January and 30 October 19870, 3,868 persons were arrested under the Northern Ireland (Emergency Provisions) Act and Prevention of Terrorism Act and detained for more than 4 hours. Yet only 11 per cent were charged. When the actual numbers of persons arrested, interrogated and released are compared and adjusted so that the figures refer to periods of the same length, they show that the number of persons involved more than doubled from 1,900 in 1978 to 4,131 in 1980.

Even those who were subsequently charged are often extensively questioned about 'other matters' not associated with the offence in question. In the most recent survey of the Diplock Courts it was found that in over 80 per cent of all cases the suspect made a confession within the first 6 hours of detention. Yet the vast majority of these people were interrogated for substantial periods after the confession.[37]

The evidence is therefore unequivocal. The powers of arrest and interrogation are being primarily used by the police to collect information on individuals and communities rather than to charge and prosecute. Policing in Northern Ireland has therefore moved from a retroactive form, where those suspected of illegal activities are arrested and processed through the courts on evidence obtained after the event, to a pre-emptive form, where large sections of those communities which are perceived as being a distinct threat to the existing *status quo* are regularly and systematically monitored and surveilled.

Monitoring and surveillance of problem groups is being extended in other directions. In January 1979 a committee was set up under the chairpersonship of Sir Harold Black to review legislation and services relating to the care and treatment of children and young persons. It recommended a comprehensive and integrated approach to provide help for children, emphasizing the important roles of the family, school, and community.[38] More specifically, it proposed a dual system of coordinating teams in schools and at district level. The school-based care teams are to be made up of the appropriate counsellor, the education welfare officer, the educational psychologist, the social worker familiar with the catchment area, as well as representatives from the police and probation service. At the district level, it was suggested that representatives of statutory agencies concerned with the interests of children should meet together to discuss the best policies to deal with identified problems. In December 1979 the government endorsed the strategy proposed by the report and accepted its recommendations in principle.

The report appears to be remarkably progressive. It begins with an analysis of the social and economic problems of Northern Ireland. Throughout, it emphasizes that the needs of children are paramount. Furthermore, it argues that it is imperative to avoid as far as possible segregating children from their families, schools, and communities, or labelling them as deviant, abnormal, troublesome, or delinquent. The report, however, is totally uncritical of its own assumptions. In particular, it assumes that the task of identifying children in need is unproblematic and that professionals and parents will agree. But how many working-class parents in West or East Belfast would view 'the lack of attainment at

school, apathy, persistent behaviour, truancy, or involvement in delinquent or criminal activity' as 'the outward manifestation of complex, personal or family problems'[39] rather than the result of their children's
position in the broader cultural and political environment in which they
are brought up?

If the strategy of a coordinated approach through school-based and district care teams is implemented in full, it will extend the monitoring and
surveillance of particular populations. It is clear from the report that this
is the principal aim of the approach. It states:

> There should be a free exchange of information among the agencies involved in
> the multi-disciplinary team. Problems manifesting themselves in the school, in
> the home or in the community, whether they first come to the attention of the
> education authorities, the social services or the police should be referred to the
> School-based Care Team for discussion and consideration of what help, if any,
> each of the agencies might provide for the child and his family to help solve the
> problem.[40]

The more efficient control of particular populations has been
attempted at other levels. There is now some evidence to suggest that
both the RUC and the army are playing a significant role in the physical
planning of Belfast. An article in the *Guardian* in 1982[41] claimed that the
Belfast Development Office, to which the Housing Executive forwards all
its proposed building plans for clearance, has representatives from the
security forces. It was also suggested that the security forces had interfered with a number of planning decisions: they had insisted that a group
of houses were removed from a planned development in the Ardoyne;
asked for reinforced pavements in the new Poleglass estate to bear the
weight of armoured vehicles; and recommended high 'security walls' in
new developments in the Lower Falls and at Roden Street in West
Belfast.[42]

Other sources have argued that the involvement of the security forces
has been more extensive. It is claimed that new housing estates have
been built with only two entrances and that factories, warehousing, and
motorways have been deliberately constructed to form barriers. The aim
of these developments, it is suggested, is to prevent residents in Catholic
areas from moving from one part of the city to another through safe
areas and to force people out on to the main roads, which are more easily
policed. If all these developments have occurred then the authorities
would appear to be making strenuous attempts to confine the problem
of violence within particular areas. In other words, they seem to be

deliberately creating ghettos in which dissident populations may be easily contained.

The role of the army in the period from 1975 has changed considerably. Its method of intelligence-gathering has altered substantially with the rise of the RUC's work in this respect. There has been a very sharp decline in the number of houses searched by the army and the large-scale screening operations have been curtailed. However, there is evidence to suggest that the army still carries out undercover and substantial surveillance operations. In addition, the army is responsible for all the bomb-disposal work.

The strategy of Ulsterization has not been without its problems. The army has resented the curtailment of its operations and has developed its own strategies on occasions to deal with those involved in political violence. In a series of incidents, a number of alleged terrorists have been shot dead. While the strains between the RUC and the army have been in existence for a long time, they appear to have deteriorated since the RUC took the dominant role. In August 1979 following the assassination of Lord Mountbatten and the killing of eighteen soldiers at Warrenpoint, the Prime Minister visited Ulster and was told that the strategy of Ulsterization had failed and that the army should once again take the dominant role. A few weeks later Sir Morris Oldfield was appointed as Security Co-ordinator. The appointment clearly was an attempt to deal with the differences of approach between the two forces.

The Diplock Court process

The strategy of relying upon the courts was made possible by the radical modifications in the ordinary criminal process which the Diplock Commission recommended in 1972 and which were enacted in the Emergency Provisions (Northern Ireland) Act 1973. These changes, however, did not become significant until the courts were relied upon as a sole method of dealing with those involved in political violence from the end of 1975 onwards.

It was abundantly clear from the Diplock Commission's report that interrogation was considered to be an essential element for the successful prosecution and conviction of those involved. The commission was critical of what it described as 'technical rules and practice' concerning the admissibility of statements. It drew attention to the 'considerable rigidity' with which the judges' rules had been interpreted in Northern Ireland. It noted a decision of the Court of Appeal in which it had been ruled that the mere creation by the authorities of any 'set-up which makes it more likely that those who did not wish to speak will eventually do so' renders any confession involuntary and inadmissible. It clearly disagreed with judgements such as these and it pointed out the whole technique of skilled interrogation is to build up an atmosphere in which the 'initial desire to remain silent is replaced by an urge to confide in the questioner'.[43]

It recommended that all statements in breach of the common law should be admitted provided that they could not be shown to have been produced by subjecting the accused to torture or to inhuman or degrading treatment. The recommendation was enacted in the Emergency Provisions (Northern Ireland) Act, 1973. The provision not only eliminated any retrospective control over the way interrogation was conducted but also legalized, in combination with the power to detain a person up to 72 hours under the Emergency Provisions Act or seven days under the Prevention of Terrorism Act, prolonged interrogation.

The commission, however, was not only responsible for legalizing prolonged interrogation. In not supporting the Court of Appeal position concerning 'set-ups' which were designed to make it 'more likely that those who did not wish to speak will eventually do so', it gave the green light to the authorities to create special interrogation centres. Two were built, one at Castlereagh and the other at Gough Barracks, and were designed to create the most conducive environment for the interrogation process. Castlereagh was opened in early 1977 and Gough later in the same year.

The subsequent history of these centres is now well known.[44] From early 1977 the number of complaints against the police in respect of ill-treatment during interrogation began to increase. The Association of Forensic Medical Officers made representations to the police authority as early as April 1977. In November 1977 Amnesty International carried out an investigation and called for a public inquiry into the allegations.[45] The government, shortly after receiving Amnesty International's report, established the Bennett Committee, not however, to investigate the allegations themselves but to consider police interrogation procedures. Notwithstanding its restrictive terms of reference the committee, however, did conclude that: 'Our own examination of medical evidence reveals cases in which injuries, whatever their precise cause, were not self-inflicted and were sustained in police custody.'[46]

Apart from the evidence of ill-treatment, the other aspect of the interrogation process which gave rise to concern during this period, and subsequently, has been the extent to which the outcome of the trial was in fact determined in the police interrogation centres. In an analysis of all cases dealt with in the Diplock Courts between January and April 1979, it was found that 86 per cent of all defendants had made a confession.[47] Of these, 56 per cent of prosecutions relied solely upon evidence of admission, and in another 30 per cent this was supplemented by additional forensic or identification evidence which pointed to the guilt of the accused, although this additional evidence would often not have been sufficient to justify a conviction on its own. In a more recent study, a very similar pattern has been found.[48] What these figures show is the extent to which the forum for determining guilt or innocence is only very occasionally the courtroom.

The Bennett Committee made a large number of recommendations to prevent abuse of the suspect during interrogation. The most important of these was perhaps the recommendation that all interviews should be monitored by members of the uniformed branch on close-circuit televisions. Most of the Bennett Committee's proposals have now been implemented. It should be emphasized, however, that all the recommendations were designed to prevent physical abuse during interrogation. The safeguards do little to curtail the extreme psychological pressures which are at the heart of the interrogation process.

Since the introduction of the Bennett Committee's suggestion there have been far fewer complaints against the police in respect of ill-treatment during interrogation. It is however hard to ascertain whether this is simply due to Bennett. The underlying assumption was that the pressure to break rules and physically assault suspects stems from the individual policemen themselves. It was assumed that they are either over-zealous or in some circumstances deviant. A similar assumption can be found in the deliberations of the Royal Commission on Criminal Procedure.[49] It is a highly questionable assumption, however. There is a considerable body of evidence which suggests that the pressure on the police to break the rules does not stem from the personality characteristics of the policemen but is located within the organization of policing. The pressures generating physical assaults during questioning tend to be developed in response to the perceived seriousness of the problem and often decisions concerning particular responses are taken at a very high level. Taylor's analysis provides some support for this view. In a chart noting the number of complaints it is clear that there was a tendency for complaints to increase when political pressure was exerted on the police to produce results, as when there was some public outrage, for example, at the La Mon bombings. When there was public concern about police behaviour, complaints tended to decrease.[50]

Apart from the centrality of confessions to the effectiveness of the Diplock Courts, there are a number of other important features of the whole process. To begin with, the Diplock system handles a large proportion of offences which do not appear to be connected with Loyalist or Republic paramilitary activity or with sectarianism. It is estimated that 40 per cent of all cases processed through the Diplock Courts have nothing to do with the Troubles.[51] In other words, a system which was widely regarded as a temporary measure to deal with the particular problems of political violence is now becoming the normal process for all offences.

A second feature of the Diplock Court system is the extent to which judges appear to have become case-hardened.[52] Since the introduction of juryless trials, the acquittal rate has been declining. There are a number of possible explanations for this. One widely stated explanation is that the prosecuting authorities are now taking greater care in the selection and preparation of cases. But when the trends for jury trials, for which the same prosecuting authorities have responsibility, are considered, no similar decline in the acquittal rate is observable. On the contrary, jury acquittals have been increasing. These very different trends provide strong support that the declining acquittal rate is principally a result of judges becoming case-hardened.

A third feature of the Diplock Court system is the extent of bargaining. This may occur in connection with either the charges, where the defence enters into negotiations to secure the withdrawal of the more serious charge or charges, or the plea, where the defendant pleads guilty to lesser charges in the expectation of a lower sentence in return for the subsequent saving of time and costs. No research has been carried out to ascertain the extent of plea bargaining, but Boyle, Hadden, and Hillyard[53] in their study of the cases which were dealt with in the Diplock Courts between January and April 1979 found specific evidence of charge bargaining. In about 20 per cent of all cases the prosecution withdrew or substituted a number of charges which were already on the indictment sheet and in which the defence pleaded to the remaining or substituted charge.

Charge and plea bargaining are, of course, features of other criminal justice systems. What is important about the phenomenon of bargaining in Northern Ireland is that the pressure to bargain is likely to be much more intensive than in other systems. The number and seriousness of cases in Northern Ireland are of a different magnitude and this will tend to place certain organizational demands upon the prosecuting court authorities to encourage bargaining. In addition, the Bar in Northern

Ireland is very small. The importance of this has been well expressed by Harvey:

Defence lawyers, both solicitors and barristers, are under their own professional, institutional and financial pressures to co-operate with the prosecuting authorities and avoid judicial disapproval. The smaller the bar the greater the pressure on its members to avoid a reputation for contesting cases with little likely chance of success.[54]

The study of the Diplock Courts in 1979 could not establish that any specific sentence had been reduced as a result of bargaining.[55] But what did emerge from the data was that the severest of sentences were imposed on defendants refusing to recognize the court, while the lowest sentences were imposed on those who pleaded guilty at the very start. In between were sentences on those who pleaded not guilty and seriously contested the case against them. The evidence suggests that the differential in terms of length and severity of sentences as between Loyalist and Republican defendants is not to be explained, as is often suggested[56] in terms of simple religious or political bias, but rather in terms of the defendant's choice whether to cooperate or not to cooperate with the system. This important point emphasizes the need to consider decision-making in this or any other criminal process not as a series of sequential phases which can be dealt with in isolation but rather as a process involving a complex series of interesting stages in which decisions taken cumulatively contribute to outcomes. Thus, the much-discussed argument of whether judge or jury is superior for normal offences should not be conducted without emphasizing that decisions as to guilt or innocence are in fact an outcome of this complex bureaucratic process where the principles of criminal law and its procedure interact with the demands of the administration. The context in which judge or jury operates is much more important than whether the final decisions are left to judge and jury or solely to a judge.

The fourth feature of the Diplock Court system which needs to be mentioned is that a higher standard of proof appears to be required in the case of charges laid against the security forces than against civilians. The Bennett Committee[57] notes that, between 1972 and the end of 1978, nineteen officers were prosecuted for alleged offences against prisoners in custody or during the course of interrogation. Of these, only two were convicted but the convictions were set aside on appeal. Another case was *nolle prosequi* and the rest were acquitted. The 1979 study of cases dealt with in the Diplock Courts between January and April 1979 found an acquittal rate of 100 per cent for members of the security forces.[58]

Special category status

The other strand in the Labour government's criminalization policy was to phase out special category status. This, as has been noted above, was granted in 1972 to members of paramilitary organizations who had been convicted in the courts and who had claimed to have been politically motivated. The Gardiner Committee had considered that its introduction had been 'a serious mistake' and argued that it should be abolished.[59] One argument was that the compound system in which the special category prisoners were held made it more likely that prisoners would emerge with an increased commitment to terrorism. The other argument was that it could see not justification in granting privileges 'to a large number of criminals convicted of very serious crimes, in many cases, murder, merely because they claimed political motivation'.[60] The government concurred with these arguments and announced that no prisoner sentenced for crimes committed after 1 March 1976 could be granted special category status. In March 1980 it announced that this would apply to any prisoner charged after 1 April 1980 for crimes wherever committed. In practice, this meant that all those convicted would be put into a conventional cellular prison and denied the special privileges which had been granted in 1972. To accommodate the prisoners the government built 800 cells in the form of an H, hence the H-Block protest, at the cost of £19,000 per cell.

There have been many previous struggles in British prisons over special or political status.[61] But the decision to phase out special category status in Northern Ireland was to lead to the longest ever collective struggle over this issue.[62] The protest started in September 1976, when Kieran Nugent was sentenced to the new cellular prison at the Maze. He refused to wear the prison clothes issued to him. The authorities reacted with considerable severity. He was kept in solitary confinement, denied exercise and all 'privileges', visits, letters, parcels. In addition, he lost a day's remission for every day of his protest. He was soon joined by other prisoners. The Blanket Protest, as it became known, as the prisoners had only blankets to wear, had begun. The protest soon escalated. In early 1978, after what appeared to be considerable intransigence by the authorities combined with a desire to make life as uncomfortable as possible for the prisoners, the prisoners extended the protest by smearing their cells with their own excreta. In 1980 the women in Armagh prison joined the dirty protest.[63] On 10 October 1980 it was announced that prisoners were starting a hunger strike on 27 October, four-and-a-half years after the initial protest had begun.

Hunger strikes have a long tradition in Irish history. They had been used in previous prison struggles and under early Irish Brehon law of the sixth and eighth centuries an offended person fasted on the doorstep of an offender to embarrass them into resolving the dispute. On 27 October seven men went on hunger strike. This strike was called off on 18 December mainly because one of the seven was about to die and there was, at that time, a widely held view in the prison that the British government would make a number of important concessions. When the concessions were revealed, they failed to meet the prisoners' expectations. It was their understanding that they were to receive their own clothes and then be issued with civilian prison clothing. The British government statement, however, issued on 19 December announcing the concessions, reversed the sequence. Civilian prison clothing had to be accepted before the prisoners could be moved to clean cells.[64]

Inevitably, another hunger strike was organized but on this occasion it was decided that volunteers should begin their fasts at intervals. Sands was the first volunteer and began his hunger strike on 1 March 1981. He died on 5 May. Nine others died before the hunger strike was ended on 5 October 1981, after the government made a number of concessions. Prisoners were granted the right to wear their own clothes, and new facilities to improve association between prisoners were promised. In addition, a proportion of the loss of remission arising out of the protest was to be restored. In terms of penal reform, these concessions were trivial, but in the face of the government's intransigence over the five-and-a-half years of prison protest, they were considerable.

Throughout the length of the protest numerous attempts were made by various individuals and organizations to seek a solution to the problems. In 1978 a number of protesting prisoners initiated procedures before the European Commission of Human Rights. They claimed that the regime under which they lived amounted to inhuman and degrading treatment and punishment in breach of Article 3 of the European Convention. They also claimed that their right to freedom of conscience and belief under Article 9 of the Convention was denied to them because the prison authorities sought to apply to them the normal prison regimes. The British government's case was that the conditions were essentially self-inflicted and that the Convention afforded no preferential status for certain categories of prisoners.

In June 1980 the European Commission declared that the major part of the case was inadmissible. It concurred with the British government's view that these conditions were self-inflicted. It also agreed that the right to preferential status for certain category of prisoners was not guaranteed by the Convention. The Commission, however, was critical of the authorities:

The Commission must express its concern at the inflexible approach of the state authorities which has been concerned more to punish offenders against prison discipline than to explore ways of resolving such a serious deadlock. Furthermore, the Commission is of the view that for humanitarian reasons, efforts should have been made by the authorities to ensure that the applicants could avail themselves of certain facilities such as taking regular exercise in the open air and with some form of clothing [other than prison clothing] and making greater use of the prison amenities under similar conditions.[65]

The decision, however, did nothing to end the protest. As the confrontation between the authorities and the protesting prisoners intensified, Provisional Sinn Fein began a political campaign in support of the prisoners' claim to political status. An H-Block information centre was established to supply local and foreign journalists with information. The authorities on their part increased their efforts to emphasize the criminality of the activities of the IRA. They issued numerous press releases as well as glossy brochures entitled 'H-Blocks: The Reality', 'Day to Day Life in Northern Ireland Prisons', and 'H-Blocks: What the Papers Say'. In August 1981 they began to issue 'fact files' on each of the hunger strikers. These included a brief description of the activities leading to conviction and a montage of selected newspaper reports on the case.

All these activities emphasized the extent to which the authorities were prepared to go to maintain its policy of criminalization. They were largely successful in convincing the British media of its case as almost without exception all newspapers and the media accepted the government's position.[66]

The policy of eliminating special category status, however, was fraught with contradiction. To begin with, those involved in political violence are dealt with in a very different way from the ordinary person who gets involved in crime. They are arrested under emergency powers and convicted in radically modified courts. Secondly, the motivations for their activities are very different from those of 'ordinary' criminals. They carry out their activities for deliberate political purposes. They do not regard themselves as 'ordinary' criminals, nor are they seen as such by the communities from which they are drawn. Neither does the law under which they are convicted define them as 'ordinary' criminals. Most were arrested under suspicion of being a 'terrorist'. 'Terrorism' is defined as 'the use of violence for political ends'. As Tomlinson points out, 'they are considered as political in the courtroom but criminal for the purposes of punishment'.[67]

Third, the abolition of special category status created the anomalous situation in which hundreds of prisoners who had committed similar offences, but at different times, were serving their sentences with special category status in compounds in the very same prison.

Fourth, the penological justifications for the elimination of special category status, namely that the compound system made it more likely that prisoners would 'emerge with an increased commitment to terrorism', was not supported by any empirical evidence. All the evidence which now exists tends to support the opposite conclusion. The 1979 Diplock Court study found that only 11 per cent of all those who came before the courts had previous convictions for scheduled offences.[68] In other words, very few people who had been released from the Maze were subsequently reconvicted. Further support for the view that the compound system does not encourage 'terrorism' is presented in the only sociological study of the Maze, carried out by Crawford. He found that of a cohort of prisoners leaving the compound between 1976 and 1979 only 12 per cent had been reconvicted for either political or non-political offences.[69]

Fifth, the claim that the prison system in Northern Ireland is the best in the world is only part of the truth. Certainly the facilities are better than most but the regime within the prisons, particularly the Maze, is repressive.

When the first hunger strike began, it received widespread support. There were huge demonstrations in Belfast and Dublin. In the North there were 1,205 demonstrations requiring 2½ million hours of police duty. The total cost of policing these parades and ensuring order was over £12 million.[70] During the period 100,000 rounds of rubber bullets were fired, 16,000 in one month alone. The hunger strikes and the authorities' response did more to unite Catholic opinion than any other single event since internment in 1971 or Bloody Sunday in 1972.

One very significant feature of the rioting and marches which took place during this time was the extent to which they were confined to the Catholic areas and away from the centres of Belfast and other towns. Any attempt to march to the Belfast city centre was strenuously resisted. The Troubles and the protests have now become ghettoized. The barriers across certain roads and the huge security gates on the roads leading out of the city centre to the Catholic areas are physical reminders of the extent to which this process has taken place. It shows how possible it is for the authorities to confine the problem of street violence to specific areas while life goes on 'normally' elsewhere.

The struggle which developed out of the authorities' attempt to deny the political nature of the conflict in order to curtail support for the paramilitaries had considerable unintended consequences. Ironically the policy had the effect of depoliticizing the IRA campaign to the extent that it pushed the central aim of the IRA's struggle, its object of achieving Irish unity, into the background. But in its place it provided a powerful humanitarian issue around which to mobilize support. The H-Block issue to the Catholic community was yet another example of a long line of injustices which had been inflicted upon them by Unionist and British administrations.

1982–6: Supergrasses and 'shoot to kill'

There were further radical changes in the security strategy at the end of 1981 and the beginning of 1982. First, the authorities began to rely extensively upon the use of supergrasses as the principal method of securing convictions. Second, there appears to have been a deliberate policy to 'shoot to kill'. Although the use of supergrasses has a long history in Ireland,[71] and there were at least four paramilitary supergrasses in the ten-year period before 1981,[72] the start of the supergrass policy began with the arrest of Christopher Black in November 1981. Just over a year later thirty-eight people appeared on trial accused of 184 separate charges arising out of forty-five alleged separate incidents and Black was the principal witness. Thirty-five were subsequently convicted mainly on the uncorroborated evidence of Black. Since then there have been other trials based on the evidence of supergrasses. Greer has calculated that between 1983 and the end of 1985 there were three loyalist and seven Republican supergrasses who were responsible for 223 people being charged with offences connected with paramilitary activities. Of these, 120 were subsequently convicted, over half on the uncorroborated evidence of the accomplice.[73]

The most obvious reason for the introduction of the supergrass policy was the public outcry and adverse publicity over the methods used by the police at Castlereagh and Gough interrogation centres. But other factors were also important. It is known that Sir John Hermon, who succeeded Sir Kenneth Newman as Chief Constable of the RUC in 1981, was very much opposed to rough treatment during interrogation and he certainly would have had an influence in developing the new policy. An equally important factor, however, was what may be called 'the European connection'. In 1978, following the kidnapping of Mr Aldo Moro, the Italian government introduced a new measure which provided for a substantial reduction in the punishment where accomplices dissociate themselves from others and endeavour to release the victim. Subsequent legislation extended the notion of dissociation and collaboration still further. The British authorities would have been aware of these developments through the regular meetings of the Ministers of Justice under the auspices of the Council of Europe and it is probable that the success of the measures in dealing with political violence in Italy influenced the development of the supergrass strategy in Northern Ireland.

Two particular points add support to this contention. First, at the heart of the Italian legislation was the notion of the 'repentant' terrorist and Sir John Hermon used a similar term 'converted' terrorist to refer to a supergrass.[74] Second, only a year after the introduction of the supergrass policy in Northern Ireland in 1982, the Ministers of Justice held a meeting at which it was proposed that the Italian strategy should be adopted by all European countries.[75]

The opposition to the supergrass system has been considerable. It has been opposed by both Republican and Loyalist communities, large sections of the legal profession, civil liberty organizations and various other groups. The criticisms have covered all aspects of the system: the methods of recruitment, the type of people recruited, the extensive preparation of the supergrasses for trial, the inducements and offers of a new life elsewhere and, above all, the preparedness of the judiciary to accept the uncorroborated evidence of supergrasses even in the face of credible alibis—on one occasion the judge described the evidence as 'contradictory and bizarre and in some respects incredible', yet he still convicted on the basis of it.[76]

The apparent 'shoot-to-kill' policy of the RUC emerged at about the same time as the supergrass system. In 1980 the RUC set up a Special Branch unit called E4A with about thirty to forty members. It is intended as a deep surveillance unit and is apparently trained by the Special Air Services unit of the army. The emphasis in training is upon, as a senior RUC officer has expressed it, 'firepower, speed and aggression'.[77] Sometime a little later the RUC established a number of Headquarter Mobile Support Units (HQMSUs). These are composed of thirty members, split into quick-reaction squads under a sergeant, and each unit having its own small surveillance team. It is thought that there are now twelve such units and all of them are trained under simulated fire and in tactics which abandon the concept of minimum force.

Both units have been involved in a number of disputed killings and six of these, which occurred over a five-week period in 1982, have now been investigated by the Stalker inquiry. This was begun in 1985 following widespread concern about the shootings and the failure of an internal RUC inquiry to satisfy the Director of Public Prosecutions in Northern Ireland, Sir Barry Shaw, who brought further pressure on the RUC. In the end, Sir John Hermon consulted the Chief Inspector of Constabulary for the North-west area of England whose responsibility also includes Northern Ireland. He in turn consulted the Chief Constable of Manchester and Mr Stalker was appointed to head an inquiry.

The killings which Mr Stalker investigated began in November 1982 when an E4A unit opened fire on a car, killing all three unarmed occupants.[78] Three RUC officers were brought to trial for the killings but were acquitted by the judge. In his remarks he said that he considered the three were absolutely blameless in the matter and he commended their courage and determination 'in bringing the three deceased men to justice, in this case, the final court of justice'.[79] These comments were widely condemned by elected representatives of the Nationalist community, the Irish government and many others. The case was significant in another respect. It was admitted that there had been an attempt to cover up the undercover nature of the operation and that the officers involved had told detectives who investigated the killings that they were on a normal RUC patrol.[80]

Two weeks later another person was shot dead in a hay shed. An HQMSU claimed it came across two men pointing rifles at them. It subsequently emerged that neither man had any paramilitary connections, the rifles found in the shed were more than fifty years old and had no firing bolts and, most significantly, the hay shed had been staked out for a number of days. At the trial of the survivor, who was charged with possession, it was revealed that officers had lied in statements.[81]

The third incident took place a few weeks later when two members of the illegal Irish National Liberation Army were stopped by an unmarked police surveillance vehicle from an HQMSU. A police officer went to the passenger side of the car and shot dead one occupant and then went round the other side and shot dead the driver. Both men were unarmed. At the trial of the officer another attempted cover-up was revealed.[82]

Mr Stalker submitted an interim report to RUC Headquarters in September 1985 dealing mainly with the first killings. It is believed that the report was highly critical of the way the force was structured and operated and recommended several prosecutions including charges of conspiracy to pervert the course of justice and conspiracy to murder.[83] In

May 1985 Mr Stalker was removed from the investigation and suspended from duty while an investigation was conducted into a number of allegations against him, including allegations of his associations with known criminals.

His suspension received widespread press and media coverage and many aspects of his own personal life and the cases which he was investigating were widely reported. There were suggestions that his suspension was part of a broader conspiracy to undermine his work and prevent the public knowing about the way the covert security forces operated in Northern Ireland. Because of the blanket secrecy which surround the Special Branch and the secret services, the public are never likely to know whether there is any truth in these suggestions. But it is known that Mr Stalker had a difficult time with the RUC and it is reported that it was made clear to him that it had more than a passing interest in his personal life.[84] In addition, if prosecutions were brought for conspiracy to pervert the course of justice and conspiracy to murder, considerable details about the way a number of specialized forces—HQMSUs, E4As, the police Special Branch, and army intelligence—operate, would be revealed.

It would not be the first time that some section within the state attempted to cover up the illegal activities of the security forces in Northern Ireland by attempting to discredit people involved in disclosure. In 1979 the *Daily Telegraph* was fed a story by a confidential source in Whitehall concerning Dr Irwin's wife shortly after he had appeared on LWT's *Weekend World* reporting that he had seen over a three-year period between 150 and 160 people who had been injured by the police during interrogation. The paper was informed that his wife had been raped in 1976 and that he harboured a grudge against the RUC for failing to find the offender. The aim of the story was clearly to undermine the credibility of Dr Irwin's information and to question his motives.[85]

Whatever the outcome of the investigation now being conducted by the Chief Constable of West Yorkshire, the investigation into the shoot-to-kill policy has been irrevocably damaged. As Dr Ian Paisley has pointed out, the final report had to be coloured after the removal from duty, however temporary, of the principal author. According to Dr Paisley, there is no way natural justice can now be done.[86] It is also most unlikely that the public will ever be informed whether there was a shoot-to-kill policy from 1982 onwards.

In any event, it is clear that the law governing the use of deadly force is totally inadequate. It has been calculated that over 270 civilians have been killed by the security forces in Northern Ireland since 1969 and at least 155 of these were people with no known connection to paramilitary organizations or activities.[87] Included in the total are thirteen deaths caused by plastic bullets. Overall, little or no attempt has been made by the authorities to curb these deaths and the attitude of some judges amounts virtually to the endorsement of martial laws.[88]

The Anglo-Irish Agreement and beyond

In November 1985 the British and Irish governments signed the Anglo-Irish Agreement. It was a product of growing fears in the South of Ireland to the threat which the Provisional IRA and its political wing Sinn Fein, poses to the stability of the whole of Ireland. Pressure was put on the British government by the Irish government and the SDLP in the North to recognize this threat and to take some action to deal with the political impasse. How far it will assist in changing the form of law in Northern Ireland is a matter of some conjecture.

When it was first introduced it was argued that the agreement would be of benefit to both the Unionists, because it would lead to greater cooperation on security matters between the North and the South, and to Nationalists because it would lead eventually to the reform of the administration of justice. In practice the reality has been very different. There has certainly been greater cooperation on security matters between the two governments over border security. The most visible feature of this cooperation is a whole series of hill forts along the border. In addition the government in the Republic has now become a signature to the European Convention on the Suppression of Terrorism, which will now allow the extradition from the South to the North of those claiming political motivation for their activities.[89] But by the beginning of December 1986 no reforms had been announced by the government to the administration of justice in Northern Ireland. It was, however, widely rumoured that only slight modifications would be introduced and that the reforms would fall far short of a return to jury trial. In any event there are certainly no plans to deal with other aspects of the security system from which the Catholic community has suffered, such as the emphasis upon 'policing people', the normalization and bureaucratization of emergency legislation and the 'Protestant' character of the whole law enforcement process.

From a broader perspective the agreement is likely only to exacerbate the present situation in Northern Ireland. It has already united the many factions within Unionism and led to considerable opposition shown in mass marches, rallies, withdrawal from local government, organized campaigns of intimidation against the RUC and RUC Reserve, and sectarian attacks on Catholics. The present situation has much in common with that which gave rise to the establishment of the Northern Ireland state itself. Once again the unique combination of British involvement and indigenous class forces in Northern Ireland has produced a unified Protestant bloc which cuts across class lines and whose attitude to the rule of law is highly conditional. At the same time the British government through its policies of Ulsterization has created a local security force which is solidly Protestant and extensively armed.

The difficulties of confronting the Unionist opposition head-on are obvious. The authorities would be forced to use the same sorts of methods and strategies which they have used for years against the Catholic community. Moreover, the policing would have to be carried out by the almost exclusively Protestant security forces. The possibility of mutiny by some sections must be very real. The most likely policy is to back-pedal on the agreement particularly in relation to any reforms of the more overtly repressive apparatus. Although the cost of having to deal with years of internal political dissent is high, as yet it is not an electoral issue in Great Britain. In the meantime, the methods and strategies for dealing with the high level of political violence in Northern Ireland are increasingly being introduced into policing and the administration of justice in the rest of the United Kingdom.

Policing Northern Ireland and policing Britain

At the outset, two points need to be emphasized to avoid misunderstanding. First, it is not being argued that the developments have been identical, only that there are many similarities despite the vast differences in the context in which the law and order policies and practices are being pursued. Second, it is not being suggested that Northern Ireland has been used as some sort of social laboratory for testing various styles and methods of policing dissent and dealing with political violence. Such a view implies that there has been some deliberate policy to experiment using Ireland as the laboratory. On the contrary, the explanation for the incorporation of many of the policies and practices developed in Northern Ireland is less sinister but perhaps more insidious. It has occurred mainly by default principally because those responsible for developing policies in Northern Ireland have been the people who have also had responsibility for developing the same policies in Britain. For any real understanding of the impact that Northern Ireland is having on British domestic policies it is essential to study the careers of the personnel who have been involved. There has been a constant interchange between all sections of the Civil Service in Britain and Northern Ireland, but particularly between the Northern Ireland Office, the Home Office, and the Ministry of Defence. The police in Northern Ireland and Britain have also had a close relationship. Senior officers have visited Northern Ireland and studied policing tactics at first hand and many officers from the RUC have attended courses in England. Of particular importance, Sir Kenneth Newman, the (sometime) Commissioner of the Metropolitan Police, spent over eight years in Northern Ireland, first a Deputy Chief Constable and then as Chief Constable.

The first and most important area of similarity has been in the *form* of policing. There are two dimensions to this. First, the British police, like their North of Ireland contemporaries, have become increasingly militarized both in thinking and in practice. While there are still important differences between the two, for example the RUC is permanently armed and the British police are armed only occasionally or for special duties, nevertheless there are other important similarities. British police forces now have at their disposal extensive armouries which not only include lethal weapons ranging from pistols to sub-machine-guns but many forces now possess guns to fire plastic bullets and CS gas—two crowd-control weapons which have been used extensively in Northern Ireland. Much of the equipment—flak jackets, steel helmets and plastic visors, leg-guards, plastic shields and batons—which is now available to police in England and Wales is similar to that used for many years in Northern Ireland. In 1986 the Metropolitan Police took its militarization still further and ordered a number of armour-plated Land Rovers, similar to the ones used by the RUC.

Increasingly, British police forces are adopting military styles of policing. As early as 1972 Sir Robert Mark had his 200-strong SPG trained in methods used by the RUC, including the snatch-squad method of making arrests, flying wedges to break up crowds, and random stop-and-search and road-block techniques.[90] The 1984–5 coal dispute provided the majority of police forces in Britain with the opportunity to develop military methods of policing. Every weekday morning the police organized what amounted to a military campaign against the striking miners. Every day huge convoys of police Transit vans, horse-boxes, smaller vans with dogs and their handlers, and Land Rovers with arc-lights moved into position to confront the pickets. Police tactics ranging from the extensive use of road-blocks to the specific methods of crowd control clearly owed much to the experiences of policing in Northern Ireland. All the police documents which have become available since the strike reflect military thinking and tactics. They talk of targets, drawing fire, missiles, and decoys.

This military style of policing was not some aberration during the coal dispute. As in Northern Ireland, it is now the dominant style of policing and is visible almost daily from policing inner-city incidents to industrial disputes. It also characterized the policing of the Peace Convoy travellers in the West Country during the summers of 1985 and 1986.[91]

The other dimension concerning the *form* of policing which has parallels to Northern Ireland has been the way in which the focus of police work has increasingly been upon policing people rather than policing crime. It has been shown earlier how since the foundation of the Northern Ireland state the principal concern of authorities has been to police, in the broadest meaning of the term, the Nationalist population. Since 1969 this has involved a number of strands: the gathering of intelligence, monitoring and control of people in and out of Nationalist areas and the incorporation of other agencies in what has been called multi-agency policing. In Britain a similar emphasis on policing people has been emerging in recent years, particularly in relation to the black community. But it is not only the black community; many different sections of the population ranging from those who take part in industrial disputes to the travellers have been treated as suspect and subjected to surveillance and techniques of control, many of which are of dubious legality.

The second area in which the Northern Ireland experience appears to be having an impact in Britain is in relation to the organization of policing. From the setting-up of the state in Northern Ireland the police have been organized as a centralized national force. While the tradition in Britain has long been for local police forces, recent developments have been steadily eroding this principle. Two factors have been important in these developments: first, the introduction of the police national computer supplying a service to all police forces and, second, the common practice of police forces supplying 'mutual aid', which is increasingly becoming centralized through the use of the National Reporting Centre. The use and operation of the centre was particularly visible during the coal dispute and illustrated the ease with which the police in England and Wales could be nationally coordinated.

The third area in which there are similarities between Northern Ireland and Britain has been in relation to the form of the criminal justice system. The radical changes made to the administration of justice in Northern Ireland in the early 1970s involved four components: the vast expansion of the police powers of arrest, search, and detention; fundamental changes in the rules of evidence particularly in the admissibility rule; the abolition of trial by jury; and the introduction of a public prosecutor system.

Many similar changes have now been introduced into England and Wales. The Police and Criminal Evidence Act, 1984 (PACE) increases the powers of arrest and search and allows a person to be detained for up to four days. This period goes beyond the three days allowed under the emergency legislation in Northern Ireland. PACE also changed the rules of evidence concerning the admissibility of evidence. Although it does not go as far as the emergency legislation in Northern Ireland which allows all statements to be admitted in court provided that they were not produced as a result of degrading or inhuman treatment or torture, nevertheless, as in Northern Ireland, the old voluntary rule that a statement can only be admitted provided that it was obtained voluntarily, has been replaced by a less stringent rule, reducing the amount of control which the court may exert over police interrogation practices. Trial by jury has not yet been abolished in England and Wales. However, it has been under threat. There have been a number of changes which have restricted the range of cases which may go for trial and the number of challenges the defence may make has altered. In addition, there have been examples of the authorities vetting the jury before important trials.[92] Finally, the introduction of a public prosecutor system in 1985 adds further support to the view that the form of the British criminal system has increasingly become similar to the form introduced into Northern Ireland in the early 1970s.

Conclusions

From a broader perspective a number of points may be stressed about the characteristics of law and order strategies and policies adopted in Northern Ireland and similarities between developments there and in Great Britain. The first point to note is the extent to which emergency laws in all parts of the United Kingdom have become normalized. The 1973 Northern Ireland (Emergency Provisions) Act, with only minor amendments, is still on the statute book. Similarly the Prevention of Terrorism act, initially described as a temporary provision, has been extended to deal with all types of political violence, not only that connected with Ireland. The normalization, however, goes beyond the mere continuation of exceptional measures: it is now treated as permanent and all discussions of ordinary legislation assume that the exceptional measures will continue. At the same time, the exceptional measures are increasingly used in circumstances for which they were never intended. In Northern Ireland powers under the Northern Ireland (Temporary Provisions) Act are used to arrest people involved in 'non-political' crime.

The second feature of the use of the strategies in Northern Ireland has been the scant respect paid to the notion of the rule of law. Throughout all the strategies law has been used as 'an instrument of the state's security rather than justice'.[93] From the introduction of internment through to the supergrass and shoot-to-kill policies, the rule of law has been systematically abused. Legal arbitrariness has been a permanent characteristic.

The third feature has been the increased bureaucratization and professionalization of the response. Instead of a relatively informal system of the administration of the criminal law, there are a number of separate and relatively autonomous agencies with responsibilities for different aspects of the process, ranging from the police through to the judiciary. The decision about guilt or innocence is the product of a complex bureaucratic process where the principles of criminal law interact with the various demands of the separate administrative agencies which are themselves influenced by the broader political context in which the decisions are taken. The idea that the court is the forum for the determination of guilt or innocence bears little resemblance to the reality.

The fourth feature has been the decline in the power of the legislature in the development of law and order policies. The policies are increasingly being developed by the executive in conjunction with the higher echelons of the police and army. They are frequently helped in this task by judges who redefine traditional problems in technical and operational terms. Most of the strategies, as has been shown, have been developed through internal reviews. The public are never consulted and Members of Parliament are simply presented with the formulated policies. They have little or no impact on them. The role of key administrators appears to have been crucial and warrants further study.

Many of these features are also characteristic of the modern British state. Although neither the army nor a paramilitary police regularly patrol the streets, the movement towards a new form of repressive apparatus which shares much in common with that which was evolved in Northern Ireland at the beginning of the 1970s is unmistakable.

Despite the clear parallels and the obvious impact which Northern

Ireland has had on developments in Britain, Northern Ireland has been largely ignored by British academics interested in issues of policing, criminal justice and the state. It appears to have been assumed that both the social divisions in Northern Ireland and the response to them are too complex and too exceptional to provide any lessons for the study of law and order in Great Britain. This is far from the case. Although the nature of the social divisions are certainly unique and have long roots stretching over a number of centuries, the study of policing in and the administration of justice in Northern Ireland adds much to any analysis of policing and administering justice in the context of any multiracial society.

An analysis of Northern Ireland throws a very different perspective on many of the current British ideas and debates. Would the new realists'[94] concept of a state in which it is considered possible to make the police accountable to a marginal section of the working class have survived if a rigorous examination of the police in Northern Ireland had been included in their analysis? Similarly, would the new realists have been so prepared to believe in the possibility of achieving radical reform under a Labour government if they had carefully analysed previous Labour governments' record on law and order in Northern Ireland? It was under a Labour administration that some of the worst abuses occurred and a Labour government was principally responsible for the Ulsterization and criminalization policies. Similarly, would the many recent analyses of the police in Britain have reached the same conclusions if an analysis of policing in Northern Ireland had been included?[95] While the answers can only be guessed, the problem of Northern Ireland is clearly crucial to an accurate conceptualization of contemporary issues in the rest of the UK.

The final point to make in conclusion is that it is wrong to see either Northern Ireland or Britain as exceptional in terms of their evolving repressive apparatus. Many other European countries are developing systems with very similar characteristics.[96] Poulantzas identified this trend as early as 1978 when he wrote:

In western capitalist societies, the State is undergoing considerable modification. A new form of State is currently being imposed—we would have to be blind not to notice (and passion always blinds, even if it springs from the noblest of motives). For want of a better term, I shall refer to this state form as authoritarian statism. This will perhaps indicate the general direction of change: namely, intensified state control over every sphere of socio-economic life combined with radical decline of the institutions of political democracy and with draconian and multiform curtailment of so-called 'formal' liberties, whose reality is being discovered now that they are going overboard.[97]

Notes

1. Patrick Buckland, *The Factory of Grievances: Devolved Government in Northern Ireland 1921–1939* (Dublin, Gill & Macmillan, 1979), 179–205.
2. M. Farrell, 'The establishment of the Ulster Constabulary', in A. Morgan and B. Purdie, *Ireland: Divided Nation Divided Class* (London, Irish Links, 1980), 126.
3. Farrell, *Arming the Protestants: the Formation of the Ulster Special Constabulary 1920–27* (London, Pluto, 1983).
4. Farrell, (1980), op. cit. 127.
5. Ibid. 134.
6. P. Bew, P. Gibbon and H. Patterson, *The State in Northern Ireland* (Manchester, Manchester University Press, 1979).
7. Cameron Commission, *Disturbances in Northern Ireland* (Cmd 532, Belfast, HMSO, 1969), 62–3.
8. Hunt Committee, *Report of the Advisory Committee on Police in Northern Ireland* (Cmd 535, Belfast, HMSO, 1969).
9. MacDermott Working Party, *Report of the Working Party on Public Prosecutions* (Cmd 554, Belfast, HMSO, 1971).
10. K. Boyle, 'The Minimum Sentences Act', *Northern Ireland Legal Quarterly*, 21: 4 (1970), 425–41.
11. See L. O'Dowd, B. Rolston and B. Tomlinson, *Northern Ireland: Between Civil Rights and Civil War* (London, CSE Books, 1980) and D. Birrell and A. Murie, *Policy and Government in Northern Ireland: Lessons of Devolution* (Dublin, Gill & Macmillan, 1980).
12. S. O'Fearghail, *Law (?) and Orders: The Belfast Curfew of 3rd–5th July, 1970* (Belfast Central Citizens' Defence Committee, 1970).
13. F. Kitson, *Low Intensity Operations: Subversion, Insurgency and Peace-keeping* (London, Faber, 1971).
14. See, for example, J. McGuffin, *Internment* (Tralee, Co. Kerry, Anvil Press, 1973); and D. Faul and R. Murray, *Flames of Long Kesh* (Belfast, 1974).
15. Widgery Tribunal, *Report of the Tribunal Appointed to inquire into the events on Sunday 30 January 1972 which led to loss of life in connection with the procession in Londonderry on that day* (HC. 220, London, HMSO, 1972). For critical commentaries see S. Dash, *Justice Denied: A Challenge to Lord Widgery's Report on Bloody Sunday* (London, NCCL, 1972); and B. M. E. McMahon, 'The impaired asset: a legal commentary on the Report of the Widgery Tribunal'. *The Human Context*, 6:3 (1974), 681–99.
16. K. Boyle, T. Hadden, and P. Hillyard, *Law and the State: The Case of Northern Ireland* (London, Martin Robertson, 1975), 58–77.
17. See, for example, D. Faul and F. Murray, *Whitelaw's Tribunals: Long Kesh Internment Camp, November 1972–January 1973* (Dungannon, Co. Tyrone, 1973).

18. Gardiner Committee, *Report of a Committee to Consider, in the Context of Civil Liberties and Human Rights, Measures to Deal with Terrorism in Northern Ireland* (Cmnd 5847, London, 1975).

19. Diplock Commission, *Report of the Commission to Consider Legal Procedures to Deal with Terrorist Activities in Northern Ireland* (Cmnd 5185, London, HMSO, 1972).

20. Criminal Law Revision Committee, Eleventh Report (Cmnd 4991, London, HMSO, 1972).

21. F. Burton and P. Carlen, *Official Discourse* (London, Routledge & Kegan Paul, 1978).

22. Kitson, op. cit. 97.

23. See for details J. McGuffin, *the Guineapigs* (Harmondsworth, Middx, Penguin, 1974); Amnesty International, *Report of an Inquiry into Allegations of Ill-treatment in Northern Ireland*, London (Amnesty International, 1975); and D. Faul and R. Murray, *British Army and Special Branch RUC Brutalities* (December 1971–2, Cavan, 1972).

24. T. Shallice, 'The Ulster depth interrogation techniques', *Cognition*, 1:4 (1973).

25. Compton Committee, *Report of the Enquiry into Allegations against the Security Forces of Physical Brutality in Northern Ireland Arising out of Events on 9 August 1971* (Cmnd 4823, London, HMSO, 1971).

26. Parker Committee, *Report of the Committee of Privy Counsellors Appointed to Consider Authorised Procedures for the Interrogation of Persons Suspected of Terrorism* (Cmnd 4901, HMSO, 1972).

27. European Commission of Human Rights, *Ireland against the United Kingdom*, Application No 5310/71, Report of the Commission (adopted 25 Jan., 1976) (Strasbourg, 1976).

28. Boyle, Hadden, and Hillyard, op. cit. 41–53.

29. Northern Ireland Information Office, Statistics on Security, 27 February 1986.

30. C. Scorer, S. Spencer and P. Hewitt, *The New Prevention of Terrorism Act: The Case for Repeal* (London, NCCL, 1985).

31. See, for example, K. Lindsay, *The British Intelligence Service in Action* (Dundalk, Co. Louth, Dundrod, 1980); B. Brady, D. Faul, and R. Murray, *British Army Terror Tactics* (West Belfast, Sept.–Oct. 1976, Dungannon, Co. Tyrone, 1977); and T. Geraghty, *Who Dares Wins: The Story of the SAS 1950–1980* (London, Fontana, 1980).

32. See C. Ackroyd, K. Margolis, J. Rosenhead, and T. Shallice, *The Technology of Political Control* (Harmondsworth, Middx, Penguin, 1977); S. Wright 'An assessment of the new technologies of repression', in M. Hoefnagels (ed.), *Repression and Repressive Violence* (Amsterdam, Swets & Zeitlinger, 1977); and S. Wright, 'New police technologies: an exploration of the social implications and unforeseen impacts of some recent developments', *Journal of Peace Research*, 15: 4 (1978), 305–22.

33. R. Harvey, *Diplock and the Assault on Civil Liberties* (London, Haldane Society, 1981), 6.

34. Hillyard and Boyle, 'The Diplock Court strategy: some reflections on law and the politics of law', in *Power and Conflict*, M. Kelly, L. O'Dowd, and J. Wickham (eds.) (Dublin, Truroe Press, 1982), 8.

35. Bennett Committee, *Report of the Committee of Inquiry into Police Interrogation Procedures in Northern Ireland* (Cmnd 7497, London, HMSO, 1979).

36. Hansard, 7 December 1980.

37. D. Walsh, *The Use and Abuse of Emergency Legislation in Northern Ireland* (London, Cobden Trust, 1983), 70–1.

38. Black Review Group, *Report of the Children and Young Persons Review Group* (Belfast, HMSO, 1979).

39. Ibid. 6.

40. Ibid. 9.

41. *Guardian*, 13 March 1982.

42. D. Alcorn, 'Who Plans Belfast?', *Scope*, 52: 4–6 (1982).

43. Diplock Commission, op. cit. 30.

44. P. Taylor, *Beating the Terrorists? Interrogation in Omagh, Gough and Castlereagh* (Harmondsworth, Middx, Penguin, 1980).

45. Amnesty International, *Report of an Amnesty International Mission to Northern Ireland* (London, Amnesty International, 1978).

46. Bennett Committee, op. cit. 136.

47. Boyle, Hadden, and Hillyard, *Ten Years on in Northern Ireland: The Legal Control of Political Violence* (London, Cobden Trust, 1980), 44.

48. Walsh, op. cit. 92.

49. P. Hillyard, 'From Belfast to Britain: The Royal Commission on Criminal Procedure', in *Law, Politics and Justice* (London, Routledge & Kegan Paul, 1981), 86–7.

50. Taylor, op. cit. 323.

51. Walsh, op. cit. 81–2.

52. Boyle, Hadden, and Hillyard (1980), op. cit. 60–2.

53. Ibid. 72.

54. Harvey, op. cit. 32.

55. Boyle, Hadden, and Hillyard (1980), op. cit. 73.

56. Workers Research Unit, *The Law in Northern Ireland* (Bulletin No. 10, Belfast, 1982).

57. Bennett Committee, op. cit. 82.

58. Boyle, Hadden, and Hillyard, op. cit. 79.

59. Gardiner Committee, op. cit. 34.

60. Ibid. 34.

61. L. Radzinowicz and R. Hood, 'The status of political prisoners in England: the struggle for recognition', *Virginia Law Review Association*, 65: 8 (1979), 1421–81.

62. T. P. Coogan, *On the Blanket: The H-Block Story* (Dublin, Ward River Press, 1980).

63. N. McCafferty, *The Armagh Women* (Dublin, Co-op Books, 1981).

64. V. Browne, 'H-Block crisis: courage, lies and confusion', *Magill* (August 1981).

65. European Commission on Human Rights, *McFeely v. United Kingdom* Application No. 8317/78 (Partial Decision, adopted 15 May 1980) (Strasbourg, 1980), 86.

66. See Hillyard, 'The media coverage of crime and justice in Northern Ireland', Cropwood Conference Paper (1982); P. Elliott, 'Reporting Northern Ireland' in J. O'Halloran *et al.* (eds), *Ethnicity and the Media* (Paris, Unesco, 1977); P. Schlesinger, G. Murdock, and P. Elliot, *Televising 'Terrorism': Political Violence in Popular Culture* (London, Comedia, 1983); and Information on Ireland, *The British Media and Ireland* (London, Information on Ireland, 1980).

67. O'Dowd, Rolston, and Tomlinson, op. cit. 193.

68. Boyle, Hadden, Hillyard (1980), op. cit. 22.

69. C. Crawford, *'Long Kesh: an alternative perspective'* (MSc thesis, Cranfield Institute of Technology, 1979).

70. Royal Ulster Constabulary, Chief Constable's Report, Belfast, RUC, Annual, (1982), p. xii.

71. See P. Hillyard and J. Percy-Smith, 'Converting terrorists: the use of supergrasses in Northern Ireland', *Journal of Law and Society* (1984), 11; and Hillyard, 'Popular justice in Northern Ireland: continuities and change', in S. Spitzer and A. Scull (eds), *Research in Law, Deviance and Social Control*, 7 (Greenwich, Conn., JAI Press, 1985), 247–67.

72. S. Greer and T. Hadden, 'Supergrasses on trial', *New Society*, 24 November 1983.

73. Personal communication from Steven Greer.

74. Royal Ulster Constabulary, op. cit., p. xi.

75. Hillyard and Percy-Smith, op. cit. 342.

76. Ibid. 350.

77. K. Asmal, *Shoot to Kill: International Lawyers' Inquiry into the Lethal Use of Firearms by the Security Forces in Northern Ireland* (Dublin, Mercier Press, 1983), 41.

78. Ibid.

79. Ibid.

80. Ibid.

81. *Guardian*, 16 June 1986.

82. Asmal, op. cit. 81.

83. *Guardian*, 16 June 1986.

84. Ibid.

85. Taylor, op. cit. 319.

86. *Guardian*, 16 June 1986.

87. Asmal, op. cit. 87.

88. Ibid.

89. The Act ratifying the Convention was passed at the beginning of 1987 and its date of introduction was December 1987. For a full account of Irish extradition see M. Farrell, *Sheltering the Fugitive* (Dublin, Mercier Press, 1985).

90. T. Bunyan, 'The police against the people', *Race and Class*, 20: 2/3 (1981), 165.

91. National Council for Civil Liberties, *Stonehenge* (London, NCCL, 1986).

92. See H. Harman and J. Griffith, *Justice Denied* (NCCL, 1979).

93. P. J. McCory, *Law and the Constitution: Present Discontents*, A Field Day Pamphlet, no. 12 (Derry, 1986), 16.

94. For example, J. Lea and J. Young, *What Is to Be Done about Law and Order?* (Harmondsworth, Middx, Penguin, 1984); and R. Kinsey, J. Lea, and J. Young, *Losing the Fight against Crime* (Oxford, Basil Blackwell, 1986).

95. For example, R. Reiner, *The Politics of the Police* (Brighton, Wheatsheaf, 1985).

96. See European Group for the Study of Deviance and Social Control, The Expansion of European Prison systems, Working Paper No. 7 (1986).

97. N. Poulantzas, *State, Power and Socialism* (London, New Left Books, 1978), 203–4.

Constructing the Case for the Prosecution

ANDREW SANDERS

One of the central paradoxes of the Anglo-American criminal justice system is that courts in virtually all criminal cases are able to reach a verdict (usually guilty) without any apparent reasonable doubt, despite the elusiveness and complexity of 'truth' and 'reality'. Doreen McBarnet has argued that the key to this conjuring trick is the adversary system. Each side argues its own side of its case, and no one need try—or is even allowed—to re-create the totality of 'what happened': 'The search for truth is replaced by a contest between caricatures. Advocacy is not by definition about "truth" or "reality", or a quest for them, but about arguing a case.'[1] McBarnet was primarily concerned to show how the courts come to be routinely satisfied by the prosecution case. She shows that convictions are not produced in defiance of the duty to prove cases beyond reasonable doubt, but nor does the high level of conviction necessarily indicate that prosecution cases are generally more 'truthful' or 'accurate' than defence cases. Convictions, in contested cases at least, are generally strong prosecution cases, but strength is a product of pre-trial criminal procedure.

Although McBarnet opens up the legal framework she does not discuss police processes: how the police produce their 'biased constructs', whether they do so routinely, nor how prosecutors are persuaded to present them to the courts. The generalizability of her analysis has to be taken on trust, which is problematic now that the Prosecution of Offences Act, 1985 has been implemented in England and Wales. From 1 October 1986 an 'independent' Crown Prosecution Service (headed by the Director of Public Prosecutions) has been responsible for virtually all police prosecutions. In order to 'promote consistency and fairness' and to 'reduce the proportion of cases pursued despite lack of sufficient

Large numbers of friends, colleagues, police officers, and prosecutors have helped me. I am particularly grateful to Roger Leng, Mike McConville and David Nelken for their comments on an earlier draft of this paper, and to ESRC for funding the research.

evidence', the White Paper that preceded the Act insisted that police control of prosecutions be broken by introducing an independent prosecution system.[2] The government also presented the Crown Prosecution Service as an important counter-balance to the increased police powers provided by the Police and Criminal Evidence Act, 1984. If advocacy is about arguing a case rather than about 'truth' we can expect role conflict, at the level of rhetoric at least, in the Crown Prosecution Service. For the Crown Prosecution Service, like prosecutor-barristers past and present, occupies a dual role of police advocate and Minister of Justice.[3]

In this article I shall go behind the notion of evidential sufficiency, setting aside 'consistency and fairness' in the interests of brevity. First, I shall examine the place of the police in the adversary system and then the processes by which the police construct their cases. Finally, I shall discuss the implications of this for the role of the Crown Prosecution Service. At the heart of the issue is the legal fact that it is not the 'truth' that is at issue in court, but the veracity of competing stories. This means that control of the means by which to judge veracity is crucial. The outcome of this struggle determines who or what controls prosecutions, and therefore determines whether McBarnet's thesis is generally applicable in adversary systems like that of England and Wales.

The accusatory structure

The English criminal process is adversarial in structure. Once the police reasonably suspect that a crime has been committed by a particular person they are expected to gather evidence against her or him and then, on reaching a certain point, charge or summons the suspect. This point is the evidential sufficiency threshold. The test used to be whether there was a prima facie case. However, a 'reasonable prospect of conviction' (the Director of Public Prosecution's 51 per cent rule) is now expected.[4]

It is the duty of the police to gather together as much evidence *against*—not about—the suspect as possible, particularly now that stronger evidence is required than previously. As Lord Devlin put it:

The face of the police officer is not 'sicklied o'er wit the pale cast of thought', and, once he finds a reasonable quantity of pros, he will act decisively without too much anxiety about the cons. When a police officer charges a man it is because he believes him to be guilty, not just because he thinks there is a case for trial.[5]

The state recognizes the interest that the police have in successfully prosecuting by providing legal aid in most cases. This recognizes that the police will not seek to provide *balanced* evidence, and that the defendant will need her or his own resources to gather evidence favourable for the defence. However, the two sides do not have equally matched resources and the defence case is necessarily reactive. It does not choose the terrain of argument, for the argument is about the *charge* which is, of course, selected by the police and abstracted from the concrete situation in which the incident(s) in question occurred. Cases are constructed to 'prove' or 'refute' the charge and so McBarnet quotes jurors and advocates who relate how they convinced others to believe stories that they did not believe themselves.[6]

The dual role of the police

Although it is the duty of the lawyer to argue her or his client's case regardless of the merits, the police are not allowed this cynicism for their role is quasi-judicial. If, for instance, they take witness statements which favour the accused the police are obliged to disclose the witnesses' names and addresses to the defendant. But the judicial role does not extend to having to provide the statements.

Thus, the police have, on the one hand, a (limited) responsibility to assist the defence, yet they must also prepare the case for the prosecution. This must produce role conflict.[7] The police generally resolve it by believing that their case is itself a fair and balanced reflection of the evidence. Devlin points to one consequence of this: 'the tendency of the police, once their mind is made up, to treat as mistaken any evidence that contradicts the proof of guilt.'[8] Take the 'Confait Affair'.[9] Of three suspects arrested for murder and arson, one had a strong alibi for the time at which the victim was estimated to have died. The police then raised sufficient doubt in the pathologist's mind about the likely time of death to persuade him to 'stretch' the possible period in which he could have died, thereby nullifying the alibi. The logic of the police was faultless: if the suspects were guilty and the alibi could not be disproved then the alibi had to be inapplicable. Unfortunately for the police, logic is double-edged and worked in the reverse direction in this instance: the alibi was applicable and the suspects were eventually exonerated.

Despite their dual role, the quasi-judicial duty of the police to disclose does not go far. The police acted lawfully in not disclosing their negotiations with the pathologist over the time of death in *Confait*. Similarly, in the *Virag* case the absence of Virag's fingerprints on crucial articles was not disclosed to the defence. This was important because the inability of at least one witness to identify Virag was only significant in the light of the fingerprint evidence.[10]

The great faith which the police have in their own cases is illustrated here:

H was summoned for assaulting a police constable. H had been 'attacking' a moving car and the police constable had taken hold of him to stop him. He alleged that H kicked him in the leg. They were both dragged along the road before falling from the car. There were three prosecution witnesses: the victim, a policeman who assisted the victim, and a club doorman. Only the victim claimed to see the defendant kick him, while all three defence witness (H plus two friends) all claimed that H did not kick the police officer, and that the latter's injuries were caused by falling to the ground. H was acquitted. (SW168)[11]

The police discounted the defence case and chose not to obtain 'independent' evidence from H's friends or the occupants of the car which H had originally attacked. Since H was bailed for further enquiries and then reported for summons there was ample opportunity to investigate the case fully and the decision to prosecute was not actually that of the victim police officer. Presumably, then, the decision to prosecute was not simply one of revenge or face saving. Made coolly in the face of contrary evidence, it implicitly discounted that contrary evidence. As I said before, once the police reach a certain threshold of evidence against a suspect, they rarely look further into the matter. This was the problem in Erroll Madden's case, where a black youth was charged with theft of a toy car which the police found on him. Although Madden told the police where he had bought it they did not find his receipt, and nor did they interview the shop assistant.[12]

The potential for discounting evidence is particularly high when that evidence relies on lay assessment. Scientific evidence (as in *Confait*) is more difficult to discount, but few cases turn on evidence of this kind. Most crimes are 'solved' by direct observation on the part of police officers or victims, or by a confession,[13] but both methods raise difficulties.

In many cases some witnesses do identify a suspect while others do not. This is, statistically, worthless, but the police tend to regard positive identifications as significant and negative identifications as mistakes. Even if the negative identifications are disclosed to the defence the *case* can none the less be built around the positive identifications, and in such a way as to eliminate the significance of the negative identifications. On the other hand, the police are not obliged to hold identification parades. So if they do not believe that their witness(es) will identify their suspect(s) their accusatorial role sometimes pushes the police into not holding a parade, as in Ian Woolmore's trial for rape in 1982. Woolmore was convicted despite being 6 ft. 8 ins. tall when the rapist had been described as around 5 ft 8 ins.[14] Confession evidence is also unreliable yet, as we shall see, it is the crucial element which the police have to rely upon or discount in many cases. Thus, even where objective facts (such as someone's height) are in issue, the actual arguments at trial usually revolve around *subjective opinions* about these facts. The police have to pursue their dual role by eliciting and evaluating those opinions and statements.

Seeking evidence of guilt

McConville and Baldwin argue that however much the police may deny it, 'once a police officer is satisfied that he knows who is the guilty party, his main concern is likely to lie in assembling a case that has good prospects of standing up in court'.[15] This means that the police will not seek information that could establish innocence. This occasionally emerges in court:

R and several friends were charged with criminal damage. All had been in the same car. According to the notes of R's interrogation (which R refused to sign) R accepted that he was in the car but said that the offence was suggested by one friend and carried out by another. R pleaded not guilty. In court the arresting police constable accepted, under cross examination, that he did not ask R whether or not he knew what was going on:

PC: '. . . that's for them to tell me.'
DEFENCE SOLICITOR: 'But surely it's your job to collect all the evidence there is to assist the court in coming to a fair decision.'
The police officer agreed. (EC140)

Despite the police officer's formal acceptance of the defence solicitor's position, we should not assume that the officer's original attitude deviated from general police practice. This attitude was, after all, endorsed by senior officers in WS168 (above), ED056 (below), and the following case:

It was alleged that D1 and D2 were shouting and swearing outside a police station. PCX said that when he told D1 to be quiet D1 became more abusive and aggressive, and he therefore tried to arrest D1. D1 resisted arrest, as a result of which he was bitten by PCX's dog. D2 followed PCX and D1 into the police station whilst abusing PCX, and he too was arrested. An order that both be bound over was sought by the police, and both were kept in custody. In court D1 and D2 said that they were originally shouting to each other about a telephone call. PCX came out with his dog, which bit D1. It was only then, they said, that they became abusive, after which they were arrested. The Magistrate refused to bind them over, and the prosecuting solicitor had had no idea that this side to the case existed. (MC029/030)

Presumably D1 and D2 could have told their story to the charge sergeant before being kept in custody, but it was not sought. A detective inspector from another force summed up the position, 'we are seekers after truth, but we are also prosecutors. We have to try to put together a case'. The accusatorial style is *expected* of police officers, as their place in the adversary system would suggest. That a full interrogation covering every point might *reveal* a defence (as distinct from producing a fictitious one) is clearly seen as either irrelevant or undesirable.

So far, we have been concerned with suspects whose actions may or may not be criminal. The same points can be made about whether the criminal was actually the suspect. As Smith and Gray comment, regarding a string of robberies and thefts on a particular estate:

> They had very little real evidence, so far, to implicate these youths . . . [but] they 'knew this lot were at it'. . . . It was because they were locked into this mental set that the PCs did not attend to the details of the evidence. . . . It was not so much that they wanted to falsify the evidence as that they were not really interested in what that detailed evidence was.[16]

In the end the youths were not charged, but only because the victim was convinced that they were not her attackers. Had she been ambivalent they might have been charged since one youth 'confessed' even though 'it was later proved beyond doubt that he was not guilty'.[17] Not all suspects are so lucky:

> G was arrested while driving a car which had been stolen the previous day. G. claimed that he had bought it in good faith from someone he did not know. He was charged, inter alia, with taking the car without consent. The sergeant endorsed the file: 'In the unlikely event that G's account is true the fact that he is charged with the offence should galvanise him into some sort of action to discover the unknown vendor.' G was found guilty following a Crown Court trial. (WS034)

The police do not see the duality of their role extending to checking the defence story if doing so would be difficult—even when following up the story is beyond the resources of the defence:

> A considerable quantity of equipment in a tent at a fête was smashed. D1 and D2 were found, drunk, nearby some time later. Both were alleged to have made written confessions, but they pleaded not guilty, claiming the confessions were false. Evidence that one or more unidentified person(s) (X) had been in the tent earlier in the day in question was produced at the trial, but it could not be proved that X had smashed the equipment. In the absence of this proof, D1 and D2's confessions were the 'hardest' evidence available. They were convicted. (WS008/9)

Clearly, the way the police handle their dual role in the adversary system is a crucial area of future research. The position of the charge sergeant is particularly interesting now that this officer is both an adversarial police officer and an 'independent' custody officer under the Police and Criminal Evidence Act, 1984.[18] It must, nevertheless, be recognized that adversarial demands upon the police are generally far more influential than justicial demands.[19] Whether a case is 'weak' or 'strong' will depend, in large part, upon the nature of those demands in the incident and circumstances from which the case arises.

How cases are constructed

I have established that cases are not simply sets of objective facts which can be ascertained once and for all. Cases have to be *built* out of what people say or think about those facts. The content of cases is, therefore, fluid and uncertain. The police (and, of course, the defence) find that some cases change over time when crucial witnesses change their minds or disappear. Sometimes they make their cases change by *eliciting* thoughts and statements. Evidential strength is, therefore, determined by a complex and variable interaction between the events in question, witnesses to those events, and the police.

The witness whose thoughts and statements are frequently most significant is the defendant. Some years ago McCabe and Purves identified the mental element in the 'crime' as a frequent source of dispute in contested cases.[20] This was true of my own research too. The following claims, some of which were accepted by courts or the police themselves following the decision to prosecute, are by no means exhaustive: taking goods as a joke (ED192, MB002), taking goods through forgetfulness or confusion (ED044, ED155, WS048, WS082), taking goods thought to be abandoned (ED137, MC153, WN168), peering inside a toilet cubicle to see if it was occupied (ED129), loitering in the streets to keep an appointment with a friend rather than for prostitution (ED026, MC142, MB178), finding money and discarding it (rather than handing it in) for fear of being accused (EC166), being unable to stand due to injury/illness rather than drunkenness (EC157, WN088), fighting in self defence (EC002, EC103, EC134, MC126, WN143), losing temper and accidentally injuring wife or children (MB199, EC053, EC113), swinging chains absentmindedly rather than to intimidate (EC076), trespassing in order to sleep rather than to steal (EC017, MB172), accidentally damaging (MC115, WS021, WS035, WS152, WN091), not knowing goods were stolen

(MC011, MC038, MC059), taking or damaging jointly owned goods and hence no dishonesty claimed (WS043, MB144).

In all these cases there is no dispute about objective facts—what was done, who did it, the damage caused, and so forth. The contentious issues are whether a suspect *meant* to do the act in question, and *why* she or he wished to do it. The evidence which makes a case weak or strong, then, frequently has to be constructed from what suspects and witnesses say, or has to be inferred from 'all the circumstances' (that timeless legal phrase!). The police have no choice but to draw inferences and prod others into drawing inferences, to select and to interpret; the question is how and why they do this in their particular way.

Interrogation and confession

A clear relationship exists between confession and conviction, either by plea or following a trial. In McConville and Baldwin's Crown Court cases in Birmingham and London only 2.4 and 5.2 respectively of those making written confessions were acquitted. Convictions were also statistically significantly higher when there were oral confessions than when there were none.[21] Although rarely essential for conviction, McConville and Baldwin claim that confession is 'frequently decisive'.[22] They argue that this is as much because confession evidence dissuades the defence from contesting the case in the first place as because of its evidential value when put to the test. This may well be true, but given the frequency of *mens rea* disputes it is not surprising that the police rely so heavily on confessions to strengthen, or indeed to create, their cases. It is difficult to prove that a defendant had a dishonest intent unless she or he admits it. Moreover, as McConville and Baldwin do point out, confessions remove doubt and ambiguity, allowing the police to pursue their adversarial role of *proving* the case against the defendant. Irving's findings, that in twenty-five out of sixty interrogations confessions were sought as the main evidence in the case, are therefore not surprising.[23] Indeed, the police sometimes rely solely on confessions:

D was arrested for an alleged offence of violence, but was eliminated from the enquiry. In the course of the interrogation he 'confessed' to a burglary two and a half years before, and was accordingly charged. The victim had moved since then, and since D said that he had stolen nothing the police made no further attempts to contact him. At court D pleaded not guilty. The police dropped the case since they had no evidence with which to support the now-disputed confession. (MB024)

This is an example of the police relying on confession evidence because it is easy for them, rather than because they need to do so. But the point remains valid: the police try, where possible, to make confession evidence the basis of their cases. This is why the police insist on having freedom to detain suspects without charge and refuse access to solicitors—practices which are all now legitimated in the Police and Criminal Evidence Act, 1984.[24]

The truth or falsity of a confession, or the correct inference to be drawn from an incriminating statement, can rarely be established definitively. For as I showed earlier, in most contested cases the argument is not about physical facts or facts known to several people, but about aspects of *mens rea* or facts known only by the defendant and perhaps people whom only the defendant can identify:

> An air rifle was seen to be taken from a stall by some unidentified young men. It was later found in D1's van. He refused to name his friend(s), but said 'we took the air rifle with us . . . I'll take what's coming to me'. He was charged with theft. The charge was dropped two months later when D2 told the police that he (D2) had taken the rifle and put it in D1's van, and that D1 had been with D2 but had taken no part in the theft. (WS46/7)

Since the truth or falsity of confessions and incriminating statements can rarely be directly established, arguments in court frequently concern how the statement was obtained. It is not so much the 'facts' which are directly disputed, as what was said about the facts or how the police persuaded the defendant to make a confession statement. Since many defendants claim that they are tricked into false confessions the arguments frequently revolve around the alleged trickery:

> G was charged with burglary. Under interrogation he made an ambiguous incriminating statement. In court he alleged that he became confused in the interrogation and that the police put words in his mouth.
>
> AS: 'Do you think it is plausible that the police prompted G to say that he intended to steal?'
> PROSECUTING SOLICITOR: 'Well, that's the idea of the interview isn't it? . . . they all deny it at first.' (FC005)

Here the prosecutor acknowledges that confessions are a *product* of police work, rather than an objective fact of the case lying around waiting to be discovered. This has been noted by researchers from a number of jurisdictions (and theoretical perspectives). Ericson, Irving, Softly, and Holdaway each separately document an enormous variety of 'manipulative tactics' and 'threats' used (in Ericson's words) 'as a means of generating information and confessions'.[25] Irving and Softly's research convinced the Royal Commission on Criminal Procedure that the whole concept of the 'voluntary' confession was unreal.[26] The Royal Commission therefore recommended that voluntariness no longer be used by the courts to decide admissibility.[27] For the whole point of interrogation is to persuade someone to tell the police things which, usually, she or he does not wish to tell them. 'Manipulative tactics' are, in a broad sense, required of the police if interrogation is to be allowed at all. What this means is that where 'the case' is little more than a confession *'the case' itself* will be a product of police work.

The problem for the police about confessions is that they only 'work' if they appear to be voluntary. Nothing undermines apparent voluntariness more than an earlier denial. Confessions are therefore sometimes presented in the absence of prior denials in order to boost their evidential strength. And why concede to the defence useful information that could be concealed?

H was arrested for shoplifting. The prosecution file contained a statement from the store detective alleging that he hid two pairs of trousers under his coat and left the store without paying. When apprehended outside the store he ran back in. When caught again he no longer had the trousers. There was also a statement from the arresting officer alleging that H made a verbal confession. In court he claimed that he had picked up some trousers, but that he had put them down again before leaving the store. He claimed that he had told the police this originally although this was not recorded in the police officer's statement. The police officer agreed with H. He said that he had told H that he 'would start writing things down when he started telling the truth'. (EC121)

The prosecuting solicitor in this case said that he had never heard such an admission from a police officer in court before, but it is not actually unique:

B was alleged to be involved in a shoplifting conspiracy. She was implicated by her co-defendants, and the police file presented an incriminating statement by B. The case therefore appeared strong. In court she alleged that she had been interrogated twice. She said that she had initially denied involvement in the shoplifting; but that after four hours in the cells, without contact with her family, she falsely incriminated herself in order to secure release. The officer in the case agreed that this was true and that the record of interrogation was incomplete. (ED176)

It is common for defendants to claim that they denied being involved in the offence during interrogation but that only their eventual confession—

made under pressure—was recorded. Cases like ED176 show that these claims are *sometimes* correct, and Holdaway's research revealed isolation to be one of several tactics routinely used to elicit 'confessions'.[28] These can sometimes be ludicrous as in one case where the defendant 'confessed' to a number of burglaries which were withdrawn in court:

PC: 'Some of these things he just could not have done.'
AS: 'What, was he in jail at the time?'
PC: 'Something like that.' (WS178)

Errol Madden's case was similar.[29]

ED176 shows one way in which cases are 'built' by the police. But the attitude of the prosecuting solicitors in that case was equally significant: they condemned the police officer, not for falsifying the record, but because he 'ratted on us' when he changed his story in court. Most important of all, his initial attempt to build the case up should be understood as a reflection of institutional practice rather than individual deviation. A detective inspector in another force was relating a case where an 'old lag' made verbal admissions but a written denial to a young officer. He said that an experienced officer would not have written down the denial.

AS: 'Don't all statements have to be taken down by the police?'
DI: 'No—there's no point taking down a statement that is a pack of lies and that contradicts what he'd said in the interview. There's only any point taking statements if they tell the truth.'

The irony of this appeal to the 'truth' is that it represents a shift from an accusatorial to an inquisitorial mode of thought. But it is not necessarily self-delusory. The police must evaluate what they are told, by defendant and victim alike. The problem is not so much the basis on which that evaluation is made, but the subsequent practice of concealing the process of evaluation which enables the case to be presented as clear and unambiguous. Among other things, this prevents prosecutors from evaluating cases realistically.

Of course, concealment is difficult since it is open to challenge by defendants. Nevertheless, as Smith and Gray say, 'officers have good opportunities to make threats and inducements without this appearing in the official record.'[30] A common police tactic is to have two officers present during an interrogation. As usual in the criminal process, the defendant is not allowed to choose the terrain of struggle. Contemporaneous notes are taken by the police and each officer generally makes a statement testifying to their accuracy. Just as Fisher believed that the defendants in *Confait* were lying because he was unwilling to accept the alternative (that considerable numbers of police officers were lying), so in everyday criminal justice processes the words of two police officers are generally more plausible than those of one defendant. The 'hierarchy of credibility' which is a natural feature of stratified societies[31] enables the prosecution case to be constructed safely.

Selecting the case

Given that the police must necessarily be creative in building their cases, it follows that a number of different structures of fact could arise from a particular incident. What this means is that within an incident there could lie more than one kind of case. A case has to be *selected* by the police, and choice of a particular case may determine the particular facts which are selected and presented. But it can work the other way around too: choice of a particular case may itself be influenced by the existence of facts which the police feel they need to justify or explain away. In other words, the cases which the police eventually bring can be influenced by a wide range of factors going far beyond legal-evidential considerations. The case which is constructed is not always the most serious, or the most winnable.

The desire to neutralize unpalatable, but undeniable, facts is often important. Some cases are selected in order to justify (after the event) unjustified arrests. Smith and Gray discuss the arrest of a black suspect:

> The reason the officers stopped Delroy was that they suspected him of loitering with intent to commit burglary. When this suspicion was not confirmed they looked for some other reason to arrest him, settling on the charge of carrying an offensive weapon.[32]

Since large numbers of stops and searches on the street are like this, it is likely that many cases are selected for these reasons, despite the high percentage of stops which do not lead to arrest.[33]

The notion of discrediting complaints against the police put forward by Box and Russell is similar. Complaints alleging assault by the police, for instance, can be neutralized by police assault charges against the complainant.[34] A civilian's black eye is difficult to deny, but the reason for its existence can be debated endlessly:

> The allegation was one of assault against two police officers by a civilian. The only witnesses were the two complainant police officers, policeman Z and the defendant. The defendant claimed that the complainant policeman assaulted him

first, and that his blows upon them were in self defence. This was corroborated by policeman Z, who later changed his statement so as not to be inconsistent with the complainant policemen. The prosecuting solicitor said that although she strongly suspected that the complainant policemen were lying and that the defendant was telling the truth she nonetheless prosecuted the case because she did not think she was entitled to refuse to prosecute on the ground of suspicion, however strong.[35]

The evidential strength of an assault case chosen in this way is of little importance to the arresting officer. As far as the officer is concerned, the case justifies its existence if it deflects the complaint.

Another influence on the case to be selected will be the desire to deal with certain policing problems:

An area suffered from drunken youths on holiday. Two drunk, but not disorderly, youths refused to move on when told to do so. They were arrested and charged with obstruction of the highway, despite this charge being difficult to prove because of, inter alia, the width of the pavement. The prosecuting solicitor advised that 'there could be difficulties in proving an actual or potential obstruction in these cases but in view of the conduct of the defendants recommend that the proceedings continue'.[36]

Sometimes the police feel they are unnecessarily involved in a policing problem. A number of strategies are then open to them. Ericson cites one case which was selected so that it would not be pursued further. Y made sexual advances to Mrs X, whereupon Mr X attacked Y with a flick knife. A patrol officer was sent to the scene which was originally defined as a 'fight'. He wrote a report labelled—and constructed—'possible sex offender' because Y had disappeared and he felt that the 'score' was even.[37] Sometimes, too, the police want something to show for all their effort, and try to select a case that can justify the arrest:

D had an argument with his girl friend and her parents at the parents' house. He was ejected and smashed a glass door. The parents called the police. He resisted arrest, claiming the damage was accidental. Later, when they were all at the police station, the parents withdrew their complaint against D. The police felt unable to charge him with criminal damage, and so charged him with being drunk and disorderly. The civilians' statements did not mention drunkenness, and D denied it.

The arresting officer wanted to pursue the allegedly criminal damage, and argued that 'consideration should be given to summonsing him (the father) to give evidence in view of the amount of trouble that was caused and police time that was wasted'. His sergeant agreed: 'Quite simply it is just not acceptable for a complainant, after action by the police has had the desired effect, to just "drop the charges".' His Inspector, however, did not believe this action to be 'appropriate', but did endorse the drunkenness charge (which was later dropped). (WS021)

Although police policies can influence whether to charge a suspect, and what to charge the suspect with, sometimes a particular policy requires the police to choose *who* will be charged out of a larger pool of equally viable suspects:

P was alleged to be at the centre of a large drug ring selling drugs to, among other people, C (who was reselling the drugs on the street). P and many others were arrested for being involved in the conspiracy. Some of them, including B, were not going to be prosecuted initially; they were seen as peripherally involved and useful as prosecution witnesses. However, the police then decided to prosecute B in order to clearly bring out the links between P and C. (WS104/5/6) (Also see EC103 and WS166/7 below.)

In this case the police did not care whether their case against B was strong, for its purpose was only to convict P. Had they aimed the case at different members of the ring both the nature of the case, and the strength and weakness of its component parts, would have been different. In short, the situation provided the basis of several different cases. The question of which case to select involves both choice of charge and choice of suspect.

Creating the facts

We have seen that crucial facts can often be far from concrete. Where, for instance, a suspect had been loitering it was not necessarily with any criminal intent; where someone refused to move along a pavement he did not necessarily obstruct it. These are matters of judgement, and judgements do not emerge from thin air. They are sought and provided in contexts that influence their very content. The judgement involved in eyewitness identification, for instance, is now known to be a partial product of promptings, expectations, and preconceptions.[38]

Some facts are almost entirely lacking in substance. They are simply statements about facts—a confession, perhaps (which could be true or false), or an *opinion* about a fact. In *Confait* the police knew that their case against one of the defendants (Lattimore) would fail unless his alibi could be neutralized. Lattimore's alibi covered the whole period in which the pathologist originally estimated Confait had died. The police therefore persuaded the pathologist to alter his estimate. The time of death was a fact that was necessarily unprovable; the next best fact was an expert's opinion as to when that fact had most probably been. The police case against Lattimore rested on the successful re-negotiation of the pathologist's estimate of Confait's time of death. In other words, the strength of the police case rested on the police's ability to transform one set of facts (the pathologist's opinion) in order to nullify the effect of another set of facts (Lattimore's alibi).

Sir Henry Fisher was critical of the police in *Confait*.[39] But to criticize individuals, rather than an institution balancing a dual role, was misconceived. We know that the police are entitled to try to build a case if it has a legally valid basis, and since most facts are vague and malleable one could argue that there is no distinction to be made between building and manipulating a case. This is as true of other law enforcement agencies as it is of the police. David Nelken, in his study of law enforcement by local authority harassment officers, comments that decision making 'involves both making the decision fit the facts and making the officially selected facts fit the decisions taken'.[40] Although this aptly characterizes many of the cases discussed earlier (for example, WS201) facts sometimes, as in *Confait* have to be created as well as selected:

V and J had been friends. V had left his radio in the street by his car. From inside his house, he said, he saw J drive up and take his radio. J claimed that he had taken from the road by V's car some car components which he had lent to V earlier. The strength of the case rested in part on whether or not there really had been those components by V's car, for they provided J's reason for being in the vicinity of the alleged theft. After reporting J for the theft, the officer in charge was ordered to ask V about the components. In reply, V said that there had been none there. (WS091)

As in other contexts where evidence is sought by the police, in the absence of knowledge about a fact (whether the components were there or not) an opinion had been sought. V's opinion, though, had to be *created* in the sense that he had to be asked specifically about the components; but in doing so, it would have been difficult for the officer to hide the significance of the question from V. The police cannot be criticized for asking V about the components, but it would be naive to assume that V's answers were unaffected by their context. Nelken provides a similar example in which the eventual statement of the 'victim' not only conveniently covered all legal requirements, but also managed to rebut the landlord's version of the facts.[41]

Since the essence of some cases is a set of facts which have to be created through police questioning, the police have also to be careful *not* to create certain facts:

H, a 64 year old man, was seen shoplifting. The arresting officer (X) asked him about psychological or medical problems in the interview. H replied that 'I had a lot of trouble with nerves'. He was cautioned. The sergeant said that he would 'talk to' X. When asked what this meant the Chief Inspector replied that X was wrong to ask H about his problems for it was 'giving him (H) a defence if it goes to court and he pleads not out.' (ED056)

Constructing the file

Just as a case is not a simple summary of an incident, so prosecution files are not simply factual dossiers. They are argumentative documents, cast in a factual unidirectional mould. As Chatterton says, they present the action taken (for our purposes, the prosecution) 'as the only reasonable course of action available'.[42] The 'Confait Affair' was, of course, an excellent example of this.

There are at least two reasons why files are generally constructed in this unidirectional way. First, supervisors prefer it when 'the thrust of the presentation is towards minimising uncertainty and maximising the strength of the case for the prosecution'.[43] As one sergeant put it, it is no use having a file that 'left too much in the air'.[44] This is why in ED176 (above) the officer in charge ignored the suspect's initial denial: it would have created uncertainty. As Nelken puts it in relation to harassment reports, 'whether or not to recommend prosecution is presented as no more than a technical matter of evidential sufficiency'.[45] This is because the officer's adversarial task is to build his case clearly and unambiguously. So, in one case where several defendants could have been charged, the evidence against those not charged was simply 'discounted . . . to prevent causing damage to the main charge' (officer in charge, EC103). This, of course, begs the question of what is the 'main charge'. The case which is selected to fulfill that role can only have its status questioned if something is known about *other* possible cases; but prosecution files are directed only at the case in question, and not any others:

D1 had an argument with D2, the father of D1's girlfriend (X). It was alleged that D1 hit D2 and that D2 damaged D1's car. Both the arresting officer and X stated that there was damage although they did not see it being done. Similarly neither saw the alleged assault. The Superintendent decided to summons D1 for assault and possession of an offensive weapon, and not prosecute D2. He then agreed with the Detective Inspector to 'strike from the statements all references to alleged criminal damage' by D2. (WS166/7)

A second reason for files being unidirectional is that it minimizes the opportunities for criticism if the decision of the officer in charge turns out

to be poor. The best thing to do about a poor choice is to pretend that
there was no choice at all! The choice in question might be the prosecution decision, but it could also be a line of questioning leading to a
defence (as in ED056) or a denial. Hence, denials are sometimes omitted,
as in ED176 and EC121. Nelken perhaps sums it all up in observing that
material which could 'confuse' the issue is 'scrupulously rejected or
amended in preparing court presentations'.[46] Officers who do not do this
thoroughly pay the penalty:

P, a 38 year old woman with no record, stole items worth £10 from a store. It
appeared a typical shoplifting, although P's confession stated that she took the
goods to cheer up her daughter, her other daughter having recently died. She was
arrested and charged with theft. When the Detective Chief Inspector saw the file
he asked why the charge sergeant accepted the charge under these circumstances,
whether P had medical problems, and what were the circumstances of the daughter's death. The officer in charge replied as follows: P was having medical treatment; the circumstances of the daughter's death were very distressing; P had told
him all of this even though it was not recorded in her 'statement'; and the officer
in charge had told the charge sergeant none of this. The case was dropped.
(ED115)

The arresting officer secured the charge by presenting a stereotyped oral
report to the charge sergeant. This practice is not unusual.[47] Had he constructed the file in the same way as his oral report no one seeing the file
would have had any reason to question it. Consequently, we cannot ever
learn how many cases of this kind there are, for it is precisely the absence
of information in the files that makes their number unquantifiable.
Constructions remain hidden forever in many guilty pleas where defendants simply wish to be rid of their cases as quickly as possible.

Ambiguity is eliminated by amending, as well as omitting, material.
The safest way of doing this is by stereotyping, for the accused is then
characterized as acting 'normally' in the alleged circumstances.[48] Charges
of soliciting for the purposes of prostitution, for instance, are typically
based on three observations of the defendant 'bending over and peering
into cars', since a formula on these lines is required by the courts; drunkenness cases always include the smell of alcohol on the defendant's
breath, inability to stand up straight, and 'glazed eyes'; cautions after
arrest in accordance with the Judges' Rules (now the Police and Criminal
Evidence Act) are always provided. Some insight into the construction of
reports is provided by a Detective Inspector's comments on this prosecution report on a burglary (WS184/5): 'PC*. Before I submit this file you
might think it advisable to insert a "caution" in your verbal exchange

with C. . . .' This statement was 'amended as requested' by PC*. A case from another force also illustrates the point:

The defendant was charged with shoplifting. The supervising sergeant wrote in the prosecution file to his superior, not seen by the prosecuting solicitors, that 'there are slight differences in the verbals as used by the store detectives in their respective statements. . . . In view of the court date I have not had the original statements amended to correspond with each other, and therefore left the typed copies as shown.' (ED149)

These cases show that it is not just in *causes célèbres* like *Confait* that confessions (especially verbals) have to be treated with circumspection. McConville and Baldwin's findings are similar. In one case, for instance, where a defendant was acquitted of going equipped for theft, one of the officers in the case commented to the researchers that:

the other police officer got into the witness box and swore that the defendant had tried several doors. . . . The prosecution barrister said to me afterwards 'he had given evidence of a different deposition completely'. We had got our stories together beforehand and if he had stuck to what we had agreed it would have been alright.[49]

The point here goes beyond confessions alone. Nelken points out that, 'harassment officers themselves give accounts of the harassment cases they have dealt with which differ from those they record in their enforcement reports'.[50] Accounts are carefully assembled to produce a scenario in which the decisions taken were self-evidently correct:

Decision making . . . may be much more preoccupied with the problem of assigning outcomes their legitimate history than with the question of deciding before the actual occasion of choice the conditions under which one, among a set of possible alternatives, will be selected.[51]

This process of construction is hidden from everyone other than the law enforcers themselves. Assigning 'legitimate history' is made easier by using the stereotyped accounts discussed earlier and by standardization. Standardization is facilitated in many police forces for certain traffic offences, for instance, such as drunk driving, by special pre-printed forms. All the officer has to do is to fill in the gaps and all legal requirements are automatically fulfilled.

This type of standardization is noted by Chatterton who comments that the charge sergeant is effectively prevented from refusing charges in the face of such cases. As long as reports follow routine formats they are not questioned. But when standard procedure is not revealed by a report a supervisor can take control—either rejecting the case or, as in WS184/5, making such changes to the report as are appropriate. One consequence of this is that officers learn to provide accounts that conform to the rules of their organization, which can only mean that radical reconstruction of cases for prosecution files is routine.[52] Becoming 'repeat players' over time,[53] officers learn to construct their cases ever more effectively. Moreover, standardization means depicting the criminal as unequivocally criminal—for which, in most cases, an unequivocal victim is required. Hence, once the police decided, in WS166/7 (above), that D1 was more of a guilty party than D2 all references to D2's possible offences were 'struck from the statements'. By constructing the prosecution file in this way the eventual decision becomes beyond question. Not only is the suspect presented as one-dimensional, but the case is too. Nothing else should be expected of an accusatorial body, but the limits on manœuvre this creates for a body vetting the by-now-obvious decisions of that accusatorial body will be very tight, as I shall show in the next section.

Independent prosecutors in an adversarial system

All police proceedings, up to and including the initial decision to prosecute, remain unchanged by the Prosecution of Offences Act. The introduction of the Crown Prosecution Service therefore does not directly affect decisions to arrest, charge, summon, caution, or take no further action. So officers aiming at, or seeking to justify, non-prosecution decisions still need only to construct their cases in ways that will satisfy their police supervisors. All charged or summonsed cases (apart from minor motoring matters) are passed to the Crown Prosecution Service before defendants' first court appearances. Until the case is committed to the Crown Court (if it is) the Crown Prosecution Service has complete power over whether to alter, drop, or continue with the charges. I pointed out earlier that this power to vet, or screen, cases was ostensibly provided to break control over prosecutions in order, *inter alia*, to reduce the number of weak cases prosecuted hitherto and to counterbalance increased police powers. The capacity of the Crown Prosecution Service to do this—to be truly independent of the police—is questionable for three reasons.

First, the underlying conception of the Crown Prosecution Service is incoherent in principle for it is supposed to play an accusatorial, as well as an inquisitorial, role. I argued earlier that the quasi-judicial elements of the police role are completely overwhelmed by the adversarial imperatives of 'normal policing'. Lord Devlin recognized this some years ago, long before the Police and Criminal Evidence Act increased the coercive powers of the police yet further. He therefore called for a 'judicial intermediary' on the lines of the *juge d'instruction* in France to carry out the inquisitorial functions of the police, leaving the police to follow accusatory norms unhindered. He argued for an enhanced office of the Director of Public Prosecutions, with investigatory powers, to carry out this role.[54] This line of argument, although not the proposed investigatory powers, was accepted by the Royal Commission on Criminal Procedure and the government.[55] The Crown Prosecution Service is presumably supposed to be inquisitorial when vetting cases and accusatorial when prosecuting them.

This idea fails to recognize that if the *police* cannot combine accusatorial and inquisitorial roles then the Crown Prosecution Service will also not be able to do so (the *juge* in France is, in principle at least, a buffer between police, prosecution, and defence). Vetters and prosecutors are the same people. The organizational pressure, encapsulated in the 'fifty-one per cent rule', to use 'winnability' as a criterion when vetting, rather than 'truth' or 'realism', will be overwhelming, especially as prosecutors will be judged on the basis of 'results'—that is, convictions. All organizations with dual preventive and active functions face this problem. Thus, whilst 'community policemen' might feel that high arrest rates do not adequately measure their effectiveness they none the less believe, probably realistically, that this is how they are judged.[56] It follows that for the Crown Prosecution Service to break police control and to counter-balance their accusatory powers it would need to be *completely* independent of the police—not, in other words, to be on the police side of the adversarial system. This is, of course, an absurd notion. Prosecutors can hardly be *neutral* when prosecuting a case *against* someone.

The second reason why the Crown Prosecution Service will not break police control is that even if it is capable of adopting this schizophrenic approach in principle, its functions are not separate in this way in reality. For vetting takes place during, as well as prior to, the passage of a case through the courts. This is because prosecution files often begin as mere police summaries. Full files, which need to be vetted anew, come later, if at all.[57] Prosecutors are required to wear their inquisitorial and accusatorial hats simultaneously. They will be working *on* the police at the same time as they are working *for* them.

Thirdly, the powers of the Crown Prosecution Service are an inadequate match for the resources of the police. One such resource is the new power of the police to initiate proceedings.[58] This accusatorial development exacerbates the contradictions inherent in the dual role of the Crown Prosecution Service.[59] Another is the power of the police to control the preprosecution decision-making role of the Crown Prosecution Service.[60] Yet another, and probably the most significant, is the main subject of this article: the power to control the provision of information.

Prosecutorial screening and re-investigation

I demonstrated earlier that police officers, like other enforcement officers in adversarial settings, will try to construct cases that will (*a*) justify their decisions to their superiors; and (*b*) be strong in court. This is done by eliminating ambiguity and showing a logical progression from the 'event' to the prosecution decision. Officers do not find strong cases. They make them. In so doing they attempt to remove all the features that undermine those cases. This does not mean that the police try to make strong cases out of every incident they encounter: the police frequently construct cases in ways which justify non-prosecution too.[61] Frequently such incidents would make poor material out of which to construct a strong case, but this is not the only consideration. The point at issue here is that, since initial decisions to caution or take no action are the province of the police alone, crown prosecutors are generally presented only with cases which the police want prosecuted.

The accounts which officers present to prosecutors are as near *faits accomplis* as they can manage. Prosecuting solicitors in England and Wales have traditionally been able to do little other than to endorse earlier prosecution decisions. Screening has always been perfunctory because most cases are constructed to be self-justifying. The institutional environment told prosecutors that their only job was to prosecute.[62] In what way will the Crown Prosecution Service be different? It has the inquisitorial power and duty to screen cases and to halt those that are evidentially insufficient. But the Crown Prosecution Service has no resources with which to open up, or to go behind, the carefully constructed accounts with which it is presented. Without investigatory powers crown prosecutors are not even judicial intermediaries in Devlin's terms. Devlin saw investigatory powers as necessary in order to open up cases—which is the essence of the judicial function. Screening does not, by definition, open up a case, but merely scans it for internal inconsistencies and measures it against the 'probability of conviction' yardstick. Screening merely identifies cases which are not self-justifying.

McConville and Baldwin point out that to expect prosecutors screening on this basis to effectively control the police is a pious aspiration.[63] For the Crown Prosecution Service has no more powers or resources to open up or go behind cases than the Director of Public Prosecutions and prosecuting solicitors had in the past. Fisher aptly summed up the problem as it then was, and as it will remain:

And there is nobody outside the police who regards it as his duty to spur the police on to question the case and to follow lines of enquiry which might be inconsistent with it.[64]

Confait was the original impetus behind the Crown Prosecution Service via the Royal Commission on Criminal Procedure. So it is ironic that not only were the processes of construction and initially successful cover-up in *Confait* normal rather than aberrational, but also the normality of this will be unaffected by the 'new' system.

This is not to say that investigative powers would affect the outcome of most cases. The problem is not that prosecutors see a need for re-investigation which the police refuse to act upon. In ED176, remember, the prosecutors felt *betrayed* by the police officer changing his story, and in EC121 the prosecutor was surprised that what had begun as a 'typical' shoplifting case took an unusual direction. The whole point about the way cases are constructed is that all hints of other suspects and other courses of action are censored from the file. There is no more reason, initially, to re-investigate one case (which later turns out to be problematic) than any other. The point is well made by Moody and Tombs in their study of Scottish Procurators Fiscal who, of course, *do* have the investigatory powers recommended by Devlin. They could be talking about English prosecuting solicitors:

The idea that the prosecutor is there to prosecute is fundamental to the Fiscal's definition of his function: in most cases not to proceed would be out of the question'.[65]

Only some 8 per cent of cases are dropped by Scottish prosecutors at any stage.[66] As Moody and Tombs point out, different practices in jurisdictions like the Netherlands show that these attitudes are not universal. But my argument is that they are universal to adversarial systems where it is the job of the police, rather than the prosecutor, to construct the case. In a skilfully constructed case no lines of re-investigation are visible to the prosecutor for there are apparently no loose ends. They will all be neatly blocked or eliminated. Consequently, in only 6 per cent of police reports did Moody and Tombs find that further information was requested by prosecutors and it only occurs 'if there is some glaring evidential flaw or very obvious mistake in police procedure'.[67] This is despite Scottish prosecutor knowing that the police are highly selective about what they include in the other 94 per cent of cases:

'the police can withhold information' . . . 'we have to rely on the police doing more and more' . . . 'we're giving up our true constitutional function of investigating crime and are almost acting as a rubber stamp for police officers'.[68]

Ericson sums up as follows:

While in theory the crown attorney can still inquire deeply into how the police produced the charges and constructed the facts . . . the truth about a case and the charges involved in it are usually synonymous with the police version of the truth.[69]

To be fair to the Royal Commission, it did recognize that in Scotland and the United States of America prosecutors generally do little more, with regard to the initial prosecution decision, than endorse police action. It therefore said that the Crown Prosecution Service would 'act as a long stop'.[70] This, however, reduces the idea that the Crown Prosecution Service can break police control of prosecutions to an absurdity. The Royal Commission was either hopelessly confused or less than honest.

Mere window-dressing?

So what is the point of the Crown Prosecution Service? Is it, as McConville suggests, 'A new legal civil service giving the stamp of respectability' to current proceedings?[71] Is it mere window-dressing aimed at projecting a neutral and objective image of the criminal law 'by investing its mobilization in a seemingly neutral and disinterested institution'?[72] I believe that its impact will be far more concrete than this.

Let us return to the ostensible reason for its introduction: the problem of the weak case. Crown prosecutors are supposed to operate the 51 per cent rule, dropping weak cases which fall below this threshold. Higher evidential standards than hitherto are expected of the police, but the forces which shape current prosecution patterns (including the prosecution of weak cases) will not be changed. Thus, while the incidents which are the subject of prosecution will no doubt remain the same, the *cases* can be expected to 'improve'—that is, to be constructed more single-mindedly and unambiguously. As McBarnet argues, success or failure in court depends as much on the *case presented* as on the 'actual' case (that is, the original events). So, rather than being ineffectual, the Crown Prosecution Service will be a catalyst for higher evidential standards although not in the way presented in official policy documents. Greater strength will reside in the accounts of the events from which cases are selected, rather than in the events themselves.

Underlying the 'mere window-dressing' theory of the Crown Prosecution Service is an assumption that the police do not want their weak cases to be identified by the new service. The theory sees the fact that weak cases often fail in court (but not always, given the pressures on defendants to plead guilty, regardless of guilt, innocence, strength, and weakness)[73] as less important to the police than their original purpose in arresting and charging the defendant in question. This, however, embodies an overly static view of the nature of 'weak cases'. Since weakness and strength are *constructions* the Crown Prosecution Service can actually *assist* the police by identifying ways of circumventing weak parts of the case. In some cases prosecutors suggest that extra evidence be obtained, while in others alternative charges with more chance of success are suggested:

There was a fight between D1 and D2 on the one hand and V and X on the other. D1 and D2 were reported for assault. The prosecuting solicitor advised that there was 'insufficient evidence to proceed on the s.47 [assault] . . . if for whatever reason you feel that the matter must go to court, Bind Overs are the obvious solution'. The police accepted this advice. (EC199/200)

None of this should be taken to suggest that the police face no difficulties in constructing seamless webs of winnable cases. Prosecutors and supervising officers do find major weaknesses in some cases and therefore reject them, and some cases fail in court. There are many reasons for this. Not all officers are highly skilled. Officers have their own notion of the line between building and manipulating cases and, virtually all being honest, they very rarely cross it—after all, few of the methods the police use to construct cases which I have discussed contravene legal rules. Some cases succeed in their objectives as far as the police are concerned if they simply neutralize a dubious exercise of power. Finally, the police are not the sole sources of information and credibility. They are, as Ericson puts it, 'interdependent' with, for instance, victims, suspects, prosecutors, and defence lawyers.[74]

Conclusion

It would be easy to conclude that criminal justice will never be 'fair' until the police are subject to more restrictive rules and until a body is created with both the powers and resources to re-investigate as many cases as it wished. This crude positivist position posits a simplistic relationship between the 'incident' and the 'case', and is common among liberal lawyers.[75] Such a conclusion would be based on a selective reading of the material which I have presented. This would treat English criminal justice in a way it would understand, but it would achieve little. Few cases ever reveal themselves as obvious cases for re-investigation, and to re-investigate all would, even were it practical, simply duplicate the work of the police. This would make the new body another police force. It would have the same dual functions and internal contradictions incorporated within it.

The liberal-positivist approach presupposes that 'the case' is available for extraction from reality and capable of reproduction in a case file. Bankowski challenges this belief in 'objective facts' which are separable from the process by which they are discovered. He attributes Jerome Frank's attack on adversary procedure to an assumption that 'the facts' are available for value free examination. By contrast, Bankowski argues that seeking the truth is impossible without some criteria for the methods of seeking and evaluating it. Rationalist, empiricist, materialist, and theocratist methods are competing positions, not different routes to the same destination. Thus:

We do not have immediate access to the 'truth of the matter' . . . the facts we know are constructs, partly determined by the procedures of discovery which in turn depend upon procedures of justification.[76]

Calls for 'fair' investigation and decision-making, then, deny the need to construct criminal cases. This conclusion may sound ethnomethodological, but that is not the only way to interpret the material presented here. I do not accept that in any criminal justice system different versions of 'the case' compete freely in an unstructured environment. It is worth noting that my argument is buttressed by research conducted in many different jurisdictions.[77] This material supports McBarnet's thesis, with which I began: that not only are cases biased constructs, but also the power to construct plausible cases is unequally distributed. State power is concretized in the form of unlimited police witnesses, automatic respectability of state prosecutors, the right of the police to set the terms of the debate, and the greater number of 'repeat players'[78] on the prosecution side than on the defence side.

Not all prosecution cases succeed, not least because the defence can also construct plausible stories, especially when it too can enlist 'repeat players'. But prosecution success is far more usual because of the structure within which cases are constructed. This structure, Ericson argues, is actually designed to provide the police (detectives in particular) with more power than the agencies with whom they are interdependent. Whether designed this way or not, Ericson is justified in concluding that the police have 'the upper hand in most transactions . . . [through] . . . their control over information production, selection and use'.[79] This explanation of why the courts routinely decide that guilt is proved beyond reasonable doubt can be most plausibly situated in the context of, in Nelken's words, 'coherence without conspiracy'.[80] Along with Nelken, it seems to me that the clash of structural and interpretive approaches represents a false dichotomy.

In concrete terms, we must conclude that there is little point expecting state employees to discover whether the police are telling the truth—or, more pertinently, the whole truth. Grafting inquisitorial elements on to an adversarial system produces the confusion of roles that constitutes Scottish criminal justice. Cases cannot ever be dispassionately and accurately screened by any organization if all the information used to do the screening is provided by the organization being screened.

McConville suggests that the way forward is to open police files to the defence.[81] This would be in order to lay the processes of construction bare for all to see and challenge. In other words, the adversary nature of the system would be neither denied nor tinkered with. Rather, it would be embraced, but its internal processes made visible to all sides of a dispute.[82] Re-investigation would be undertaken by the defence. Since it would be undertaken by the agency which would benefit from it, we could expect it to be productive. For this to be at all effective the police would have to be reassured that a reduced conviction rate and the revelation of police methods would not be used against them. In practice this would be a gigantic obstacle to overcome, but any incremental steps forward in this direction could well be worth more than any 'new' system of 'independent' prosecutors.

Notes

1. D. McBarnet, *Conviction* (1981), 16.
2. Home Office, *An Independent Prosecution Service for England and Wales* (1983; Cmnd 9074) para. 6.

3. *R.* v. *Banks* [1916] 2 K.B. 621. The government's position was put by Lord Elton, Minister of State, Home Office, introducing the second reading debate on the Prosecution of Offences Bill in the House of Lords 457 *H. L. Debs.*, 1014 (29 Nov. 1984). This point is discussed by S. Uglow, 'Independent Prosecutions' (1984) 11 *J. Law and Society*, 233.

4. Attorney General, *Criteria for Prosecution* (1983). The Director of Public Prosecutions' *Code for Crown Prosecutors* (1986) endorses these guidelines. See A. Sanders, 'Prosecution Decisions and the Attorney General's Guidelines' (1985) *Crim. Law Rev.* 6.

5. P. Devlin, *The Judge* (1979), 72.

6. McBarnet, op. cit., 16–19, n. 1. As will become clear, I am not suggesting that the construction of cases is necessarily, or usually, a cynical process (although the scope for conscious cynical manipulation should not be under-estimated). For a classic ethnomethodological approach, see A. Cicourel, *The Social Organisation of Juvenile Justice* (1968). As should also become clear, however, my approach is not ethnomethodological.

7. This is even acknowledged by legal writers, although the terminology is different. See R. Munday, 'Natural Justice in the English Criminal Prosecution', *New Law J.* Jan. 1981, p. 6.

8. Devlin, op cit., p. 73, n. 5.

9. Home Office, *Report of an Inquiry into the circumstances leading to the trial of three persons on charges arising out of the death of Maxwell Confait and the fire at 27 Doggett Road, London S.E.6.* (Fisher Report) (1977; H.C. 90). M. McConville and J. Baldwin, *Courts, Prosecution, and Conviction* (1981), 190–1.

10. Home Office, *Report of the Departmental Committee on Identification* (Devlin) (1976, H.C. 338). The new obligation on the prosecution to provide advance disclosure to the defence under the Criminal Law Act 1977, s. 48, is not a change of principle, since it only creates new duties in Magistrates court cases equivalent to their pre-existing duties in Crown Court cases. Both *Virag* and *Confait* were Crown Court cases.

11. This case, along with the other unacknowledged quotations and cases used in this article, is taken from my ESRC-funded research on police prosecutions. See Sanders, op. cit., n. 4 for a description of the project. Minor details have been altered in these cases to preserve confidentiality. Any reader requiring further information about the cases should contact me, quoting reference number(s) to the appropriate case(s) in the text of this article.

12. D. Leigh, 'How the Innocent Can Still "Confess"' *Guardian*, 9 Mar. 1981. Smith and Gray cite cases which also illustrate the point: see Policy Studies Institute report, *The Police in Action* (1983), 167–8.

13. See, for instance, A. K. Bottomley, *Decisions in the Penal Process* (1973), chap. 1; M. Zander, 'The Investigation of Crime: A Study of Cases Tried at the Old Bailey' (1979), *Crim. Law Rev.* 203.

14. T. Sargant and P. Hill, *Criminal Trials—The Search for Truth* (Fabian Research Series 348, 1986), 4. On identification evidence in general see P. Hain, *Mistaken Identity* (1976).

15. McConville and Baldwin, op. cit., p. 190, n. 9.

16. Smith and Gray, op. cit., pp. 145–6, n. 12.

17. Ibid. 149.

18. Section 36. See V. Bevan and K. Lidstone, *A Guide to the Police and Criminal Evidence Act, 1984* (1985), paras. 6.06–6.11.

19. See Sargant and Hill, op. cit., n. 14, who attack the adversary system as a whole in this vein.

20. S. McCabe and R. Purves, *The Jury at Work* (1972).

21. McConville and Baldwin, op. cit., p. 110, n. 9.

22. Ibid., 'The Role of Interrogation in Crime Discovery and Conviction' (1982) 22 *Brit. J. Criminol.* 169.

23. B. Irving, *Police Interrogation—A Case Study of Current Practice* (1980) HMSO, p. 116.

24. A similar point is made in S. Holdaway, *Inside the British Police* (1983), 103–4. This, of course, partially accounts for the police not obtaining independent evidence that could assist the defence as in WS168 above.

25. R. Ericson, *Making Crime* (1981), 162. Also see P. Softly, *Police Interrogation—An Observational Study in Four Police Stations* (1980) HMSO, p. 78; Irving, op. cit., pp. 138–51, n. 23; and S. Holdaway, op. cit., pp. 102–8, n. 24.

26. Softly, op. cit., p. 81, n. 25; Irving, op. cit., p. 152, n. 23.

27. Royal Commission on Criminal Procedure, *Report* (1981) Cmnd 8092, chap. 4. Sect. 74 of the Police and Criminal Evidence Act now provides for the exclusion of evidence on grounds of 'oppression' or 'unreliability' but not involuntariness.

28. Holdaway, op. cit., pp. 104–7, n. 24.

29. Leigh, op. cit., n. 12. Also see the example cited from Smith and Gray's research, op. cit., n. 12, and B. Cox, *Civil Liberties in Britain* (1975).

30. Smith and Gray, op. cit., pp. 217–18, n. 12,

31. H. Becker, 'Whose Side Are We On?' (1967) 14 *Social Problems*, 239.

32. Smith and Gray, op. cit., p. 142, n. 12.

33. See C. Willis, *The Use, Effectiveness, and Impact of Police Stop and Search Powers* (Home Office, 1983), and I. Piliavin and S. Briar, 'Police Encounters with Juveniles' (1964) 70 *Am. J. Sociology*. Similar examples are given by M. Chatterton, Organisational Relationships and Processes in Police Work (1975, unpubl. Ph.D.) chap. 6. He calls cases like this 'resource charges'. See Sanders, op. cit., n. 4, for a general discussion.

34. S. Box and K. Russell, 'The Politics of Discreditability: Disarming Complaints Against the Police' (1975) 8 *Soc. Rev.* 315.

35. A. Sanders and G. Cole, 'The Prosecution of 'Weak' Cases in England and Wales' (1982) 7 *Criminal Justice Rev.* 23.

36. Ibid. Also see E. Bittner, 'The Police on Skid Row: A Study of Peace Keeping' (1967) 32 *Am. Sociological Rev.* 699.

37. R. Ericson, *Reproducing Order—A Study of Police Patrol Work* (1982), 129–31. The police often avoid involvement in 'domestic violence' cases. See, for example, T. Faragher, 'The Police Response to Violence Against Women in the Home', in J. Pahl (ed.), *Private Violence and Public Policy* (1985). The police are reluctant to choose a 'domestic violence' case where an incident gives rise to other alternative cases: F. Wasoff, 'Legal Protection from Wifebeating' (1982) 10 *International J. Sociology of Law*, 187.

38. Devlin Report, op. cit., n. 10; Hain, op. cit., n. 14.

39. Fisher Report, op. cit., n. 9.

40. D. Nelken, *The Limits of the Legal Process* (1983), 127. This can also mean playing down the significance of a case, in order to justify non-prosecution or relatively minor charges. This is characteristic of non-police agencies concerned with, for instance, pollution (see K. Hawkins, *Environment and Enforcement* (1984)). But it is equally true of the police in, for instance, domestic assault cases: Faragher, op. cit., n. 37; Wasoff, op. cit., n. 37; Ericson, op. cit., n. 37.

41. Nelken, op. cit., pp. 160–6, n. 40.

42. Chatterton, op. cit., p. 192, n. 33.

43. S. Moody and J. Tombs, *Prosecution in the Public Interest* (1982), 45.

44. Chatterton, op. cit., p. 192, n. 33.

45. Nelken, op. cit., p. 138, n. 40.

46. Id., p. 160.

47. Chatterton, op. cit., n. 33; Sanders, op. cit., n. 4. Holdaway comments that an officer who wishes to protect himself 'constructs the appropriate account. This asymmetrical relationship between senior and junior officers enhances the power of the lower ranks.' Op. cit., pp. 165–6, n. 24.

48. D. Sudnow, 'Normal Crimes' (1965) 12 *Social Problems*, 255.

49. McConville and Baldwin, op. cit., p. 167, n. 9. Holdaway, op. cit., pp. 108–10, n. 24, claims that while 'verballing' is rarely forced upon officers it is rarely condemned either. It is therefore an accepted part of police practice.

50. Nelken, op. cit., p. 135, n. 40.

51. H. Garfinkel, *Studies in Ethnomethodology* (1968), 110.

52. McConville and Baldwin, op. cit., chap. 10, n. 9; Ericson, op. cit., chap. 1, n. 25.

53. M. Galanter, 'Why the "Haves" Come Out Ahead: Speculation on the Limits of Legal Change' (1974) *Law and Society Rev.* 95.

54. Devlin, op. cit., p. 82, n. 5; it is unclear whether Devlin intended this for all, or just very serious, offences: in France the *juge* is concerned only in the latter. For a debate on inquisitorial systems see A. Goldstein and M. Marcus, 'The Myth of Judicial Supervision in Three Inquisitorial Systems: France, Italy and Germany' (1977) 87 *Yale Law J.* 240, plus a reply by J. Langbein and L. Weinreb (1978) 87 *Yale Law J.* 1549 and rejoinder by Goldstein and Marcus (1978) 87 *Yale Law J.* 1570.

55. I argue this more fully in my 'Arrest, Charge, and Prosecution' (1986) 6 *Legal Studies* 257.

56. D. Brown and S. Iles, *Community Constables—A Study of a Policing Initiative* (Home Office, 1985); M. Jones and J. Winkler, 'Beyond The Beat' (1982), *J. Law and Society*, 9. The distinction between likely guilt and likely conviction was identified by Glanville Williams, who criticized the Attorney General's Guidelines for embodying the latter test, rather than the former. See 'Letting off the Guilty and Prosecuting the Innocent' (1985), *Crim. Law Rev.* 115. The Director of Public Prosecutions' *Code for Crown Prosecutors* (1986) merely reiterates the Attorney General's Guidelines on this point.

57. A. Sanders, 'An Independent Crown Prosecution Service?' (1986) *Crim. Law Rev.* 16. The Director of Public Prosecutions' *Code for Crown Prosecutors* (1986) para. 10 states that 'the discretion to discontinue is a continuing one, and even when proceedings are under way Crown Prosecutors should continue to exercise their reviewing function'.

58. Prosecution of Offences Act 1985 s. 15(2)(c).

59. Discussed in Sanders, op. cit., n. 55.

60. Ibid. n. 57.

61. Ericson, op. cit., n. 37.

62. Sanders, op. cit., n. 57.

63. McConville and Baldwin, 'Recent Developments in English Criminal Justice and The Royal Commission on Criminal Procedure' (1982) 10 *International J. Sociology of Law*, 287. McConville has developed this point further in 'Prosecuting Criminal Cases in England and Wales: Reflections of an Inquisitorial Adversary' (1984) 6 *Liverpool Law Rev.* 15.

64. Fisher Report, op. cit., p. 20, n. 9.

65. Moody and Tombs, op. cit., p. 58, n. 43. Canadian researchers make the same point: B. Grosman, *The Prosecutor* (1969), 27. The evidence from the USA, where there is a variety of jurisdiction, is more confused. For a variety of studies see, for example, L. Carter, *The Limits of Order* (1974); G. Cole, 'The Decision to Prosecute' (1970) 4 *Law and Society Rev.* 331; D. Neubauer, 'After the Arrest' (1974) 8 *Law and Society Rev.* 495; B. Stanko, 'The Arrest Versus the Case' (1981) 9 *Urban Life*, 395.

66. Moody and Tombs, op. cit., p. 57, n. 43.

67. Ibid., p. 47, n. 43.

68. Ibid., pp. 47–8, n. 43. Also see Wasoff, op. cit., n. 37.

69. Ericson, op. cit., pp. 180–1, n. 37. Goldstein and Marcus, op. cit., n. 54, argue that this is true of European inquisitorial systems too, although not in the most serious cases.

70. Royal Commission on Criminal Procedure, op. cit., n. 27, para. 7–11.

71. McConville, op. cit., n. 63.

72. Uglow, op. cit., p. 240, n. 3.

73. See, for example, Baldwin and McConville, *Negotiated Justice* (1977); McBarnet, op. cit., chap. 4, n. 1; Sanders, op. cit., n. 4.

74. Ericson, op. cit., n. 25.

75. Tom Sargant of JUSTICE, for instance, advocates investigative powers for prosecutors in 'The Prosecution Process' (1981) *New Law J.* 12 March 1981, 276, and in Sargant and Hill, op. cit., n. 14. And Lord Scarman has called for 'judicial control of the pre-trial process' precisely because he does not antici-pate the Crown Prosecution Service being able to deal with the underlying causes of *Confait*-type incidents (*The Times*, 7 Oct. 1986).

76. Z. Bankowski, 'The Value of Truth: Fact Scepticism Re-visited' (1981) 1 *Legal Studies*, 257.

77. Ericson and Grosman in Canada, Moody and Tombs in Scotland, Nelken in an English non-police context, and the research from the USA cited in n. 65. Some quantitative research has come to similar conclusions, such as M. Radelet and G. Pierce, 'Race and Prosecutorial Discretion in Homicide Cases' (1985) 19 *Law and Society Rev.* 587.

78. Galanter, op. cit., n. 53.

79. Ericson, op. cit., pp. 213–14, n. 25.

80. Nelken, op. cit., p. 212, n. 40.

81. McConville, op. cit., n. 63.

82. This may sound impractical but it does happen in France: Langbein and Weinreb, op. cit., n. 54. There is, though, nothing intrinsically inquisitorial about this.

The Question of Bail: Magistrates' Responses to Applications for Bail on Behalf of Men and Women Defendants

MARY EATON

It is inevitable that the legal system should invite questions about the nature of justice. Certainly, there appears to be a basic contradiction in the position of a state apparatus which promises justice but which is committed to the upholding of the *status quo*, that is a society divided by class, gender, and racism. In this chapter I will explore this contradiction as it affects the reproduction of gender differences and the operation of sexism within the criminal justice system. I will argue that sexism is manifest not in overt disparities in the treatment of men and women but through the subtle reinforcement of gender roles in the discourse and practice of courtroom practitioners.

Sexism in the courts

Traditionally, the issue of sexism within the courts has been addressed by comparing the sentences of men and women. Much of this work is flawed and limited. It is flawed because it usually does not effectively control for factors most relevant to the phenomena being compared (e.g. sentences). It is limited because if such factors are effectively controlled, the focus is then on a narrow range of women offenders—those whose situations can be compared with men. Most women and men differ in the type of offence with which they are charged and in the number of previous convictions with which they appear before the court. Furthermore, by concentrating on the end result, or the sentence, such work neglects the process by which it is accomplished. Official statistics record the offences with which defendants are charged and the outcome of such proceedings, but such figures can be only a starting point for a sociological analysis of the processes which give rise to these figures.

TABLE 1 *Offenders found guilty at all courts by sex and type of Offence in England and Wales (1983)*

Offence	Males		Females	
	Number (000's)	Percentage	Number (000's)	Percentage
Indictable Offences				
Violence against the person	47.4	92	4.0	8
Sexual offences	6.4	98	0.1	2
Burglary	70.3	97	2.4	3
Robbery	3.8	95	0.2	5
Theft and handling stolen goods	179.5	80	45.3	20
Fraud and forgery	20.1	79	5.5	21
Criminal damage	11.2	93	0.8	7
Other (excluding motoring)	30.0	90	3.4	10
Motoring	29.6	97	1.0	3
TOTAL	398.4	86	62.7	14
Summary Offences				
Offences (excluding motoring)	390.4	83	82.4	17
Motoring	1,053.7	91	108.1	9
TOTAL	1,444.1	88	190.4	12
All offences	1,842.4	88	253.1	12

Source: Home Office (1984*a*), Table 5.1.

TABLE 2 *Type of sentence or order given to offenders over 21 in England and Wales (1983)*

Sentence or order	Males		Females	
	Number (000's)	Percentage	Number (000's)	Percentage
Absolute or conditional discharge	18.4	9	8.6	21
Probation order	13.3	6	6.8	17
Fine	100.8	47	18.6	46
Community Service order	14.3	7	1.0	2
Imprisonment:				
Full suspended	24.6	11	2.9	7
Partly suspended	3.5	2	0.3	1
Unsuspended	38.0	18	1.8	4
Otherwise	3.1	1	0.5	1
TOTAL	216.2	101*	40.5	99[a]

[a] Percentage figures do not sum to 100 as they have been rounded up or down to the nearest whole number.

Source: Home Office (1984a), tables 7.11, 7.12.

From the official statistics we can see that, officially at least, men and women differ in their criminal involvements and in the punishments they receive.

Women form a small proportion of all known criminals (about 12 per cent in 1983), and their offences are concentrated within specific areas. Given the difference in recorded offences, it is not surprising to find that men and women differ in the sentences they receive. Most offenders are fined, but a higher proportion of men receive sentences of imprisonment, while a higher proportion of women receive probation and absolute or conditional discharges.

This difference in sentencing has led many writers to speculate on the apparent leniency of the courts towards women. Ignoring the differences in gravity of offences and previous convictions, much has been attributed to chivalry on the part of judges and magistrates. One extreme example of this approach is Otto Pollak's work. Taking official statistics at their face value he concluded:

One of the outstanding concomitants of the existing inequality between the sexes is chivalry and the general protective attitude of man towards woman. . . . Men hate to accuse women . . . police officers dislike to arrest them, district attorneys to prosecute them, judges and juries to find them guilty, and so on. (Pollak 1950: 151)

Others have attempted a more systematic comparison and analysis. Among the most widely cited are the studies carried out by Nagel and Weitzmen (1971) and Rita James Simon (1977). Both studies, conducted in the USA, claim to compare the sentences of men and women. Both studies acknowledge their failure to control for previous conviction and gravity of offence. Yet neither study allows that such factors may throw doubt on the findings of leniency towards women defendants. Nagel and Weitzman conclude:

These findings seem consistent with how women are generally treated in American society. There exists a paternalistic protectiveness, at least towards white women, that assumes they need sheltering from manly experiences such as jail and from subjection to the unfriendliness of overly formal proceedings in criminal . . . cases. (Nagel and Weitzman 1971: 180)

In the research which does control for offence and prior record, the apparent benefits to women disappear. Meda Chesney-Lind has reviewed such studies conducted in the USA (Green, 1961; Rottman and Simon 1975; Pope 1975—all cited in Chesney-Lind 1978). In the UK one study notable for the rigour of its approach is the Farrington and Morris work on magistrates' courts in Cambridge (Farrington and Morris 1983*a*). Using court records, Farrington and Morris examined nearly 400 cases, including 108 women, involving sentencing for theft between January and July 1979. Carefully controlling for gravity of offence and previous convictions, they found that the lighter sentences received by women were due to the different circumstances in which men and women appear before the court. They write:

the sex of the defendant did not have any direct influence on the severity of the sentence or the probability of reconviction. Women appeared to receive more lenient sentences . . . only because they had committed less serious offences and were less likely to have been convicted previously. (Farrington and Morris, 1983a: 245)

However, while Farrington and Morris found no difference in the sentencing of men and women in similar circumstances, they did find a difference in the sentencing of married and unmarried women:

Women who were in the 'other' category on marital status (predominantly divorced or separated rather than widowed) received relatively severe sentences, as did women from a deviant family background (coming from a broken home, usually). (ibid.)

Such findings are similar to those of Nagel who examined the processing of nearly 3,000 defendants (338 women) in New York State (Nagel, 1981). Nagel found that

marital status had no significant effect for males and a strong significant effect for females—married females were considerably less likely than their unmarried female counterparts to spend any time imprisoned. (Nagel 1981: 113)

What begins to emerge from careful studies of the sentencing of men and women is the significance for the court of a woman defendant occupying a traditional role, that is being a married woman. This is a point to which I will return, after describing the case study which I carried out on a magistrates' court situated in a town on the edge of the Greater London area. The work was based on observation, interviews and document analysis.

The case study

The period of observation consisted of one or two mornings a week during 1980 and 1981. During that time I saw a total of 321 complete cases, involving 210 men and 111 women defendants.[1] Eight men and eight women appeared as co-defendants. Three of these couples were legally represented, and thirty-two of the other men and twenty-five of the other women were legally represented. Social inquiry reports were requested for thirty-seven of the men and thirty-five of the women. Applications for bail were made on behalf of five women and three men who are not included in the 'complete cases' seen.

It was unusual to find cases in which the defendants resembled each other in all respects but sex. Most of the men had previous convictions and most of the women were appearing for the first time. Family circumstances and disposable income were rarely similar for men and women, and this affected sentence. Fines are the most usual penalty, but many magistrates commented in interview on the difficulty of fining a woman with no disposable income. The women before them were usually responsible for the care and maintenance of children, supported either by social security benefits or by such small housekeeping allowances that to deduct any amount to pay a fine would be to deprive the children.

Magistrates frequently said that they responded to the circumstances of the cases and not the sex of the defendant, and my observations confirmed this. On the few occasions on which men and women appeared in similar circumstances, they received similar sentences. This applied to defendants appearing on separate charges and to those appearing as co-defendants on joint charges. In these cases the blame was not automatically ascribed to the man or the woman, usually both were recognized as equally culpable.

The majority of cases were treated in a routine manner (£10 fine for being drunk, between £15 and £40 for drunk and disorderly, £25 to £30 for possession of cannabis). Less routine matters gave rise to discussion among lawyers and magistrates with perhaps a contribution from a probation officer. Such discussions revealed something of the criteria by which decisions are reached. Here the importance of family circumstances, together with the offence and the previous convictions, was apparent. Contained in these discussions was a model of family life and appropriate gender-roles. This model is crucial to any understanding of the reproduction of gender differences by the court. Evidence of similar treatment for the few men and women who appear before the court in similar circumstances may satisfy the court's criteria of justice, but it has little to do with the way in which the subordinate role of women is reproduced by the processes of summary justice.

The reproduction of gender differences is a subtle process accomplished not by differential sentencing but by the routine processes of the court. To understand this it is necessary to go beyond those rare cases in which men and women appear in similar circumstances and consider the ways in which most men and women are presented to the court.

Summary justice and familial ideology

The language of the courtroom both reflects and reinforces the prevailing picture of the social order. It contains and communicates the attitudes and assumptions of those involved in the social construction of justice. Elsewhere I have examined pleas of mitigation and social inquiry reports to discover what they reveal of the court's expectations concerning the behaviour of men and women. (Eaton 1983, 1985, 1986). Pleas of mitigation invoke a consensual social world in which the family is the basic unit, a privileged unit and the touchstone of normality. Those whose lives conform to this pattern can more easily refute the label 'criminal' since membership of a family is recognized to involve a degree of social control. However, while the conventional nuclear family—breadwinner husband and dependant wife responsible for child-care and domestic labour—may be used in pleas of mitigation made on behalf of both men and women, the allotted roles are different. The division of labour implicit in pleas of mitigation is endorsed in social inquiry reports—not only in what they say but also in the way they are constructed. When writing a report on a woman, the probation officer would visit her at home and incorporate a description of the home in the report. When writing a report on a man, the probation officer would, where possible, visit the home in order to talk to the wife (or cohabitee) and incorporate her comments into the report. The woman's caring role is expected to extend to mediating with outside agencies which intrude into the home.

The court's concern with the playing of an appropriate gender role within the context of the family corresponds to the findings noted in the research cited above. However, while Nagel (1981) and Farrington and Morris (1983*a*) have noted the significance of marital status in the sentencing of women, they advance no explanation beyond the suggestion that courts may 'disapprove' of women in unconventional roles. To fully understand the reasons for the court's approval of a conventional female gender role, one must appreciate the degree of social control which is involved in that role.

The traditional role of the married woman is that of an economic dependant with no financial resources of her own and with domestic responsibilities which tie her to the home. Those who work outside the home are usually employed in the poorest-paid sector of the labour market as part-time employees. Furthermore, such employment does not lighten their domestic responsibilities, and so they are left with even less time which is not occupied by the demands of home, husband, and children. Recent feminist writings have analysed the degree of control to which women are subject within the home (Krutschnitt 1982; Heidensohn 1985). This control is most starkly demonstrated when one considers the court's response to applications for bail.

Bail or custody?

All defendants in England and Wales appear before a local magistrates' court. For the majority (approximately 96 per cent), this is where their cases are heard and their fates decided. A minority are committed for trial to the Crown court. These defendants either choose trial by jury or are charged with matters which are considered too serious to be dealt with by the lower courts. Those who are committed for trial face a period of remand, and it is the magistrates who decide whether that period should be spent in custody or on bail. In England and Wales there is no limit to the time spent on remand; although the average in the London area was thirty weeks in 1983 (NACRO 1985*a*), some people experience a delay of between one and two years. (In Scotland there is a limit of 110 days.) Arguments for and against bail may be put forward by the police and by the defendant's legal representative. A person held in custody while awaiting trial is, according to legal rhetoric, presumed innocent. Since the imprisonment of an innocent person is contrary to natural justice, it is deemed permissible only in exceptional circumstances set out in the Bail Act, 1976. Doherty and East (1985) describe these as follows:

Where an offence is imprisonable, bail need not be granted if there are substantial grounds for believing that, if released on bail, a defendant would fail to surrender to custody, commit an offence, interfere with witnesses or otherwise obstruct the course of justice. Bail may also be refused for the protection of a defendant, or to ensure the welfare of a defendant who is a child or young person, or where a defendant is in custody in pursuance of the sentence of a court or of any authority acting under any of the Service Acts, or where the defendant has in relation to the proceedings absconded or breached bail conditions. Finally, bail may be refused where the court is satisfied that it has not been practicable to obtain sufficient information for the purpose of making such decisions, for want of time, since the institution of proceedings against the defendant. (Doherty and East, 1985: 252)

Despite the apparent safeguard of the Act, many of those held in custody are given non-custodial sentences or are found 'not guilty'. In 1982, of the 52,606 prisoners held in custody, 36 per cent (19,464) were given non-custodial sentences, and 3 per cent (1,578) were acquitted (Peckham 1985: 240). The conditions endured by remand prisoners have been described elsewhere (King and Morgan 1976). Audrey Peckham gives a graphic account of her own experience in Pucklechurch (Peckham, 1985). Noting that 62,871 people were held on remand in 1982 she writes:

I cannot understand why so many people are remanded in custody. Of the people with whom I spent my five months on remand, it seemed to me that very few represented any kind of threat to society. Most were either ill, or inadequate, or had made one mistake. I am not arguing for the abolition of remand centres. I understand that there are some criminals who do represent a threat and should be kept in custody. What I am saying is that the population of our remand centres could be reduced today by between 50 and 70 per cent, without anyone being adversely affected. (Peckham 1985: 240)

This is clearly an area in which the discretion of the magistrates operates. It is at such non-routine points in the criminal justice process that discussion takes place and assumptions are revealed. What emerges from a consideration of the men and women whose applications for bail I heard, was a concern with social control and an implicit recognition of those social arrangements, family structures, which offer effective control. The choice for the magistrates is between the formal controls of the prison system and the informal controls of the community, or more precisely, of the family.

The first case concerns someone with no family ties and therefore nothing to offer for surety of good behaviour. Neil Brown (aged 24) was charged with the theft of several items from local shops, valued at £55.45.[2] These included three pairs of trousers, a purse, three toy cars, and cosmetics. The police objected to bail saying that they feared the defendant would continue to offend as he had had twenty convictions in twenty-four years; they feared he might abscond, and the defendant had previously committed offences while on bail. Furthermore, the defendant had left prison only three days prior to this appearance in court. Neil Brown was legally represented, and his lawyer told the court that his client feared that if he was immediately returned to prison he would lose what little confidence he had gained. The lawyer added that his client had found a room to rent and was looking for work. Bail was refused.

A similar fate awaited Joan Smith (aged 18) who was also without family commitments. She appeared on several charges of shoplifting. The first concerned the theft of a dress and shirt valued at £20.99, the second a pair of trousers valued at £17.99, the third a large amount of toiletries and cosmetics. The police applied for a renewal in order to establish the full details of the case, and they opposed bail. They described a violent struggle which had taken place when a shop assistant had apprehended Joan Smith, who had then given the police a false name and address. On learning her true name and address the police found that the room in which she lived was full of goods and correspondence, which led them to believe that she had ordered goods from mail-order companies and moved before paying for them. This appeared to have occurred several times since she first came to London one year previously. The police said that they believed she would fail to appear for trial and would re-offend if given bail. In support of their argument they cited her five previous offences of shoplifting, which had been committed in Derby, where Joan Smith had lived with her parents. There was also an assault on a woman police constable and the defendant was in breach of a supervision order.

The legal representative then told the court that he had been instructed to make an application for bail on behalf of the defendant. By using this wording rather than beginning to make the application, or saying that he wished to make an application, the solicitor distanced himself from the procedure and seemed to withhold his professional involvement—he was acting merely as a mouthpiece. He then told the court:

Miss [Smith] is prepared to help police in finding receipts and witnesses to the purchase of the goods, and she could do this better on bail when she could contact the relevant people.

Bail was refused, and the magistrates gave the reasons:

she might fail to surrender to bail, we fear she might re-offend, and there is the nature and seriousness of the offence, her character, antecedents and community ties.

The second woman in my sample offers an interesting point of comparison with the women with domestic responsibilities who are considered later. In the case of Janet Bailey (aged 21) the local mental hospital does not promise the degree of control which in another case is attributed to the institution of marriage. Janet Bailey was charged with theft and burglary, that is with taking £21.50 from a church. She gave her address as a local mental hospital, but was, at the time of her appearance, in custody. Her case was to be further remanded for medical reports on her fitness to plead. The police objected to bail and told the court that the defendant had stated her intention of going to Ireland, and had offended while on bail for another matter.

In reply, her lawyer said that at the mental hospital Janet Bailey had been receiving treatment which was not available at Holloway. However, he added that there had been no change in her circumstances since she was last refused bail. Like the solicitor in the case of Janet Smith, he seemed to distance himself from the application;[3] he was almost inviting the magistrates to repeat an earlier decision. This they did. In both cases the lawyers were unable to present their client as an acceptable family member and were unable or unwilling to find other reasons why bail should not be refused. Their lack of commitment to their cases contrasts sharply with the enthusiasm manifested by the lawyers in the next two cases. In these cases there is reason to believe that re-offending, and interfering with the course of justice, might take place. However, the lawyers use the family circumstances not only to demonstrate their clients' fitness for bail, but also to reduce the seriousness of the offences which they describe as 'family disputes'.

Brenda Cartwright (aged 39) was charged with threatening to cause criminal damage, and of going equipped to cause criminal damage. The case was to be heard by the magistrates, but since the defendant was pleading 'not guilty' there was to be a remand for three weeks. The police opposed bail. An officer told the court that the defendant was accused of going to her mother's home where her daughter, aged 18, lived with her grandmother who had adopted her. At the home Brenda had, it was alleged, threatened to burn down the flat. The objection to bail was based on a fear that the defendant would interfere with witnesses as she had done in the past.

The solicitor representing Brenda asked the police officer what they thought she would do. The officer replied that in the past there had been threats to the daughter's life and health. The solicitor then told the court:

This whole matter is really a family feud which has come before the court from time to time. On some occasions allegations were proved, on some occasions not. A recent robbery with threats resulted in the money being returned and my client was co-operative with the police.

To this the police officer replied:

She recently visited her daughter's place of work and made threats. In the past bail was allowed because there were young children in the home. These children have now been placed in the care of the local authority.

As far as the police officer was concerned, in forfeiting her role as mother, Brenda forfeited her right to bail. Her lawyer argued that his client would not interfere with witnesses. In an attempt to re-establish her identity as a respectable family member, he argued that she was on good terms with her brother (i.e. an adult male who could be seen to have some control over her) and she would keep away from the others. Bail was granted on condition that the defendant did not go within 100 yards of her mother's block of flats, and that she contacted neither her mother nor her daughter.

The second case in which the family context was emphasized to reduce the gravity of the offence concerned Wayne Ross (aged 21). He had been charged with malicious wounding and held in custody since the incident two days earlier. The police told the court that the victim had withdrawn his complaint, but papers were with the police solicitors as the matter was serious. The victim was the defendant's brother-in-law and the police considered that pressure had already been brought to bear. They opposed bail because they feared interference with witnesses.

In the application for bail, Wayne's legal representative emphasized that this was a family dispute. He told the court, 'it came within the ambit of the family. . . . The defendant is not a danger to the public . . . both sides have cooled down now.' Bail was granted on condition that Wayne stay out of the area in which his brother-in-law lived. In both cases the family context of the offence was used to mitigate the gravity of serious assault and threatening behaviour. The expectation of the lawyers using these arguments is that what happens within a family will be viewed rather differently from similar occurrences between strangers. The assumption is that less official intervention is appropriate in family matters which are privileged by privacy. The confidence of the lawyers in making such pleas is well founded—the response of the magistrates is to endorse the privileged and private nature of the family.

If the family is privileged in matters of outside interference, it is because families are expected to police themselves—that is, to be responsible for the social control of the members, especially the structurally subordinate members, like women and children. The degree of control which is expected to reside in the conventional family structure is illustrated by the court's differing responses to the three defendants in the final case.

Eileen Boyle (aged 37), Denis Green (aged 30), and Joanne Day (aged 33) appeared as co-defendants on a charge of stealing eight garments valued at £472.60 from a department store, and of going equipped to steal. (They had some of the store's bags hidden about their persons.) Eileen Boyle had no previous convictions; Denis Green and Joanne Day had several previous convictions, and histories of offending while on bail. Since their arrest the previous day they had been held in custody. The case was to be committed to trial and the magistrates had to decide what to do with the defendants in the meantime.

A police officer told the court that the three had been seen acting in a suspicious manner. The store detective called the police. When the defendants left the store they were followed by the store detective, and a police officer, who saw them put the garments into a car. When arrested, one of the women, Joanne Day, gave several false names and addresses. The police asked for a remand for a week 'to sort out identity from fingerprint evidence'. There was no objection to bail for Eileen Boyle, although there was a request that she should report daily to her local police station. She was described as a single mother of four children who lived in a neighbouring district. The other two defendants were described as 'professionals' who had come some distance to shoplift on a large scale. There were objections to bail for both of these defendants. Speaking of Denis Green, the police officer said,

His wife claims that he no longer lives at the address he gave us, and we could find no evidence, such as clothes, of his being there. There were only bills in his name.

Joanne Day was described as someone who had come from Birmingham to shoplift in the London area, and who had given numerous false names and stories to the police. At this point a man stood up in the court, identified himself as Joanne's husband and asked if he might speak. He was invited to take the stand. He then pleaded that his wife should not be kept in custody. He said that he could not cope without her and that she could not cope with custody as she was a nervous person, and he said that there were children to look after. The senior magistrate then asked how she looked after the children and was told that she was an excellent wife and mother. Her husband added that she probably lied because she was frightened that he would leave her if it happened again. He admitted that he had threatened to, but said that he would not do so. He assured the court that his wife would not commit another offence and that she would come to court to face the charges. The magistrate asked if he had any money with which to stand surety, and he said that he had and he was willing to take the risk. The magistrate commented that 'Children place a different complexion on it.' Having conferred, the magistrates announced their decision. Denis Green was remanded in custody. Eileen Boyle was given bail on condition that she reside at her home address and report to her nearest police station. The police had asked that she report twice a day, but this was reduced to once a day when she told the court how much of her time was spent taking children to and from school. Joanne Day was given bail on condition that she reside at her home and report twice a day to her local police station, and her husband was to act as a surety for £500.

The importance of a family in assuring the court of the stability of a defendant is apparent here. However, on the second hearing in connection with this case a further factor became apparent—that is, the role of social control exercised by the acceptable model of family (male breadwinner and dependents) but not found in other family forms (e.g. single mother and children).

On their next appearance, a week later, both women applied to have their reporting conditions lifted. Joanne Day's application was granted 'since she has four children and a surety of £500'. Eileen Boyle told the court that reporting each evening meant that her son had to babysit and this was disrupting his evening classes and his social life. The magistrate asked why she did not take the younger children with her when she reported since it would not take long. He had turned to his colleagues as she replied and did not seem to hear her say that on the previous day it had taken one and a half hours. Her bail was renewed with the existing conditions.

So at the end of the second hearing the woman who was originally represented as the more 'criminal'—Joanne Day—was subject to less formal control than the woman who was originally seen as less of a problem and for whom the police did not oppose bail. Both women had domestic responsibilities—both had four children. The difference in the court's response is clearly not due to a difference in the extent of such responsibilities since, as a single mother, Eileen Boyle could claim to have a greater degree of responsibility than the married woman, Joanne Day. However, to a court concerned with issues of social control, Joanne Day is clearly in a more secure situation. In responding as they did, the magistrates recognized the degree of social control, particularly of women, which is inherent in the traditional family. This may well explain the finding noted by Farrington and Morris, and by Nagel, that a woman occupying a traditional gender-role is less likely to be subjected to formal social control. The control inherent within a traditional form of family structure was implicitly recognized by those lawyers who seemed reluctant to support an application for bail on behalf of defendants without such family ties (cf. the cases of Neil Brown, Joan Smith, and Janet Bailey above). It was also recognized by the lawyer in the case of Brenda Cartwright, where the defendant's brother was cited as an adult male who might be seen as someone with the ability to police her behaviour in the absence of her husband.

Conclusion

Throughout the process of summary justice a model of the family is employed when dealing with both men and women defendants. This model, with a male breadwinner and a dependent woman, responsible for child-care and domestic labour, is used in pleas of mitigation and social inquiry reports. The same model also underlies current legislation on taxation and benefits and traditional policies in providing for and responding to the family. It is a model based on a sexual division of labour. For many women it means deprivation and isolation.

In the labour market, men may expect to earn a 'family wage' since it is assumed that their earnings provide for others. Women find that the jobs available to them do not offer the same earnings. In 1982 the average full time wage for a woman was 72 per cent of a man's wage. Women in part-time work, who constitute two-fifths of the female labour force were even worse off; their hourly rate in 1982 was, on average, 57 per cent of the hourly rate paid to men in full-time work (Kahn 1985: 81). As part-time workers these women have fewer rights to sick pay, holiday pay, or pensions. While many married women work to keep the family above the poverty line, they are usually unable to claim for dependants if they become unemployed. Domestic responsibilities bring long hours of work for most women. One survey revealed that women with young children worked an average of 77 hours a week—nearly twice as long as an indus-trial working week of 40 hours (Oakley 1974*b*: 33). Child-care and house-work are still assumed to be the woman's work even if she has paid employment outside the home (Young and Willmott 1973). The choice facing many women is the 'double shift' of paid employment and domes-tic labour, or the isolation and lower income of full-time housework.

Isolation is not just the result of the social organization of housework. It is also a consequence of the traditions of privacy which surround the family. In the cases of Brenda Cartwright and Wayne Ross, discussed above, the fact that the offence involved members of the same family was used to mitigate its gravity. The same attitude is manifest in police reluc-tance to respond to instances of wife assault (Dobash and Dobash 1979; McCann 1985). Those relegated to the domestic sphere are most vulnera-ble to the abuse of power within that sphere. Even where women do not suffer physical abuse, mental illness may be a response to the conflicting demands placed on them. Depression is more likely among women involved full-time in housework than it is among unmarried women and married women with jobs outside the home (Procek 1981; Brown and Harris 1978).

Within the family women are vulnerable to violence, depression and poverty and for these reasons it has been subject of much feminist cri-tique (Gittins 1985; Land 1978, 1980; Pahl 1980; Wilson 1977). Only by questioning the position of women within this structure is there any chal-lenge to the continual subordination of women—a subordination learned and reconstituted daily within the family. Of course courts do not ques-tion the gender roles of women within the family—these are accepted as normal and natural. They are implicit in the model of family which underlies pleas of mitigation and social inquiry reports, as they are in applications for bail. But applications for bail go further than other exam-ples of courtroom rhetoric. In applications for bail we have more than a description of an acceptable model of the family and its associated gender roles: we have an acknowledgement that such a family structure may offer a form of control comparable to that offered by the prison system.

Notes

1. The large proportion of women defendants is the result of selecting court-rooms with cases involving women.
2. Pseudonyms are used when referring to defendants.
3. This was the second application for bail and so not subject to the decision in the Nottingham Justices case of 1980 that an application for bail need not be heard on or after the third application unless there are new circumstances to consider (NACRO 1985*a*: 3).

Bibliography

Brown, G. W. and Harris, T. (1978), *Social Origins of Depression*, London: Tavistock.

Chesney-Lind, M. (1978), 'Chivalry Re-examined: Women and the Criminal Justice System', in L. H. Bowker (1978).

Dobash, R. and Dobash, R. E. (1979), *Violence Against Wives*, London: Open Books.

Doherty, M. J. and East, R. (1985), 'Bail Decisions in Magistrates' Courts', *British Journal of Criminology* 25 (3), 251–66.

Eaton, M. (1983), 'Mitigating Circumstances: Familiar Rhetoric', *International Journal of the Sociology of Law* 11, 385–400.

—— (1985), 'Documenting the Defendant', in J. Brophy and C. Smart (1985).

—— (1986), *Justice for Women? Family, Court and Social Control*, Milton Keynes: Open University Press.

Farrington, D. and Morris, A. (1983a), 'Sex, Sentencing and Reconviction', *British Journal of Criminology* 23 (3), July, 229–248.

Gittins, D. (1985), *The Family in Question: Changing Households and Familiar Ideologies*. London: Macmillan.

Green, E. (1961), *Judicial Attitudes in Sentencing*, London: Macmillan.

Heidensohn, F. M. (1985), *Women and Crime*, London: Macmillan and New York University Press.

Kahn, P. (1985), 'Unequal Opportunities: Women, Unemployment and the Law', in S. Edwards (1985).

King, R. D. and Morgan, R. (1976), *A Taste of Prison*, London: Routledge & Kegan Paul.

Krutschnitt, K. (1982), 'Women, Crime and Dependency', *Criminology* 19 (4), 495–513.

Land, H. (1978), 'Who Cares for the Family?', *Journal of Social Policy* 7, 257–84.

—— (1980), 'The Family Wage', *Feminist Review* 6, 55–77.

McCann, K. (1985), 'Battered Women and the Law: The Limits of Legislation', in J. Brophy and C. Smart (1985).

NACRO (1985a), 'Bail and Remand in Custody', *NACRO Briefing*, London: National Association for the Care and Resettlement of Offenders.

Nagel, I. (1981), 'Sex Differences in the Processing of Criminal Defendants', in A. Morris (1981).

Nagel, S. S. and Weitzman, L. J. (1971), 'Women as Litigants', *The Hastings Law Journal* 23 (1), 171–98.

Oakley, A. (1974a), *Housewife*, London: Allen Lane.

Pahl, J. (1980), 'Patterns of Money Management within Marriage', *Journal of Social Policy* 9, part 3.

Peckham, A. (1985), *A Woman in Custody*, London: Fontana.

Pollack, P. (1950), *The Criminality of Women*, Philadelphia: University of Pennsylvania Press.

Pope, C. E. (1975), *Sentencing of California Felony Offenders*, Washington DC: Criminal Justice Research Centre.

Procek, E. (1981), 'Psychiatry and the Social Control of Women', in A. Morris (1981).

Rottman, D. B. and Simon, R. J. (1975), 'Women in the Courts', *Chitty's Law Journal* 23 (52).

Simon, R. J. (1977), *Women and Crime*, Lexington, Mass.: D. C. Heath and Co.

Wilson, E. (1977), *Women and the Welfare State*, London: Tavistock.

Young, M. D. & Willmott, P. (1973), *The Symmetrical Family: A Study of Work and Leisure in the London Region*, London: Routledge & Kegan Paul.

Regulating Pre-Trial Decisions

D. J. GALLIGAN

The subtitle of this essay might well be 'Pre-Trial Decisions as Administrative Discretions' since my object is to consider the application of public law ideas to pre-trial decisions. Legal attention is normally concentrated on the trial, but the fact that only a small percentage of the crimes investigated go to court is good reason for paying more attention to what happens beforehand. The range of decisions is extensive: whether to investigate, to question, to search, to arrest, to caution, to charge, to prosecute; what charge to bring, whether to negotiate over pleas and other matters; which judge or bench of magistrates to put the case before. These are only some of the decisions that have to be made, and the outcome of any one may settle or greatly influence the disposition of the case. Yet it is only recently that these areas of official decision-making have begun to be recognized as administrative powers which are capable of being misused, and which, accordingly, ought to be subject to the regulatory principles of public law. In determining the application of those principles, each area of decision-making needs to be examined carefully, but there is room for a general, preliminary survey of both the potential and the problems in approaching pre-trial decisions as administrative discretions.

Two preliminary points. First, I shall use the term 'discretion' without being too precise about its meaning. It is a convenient term to refer to the fact that in making decisions there are varying degrees of scope for officials to make assessments and judgments as to what constitute good reasons for deciding on a course of action. Discretion may occur because of the absence of standards, the looseness or ambiguity of standards, the conflicts of standards, or the unacceptability of standards. Discretion may occur officially within governing standards; it also often occurs unofficially in the sense that it consists in departing from, ignoring, or using standards selectively. Official rules often give little idea of where the real pockets of discretion are, and, in order to understand that, it is necessary to consider decisions not only from the standpoint of the legal rules but also from the point of view of those making them.[1]

The second point concerns the objects of legal regulation. There are several which are pertinent to pre-trial decisions: preventing the abuse of power; ensuring some notion of fair government; protecting rights and other important values. These broad objectives have been translated into more specific strategies: to ensure that officials pursue the objects of their powers; to ensure that within those objects they act for good, non-arbitrary reasons; to uphold fair procedures in the sense of natural justice and in the sense that there are other values to be given their place in pursuing the overall goal of crime control; and to uphold a residue of moral and political ideas based on notions of fairness, equality of treatment, and non-discrimination. Whether there is any general concept which covers these various strategies is unclear. Lawyers traditionally express this idea in terms of the rule of law, but the difficulty with that is in knowing what the rule of law means in the modern state. Classic formulations like Dicey's contemplated a different role for the state than exists today and do not fit easily into discretionary contexts. Accountability is a more accommodating and less precise idea, embracing an ideal of modern, constitutional government to the effect that the legitimacy of actions by government officials depends partly on their being accountable. Compliance with a framework of legal principles is one aspect of accountability. These are complex ideas which cannot be developed here, except to note that there is more to accountability than legal regulation, and there is more to legitimacy than accountability. But legal accountability, in the sense of ensuring compliance with a framework of values, is an important element of legitimate authority.

The regulation of policies and purposes

Two images of criminal justice

The first type of legal regulation relates to the content of discretion, to goals, purposes and policies. In considering the possibilities for regulation of these matters, it is useful to present two different images of the criminal justice process. One image is of a system of officials and institutions linked together for the pursuit of clear, harmonious, and common purposes. The emphasis is on system and co-ordination; within the system each set of officials has defined tasks which fit in with the tasks of each other set, and which, taken together, constitute a whole.[2] The general object of pre-trial decisions might be to prepare the way for the trial; each decision then would be a step towards that end. The pursuit of specified purposes would provide the link between each authority and the representative, political system. The legitimacy of actions would depend on compliance with purposes, and the legitimacy of those purposes would flow from the constitutional order. The general strategy for legal regulation would be to ensure compliance with purposes.

The second image of the criminal justice process is different and rather more realistic; it emphasizes the various processes but denies that they form a system. Consider the many areas of pre-trial decisions: to initiate an enquiry, to search the person or his property, to question, to arrest or caution, to charge or caution, to bail, to prosecute, to select the offence, to take into account a guilty plea and other such factors, to prepare a list for hearings. These processes are characterized by two general features. One is that decisions are made by individuals and sets of individuals who often act independently of each other, and often in ignorance of the actions of each other. The other is that each sub-unit acts under delegated powers, but generally without clear guidance from the legislature or other delegating authority. Where objectives can be discerned, they are likely to be fairly abstract and so open to varying interpretations; they are also often in mutual competition. Take as an example the dispensing power of the police, that is, the power which can occur at various points to divert an offender from trial and punishment. The object might be to punish the guilty, to reward the remorseful, to make and act on predictions about future behaviour, or simply to divert as many offenders as possible from the criminal process. The same tensions, dilemmas, and inconsistencies in attitudes towards these matters that are to be found at the macro-social level are transferred to each micro-level of decision-making.

The result is that each decision-making unit is left to work out an approach to its tasks, to make sense of its powers within an environment of constraints, and to deal with the problems it encounters. Within some broad notions of purpose, such as controlling crime, or punishing the guilty, each sub-unit of authority has to accommodate a range of influences: structural and organizational, the limitations on resources, and the constraints of numerous moral and political factors.[3] The importance of these factors is shown in studies of practical decision-making to be a recurring theme; they are constant and powerful in shaping the way that purposes are translated into practical decisions. In order, therefore, to understand the true variables in decision-making, it is necessary to study the internal attitudes of the different officials. Within the given parameters, officials are likely to devise their own operating goals and strategies in a rational and organized manner. But the point is that those goals and strategies may coincide only loosely with macro-goals, or with the goals being pursued by other sub-systems. It is to be noted, moreover, that the internal factors may be potent in their influence on decisions. The result is a serious tension between those internal factors on the one side, and legal norms and directives flowing from the wider system on the other. Indeed, the relationship between the two is one of interaction and complexity, and the tension between the two is likely to result in widespread, unauthorized discretion, that is discretion, which officials assume without authority to depart from, modify or selectively apply legal standards.[4]

Approaches to regulating policies and principles

On the basis that the criminal justice process, and in particular pre-trial decision, is reflected more accurately in the second of these images, the next question is to consider different strategies of legal regulation. Roughly matching those two images are two types of approach to legal regulation: one based on the 'rational reconstruction of purposes'[5] and in ensuring compliance with them; the other based on minimal threshold requirements which avoids entering into questions of content except in the most peripheral way, but which concentrates on notions of non-arbitrariness, gross unreasonableness, and formal and procedural fairness.

The idea central to the first of these strategies is that governmental institutions and officials act for purposes, and that the purposes can be extrapolated from the evidence of history, political theory and opinion, and actual practice. So, even where purposes are not specified, they can be reconstructed by rational extrapolation from evidence. The most interesting account of this approach is given by Nonet and Selznick;[6] they recognize that the image of authority in terms of relatively autonomous sub-systems accurately describes many aspects of the modern state and creates grave problems of accountability and legitimacy. The solution, they suggest, is in developing responsive law, and the key to responsive law is purpose. According to their account, the purposes of any sub-system of authority can be made objective enough to provide guidance in designing the institutions and procedures for decision-making, and in settling the substantive ends to which decisions are to be directed. So, while purposes guide decision-making, they also provide the basis for external scrutiny. If purposes can be reconstructed in an objective manner, then it would be for legal authorities, in particular the courts, to ensure compliance. Nonet and Selznick certainly envisage the courts having a substantial role in settling purposes and ensuring conformity.

This is a simplified sketch of a complex and imaginative attempt at a strategy for legal regulation; but enough has been said to reveal two basic difficulties that any such approach encounters. The first is the problem of identifying purposes with any degree of objectivity and specificity. In the absence of further evidence, it is hard to be persuaded that underlying pre-trial decisions there are purposes which flow from an overall scheme of things, and which are consistent from one sub-system of decision to another. The idea is attractive, but the evidence tends to show that while each sub-system does have goals and purposes, they are the product of a range of factors, rather than the logical application of an authoritative objective. Moreover, those purposes are mixed, often incompatible, variable over time and from one decision-maker to another. There may be scope for more authoritative direction from the political system, but the various factors noted earlier will be stubborn obstacles not to be easily overcome. There is also the general point that the wider society is itself divided about many of the basic issues regarding crime control, so it is not surprising that those divisions and tensions are reflected in the various processes of criminal justice. The second general question concerns the agency that is to be responsible for the authoritative extrapolation of purposes. If there are tensions and divisions then any definition of purposes is likely to be contentious; and if that decision is to be left to the courts, there is no guarantee that their stipulations will command authority, or that it will be accepted and applied in practical decisions.

Approaches based on the objective extrapolation of purposes rest ultimately on a view of society as highly consensual and harmonious. The cornerstone of that faith is the supposed existence of a substratum of deep principles which will command universal allegiance once the obstacles have been cleared away; within this vision the law could be a potent instrument. The difficulty, however, is in finding support for that view. Much of the evidence points to the contrary, supporting a view of dissensus, conflict, and confusion. Indeed, an emerging theme in social theory is that there is limited scope for agreement in any deep sense about the purposes and principles of social institutions. Society is seen rather in terms of colliding and interacting sub-systems, each performing a number of rules and functions, where the primary task for law is directed to reducing conflict through procedural forms rather than attempting to specify and enforce substantive outcomes.[7] The legitimacy of decisions comes to depend partly at least on the processes by which they are made. This view fits in with the semi-autonomy of administrative bodies and officials according to which they are left to a substantial extent to devise and implement their own goals and purposes.

If there are difficulties, however, in making the regulation of administrative powers depend too much on the objectivity of purposes, what are
the alternatives? The one most familiar is that taken by the English
courts. This could be placed virtually at the other end of the spectrum; it
is couched in terms of purposes, relevant factors, and unreasonableness,
but these are in general directed to defining the outer limits of purposes,
reasonableness, and relevance. Despite judicial pronouncements that
decisions must be based on correct purposes and that they must be neither irrational nor arbitrary, the courts have demonstrated a marked
reluctance to involve themselves in the merits of administrative decisions; an interpretation is adopted which erects minimal thresholds rather
than examining inner content.[8] The yardstick for review is still the
Wednesbury principle according to which (*a*) the court must not substitute
its own view of the way the discretion should have been exercised for
that of the original authority; and (*b*) the court is to ensure only that certain minimum requirements are upheld, namely, that the authority stays
within its powers, does not act on extraneous factors, and does not come
to a decision that is overwhelmingly unreasonable.[9] This general
approach becomes particularly noticeable in criminal justice. In *Re
Findlay*,[10] the courts had an opportunity to look into the parole decision,
to examine both its procedures and its purposes; but they resisted any
such temptation and in effect declared parole to be beyond scrutiny. The
same attitude applies in general to pre-trial matters.[11]

The result is that judicial review has a very limited application to decisions within criminal justice, especially the elements of those decisions
which touch on purposes, relevance, and reasons. There are two general
points about this approach. In the first place, the thin interpretation given
in judicial review to purposes, relevance, and reasons, is one that the
courts have chosen for themselves; the heads of review are able to
accommodate different interpretations ranging from the minimal
requirements of the *Wednesbury* principle, through a greater scrutiny of
reasons, to the exacting standards of the hard-look doctrine of American
courts.[12] Part of the explanation for the restrained approach of English
law is likely to be a recognition by courts of the difficulties, for the reasons we have noted, in getting involved in the reconstruction of purposes
and the examination of merits. Another part of the explanation is the constitutional point that such matters are considered to be for determination
by Parliament or those agencies to whom it has delegated the task. This
is a major restraint since courts should not be seen to be usurping the
functions of those bodies linked to the democratic process. The dangers

of this approach, dangers which appear to have become to a large extent the reality,[13] is that the agencies and officials in the pre-trial process fall between the two points of accountability, Parliament on the one hand, the courts on the other. If the lines of accountability to Parliament are disrupted and the courts maintain an attitude of abstinence, then the autonomy and independence of officials and agencies is strengthened.

The second general point is that failure by the courts to consider the purposes and policies of pre-trial decisions affects other notions like fairness, consistency, and equality before the law. These concepts have an important role in the administration of justice; and yet unless they are attached to substantive policies it is hard to give such ideas any hard core of meaning. A useful analogy can be taken from sentencing: much has been made in recent years of fairness in sentencing to the extent that whole reform movements, like the guidelines approach, have been directed towards it. But the failure of these movements to achieve their aims is largely the result of their failure to notice that fairness in the distribution of punishment depends on fairness in the substantive purposes of punishment, two issues which are usually kept apart.[14] The result is that fairness takes on a narrow and rather empty meaning, requiring simply that whatever the policies may be, they should be applied even-handedly. The same applies to consistency and equality. It is often said that 'treat like cases alike' is a basic tenet of justice,[15] but whether that is true, independently of the substantive justice of the treatment, is doubtful.[16] Moreover, if issues of policy and substance are left to the deciding authority and are immune from judicial scrutiny then it may be very difficult to know what counts as equal treatment.

To sum up then, while there are limitations on the legal regulation of goals and purposes, there is considerable scope nevertheless for increased scrutiny of the policies followed in pre-trial decisions. The present approach of the courts is so restricted that it is largely ineffective. It may be necessary to invest authorities other than courts with powers of review. Lessons can be learnt from other systems, and the Administrative Appeals Tribunals of some Australian jurisdictions are especially instructive. They are of mixed membership consisting of lawyers and non-lawyers, easy of access, and informal in procedure; but the main point is that they may scrutinize policy and merits, and although there are potential problems of conflict with ideas of political responsibility, the Tribunals appear to be working well, without serious challenge to their legitimacy. There is no good reason for pre-trial decision-makers being immune from scrutiny as to both substance and procedure; the only real issue is in devising suitable methods and authorities for taking on the task.

Structuring discretion through guidelines

A combination of the factors considered above has led to a greater emphasis on regulating discretion through guidelines. The existence of sub-systems of power, substantially free of political or legal regulation, the difficulties of specifying or identifying purposes, and the potential for abuse that accompanies discretionary powers, have each contributed to the guidelines movement generally and in criminal justice in particular. There is now wide support for the idea that in any context of discretion, guidelines in the sense of rules, policies, and factors, ought to be laid down, if not by Parliament, then by the officials making the decisions. Whatever the policies being followed, guidelines formalize and open up the decision process, and provide a basis for scrutiny of individual decisions.

Guidelines and their advantages

The idea of guidelines is not new, but much of the modern impetus stems from the work of K. C. Davis.[17] He argues: (*a*) that much discretion is unnecessary and should be governed by rules; (*b*) that much discretion is without rules because nobody knows how to formulate rules; (*c*) that sometimes discretion is necessary for reasons of individualized justice.[18] The suggestion is that unnecessary discretion should be removed, and that an optimum balance should be sought between rules and discretion. Davis in fact offers little guidance for deciding whether discretion is necessary or how the optimum balance is to be found. One difficulty is that there may be factors, which have an important place in decision-making, but which pull in different directions; the tension between consistency and individualization being an example. There is also a problem in posing the question as if the alternatives are between rules on the one hand and discretion on the other, since there are other considerations, like allowing scope for participatory procedures, which cut across the dichotomy. However, it is not my concern to offer a detailed analysis of the rules-discretion debate, but merely to make a number of comments about the advantages and disadvantages of structuring pre-trial discretions.[19]

Guidelines carry a number of clear advantages. In the first place they open up the basis for accountability. Assuming that they are public, guidelines can be a yardstick for testing decisions, and in that way reduce the scope for reliance on irrelevant, improper, or arbitrary factors.[20] Secondly, the need to formulate guidelines may be an incentive to officials to think more carefully and critically about the objects to be attained and the policies to be followed. The public articulation of the criteria for decisions is clearly preferable to proceedings in secret. Thirdly, the setting down of reasonably specific guidelines may advance a sense of procedural fairness. Public guidelines enable the citizen to know in advance how he is likely to be treated; they may also encourage consistency in treatment. These are both procedural values of importance.

The disadvantages of guidelines

The case for guidelines is a strong one; they seem to reduce some of the worst features of unchecked discretion by promising more open and rational decision-making. But there are also difficulties. In the first place there is something of a paradox: if guidelines for pre-trial decisions are stipulated by a superior political authority—Parliament or a body directly responsible to Parliament—then the guidelines will have good credentials in terms of legitimacy. The problem then is to ensure compliance in practical decisions, bearing in mind the problematic relationship between standards imposed externally, and norms, conventions and mores produced internally. Earlier mention was made of the difficulties in having external norms assimilated in decisions. In some of the notable attempts to change the behaviour of officials by external norms, such as the Supreme Court directives to the police concerning the treatment of suspects, the evidence seems ambiguous and controversial.[21] More information has to be gathered, but it is clear that there are serious hurdles to be overcome in making external standards efficacious; it is also safe to conclude that the mere declaration of standards by one authority to be followed by another is unlikely to be effective, unless supported by resources, procedures, and controls. Indeed, the application of the codes of practice under the Police and Criminal Evidence Act, 1984 in dealing with offenders will provide a good testing ground in the context of pre-trial decisions.[22] But the general point is that if guidelines are to be used more widely in that context, there is a great need to know more about the conditions necessary for effectiveness.

The other part of the paradox is that if each sub-system of authority devises its own guidelines, in a manner compatible with other operational constraints, the guidelines are likely to be more effective in structuring decisions. Then the problem is the legitimacy of the policies on which the guidelines are based, since the various authorities involved in pre-trial decisions are unlikely to have direct lines of accountability to Parliament or other democratically based institutions. An examination of the decisions of the police, the courts in matters of bail, and the prosecutors, shows that the policies applied are developed largely by those authorities themselves with small guidance or scrutiny from Parliament. The new prosecution service will be a particularly interesting study; here is an opportunity for Parliament to provide guidance on basic matters of policy, but there is little evidence that it will.[23] Rather policy will be left to each local area with occasional guidance from the Director of Public Prosecutions, the result being that the lines of political responsibility will be highly fragmented.

Moreover, scrutiny of policy by the higher courts occurs only on rare occasions. Mr Blackburn was able to persuade the judges that they ought to require a change in the policies of the Metropolitan police in prosecuting the display of pornography, but this was achieved through the procedural doctrine against fettering discretion rather than by direct examination of policy.[24] The more typical attitude towards the contents of a policy is that displayed in Re Findlay, the parole case, to the effect that issues as to the goals, purposes, and policies of agents within the criminal justice system are not for the courts.[25] It is doubtful that this paradox can be resolved, but steps can be taken towards that end. This would require that there be guidelines which are both efficacious and politically legitimate; to even approach that end, guidelines must be articulated publicly, and the scope for external scrutiny must be enlarged, partly by the courts, but also possibly by other review agencies which better understand the problems and processes of criminal justice, and which are themselves to a greater degree politically responsible.

A second general difficulty with guidelines is that by their very nature they restrict the facts that can be considered in decisions. We might recall Weber's distinction between formal and substantive rationality, the former suggesting decisions according to rules, precisely formulated, and applied coolly and logically, without reference to underlying purposes; the latter suggesting decisions which, in the circumstances, best advance some goal or serve some important value.[26] We would not expect guidelines in pre-trial decisions to resemble strict rules, but the point remains that as guidelines become more precise and conclusive, more like rules, they exclude or restrict consideration of other factors. One consequence is that in individual cases, by following guidelines, the level of attainment of goals may be reduced. There is a certain tension between formal rationality and substantive, between the advantages of precise, binding rules on the one hand, and the ability to mould decisions according to underlying purposes on the other hand without particular regard to what has been done in other cases. Normally the tension can be eased to some degree by accommodating both through open-ended standards, and by making provision for exceptions and qualifications. But if guidelines are to be genuinely determinative in decisions, the tension remains and choices have to be made in designing the framework of decision-making.

Another consequence of guidelines is the risk that, once formulated, they tend to ossify, and instead of being reassessed in the light of experience and purposes, they come to be regarded as immutable. Experience shows that it is difficult to formulate guidelines in the abstract and to maintain critical reappraisal of guidelines once they are established, a point which is perhaps reflected in the fact that where sentencing guidelines have been adopted, they tend to be the formalization of existing practices. This can be linked to a more general point about the difficulty of formulating guidelines in contexts of complexity. Indeed, the idea of complexity has become critical in some strands of social theory, the argument being that sub-systems of authority operate within highly complex environments, making it difficult to devise criteria which provide authoritative guidance in decisions and at the same time take adequate account of the factors and forces in play.[27] The result may be that the formalized guidelines end up being too loose to be a real guidance, while the real decision-factors are left to individuals and agencies, without public involvement in their formulation or scrutiny. The Attorney-General's guidelines on prosecution provide an example; they draw certain parameters around the decision whether or not to prosecute, but within these parameters, there is minimal guidance, the more precise factors being left to the prosecutors and the police.[28]

The final point is that guidelines may enhance a sense of fairness through consistent treatment. This was one of the main claims made for guidelines in sentencing: they would do much to remove disparities and thereby ensure fairness in punishment. However, the fairly obvious point has already been made that this is a very narrow sense of fairness, and that fairness in distribution of punishment depends on the fairness of the substantive principles on which guidelines are based. If the substantive principles are unfair in the sense of unjust or unjustifiable, then the guidelines merely perpetuate the unfairness. There may be a very primitive sense of fairness in applying the rules whatever the rules may be, but at best it is of little weight unless the rules are themselves sound. There is a real risk, as shown in sentencing, that guidelines reflect existing practices, perpetuate the injustices of those practices, and indeed, by advancing a thin sense of procedural fairness, deflect attention from more penetrating reform.[29]

The legal approach and the potential

The present legal position regarding guidelines in pre-trial decisions can be stated briefly.[30] There is no general duty on the various agencies involved in decision-making nor on other superior or external authorities to stipulate or develop guidelines. However, officials and agencies are generally free to formulate guidelines (subject to the two principles stated below), and there exist some powers whereby superior authorities, such as the Attorney-General, the Director of Public Prosecutions or the Home Secretary, may make guidelines to be followed by agencies and officials such as police and prosecutors. The courts have not so far taken an active role in the area, but the usual common law principles would apply. These are: first, that the policies of guidelines must be within powers in the sense that they are not based on irrelevant considerations, advance improper purposes, or are totally unreasonable; secondly, guidelines must not be applied so strictly that they amount to a fettering of discretion, in the sense that decisions are made by simply applying the guidelines. There must be some attempt to consider the merits of the individual case, even if that means departing from the guidelines. In general, the law has had little impact on the issue of guidelines: it does not enter into the question of whether guidelines should be adopted in different areas of decisions; rarely is the content so clearly outside the bounds of reasonableness to warrant judicial intervention; and the no-fettering doctrine is a procedural hurdle easily enough surmounted.

What attitudes then should be taken towards guidelines in pre-trial decisions? The first point is that pre-trial decisions at present are not typically subject to guidelines officially formulated and publicly announced. There are exceptions, but a plea regularly heard from researchers into criminal justice is for wider reliance on guidelines.[31] However, it is a common characteristic of decision-making, especially where the same types of decisions are being made regularly, to find that there are fairly settled criteria or guidelines, and it is likely that this is the case in pre-trial decisions. What really is being called for, then, is that the making of guidelines be put on a more formal basis. The call for the structuring of discretion has become a standard part of any reform package, often without taking full account of the drawbacks discussed. But even considering the disadvantages, it is hard not to be in favour of structuring through guidelines, particularly if it is seen as part of a package which includes greater involvement by other agencies and organizations in shaping the policies of guidelines, and which provides wider external scrutiny by the courts, special tribunals, or other authorities. The case for structuring, taken in this way as part of a package, rests finally on the gains made in opening up pre-trial processes. That in turn clears the way for more rational and justifiable policies, reasoned decisions, and for a broader basis of external scrutiny. Structuring is only part of a general commitment to greater openness in pre-trial processes, and once that step is taken, the problems that come with structuring can be more easily tackled.

Regulation through procedures

It is useful to recall Herbert Packer's two models of criminal justice, the crime control model and the due process model.[32] According to the first, the general objective is to control and reduce crime, and this is to be achieved as efficiently as possible through informal, administrative processes. Applying the model to pre-trial decisions, ranging from the first encounter with the police to negotiations over pleas, the overriding concern in each would be to take whatever action is most effective in achieving that goal. By contrast the due process model can be seen as a set of constraints on the way the general objective of crime control is advanced, constraints which derive from values independent of crime control and which may have the effect of reducing the level of crime control. Now Packer's dichotomy has been much discussed and criticized, but it still serves as a useful way of identifying a basic source of tensions within criminal justice.[33] The general case for due process is that the values it serves are important enough to be upheld in criminal justice even if that means, as it sometimes may, reduced efficiency in preventing crime; moreover, procedural constraints form part of the framework of accountability, and so reduce the scope for the abuse of powers.

Procedures instrumental to outcomes

However, due process is itself a complex notion which contains a number of different ideas. The first and most important is the relationship between procedures and outcomes: procedures are instrumental in achieving required outcomes, so that the measure of a good procedure is the likelihood that it will lead to the right outcome. The trial is a good example: the required outcome is to distinguish guilt from innocence;

trial procedures are good and effective to the extent that the verdicts are accurate assessments of guilt and innocence. But procedures of this kind are imperfect in the sense that the wrong outcome might be reached, the guilty acquitted or the innocent convicted. There is no way of being sure that the outcome is the right one, but the risks of error can be reduced by ensuring that sufficient resources are devoted to the task. However, there remains the question of what level of accuracy is acceptable for each type of decision. It is wrong to acquit the guilty, but it is a more serious wrong to convict the innocent, and accordingly the trial reflects a concern to avoid wrongful convictions, even though this puts heavy demands on resources, and even though there is a higher risk of acquitting the guilty. In other words, it is necessary to build into procedures some proportion between the gravity of the consequences when an error does occur, and the level of accuracy aimed at through appropriate procedures. So, for example, there should be a relationship of proportion between the harm caused by a wrongful conviction and the level of accuracy aimed at through procedures. By way of aside, it may be noted that this approach can be used to generate procedural rights, that is, one has a right to procedures which are proportional to the gravity of the consequences of a mistaken outcome.[34]

Applying this view of due process to pre-trial decisions, the first issue is to ascertain the desired outcomes. On one approach, pre-trial decisions might be regarded as preliminary steps towards the trial, and, therefore, as instrumental to the accurate determination of guilt or innocence at the trial. However, we have seen that this is an unrealistic view; the different pre-trial decisions are only loosely connected, with most cases being disposed of before the trial. But if those decisions are not steps towards the trial but largely independent and dispositive, what then in each case are the outcomes sought? Consideration of guilt and innocence clearly has a role, but it may be overshadowed by other considerations, and, in many cases, guilt is assumed so that disposition of the case depends on other goals and outcomes. What level of punishment should be imposed is a major concern, especially in negotiations over pleas and charges. This is an underlying concern throughout the pre-trial processes; but that there are also other goals becomes clear when we ask what are the desired outcomes in deciding whether to investigate, to caution, to prosecute, or to negotiate. Considerations of efficiency, keeping the process working and manageable, deserts, likely future behaviour, deterrence—each of these has some place in pre-trial decisions. Or consider police interrogations: according to Baldwin and McConville the main aim of interrogation is to get a confession, confessions lead to a guilty plea, and so a trial is avoided, the only question left for the court being the sentence.[35]

It is clear that we have hardly begun to think about the requirements of due process in the pre-trial context. Because such a range of authorized, semi-authorized, and unauthorized objectives are in play, it is difficult to apply the idea that procedures are instrumental to outcomes and are to be settled according to the resulting consequences for the interests at stake. This is perhaps why at present due process has virtually no place in pre-trial decisions, and where it does, it is a shadow of the idea that pre-trial decisions are preliminary to the determination at the trial of guilt and innocence.

If due process is to be extended to the pre-trial context, there are two necessary steps: first to identify or where necessary to stipulate the objectives and outcomes of each type of decision; secondly, to identify and evaluate the interests in issue. I shall comment briefly on each. As to the first, it might be argued that the jury trial should be re-established as the centre piece of criminal justice and the culmination of pre-trial processes. This has the attraction of simplicity, but as an overall strategy its success would be doubtful. Pre-trial processes serve important goals of diversion and early disposition of cases, goals which are embedded so deeply into the structure and practice of criminal justice that it seems unrealistic to expect that they can be discarded. It might be possible to restrict the range of goals that are to be pursued and to eliminate those which are unacceptable; but a plurality of goals within the pre-trial processes seems unavoidable. The strategy then would be to ensure that the various goals are recognized, and that steps are taken to see that they are pursued according to appropriate procedures. In some cases this will mean according to procedures that ensure a high level of accuracy; in other cases, the test of accuracy may be less appropriate, the important concern then being that the interests of the suspect or accused are considered and taken into account in a manner reflecting their importance. The second step is to clarify the interests at stake and then make the link between those interests and due process. For example, pre-trial negotiations have the effect of dispensing with the trial and setting the range within which the punishment will be fixed. Since pre-trial negotiations become a surrogate for the trial, they should be subject to procedural protections analogous to those that would apply at the trial; namely, procedures to ensure that the admission or assumption of guilt is warranted, and that the process of surrogate sentencing is preceded by proper examination of the facts and circumstances. The same interests are at stake whether these issues are settled at the trial or at some prior stage; accordingly, in the case of the latter, there is a similar claim to procedural protections. Now this analysis has been brief, and each area of pre-trial decisions should be examined closely to determine the requirements of due process. But the general point is that that determination is to be made by identifying outcomes and interests, and there are no good reasons for any pre-trial decision being exempt.

Procedures and participation

A second element in the notion of due process is that procedures encourage participation by interested parties and that this is itself important. But it can be important for different reasons. One reason is the connection between participation and outcome; here the underlying principle is that participation by interested parties is likely to improve the outcome. Those who have an interest in the outcome may well be able to contribute facts and evidence which enable more rational, and therefore more accurate, decisions to be made. For this reason, participation is generally considered to be a major element in designing procedures. There may be occasions where interested parties cannot contribute anything which would not otherwise be available; but, as a working rule, it is justifiable to regard participation as a rational and efficient part of instrumental procedures. Just as the type and level of procedures are to be determined on the instrumental approach according to the consequences and the interests in issue, similar factors will provide guidance as to the type and extent of participation.

Participation may be valued also for non-instrumental reasons; here participation is considered to be of importance, not because it may affect the outcome, but because it is connected to ideas of personal dignity and respect. The idea is put by Lawrence Tribe:

The right to be heard from and the right to be told why, are analytically distinct from the right to secure a different outcome, these rights to interchange express the elementary idea that to be a *person*, rather than a *thing*, is at least to be *consulted* about what is done with one. For when government acts in a way that singles out identifiable individuals—in a way that is likely to be premised on suppositions about specific persons—it activates the special concern about being personally *talked to* about the decision rather than simply being *dealt with*.[36]

This expression of what has come to be known as the dignitary theory comes close, in the words 'likely to be premised on suppositions about specific persons', to importing an instrumental element. That, however, seems not to be the intention; but, if instrumental effects are excluded, what is left to provide the basis for valuing participation? To invoke the idea of personhood begs the question, because what we need is a normative principle about what personhood requires. According to J. L. Mashaw, the significant link is that between participation and self-respect: 'participation increases self-respect to the degree that participation gives the participant *control* over the process of decision-making.'[37] But even if it is conceded that loss of control over decisions is necessarily damaging of self-respect (a matter which is at least arguable), it does not follow that participation guarantees controls; indeed, in most contexts of decision-making it clearly does not. Control is too grand a notion, it being more realistic to link participation to the need for official decisions to be explained and justified in the light of all the evidence and argument, including that advanced by the participants. There still seems difficulty, however, in understanding precisely what it is that establishes the link between participation and self-respect. I do not wish to rule out the possibility that there is a link, but I know of no account which succeeds in its identification. And even if self-respect or dignity does require participation, this leaves open the difficult issue of deriving from the normative principle practical guidance in the design of procedures.

An alternative to the participation–dignity equation is to link participation to the concept of open government.[38] Participation is part of a package of procedures which contributes to open government, meaning in this context that decisions by government officials are available for and capable of external scrutiny. That is secured through a package which includes such factors as reasonably settled and known criteria, the evidence and facts, and the reasons for the outcome. The participation of interested parties would seem to be in turn one of various measures which help to maintain those conditions of openness. The actual importance of participation in that regard is a matter for empirical appraisal, and although I know of no evidence one way or the other, the hypothesis seems plausible, certainly sufficiently so to warrant further investigation.

Pulling together the strands of argument, the object of this section has been to examine the idea that personal participation has a value in procedures independently of its instrumental effect on outcomes. One basis for that idea is that participation protects self-respect; but exactly how it does that remains elusive. The other basis is that participation is linked to ideals of open government; this clearly needs further investigation, but it seems particularly promising in relation to pre-trial decisions, many of which are notoriously anything but open.

Procedures based on values independently of outcomes

The third element of due process relates to values which are not linked to outcomes but derive from sources independently of outcomes. Such values, which are the defining elements of Packer's due process model, may sometimes advance the cause of crime control, but they restrict the means employed to that end and may even impede the level of realization. The presumption of innocence, the right to silence, the privilege against self-incrimination, indeed the very idea that only the guilty should be punished, are the most important of these values; but there are others like the restrictions on arrest, detention, search and seizure, and indeed the general requirement that the police operate within a framework of legal restrictions. The justification for these values and the procedural constraints that result has to be made out in terms of wider moral and political ideals, depending finally on a view of the relationship between individuals and the state. The case for due process values is strong and convincing, but needs to be restated from time to time in the light of contemporary conditions.

However, assuming that due process values are embedded in legal culture, they would be expected to have considerable impact on pre-trial decisions. The presumption of innocence and the right to silence, for example, should exert a powerful influence on the conduct of police investigations and on the course of pre-trial decisions in general. It would be reasonable to expect, from the commitment to due process values, a system of rules and principles enforced where necessary by the courts. A number of obstacles, however, ensure that the reality falls short of that ideal.

One obstacle is that, despite common assumptions to the contrary, due process values do not have such a secure foundation in the law. A general commitment to due process is part of legal culture, but it remains at an abstract level which is not matched either by firm legal rules or by actual practice. After an extensive study of the law relating to due process, McBarnet has concluded that the law relating to pre-trial matters does not in fact secure the values of due process in the way or to the extent that vague and general pronouncements of law might lead one to expect.[39] My own examination of the law relating to civil liberties in the context of public protest has led to a similar conclusion; rights of speech, movement, and assembly are given high rhetorical prominence, but on closer examination the legal basis turns out to be fragmented, unclear, ambiguous, and in so many ways subject to discretionary judgments.[40] The result is that the freedoms associated with public protest nearly always give way to public and private interests of other kinds. And this is not because officials ignore or violate the law, but because that is the legal position. This is not to say that due process is a complete illusion; there are rules and occasional court decisions which do attempt to state the law clearly and firmly. The argument is that a study of pre-trial decisions will show that the translation of the values of due process into law is highly imperfect and incomplete.

The second obstacle is that even where there are legal rights and duties, they are not always enforceable. A breach of the law in such cases may have little consequence. Consider the Judges' Rules which, until replaced by the provisions of the Police and Criminal Evidence Act, governed the conduct of police towards a suspect.[41] The rules, being only directives drawn up by the judges, carried no clear legal consequences; rather breach of the rules by the police was a matter to be taken into account (at a much later time) by the trial judge in deciding whether in the exercise of his discretion to admit evidence obtained as a result of the violation. The breach might also possibly be the basis for disciplinary action against the police officer, but again this was a consequence that followed only rarely. The law was even less helpful in the event of outright illegality by the police in searches or seizures, for here the trial judge has no power to regard the illegality as a justification for excluding the evidence gained.[42] So, it may be concluded, even where due process values are reflected in legal rules, it does not follow that effective legal consequences will be available in case of violation.

The third obstacle to the application of due process values is that even where the law protects the suspect, that protection may in practice be ineffective. The right to silence provides a good example: the legal principle is that a suspect must not be coerced or induced into making a confession or other incriminating admissions, and that any confession or admission will be allowed into evidence if, but only if, it is voluntarily made. Yet, according to research by J. Baldwin and M. McConville, 70 per cent of suspects make incriminating admissions.[43] That might be the result of a voluntary waiver of the right to silence, and in a sense it is; but to understand what that really means, it is necessary to examine the context in which confessions are made. Again according to the research, that context is one in which a confession is expected; the police investigation is based around the assumption that the suspect against whom there is some evidence will speak and make damaging admissions. This expectation has a powerful influence in both psychological and institutional terms on the whole process of investigation. The resulting pressure on the suspect to confess is so great that one can be only sceptical of the real value of the right to silence, and of the idea that the suspect makes a free choice. The point to emphasize is that this position cannot be changed simply by one or two more explicit laws; effective change aimed at making the right to silence worthwhile would require fundamental re-organization of the investigatory process, and fundamental change in the attitudes of the police and the courts.

It can be seen from this discussion that due process is a complex notion offering greater potential in regulating pre-trial decisions than has so far been realized. One difficulty is that there is still much to be done in analysing and developing the very elements of due process. Another difficulty is that traditionally attention has been concentrated on the trial itself to the neglect of other decisions both pre-trial and post-trial which may in their consequences for the suspect be just as serious. The time has now come to examine the requirements of due process at each point in the criminal justice process. The final problem is that there are serious impediments in the practical workings of criminal justice and in the attitudes not only of those involved but also in the judges and legislators. It is only if those attitudes begin to recognize the claims of due process that structures and practices are likely to follow suit. Indeed, there is a certain urgency in developing due process in pre-trial decisions, since it may be those values which finally hold the line between processes of crime control which are tolerable and those which are not.

Democratic accountability

The background

The object of this last section is to consider the scope for greater accountability by the makers of pre-trial decisions to the democratic process. According to a traditional view of the constitution, the powers exercised by subordinate bodies, such as those involved in pre-trial decisions, are conferred by Parliament. Provided that it acts within the terms of its powers, a subordinate body may be regarded as acting with the authority of Parliament. Parliament in turn is the centre-piece of the democratic system, so that its actions are taken as representative of the people at large. There is then a direct line from the people, to Parliament, to administrative authorities. The legal system has only a minor role in this arrangement, its main task being to see that authorities stay within their powers.

The shortcomings of this account have already to some extent been noted, and are best summed up in the notion of administrative autonomy. Parliament provides the authority for an agency to take action within defined areas, but the agency is likely to have discretion in deciding on the policies to be applied, the strategies for achieving them, and the outcome of particular decisions. Moreover, the duties on an agency to account back to Parliament for its policies and decisions are generally less than onerous. The result is a range of sub-systems of authority, operating independently of Parliament to significant degrees. The regulatory techniques considered—content and purpose, guidelines, and due process—are ways of reducing that sense of autonomy, of opening out decisions to external scrutiny, and of improving accountability. However, these are concentrated on notions of process and procedure, and are concerned only peripherally with substantive policies and outcomes. But, ironically, a major reason for emphasizing process is that matters of content are thought to be properly left to Parliament or its delegates, that is, to the chain of authority which ends in the democratic process; whereas institutions like the courts are not linked directly to that chain. The argument was put earlier that more could be done by courts and other external bodies in improving pre-trial decisions; the issue now, however, is whether there is scope for more control over the substantive aspects of pre-trial decisions by authorities which are themselves democratically based.

Scope for democratic supervision

There are two broad lines of development. One is to increase and improve scrutiny by Parliament, either directly or more indirectly through its committee structure or by such bodies as the Parliamentary Commissioner for Administration. The present role of such authorities is very limited, hardly penetrating many areas of pre-trial action, let alone having an impact on them. There seems clearly to be scope for extending these methods of scrutiny. But no matter how effective such methods become, they are still a step removed from Parliament itself and perhaps two steps removed from the democratic process. For these reasons, a second line of development appears increasingly attractive, that is, to draw closer links between areas of criminal justice and local democracy. Here the argument is that a number of pre-trial issues raise elements of policy and planning which, rather than being left to be settled within the relatively closed world of officials, should involve local, democratic authorities. A good topical case is policing, the argument being that many aspects of policing are essentially policy matters, and that local democratic institutions should have a major role in their determination. Examples which would attract such involvement are decisions about the use of resources, the styles of policing to be adopted, the approach to public assemblies such as picketing, and the standards to govern such matters as cautioning offenders. These are often presented as matters for the police to be settled in the exercise of their professional judgment. On closer examination, however, it is clear that discretionary assessments have to be made, that the law may offer little guidance, and that matters of policy inevitably occur. There is, accordingly, a powerful case for the interests and wishes of local communities being represented in such decisions.

The case for the involvement of democratic institutions in the policy issues of criminal justice is persuasive and opens up new lines of development. A full analysis of these lines cannot be undertaken here, but it is worth setting out in brief form some of the main issues that would arise in the pre-trial context.[44] One is the problem of distinguishing matters of policy which might properly be the concern of external authorities, and those matters which should be left to the official making the actual decisions. The constable, for example, might work within guidelines based on policies devised by external authorities, but the decision as to the application of the guidelines would be left to his judgement. The difficulty is that such lines are hard to draw. The police have come to rely on the distinction between policy and operational strategy, claiming that the latter is for their professional judgement. But the distinction has been shown to be untenable, logically and in policy terms.[45] Once it is recognized that operational issues involve policy, the question is which aspects of policy are to be determined by which authorities. There are never clear lines between policy and non-policy, and even the most individualized decision is likely to involve some element of policy. I can only raise the point here, but much consideration has yet to be given to the allocation of powers and responsibilities as between those officials making day-to-day decisions, and those charged with the overall formation of policy.

Another issue concerns the division between central authority and local authority. Local institutions reflect local interests and values, but these may in some ways diverge from the broader interests and values reflected in central authority. There are obvious attractions in local accountability; local residents should be able to influence matters which affect them in important ways; local controls are likely to be more direct and effective; and it is clear that some aspects of criminal justice, such as policing and sentencing, are closely linked to local conditions. Local control also has its dangers: small communities can be repressive and intolerant of minority interests; they can be backward-looking and resistant to the most basic

Hallward Library – Issue Receipt

Customer name: Royce, Andrewdavid Lyndon

Title: Criminal justice / edited by Nicola Lacey
ID: 1000445954
Due: 31/10/2006 23:59

Total items: 1
24/10/2006 14:54

All items must be returned before the due date and time.

reforms; and they may persist in practices which are unacceptable to the wider community. A corresponding list of strengths and weaknesses can be drawn up for central government: it may be remote and hard to mobilize; on the other hand, it does represent a broad notion of the public interest and may set standards and principles for general application. The issue, then, is to work out a reasonable accommodation between the two levels of authority. For example, it would be hard to accept that local variations should affect the standards governing the questioning and general treatment of suspects; one might accept, however, that some aspects of policing are properly matters for local decision. But there are hard cases; for example, sentencing clearly does tend to reflect local conditions, but should it? Is it acceptable for a bench of magistrates to have a policy of virtually automatic imprisonment for football related offences, even though this is out of step with general practice in the rest of the country? From these examples it can be seen that the relationship between central and local authority depends on a close analysis of the various contexts of criminal justice; but it depends also on a more theoretical appraisal of the requirements of good, democratic government.

The final issue in local–central relations concerns the protection of minorities. The point has been noted that local action may be repressive and intolerant of minorities, which in the present context means those suspected or convicted of offences. It falls to central government to set legislative and administrative standards which guarantee basic protections against the claims of local majorities. But central government may itself reflect the will of dominant majorities which may also be intolerant of individual and minority interests. In one sense there is nothing more to be said since a society is only as good as its majorities. In another sense, however, this might be taken as a good argument for protecting minority rights against the majority of the day through some form of constitutional protection. This again raises issues which cannot be dealt with here, except to note that under the present law the interests of suspects, offenders, and prisoners enjoy only limited and haphazard protection against the majority and against the practices of officials.

Conclusions

Administrative law has experienced a burst of growth in recent years. It has come to be seen as an instrument of considerable worth in bringing reason and openness to the most fusty recesses of administrative action. Yet the promise has not been fulfilled; timid judges, official obsessions with secrecy, and a series of governments committed to a corporate state have seen to that. Administrative law accordingly remains at the edges, the occasional step forward being engulfed in the swamp of administration and practice. And if we were to liken different areas of official action to the circles of hell, criminal justice would be the very innermost. But it need not be like that, and the object of this essay has been to lay out a plan within which pre-trial decisions, and indeed criminal justice generally, can be made the object of administrative law. I do not wish to suggest that all the problems of good government can be turned into problems of law; there are severe limitations and drawbacks on the capacity of public law to solve issues of government and administration as I have noted at various points in the essay. Nevertheless, administrative law contains within its present doctrines and concepts a potential which is not being realized, a potential which could have a very significant effect in bringing to pre-trial decisions reasons, openness, and accountability.

Notes

1. For further analysis of discretion, see D. J. Galligan, *Discretionary Powers: A Legal Study of Official Discretion* (1986), chap. 1.
2. A former Home Secretary, Mr Leon Brittan emphasized the systematic nature of criminal justice: Home Affairs Select Committee 23.1.84.
3. For further discussion of these constraints and influences, see Galligan, *Discretionary Powers*, chap. 3.
4. Of the many studies which demonstrate these points, the following are recommended especially: J. H. Skolnick, *Justice Without Trial: Law Enforcement in Democratic Society* (1966); P. K. Manning, *Police Work: The Social Organisation of Policing* (1977); G. Richardson and others, *Policing Pollution: A Study of Regulation and Enforcement* (1982); K. Hawkins, *Environment and Enforcement: Regulation and the Social Definition of Pollution* (1984).
5. An expression used by P. Nonet in 'Taking Purposes Seriously' in Gray Dorsey (ed.), *Proceedings of the International Conference of Legal and Social Philosophy* (1975).
6. P. Nonet and P. Selznick, *Law and Society in Transition* (1978).
7. A particularly useful analysis of these ideas is in G. Teubner, 'Substantive and Reflexive Elements in Modern Law' (1983) 17 Law and Society Review 239.
8. For an account of judicial attitudes, see S. A. de Smith, J. M. Evans, *Judicial Review of Administrative Action* (4th edn. 1980), chap. 6. One of the more important recent cases is *Council of Civil Service Unions* v. *Minister for Civil Service* [1985] A.C. 374.

9. *Associated Provincial Picture Houses* v. *Wednesbury Corporation* [1948] 1 K.B. 223.

10. [1985] A.C. 318.

11. See David Williams, 'Prosecution, Discretion, and Accountability of the Police' in Hood, R. (ed.), *Crime, Criminology and Public Policy* (1974).

12. On the hard-look doctrine, see C. S. Diver, 'Policymaking Paradigms in Administrative Law' (1981) 95 Harv. L.R. 393.

13. This is the gist of a good deal of recent literature; see for example, I. Harden and N. Lewis, *The Noble Lie: The British Constitution and the Rule of Law* (1986).

14. For a critique in the context of sentencing, see D. J. Galligan, 'Guidelines and Just Deserts: A Critique of Recent Reform Movements in Sentencing' [1981] Crim. L.R. 297.

15. See H. L. A. Hart, *The Concept of Law* (1961), chap. VIII.

16. For discussion, see D. J. Galligan, 'Arbitrariness and Formal Justice in Discretionary Decisions' in Galligan (ed.), *Essays in Legal Theory* (1984).

17. The main work is K. C. Davis, *Discretionary Justice* (1969).

18. *Discretionary Justice*, 20 ff.

19. For fuller discussion, see R. Baldwin and K. Hawkins, 'Discretionary Justice: Davis Reconsidered' [1985] P.L. 570.

20. Attention should be drawn (without further discussion) to the argument that guidelines actually increase the level of discretion, since the more guidelines there are, the greater the opportunities for departing from them. See H. Pepinsky, *Crime and Conflict: Study of Law and Society* (1976).

21. See D. Horowitz, *The Court and Social Policy* (1977). For discussion of the wider issue of making external norms effective, see L. Sherman, 'After the Riots: Police and Minorities in the United States 1970–80' in N. Glazer and K. Young (eds.), *Ethnic Pluralism and Public Policy* (1983); L. Lustgarten, *The Governance of Police* (1986), 179–82.

22. Police and Criminal Evidence Act 1984 s. 66.

23. For discussion, see F. Bennion, 'The Crown Prosecution Service' [1986] Crim. L.R. 3; J. Vennard, 'Decisions to Prosecute: Screening Policies and Practices in the United States' [1985] Crim. L.R. 20.

24. R. v. *Metropolitan Police Commissioner, ex parte Blackburn* [1968] 2 Q.B. 118.

25. [1985] A.C. 318.

26. For further discussion; I. Ehrlich and R. Posner, 'An Economic Analysis of Legal Rulemaking' (1974) 4 J. of Legal Studies 257.

27. The principal exponent of this notion is N. Luhmann in *Trust and Power* (1969). See also the introduction to that book by G. Poggi and his 'Two Themes from Luhmann's Contribution to the Sociology of Law' 1981 Bulletin of the Association of Legal and Social Philosophy (Australia).

28. Attorney-General's Guidelines on Prosecution.

29. For discussion of guidelines in sentencing: D. J. Galligan, 'Guidelines and Just Deserts: A Critique of Recent Reform Movements in Sentencing' [1981] Crim. L.R. 297.

30. For a fuller account: Galligan, *Discretionary Powers*, 281–90.

31. e.g. Davis, *Police Discretion* (1975); J. Goldstein, 'Police Discretion Not to Invoke the Criminal Process' (1960) 69 Yale L.J. 543; W. R. La Fave and F. J. Remington, 'Controlling the Police: The Judge's Role in Making and Reviewing Law Enforcement Decisions' (1964–5) 63 Mich. L.R. 987; A. K. Bottomley, *Criminology in Focus* (1979).

32. H. Packer, *The Limits of the Criminal Sanction* (1969).

33. For discussion, see J. Griffith, 'Ideology in Criminal Procedure or a Third Model of the Criminal Process' (1970) 79 Yale L.J. 359; D. McBarnet, 'False Dichotomies in Criminal Justice Research' in J. Baldwin and A. K. Bottomley (eds.), *Criminal Justice: Selected Readings* (1976).

34. The basis of this approach is R. M. Dworkin's 'Principle, Policy, Procedures' in C. F. H. Tapper (ed.), *Crime, Proof and Punishment* (1981).

35. Baldwin and McConville, *Courts, Prosecution and Conviction* (1981).

36. L. Tribe, *Constitutional Law* (1978), 503.

37. L. J. Mashaw, *Bureaucratic Justice* (1983), 95–6 and 'Administrative Due Process: The Quest for a Dignitary Theory' (1981) 61 Boston U.L.R. 885.

38. See further W. N. Nelson, *On Justifying Democracy* (1980), 118 ff.; Galligan, *Discretionary Powers*, 332–6.

39. See for example D. McBarnet, 'False Dichotomies in Criminal Justice Research' in J. Baldwin and A. K. Bottomley (eds.), *Criminal Justice: Selected Readings*, and 'Arrest: The Legal Context of Policing' in S. Holdaway (ed.), *The British Police* (1979). For discussion see J. Baldwin and M. McConville, *Courts, Prosecution and Conviction*, 199–203.

40. Galligan, 'Preserving Public Protest: The Legal Approach' in L. Gostin (ed.), *Civil Liberties in Conflict* (1987).

41. See Police and Criminal Evidence Act, 1984.

42. *Sang* [1980] A.C. 402.

43. Baldwin and McConville, *Courts, Prosecution and Conviction*.

44. For a good and recent discussion, see Lustgarten, *The Governance of Police*, chap. 10.

45. Ibid. 10–24.

Two Tiers of Justice

DOREEN McBARNET

The lower courts[1] are where most of the work of the criminal law is done—they are also where the characteristics of legality and justice are least in evidence.

To enter the lower courts is to be taken aback by the casualness and rapidity of the proceedings. The mental image of law carried into the courts is shattered by observation. The solemnity, the skills of advocacy, the objections, the slow, careful precision of evidence, the adversarial joust, none of these taken-for-granted legal images are in evidence. It seems to be another world from the legal system we have learned about in books, films, and television. The statistics tell the same story. Credibility in the ideology that the scales of justice are tipped to acquitting ten guilty men rather than convicting one innocent man is stretched to breaking point by the work of the lower courts. According to 1978 statistics the conviction rate in Scottish summary courts is 95 per cent, in English magistrates' courts 95 per cent for non-indictable offences and 93 per cent for indictable crimes. The combination of pleas and verdicts of guilt brought the total of convictions in the Sheffield magistrates' courts which Bottoms and McClean (1976) studied to 98.5 per cent (p. 106).

Magistrates' courts have, perhaps because of the blatancy of this contradiction, been the courts that have most attracted the scrutiny of sociology and social policy. Dell (1971) has shown that defendants remain 'silent in court' through fear or ignorance. Hetzler and Kanter (1974) have shown how the defendant stands in court at a situational disadvantage because of the symbolic layout of bench and dock. In particular, Carlen (1976) has demonstrated how the processing of defendants is achieved *situationally*, how the court team—magistrates, clerk of court, police, solicitors, probation officers—manages to obviate due process, suppress challenges, make the defendant a 'dummy player' by ruling him, whenever he speaks, out of time, out of place, out of order, even out of mind. All of these studies focus on the situation of participants, the use and avoidance of the rules. This study fully supports Carlen's description of the operation of summary justice but it changes the focus of analysis in three ways.

First, it changes the stress from *use* of *rules* to the rules used, to the rules of procedure which actually define what is out of time, place or order, and to ironies not accomplished by the magistrate *in situ* but inherent in the structure of magistrates' justice. If the defendant, normally unrepresented, is the only one who does not know the rules, as every study of courts demonstrates, the cause must be traced beyond his ignorance, or the court team's games, to the paradox of a legal structure which requires knowledge of procedural propriety in making a case, and a legal policy which denies access to it.

Second, that paradox itself requires explanation too. A little delving into the historical development of magistrates' justice shows only too clearly that the high conviction rate in the face of all the safeguards for the defendant offered by legality is no mere situational accomplishment of the magistrates' court. Nor, indeed, is it accomplished by the High Court judges through the subtle qualifications, the ifs and buts of case law, maintaining the general rule but qualifying it for each particular case. It is the product of the heavy hand of legislation simply wiping out the rules as neither necessary nor relevant for the lower court at all.

The third concern is with Carlen's observation of the particular situational problems faced by the magistrates in presenting their work ideologically as justice. The higher courts are helped by 'rigid rules of ceremony' and 'traditional ceremonial costumes'. Magistrates have to 'produce a disciplined display of justice' *despite* the lack of solemnity and ceremony, lack of solicitors, and petty and marginal offences that characterize the lower courts (Carlen 1976: 38). This chapter suggests that the lower courts in fact have no significant ideological function,[2] that the factors Carlen points to as situational problems for the production of magistrates' justice are the very factors which, by ideological sleight of hand, screen it from scrutiny, and indeed which accomplish the ultimate irony of protecting the ideology of justice while simultaneously denying it.

Self-defence

One of the crucial disadvantages pinpointed by all the studies of the accused in the lower courts is the fact that he is normally unrepresented. In Scotland there is now a duty solicitor scheme at all levels,[3] but duty stretches only to those in custody and stops at the point of plea—legal advice is available of right only to answer a charge, not to contest it. In England the defendant only exceptionally has a lawyer: Bottoms and McClean's Sheffield study found only 19 per cent represented throughout, compared with 99 per cent in the higher courts. The reason for this is simple enough: legal aid, though virtually a right in the higher courts, is not available in any but exceptional cases in the lower courts. Nor do the recommendations of the Royal Commission on Legal Services (1979) augur well for any significant change (p. 158).[4] The Widgery Committee on legal aid denied that a professional lawyer was normally necessary in the lower courts, implying that points of law, tracing and interviewing witnesses, or engaging in expert cross-examination were not normally involved. Yet the same report insisted that a professional lawyer *was* necessary for the higher courts:

A layman, however competent, can rarely be relied on to possess the skill and knowledge necessary to put forward the defence effectively tried on *indictment* without the guidance of a lawyer. (Widgery 1966: 79, my emphasis)

Were the structure and rules of procedure essentially different this distinction might be valid; differences there are, as we shall see, but not in the proof of a case. The trial, and with it the method of proof and the criteria of proof, remain exactly the same. There is the same adversarial structure, the same structure of proof by examination, cross-examination, the same requirement of direct witnesses to provide that proof, the same rules of evidence, *and the same requirement that the procedures be rigidly adhered to*. These are not laymen's courts but highly legalized proceedings.

The bench may be composed of lay magistrates, of course, though there is an increasing number of stipendiary magistrates in England, and in Scotland lay magistrates operate only on the fringes of criminal justice. But lay magistrates have clerks in England, assessors in Scotland, to keep the proceedings legally in check (both, according to Carlen's study, and this one, keen to stress legal technicalities exactly because that is their only justification for being there), while even the lay magistrates are themselves 'repeat players' with knowledge—or belief in their own knowledge—of the law. The prosecutor is *always* a professional lawyer in Scotland, while in England more and more police forces have prosecuting solicitors' departments to do the job professionally; and at worst the prosecution will be conducted by a policeman, a repeat player, and a legal professional. All of this is at the state's expense, of course, which makes Widgery's conclusion on the provision of professional representation for the defence that 'there is a limit both to the number of practitioners who can provide legal assistance and to the funds that the state can reasonably be expected to make available' (Widgery 1966: 14) appear something of a one-sided view. The provision of a prosecution is taken for granted; the provision of a defence is not. Yet the trial remains adversarial, and the legitimation of the adversary structure is exactly that it must be conducted by *equal* adversaries. To declare a professional defence unnecessary in this context is to put the accused into the ring as an amateur flyweight against professionals or heavyweights or both.

The plight of the unrepresented defendant in the magistrates' courts has often been put down to his lower-class background, and consequent lack of speech skills, articulateness, understanding. But as sociologists of education and speech have demonstrated, there is little essentially inarticulate about lower-class speech, and these same defendants recounting the same event of a Friday night in the pub as a story not as a case might do so with great aplomb. Nor is it necessarily fear (Dell 1971) that prevents them getting their story across. Certainly surveys[5] have noted that more than half of defendants found the experience an ordeal, but that does not necessarily silence them. Fear might explain why so many people plead guilty: but all of those who pleaded *not* guilty in this study were prepared to tell their story to the magistrate. The problem was in fact that they were *too* prepared to do so to be mindful of courtroom procedures. Carlen describes how any challenges by the defendant to the actual administration and legitimacy of the law result in them being portrayed as 'out of place, out of time, out of mind, or out of order' (Carlen 1976: 104). But the rules of time, place, and order are invoked much more routinely than this: they are not just emergency measures; but the very things which make a trial a trial, and the result is that the defendant is not only prevented from challenging the law but is routinely prevented from participating in the trial.

The trial is organized into a quite definite order of events and at each stage different rules pertain:

(1) the defendant makes his plea;
(2) the prosecutor calls his witnesses—usually policemen—and examines them;
(3) the defendant can cross-examine each witness, immediately after the prosecution has examined him—at this stage the rule is that he can only ask questions of the witnesses not make statements on his own behalf;
(4) the defendant can, but only at this point and only if he moves from the dock to the witness box, make a statement;
(5) he is cross-examined in turn;

(6) if he has any witnesses he can examine them (again ask questions only) to elicit support for his story;

(7) they are cross-examined by the prosecutor;

(8) each party may sum up.

The defendant's first admissible opportunity to make a statement is at stage (4). But repeatedly he takes up the first invitation to speak, at stage (3), to deliver a statement to the magistrate, only to be rebuffed on procedural grounds. He is likewise interrupted or silenced with each witness until when it comes to his turn to enter the witness box (and often he starts his statement again in the dock only to be rebuffed or moved), he often rejects the chance or is quite taken aback to have a say. When he does speak he may well find his story interrupted and what seem to be crucial points excluded by the rules of evidence.

MAGISTRATE: How do you know what they [the police] said to Pauline [co-accused]?
ACCUSED: She told us.
MAGISTRATE: That's hearsay. (Case 29).

ACCUSED: Sir I'd left before closing time to go to another pub.
MAGISTRATE: That's an alibi defence. You didn't intimate that. [In his summing up later he declared it inadmissible because no warning had been given.] (Case 1)

In Case 27 the accused's defence depended on his having good reason to use a police phone:

MAGISTRATE: Would you like to ask the officer any questions Mr McC?
ACCUSED: Do you know why I was on the phone?
PROSECUTOR: He can't answer that.

The unrepresented accused is not only denied access to knowledge of procedures but to the opportunity of being questioned. It may be easy to tell a long story in relaxed surroundings where the odd omission, carelessness, or exaggeration in detail is irrelevant, but where all these things are likely to be picked up by an opponent, without an opportunity to redress them, it is easier to sustain a long detailed account via questions and answers, as indeed is sometimes made explicit in court. In Case 25 the prosecution witness was telling a long confused tale. The magistrate intervened to invoke the prosecutor into a more active role:

MAGISTRATE: Do you think you could question him and get it a bit more clearly?

Defendants have the same problem. But with no lawyer representing them, there is no-one for the magistrate to call on to get the defence case clear. What is more, a lawyer with an eye to legal relevance will ask questions that make the account into a case, something a layman might simply lack the knowledge to achieve.

Indeed, a case is not made simply by presenting an account of one's own version of events. Proof in the adversary trial is achieved not just by building up the strong points in one's own case but by pointing out the weak points in one's opponent's. Proof has to be built up by countering the persuasive points in the opposing case or by destroying them, and given the nature of the evidence in minor offences, it is very often a necessity for the defendant not simply to remain silent or present an account that does not challenge police evidence, but actively to raise reasonable doubts in the prosecution case—remember the magistrate's conclusion: 'I see no reason to disbelieve the police' (Case 8). One way to raise such doubts is by cross-examination. Yet the Widgery Report (1966) sees professional cross-examination as rarely needed in summary cases (p. 47). This ignores the fact that in a good many cases this only denies professional cross-examination *of the prosecution case* since the prosecution will have a professional advocate to subject the *defendant* to professional cross-examination. Perhaps the implication is that the police do not need to be cross-examined because their version is correct. In any case that is the net result. Yet cross-examination is one of the essential weapons of the adversarial trial. With no cross-examination there is in a sense no trial and with no professional lawyer there tends to be no cross-examination, as observation in court demonstrates.

In order to be allowed to cross-examine his opponent just as in presenting his own story, the defendant must do so according to the rules and at the right stage of the procedure. But he is not necessarily told the procedure or the varying rules at each stage, and indeed he may not understand the distinctions in the rules between questions and statements, or be too intent on getting his story across to the magistrate at the first opportunity to abide by the formal rules of the court. His confusion of stages (3) and (4) of the trial's procedure not only tends to foil his attempt to present the case, it also foils the possibility of cross-examination taking place at all, so that the prosecution goes unchallenged. Take Case 1, for example, where four young men and one elderly man of no fixed abode were charged with breach of the peace. Only two were individually identified but they were all collectively identified as part of an aggressive crowd:

MAGISTRATE: Would you like to ask any questions?
ACCUSED 1: [the elderly man]: All I said was 'what's happening?'
MAGISTRATE: [to policeman] Are you in any doubt that this man was committing the offence?

POLICEMAN: No.
ACCUSED 1: I never opened my mouth except to ask what was happening.
MAGISTRATE: You can't deliver a peroration at this point. Have you [moving on to
     Accused 2] any questions?

Accused 1 is left still on his feet looking baffled. Accused 2 shakes his head
and the magistrate moves on to Accused 3.

ACCUSED 3: What time was this?
POLICEMAN: 10.15.
ACCUSED 3: Sir, I'd left before closing time to go to another pub.
MAGISTRATE: That's an alibi defence. You didn't intimate that. Stay on your feet.
     Don't talk [to Accused 1 who was asking Accused 2 something in an agitated
     manner].
ACCUSED 2: [one of the two identified]: Sir, I had a beard that night.
MAGISTRATE: Ask him, don't tell me.

Accused 1, having had his response to the police story ruled out at the
point of cross-examination with the first witness did not wait so long
with the second one, but simply intervened to say that what was being
said was not true. That attempt was ruled out too:

MAGISTRATE: I wish you wouldn't interrupt. It's bad manners.
ACCUSED 1: But I wasn't with them, I'm a stranger. They'll tell you if you ask
     them.

(This procedural heresy was of course ignored.)
     Case 21 involved an Italian who could not speak English and therefore
had an interpreter. When it came to stage (3) the assessor to the magistrate invited the accused to ask questions:

ASSESSOR: You'll realize it's difficult, but ask questions to the interpreter.
ACCUSED: No, I don't want to waste the court's time with language problems.

Magistrate and assessor both leapt in at this undermining of courtroom
rhetoric:

MAGISTRATE: Oh we have all the time in the world.
ASSESSOR: The court's time is not wasted.

But the accused's 'question' was a statement; he simply stated what was
incorrect in his view about the testimony. So it did not count; it did not
have to be answered since it was not a question and since it was too early
for a statement it lost him his turn. The magistrate, having gone overboard to invite him to speak, now simply stopped him: 'You'll get your
chance later.'

Case 35 involved two teenage girls on a breach of the peace charge:

MAGISTRATE: At this time you ask the officer questions from the evidence he's given. Have you any questions?
ACCUSED: We were just standing talking.
MAGISTRATE: [to policeman] She says they were just standing talking. Is this so?
POLICEMAN: No.
MAGISTRATE: That's the answer to your question. You may not like it but that's it. Move on to the next question.
ACCUSED: There's nothing else.

Case 30 was the 'jumping on and off the pavement in a disorderly manner' case. The accused's 'cross-examination' consisted of no more than a series of statements of denial that he was part of the disorderly group, and the magistrate ultimately interrupted:

MAGISTRATE: Are you satisfied, constable, that the boy was in the original group?
POLICEMAN: Yes.
MAGISTRATE: Right. Any other questions?

Case 2 was about the theft of lead and involved 'verbals' which the accused denied:

POLICEMAN: He said 'I took the chance because the sheriff comes to the house tomorrow and I need the money.'
ACCUSED: I said I got it from the coup [rubbish tip]. I didn't show him a sheriff's letter.
MAGISTRATE: Well he says he saw a letter that you produced. Next question.

Case 29:

ACCUSED: We were playing football and he came up and asked our name and about a TV.
ASSESSOR: [to policeman] Did you say this?
POLICEMAN: No.
MAGISTRATE: There's your answer. Any other questions?

Case 5:

MAGISTRATE: Any questions?
ACCUSED: I was only violent because I was being punched.
MAGISTRATE: Was he being assaulted?
POLICEMAN: No. We put him on the floor when he entered to await assistance.
MAGISTRATE: That's your answer. Any more questions?

Case 25:

ACCUSED: [to magistrate] Well all I can say is . . .

MAGISTRATE: It's him you ask the questions.
ACCUSED: No questions then.

And so on. There are dozens of examples from the data—these are not peculiar cases but *typical* of the lower courts, as indeed the Lord Chancellor's office recognizes in a series of lectures to magistrates:

cross-examination and re-examination are difficult matters for unrepresented parties, and the help of the court is often necessary, just as it is necessary in most cases for the court to conduct the examination-in-chief. (1953, p. 38)

Several points are to be drawn from such examples. First, they demonstrate how the accused's ignorance of the procedures, inability to handle them, or indeed unmindfulness of them in his indignation or nervousness, leads to the magistrate simply silencing him. It is partly procedural nicety and grammatical pedantry that defines this as out of court because making a statement rather than asking a question is *not* cross-examination. It is also a matter of substance. For, and this is the second point, approaching an opposition witness with a direct denial and a clear statement of one's own case is *not* cross-examination in that it does not achieve the job cross-examination is fashioned for in the adversarial trial. It does not search out (or create the impression of) weakness in the opponent's evidence, or undermine the credibility of the witness. On the contrary it *underlines* the opposing case by giving the witness an easy opportunity to simply *deny* the defence. Professional cross-examination proceeds by quite different means, by direct approaches, by a series of questions on apparently peripheral matters, with a crucial issue casually dropped in *en route*, by a series of questions leading the witness to an accusation which the witness cannot *logically* deny without discrediting his previous answers. The methods recommended by manuals on advocacy and used routinely by lawyers in court, are indirect and subtle. They may contradict the methods used in *non-legal* situations to establish truth but they *are* the stuff of cross-examination.

The unrepresented accused then all too often does *not* cross-examine; neither—and this is the third point—does the magistrate. An Act in 1903 for helping 'poor prisoners' to be legally represented, offered help only in exceptional circumstances on the grounds that 'where a prisoner was not defended by counsel his interests were safe in the hands of the presiding judge.' (Widgery, 1966, p. 2). And the lectures from the Lord Chancellor's Office already referred to remind the magistrate he may well need to help.

If the defence when told he may cross-examine begins to make a statement and persists in doing so when told he must ask questions, the court will usually be able to turn his statements into questions on his behalf. (1953: 38)

But as these examples from court observation show, putting cross-examination in the hands of the magistrate does not resolve the problem. This is not just because of the team games played out in court, nor indeed because of the personal characteristics, the impatience, hostility, or sarcasm of the magistrate, though they undoubtedly play a part, but precisely because the magistrate cannot cross-examine for the accused by turning his statements into questions. For a start it is too late: once the statement is put the surprise is lost. What is more, once the translated direct question is put it creates an impasse, a categorical denial, with nothing to pursue further. A competent professional advocate would never take this route. For the magistrate to do so does not therefore help the unrepresented accused conduct his cross-examination as a professional might, it simply ensures that his amateur cross-examination both terminates and fails. The magistrate's 'help' is therefore no substitute for defence advocacy. Nor could it be: that is not his role. The magistrate can, as all judges can, ask questions, but his role remains that of independent judge, he has no involvement in the preparation of cases and he may not take sides. And of course he does not know the defendant's version beforehand, so the questions he asks are necessarily coloured by the only version he has heard, the prosecution's. With the best will in the world he is not in the structural position to do the job of defence advocate.

Neither, for that matter, is the defendant. Indeed, the unrepresented defendant is truly in a dilemma. Without exercising the skills of the advocate or knowledge of the law he cannot participate in his trial, and there is no *defence*, but if he *does* demonstrate such skills he is caught in the double bind that he is not supposed to. Implicit in the notion of professional expertise is an unspoken closed shop which fosters the idea that only professionals *can* or *may* do the job. This indeed is an expectation promoted not only by experience of scores of baffled defendants but by authoritative sources, like the matter-of-fact observation in the Chancellor's lectures for magistrates, that: 'cross-examination and re-examination are difficult matters for unrepresented parties . . .' (1953: 38). The result is that the accused who *does* cross-examine rather than make statements invites interruption and criticism, even though he is often pursuing only, if perhaps a little more agitatedly, the same lines that the professional would. In Case 6 the accused is invited to cross-examine for the second time with the quip: 'We don't want a breach of the peace here.' When one of the accused in Case 1 caught out the police witness on a detail of location, exactly the kind of detail advocates rub their hands over, he was interrupted by the magistrate (who after all had to decide his fate) with the comment: 'I wish you wouldn't be so aggressive—you're slightly offensive.' The same man had been cross-examining police witnesses as to identity with the trump card up his sleeve that he had a beard then and none now, yet this was not being noted when he was identified. Having tried to cross-examine the preceding two witnesses on this somewhat convolutedly but with enough grasp of the advocate's style to keep surprise on his side, he began on the third, only to be beaten to it by a direct question from the magistrate: 'How was he facially? Did he have a beard?' It is not at all unusual for prosecutors to conclude cross-examination of the accused with the suggestion that he is 'telling a pack of lies'. The same attack by an accused on the police is seen as insolent:

ACCUSED: [to police] I think you're a liar.
ASSESSOR: That's enough! (Case 29)

Ascertaining and trying to catch opponents out on details of time and place often take up a good deal of court time in represented cases but the unrepresented accused may not play the same game. In Case 9, one of the defendants tried to establish that the police could not, from their vantage point, have seen them 'touching cars' even if they were. The prosecutor in cross-examining him, reproved him:

PROSECUTOR: So the story of touching cars is all lies.
DEFENDANT: Aye, that's all lies. I never touched it.
PROSECUTOR: Why did you not ask the police that when they were here instead of about walls and curves in roads?

The magistrate had his say too:

MAGISTRATE: You're still a cocky young whippersnapper. When's your bubble going to burst? You're a very confident self-opinionated young man.

Dell may point to nerves as a problem for defendants but it would appear from such comments that confidence fares them little better. Defendants *may not* play the role of the confident punch-pulling advocate because it clashes not only with the incompetence and deference routinely demanded of the lower-class people who dominate the courts, but because it clashes with the role expected of the *defendant*. The defendant may be diffident, nervous, excited, contrite; he may not be confident, aggressive, cool, calculating, tricky—unless of course he is that rarity, an unrepresented middle-class defendant in the lower courts. The inherent characteristics of the competent defendant and the competent advocate make it structurally difficult to get away with playing both roles at once.

Defendants occasionally succeed in cross-examination, managing to suggest an alternative case without stepping over the threshold of the professional closed shop, succeed at least in the sense of winning judicial tolerance, if not of winning the case, as in Case 21. But this case ended as not proven on a technical lack in the prosecution case, not on the strength of the defence, while it was not only marked by exchange of smiles throughout between magistrate, assessor, and prosecutor but by comments among the court team at the end on how well the defendant had done, which rather suggested this was a phenomenon that was neither expected nor typical.

It is a normal technique of advocates to cross-examine on matters which appear to be peripheral as a way of catching the witness on a crucial matter unawares, or indeed to make something significant of a matter which may not seem so to the witness. Either way the crucial elements are surprise and a continuity of flow in the questioning, and a judge would be unlikely to intervene. Unrepresented defendants are not so readily accorded this privilege:

MAGISTRATE: What's that got to do with it? Next question. (Case 1)

Repetition, near-repetition, or persistence with a particular line, normal enough advocacy styles, invite termination:

ASSESSOR: I think you've covered that. I think we've got the picture. (Case 21)

—though the assessor, having stopped this defendant, then went on to ask questions on a new line only to tell the defendant when he interrupted:

ASSESSOR: You sit down—you've had your turn to cross-examine. This is the court's turn.

Or the defendant's cross-examination may be ended by a simple 'Anything else?'—simple, but from *the* powerful court figure, be it brusque, bored, or kindly, undeniably final. Magistrates exercise much more control over defendants representing themselves than over lawyers. Not only is there no professional etiquette to get in the way but there is more of an immediate power relationship between the defendant and the magistrate who holds the key to his fate than between magistrate, or indeed judge, and lawyer.

It is not therefore just as simple as lawyers being able to do things that laymen cannot. Even among defendants competent in the art of self-defence it is harder for the unrepresented defendant to *get away with* the same methods as a lawyer. Indeed, to be too *au fait* with law, procedure, and advocacy can mean inviting not just ridicule or interruption but suspicion:

ASSESSOR: Your vocabulary's very expressive, isn't it? You know all about the powers. (Case 29) (General Powers Act)

Or:

MAGISTRATE: It seems strange a young girl like you should know all this jargon if you've not been in trouble before. (Case 29)

The implication was made explicit when assessor, magistrate, and prosecutor chatted together after the case:

PROSECUTOR: They've been at it so often they know the score.

The accused is thus put in an absurd double bind—damned if he is knowledgeable in the rules, competent in advocacy; damned if he is not.

This analysis has examined the *situation* of the unrepresented defendant in court, as others have, and it has set it in the fairly obvious context of a structural paradox. The trial is predicated upon professional knowledge, expertise, and adversarial advocacy, but legal policy denies access to professional representation. Indeed, even status differentials in the lower courts can be explained in part by legal policy. Not only are the occasional middle-class defendants more likely to be articulate and competent, more likely than their working-class counterparts, to be *expected* and *allowed* by court personnel to be articulate and competent, and more likely to be able to afford a lawyer themselves, but they are also more likely, if they cannot, to be awarded legal aid. The Widgery Committee noted that assessment of the need for a lawyer should take account of variations in the consequences according to the social status of the person involved:

the seriousness of the consequences likely to result from loss of employment will also differ widely in different circumstances. A young labourer who loses his job in conditions of full employment will obviously not suffer to anything like the same extent as a middle aged black-coated worker who in the loss of his job, sacrifices career prospects, pension rights and may have the greatest difficulty in finding other comparable employment. (Widgery 1966: 46)

Thus speaks the middle-aged black-coated judge. Likewise, though the jeopardy of mere stigma resulting from a case is not of itself enough to allow legal aid, it can be taken into account where it is, say, 'a *respectable* housewife charged with shoplifting' (my emphasis).

One policy implication of analysis at this level might seem clear enough: if legal policy denies the defendant—and particularly the working-class defendant—a lawyer, on the mistaken assumption he does not need one, and if empirical evidence shows he is at a disadvantage without one, then perhaps legal policy should remove the disadvantage by providing a lawyer. Leaving aside the financial consideration which undoubtedly motivated the Widgery Committee to minimize legal aid in the lower courts this seems simple. But the simplicity is in the analysis. The lack of a lawyer for the lower court defendant cannot be analysed simply as causing his problems nor indeed as *caused* by a paradox of policy and structure. That paradox is itself a symptom of a deeper structural and ideological distinction between higher and lower court justice, which implies that even with a lawyer the defendant in the lower court would have the odds weighted against him. To raise questions about the need for lawyers or the quality of their service before magistrates is to confuse the social roles of higher and lower courts. The lower courts are not there to stage grand ideological scenarios of proof by adversarial advocacy; they are simply in the business of summary justice.

Summary courts and the ideology of justice

Until the name was changed in 1952 the magistrates' courts were called courts of summary jurisdiction, as in Scotland they (and the Sheriff Courts operating without a jury) still are. What they offer is summary justice. Summary justice is characterized precisely by its *lack* of many of the attributes of the ideology of law, legality, and a fair trial. The *Oxford Dictionary* defines summary law as 'proceedings in a court of law carried out rapidly by the omission of certain formalities required by the common law'. The lack of representation is but one of many omissions. The judicial definition in Scots law is a procedure:

without *indiciae* and without indictment and further without any notice to the party of the names of the witnesses that are to be called against him and without the accused being represented by legal adviser unless he chooses to provide himself with one. (*Lamb* v. *Threshie*, 1892)

The judge might have added, without a record of the proceedings and of course without a jury. Summary justice is thus characterized legally not by positive attributes but by negative ones: it negates many of the procedures held to be necessary in the ideology of due process.

Controls are not very much in evidence either. Indeed, until 1953 the accused could not even appeal against a magistrate's decision. Now he can appeal against sentence and have the case reheard at the Crown Court, so long as he does so within twenty-one days, and with the proviso that the sentence may be increased if he does appeal, something that is not possible for appeals from higher courts. He can also appeal against conviction on a point of law, though the method by which this is done in the lower courts, 'by case stated', is somewhat illogical as a method of control. Appeal against a magistrate is made by that magistrate stating the facts of the case to a higher court. There are no official records against which to check the magistrate's version. Nor does the defendant have an opportunity to give his own version of what occurred to cause him grievance. Thus in contradiction to the rest of the criminal justice system, the complaint is stated not by the complainant or independently by both complainant and defendant, but only by the person being complained against. Since all adversary legal procedure is geared to the idea that there are two contradictory versions of the facts in any dispute this is a total violation of its own assumptions. In law it is not stated like this of course. The appeal is presented as an appeal against the *prosecutor*: he is the 'respondent', and the magistrate is merely the independent judge. But it is of course the *magistrate*'s decision that is in question, and control would seem to be put in the hands of those whom it is supposed to control. Not surprisingly only 0.3 per cent of summary defendants on indictments, 0.4 per cent on non-indictable offences, appeal against conviction, and only a quarter of those succeed.

In all sorts of ways the formality of the higher court is abandoned. The indictments by which prosecutions are launched in the superior courts require absolute precision—even the size of the paper and margins are specified in the 1918 rules, but the 'information' which initiates the lower court prosecution has no set form, it need not even be written, though it usually is, and not all the elements of the offence need to be stated. Nor can any objection be raised to an 'information' on the grounds of defect of substance or form or because the evidence given at the trial varies from it (Arguile 1969: 55). Hence the administration of the lower courts is often presented as less formal and legalistic than that of the higher courts. But the 'informality' would seem to be rather one-sided: the defendant's *role*, as this chapter has already shown, is still governed by formal procedures, but the defendant's *rights* are greatly reduced.

If the lower courts seem to present a different world from the image we carry in our heads of the higher courts then, it is hardly surprising; in law that is exactly what they are. The law has created two tiers of justice, one which is geared in its ideology and generality at least to the structures of legality, and one which, quite simply and explicitly, is not.

State struggles and the two tiers of justice

The positive characteristics of summary justice are not legal so much as economic and bureaucratic: summary justice is fast, easy, and cheap. The Scots manual, Renton and Brown (1972), notes 'the facility and rapidity of summary process' (p. 184), while a handbook for English law students observes that 'summary offences, being both more numerous and less serious than indictable offences, are tried by a simpler and cheaper method' (Price 1979: 74).

But the appropriateness of simpler, cheaper procedure for minor offences has not always been quite so taken for granted. In the early days of the liberal democratic state after the 1688 Revolution the judiciary viewed with considerable suspicion the operation of summary justice, and convictions by JPs were constantly quashed throughout the eighteenth century.[6] The grounds were often technical, an inaccuracy in the form of the 'information' (the JPs acting in the absence of an organized police force, on the word of anonymous informers). Eighteenth-century justice was thus not only marked by merciful pardons, as Hay (1975) has demonstrated, nor indeed by technical acquittals by jurors, which have been put down to the severity of the penalties, but by technical acquittals by the judiciary of the higher courts. The reasoning displays not so much a fetish for technicality, 'mere form or formality is not required in these nor any other summary proceedings' (*R. v. Chandler*, 1700), but as a deliberate policy of strict control over the summary courts: 'a tight hand ought to be holden over these summary convictions' (*R. v. Corden*, 1769). This may have been because the theories from which democratic ideology emerged were still recent enough for that ideology to be believed in and fervently upheld. The seventeenth-century common lawyers had, in their challenge to the monarchy, traced the pedigree of common law justice to no less than the Magna Carta and the famous dictum of Chapter 29 that

No free man shall be taken and imprisoned or disseised of any free tenement or of his liberties or free customs or outlawed or exiled, or in any other way destroyed, nor will we go upon nor send upon him, *except by the lawful judgement of his peers* or by the law of the land.[7] (My emphasis)

Such rhetoric certainly jarred with the trial by 'a single justice of the peace in a private chamber upon the testimony of one witness' that summary justice offered:

Everybody knows, that this being a penal law ought by equity and reason to be construed according to the letter of it and no further; and that this Act is penal is most plain, . . . and what is highly so, the defendant is put to a summary trial different from Magna Carta, for it is a fundamental privilege of Englishmen to be tried by jury, which privilege has been secured to us by our ancestors . . . (R. v. *Whistler*, 1699)

But summary jurisdiction was an affront to the common law judges not just because it violated the concept of justice celebrated in Magna Carta but by the fact that it was not a common law creation but was *statutory*. It had historically been introduced by the monarch, used oppressively by Henry II in particular, and thus, in a state now geared to keeping the monarchy in its place, must have had unfortunate connotations. But it was not done away with. On the contrary there were new interests involved. The new state was based on an idea of divided sovereignty, the separation of powers, but what that meant remained to be determined and there was still a battle to be fought out on the division of spoils. In the judiciary's technical acquittals on appeal from summary courts we may be witnessing a battle over the meaning of the separation of powers, with the judges claiming, on the basis of pre-parliamentary authority (hence the rhetoric of Magna Carta), exclusive rights over the operation of justice. Summary jurisdiction as a statutory creation offended this claim by being the prerogative of parliament. The summary courts may thus have become one of the battlegrounds in the struggle over the form of the modern state; through such minutiae are the great battles of history fought out.

If this is correct, and it would require a deeper historical study than this to find out, it was a battle which the judges lost. By 1787 in the summary justice skirmish at least they were beginning to assume the role of the interpreters of Parliament rather than its challengers and watchdogs, to define their role within the compass of parliamentary authority rather than as derived from a different tradition:

As to the principle drawn from the old cases that the court will be astute in discovering defects in convictions before summary jurisdiction there seems to be no reason for it. Whether it was expedient that those jurisdictions should have been erected was a matter for the legislature; but as long as they exist we ought to go to all reasonable lengths to support their determinations. (R. v. *Thompson*, 1787)

In any case by the mid-nineteenth century in Acts 'to facilitate the performance of the duties of the Justices of the Peace' Parliament had intervened decisively by simply removing the means by which convictions could be quashed. The judges had always insisted as the superior courts that detailed records were kept by the JPs. The more complete the more likely they were to disclose technical errors. Parliament now removed the need to keep a note of the evidence on which the conviction was based, and so made appeal and judicial control well nigh impossible. This move from excessive technicality might be seen as a simple—welcome—triumph for common sense over legalism. But for its full implications to be understood it should be set in the context of *why* the judges quashed summary convictions on technical grounds. One might speculate from the sparse evidence offered here that this represented not just mindless procedural fetishism but a means of upholding justice based on the ideology of the 'ancient rights of free men'. Technical acquittals may have defied common sense but they may also have been no more than a front for challenging not the case but the procedure *per se*. The irony is that the front itself, especially in the 'common sense' *par excellence* of Benthamism, became an easy justification not for removing summary procedure but for removing the judges' control over it, by declaring technicalities irrelevant.

The Justices of the Peace lost their administrative role with the Municipal Corporation Act of 1835 but their judicial role began to expand. The 1847 Juvenile Offenders Act and the Summary Jurisdiction and Indictable Offences Act of 1858 allowed summary justices to deal with an increasing range of indictable offences. By the mid-nineteenth century more and more offences were being diverted from the higher courts to the summary courts (a process that continues one hundred years later in, for example, the James Report 1975). Summary courts were also well established by the same period as courts freed from the due process of the common law. The apparent contradiction in the dictionary quotation cited earlier, 'proceedings in a court of law' which omit 'formalities required by the common law', may now be clearer. Courts of law can operate *without* what is required by law precisely because the courts in question are created by one strand of the state, Parliament, and the rules by another, common law. The separation of powers thus provides the structural background for democratic ideology to operate despite its internal contradictions. The principles of one strand have remained as the dominant image of law and as the rhetoric of justice, but the existence of the other allows the legal system to deal with the vast majority of offenders in a way which flouts the principles of justice *legally*.

The short-circuiting of justice as traditionally defined required not just structural manœuvring, however, but legitimation. Due process was and is ruled out of the lower courts as unnecessary on two grounds: first, both the offences and the penalties are too trivial; second, the issues and processes are such that the niceties of law and lawyers are irrelevant. The next sections analyse these legitimations to demonstrate their ideological nature, and their ideological accomplishments.

The ideology of triviality

To read law books for information on the magistrates' courts is to come away with the clear impression that what goes on in them is overwhelmingly trivial. They deal with 'minor offences', 'everyday offences', 'the most ordinary cases', 'humdrum' events.[8] Legal academics even go so far—rare event—as indulging in jocularity. Coull and Merry's text gives the Scottish police courts, very much the lowest tier of justice, seven lines, largely taken up with the fact that they are empowered,

inter alia to impose a fine of 50p for 'allowing a chimney to catch or be on fire' or a penalty of £2 for throwing 'any snowball, to the danger or annoyance' of any person. (Coull and Merry 1971: 25–6)

This dominant image of the triviality of the work of the lower courts is shared by the Press. The Press benches in magistrates' courts are rarely occupied. The column of offenders and penalties that every local paper carries is the result of a phone call for results. The proceedings themselves are of no interest, except perhaps to provide this week's funny stories for the Diary column, institutionalized indeed in one Scottish paper[9] as 'little stories from the police courts' where the comic antics and Glaswegian patter in the dock of Big Bertha and Wee Annie are recounted for laughs. And why not? Much of what happens in the court is—as Pat Carlen demonstrates—funny or pathetic or absurd, and so very trivial, too trivial to attract any serious attention from the Press.

Nor indeed from the public: so rare is it for a member of the public to attend summary courts that the public benches are often used as a waiting room for the morning's batch of defendants, from which they can observe their predecessors' fate and shuffle along to each newly vacated space till their turn comes for the dock. To go to these courts as a member of the public is to become an object of curiosity; to sit there taking notes is to invite paroxysms of paranoia. I have been asked by one police officer on duty if I was 'from one of those radical papers' by another if I was 'just here to practise your shorthand, dear?' I've been called before the bench to explain myself, had a policeman sent by the magistrate to ask me what I was doing there, been advised not to take notes by a policeman on duty, told by another that taking notes was illegal, and instructed by yet another, not to note down an altercation between an assessor (the legal adviser to a lay magistrate in Scotland) and a solicitor—it wasn't 'done'. The 'public' in the lower court is an unusual phenomenon, and the purveyors of magistrates' justice are somewhat sensitive to anyone seeing their particular brand of justice being done. More than that, some were just genuinely concerned that I should be wasting my time at the lower courts when I could be watching 'juicy cases' and 'real judges' elsewhere. *Their* assumption was that the work of *their* court was too trivial to be of interest. So the image of triviality that pervades the lowest ranks of criminal justice has the consequence of removing yet another requisite of due process: that the administration of justice should be public. One of the objections of the eighteenth-century judges to summary justice was that it was 'in a private chamber' behind closed doors. The doors were opened in 1848 but the dominant image of triviality helps ensure that the public benches remain empty. It is not just the offences that are deemed trivial—drunkenness, swearing, petty theft (a report by the Chief Constable for Glasgow (1975) noted that 47 per cent of all thefts were of goods valued under £10)—but the penalties, and the triviality of the penalties may help in particular to explain public apathy. Not only is it difficult to work up a moral panic over someone 'jumping on and off the pavement in a disorderly manner', taking lead worth 20p from a rubbish tip or touching cars, but the life-and-death decision of Hay's eighteenth-century courts is missing. The salacious fascination of whether the scales would tip to the gallows or mercy can hardly be matched by crimes whose *maximum* penalties are six months in prison or a fine of £1,000.

More specifically, it is the relative triviality of the *penalties* that provides the crucial legitimations in law for the lack of due process in summary justice. Due process of law is required in the ideology of democratic justice before a person's liberty may be interfered with. The reasoning which legitimizes reducing due process in the lowest courts is based on this premise, but with a refinement. 'Liberty' ceases to be an absolute and becomes subject to a measuring rod. The limited penalties available to magistrates means they can interfere less with one's liberty than the higher courts, so defendants in these courts need less due process. The less one's liberty is at risk the less one need protection. This is perhaps most explicitly stated in the criteria for awarding legal aid. One important condition is where the defendant is 'in real jeopardy of losing his liberty or livelihood or suffering imprisonment' (Widgery 1966; Royal Commission on Legal Services 1979: 158).

More generally this is in many ways a strange argument. 'Trivial' offences after all still involve state intervention in the citizen's liberty. Indeed, if the same due process is not to be awarded to all defendants, it might seem a bit illogical to minimize the legal rights for those who have allegedly infringed least on law and order and maximize them for those who have infringed most. Perhaps it is just that the more unusual the crime, and the larger the penalty, the more public interest is likely to be aroused and the more justice will be willy-nilly on display. The more criminality in the offence, the more legality in the proceedings might be an odd equation. The more *publicity*, the more legality, is in ideological terms, perfectly understandable. Publicity is not an issue that need trouble lower court justice, closeted from the public eye by its own triviality—or more accurately, by its own ideology of triviality. Triviality is not just a description but an interpretation, an assessment, and the work of the lower courts could be viewed quite differently.

For a start, offences and penalties may seem trivial from the outside but far from trivial from the perspective of the accused—unless they have become so only through the folk memory[10] of the lower-class people who pass through the court, to whom police and law have become enemies, and prosecution for trivial offences a risk of everyday life. The James Report rejected the perspective of the defendant as a way of categorizing which offences and penalties were serious and which were not, on grounds which stressed its significance but also its bureaucratic inconvenience: 'It would be impracticable . . . since that importance varies according to his character and position in society' (James Report 1975: 20), though the same reasoning is used in the Widgery Report to do the opposite; that is, to use the defendant's perspective, *as it varies according to his social status*, to justify discriminating in favour of the middle class in the award of legal aid.[11] Thus the very people who are *expected* rightly or wrongly to be more competent in handling both authorities and formal, verbal situations, are the ones who are also made the exceptions who need additional professional help. One is tempted to conclude from such careful exceptions that the ideology of triviality may ultimately derive less from the triviality of the offences or the penalties but from the triviality in authoritative eyes of *the people*, the lower class and lower still, the unemployed, homeless, feeble, who provide the fodder for the lower courts—an implication indeed which is supported by the fact that the only time the lower courts become news is when, for example, Mark Phillips is charged with speeding.

Nor is it just a question of perspective but a question of focus. There is an inherent paradox in the very idea of prosecuting trivial offences. They are too trivial to interest the public but not too trivial for the state to prosecute in the name of the public; too trivial to merit due process of law but not too trivial for the intervention of the law. The ideology of triviality focuses on the offences and penalties, not on the question of prosecution itself. It is these trivial offences after all which are: first, most open to the direct intervention of the state in the sense that the police are the *only complainants*; second, most open to the imposition of a criminal label on 'marginal' behaviour; and third, most open—because their content is so open—to *post hoc* law-making. In short, it is exactly in the area of minor offences that the operation of the law, in terms of democratic justice, becomes most suspect. If the behaviour involved in the offence is not intrinsically interesting, perhaps, as the eighteenth-century judges felt, the law's processing of that behaviour into an offence is. But contemporary official discourse is more concerned with the quantity of crime than the quality of justice, and the lower courts remain something to be laughed at or yawned over for the pettiness of their crimes, not watched with care for the marginality of their legality.

Legal relevance

The second justification for reducing the strictures of due process—a view indeed taken for granted by socio-legal writers like Mungham and Thomas (1979)—is that the offences dealt with in the lower courts do not involve much law or require much legal expertise or advocacy. They can therefore be safely left to be dealt with by laymen[12]—by lay magistrates and by the defendants themselves, with lawyers seen as normally unnecessary in the lower courts. According to the Widgery Report, legal aid is rarely necessary for summary offences since: 'The large majority of cases are straightforward and the facts are uncomplicated and clear-cut' (Widgery Report 1966: 47).

But this view of the lower court is inaccurate in two ways. First, empirical study, as already demonstrated, shows that the lower courts are permeated by legalistic and professional consciousness. Second, it is logically confused—it confuses cause and effect. The reasoning in the Widgery Report, and Mungham and Thomas's essay, verges on tautology. It might just as readily be argued that minor offences are characterized by simple facts and straightforward cases because lawyers are so rarely involved. The 'case' is a construct from an event, not a reproduction of it. The construction of a case as straightforward or as involving points of law is very much the product of the advocate's trade. Case law, after all, develops exactly because advocates present cases which draw subtle distinctions and shades of meaning; in short, complicate the simple, in arguing for the treatment of the case in hand as different from previous cases. What is more, case law and the development of complicated and difficult legal issues in specific types of offence and case, is predicated largely on the right to appeal on points of law, and both the nature of the appeal procedure in the lower courts and the lack of lawyers to formulate an appeal on a point of law, means that there is little opportunity to develop difficult and complex case law on minor offences. It is not in the nature of drunkenness, breach of the peace, or petty theft to be less susceptible than fraud, burglary, or murder to complex legal argument; it is rather in the nature of the procedure by which they are tried. Indeed, the James Report implicitly recognizes this when it notes that: 'trial on indictment takes longer than summary trial even for a case of similar gravity and complexity' (James Report 1975: 13). And of course the eighteenth-century judges found plenty of legal niceties in the work of the summary courts, until they were explicitly deprived of the means to intervene. The comment in the Lords' debate on the 1952 Magistrates' Act that the high courts were not aware of what went on in the magistrates' courts because: 'in the nature of things their professional skill has led them into the higher reaches of the law rather than the more humdrum reaches of the magistrates' courts' (Hansard 1952: 1223) ignores the use to which professional skill was put historically, and the legislative axe that ended it. The 'straightforward cases' of the lower courts are themselves legal constructions.

The same is true of the 'simple facts'. The facts of a case—a case of any sort—are not *all* the elements of the event, but the information allowed in by the rules, presented by the witnesses, and surviving the credibility test of cross-examination. The facts of summary cases may not be simple because of the nature of the offence but because of the lack of professional expertise in manipulation of the rules, persuasive presentation of one's own case and destructive cross-examination of the other side's. It is not that complex facts need lawyers, but that lawyers can make 'facts' complex. That is exactly their trade.

Or the facts may be 'simple' not because of the nature of the behaviour in the offence but because of the nature of the *definition* of the offence. The openness of the legal definition of what constitutes an offence, along with the fact that these offences are normally the result not of citizens' reports but of police-accused encounters—with only the accused's word against the policeman's constituting the case—means that it is extremely difficult to establish a defence. In short, the facts are simple only because they are legally so difficult for the defendant to contest.

Indeed, it might be suggested that the openness of the laws defining summary offences argues not for less legal expertise but for more. If the police can legally define almost anything as an offence, then the facts cannot be in dispute and the only way to establish a defence is on a point of law. Remember Case 30, the 'jumping on and off a pavement in a disorderly manner' case. One reaction to being charged for that, even if one *was* doing it, might be total disbelief and a defence on the basis of it being absurd to be taken to court for such behaviour at all. But that of course is not a legal defence, just a cut-and-dried admission of guilt. The accused in this case, the only one of the group charged who pleaded not guilty, defended himself by saying he was not doing anything disorderly, that indeed he had just crossed the road to talk to the group collected at the tenement entrance, and that he did not run away because he 'didn't expect to be lifted'. That was his mistake. The prosecution even noted in his concluding speech that: 'he may think he wasn't misbehaving as much as the others *but he stayed with them.*' And that was all that was necessary in law. There was therefore no legal defence in denying his behaviour was offensive, not only because that was difficult to maintain against two policemen but because in law it was irrelevant. A relevant defence would have to take on the meaning of the law; for example, contending that to be 'part of a disorderly crowd' requires not just one's presence but active participation. But that would be a point of law: it would require a more sophisticated knowledge of law and legal reasoning than this layman had, and of course, as we have already seen, might require representation by a lawyer to be given a hearing at all. The irony is then that because there is so little case law to specify meaning, the best route to a defence is to challenge on a point of law. This of course could *establish* that missing case law, but it cannot be readily done because no need for lawyers is perceived, and the means to raise a point of law are denied. The image of the lower courts as not needing lawyers, which justifies not providing lawyers, is itself a *product* of their absence. The defendant is thus caught up in the vicious circle that lies behind the image of 'simple facts' and 'straightforward cases'.

But, and this is why situational analysis needs to be set in its deeper structural context, providing lawyers would not necessarily make any difference: the ideologies of non-law and triviality pervade the origins and structure of the lower courts and so pervade the attitudes of those who work in them. Remember the police official who helpfully suggested I go to the higher courts for 'juicy cases' and 'real judges'. And lawyers themselves often operate with different style in the lower courts. Indeed, they are different lawyers. The non-law ideology has its structural expression in the idea that only barristers can act in the higher courts but only solicitors can usually be provided on legal aid in the lower courts. This is not to suggest insidious comparisons between the skills of solicitors and barristers, but merely to indicate that whatever the personal attitudes or competence of the solicitors who do appear in the lower courts the standard of advocacy *required* is pre-set as second class. Likewise there is a structural expectation that lower courts do not need cases that are well prepared, or indeed prepared beforehand at all, by either side. With no committal proceedings the defence has no advance warning of the prosecution case it will have to face anyway, while Arguile's book on criminal procedure notes that if a matter arises in the defence evidence that takes the prosecution by surprise he may call evidence in rebuttal of it *afterwards*:

This is permitted because summary trials usually owe very little to advance preparation of the case, and the prosecution is therefore more likely to be surprised by unexpected defences. (Arguile 1969: 164)

This is certainly borne out by observation, as indeed is the idea that lawyers consider lower court cases too trivial, or too simple, to be worth much bother. In Case 17 two brothers charged with breach of the peace while on business in Scotland had pleaded not guilty and came all the way from London to stand trial. They had hired a solicitor and provided him with the details of their case. He did not turn up. The brothers were adamant they would not continue without a solicitor, though they earned themselves a few rude comments as a result. A solicitor from the same firm who happened to be in the building agreed to step in, and began to find out about the case there in court, suppressing one of his new clients' indignation at these proceedings with the reprimand that *he* should have reminded the solicitor of the date and venue of the trial: 'I'd have thought someone who knows as much about the law as you would know that.' And he added the ultimate put-down that in any case: 'Breach of the peace isn't a serious charge.'

There were lawyers who operated as advocates, prepared efficient cases, organized witnesses. They tended to be young, one was a woman, all were patronized by the court officials as new to the game and trying a bit too hard. *The reaction of the court* suggested they were not typical. There was even one who launched into technicalities, refusing to let his client stand trial because he had turned up on the due date given him and the court had not tried him—the clerk had got the date wrong and made it a Sunday (Case 18). He was, in a tired tone, given a new date: such technical details are expressly ruled out as unimportant in the lower courts. Another, representing the middle-class owner of a pub on a strict liability licensing charge, even raised a point of law, cited precedents and got the court very excited. This was such an unusual occurrence they had to adjourn to find the relevant books (Case 14). There were others, however, who simply left their clients as dumbfounded as the defendant in Case 8. McD. had been so adamant he was innocent that he and his mother had hired a lawyer at their own expense. And in their view, 'it was the easiest £30 I ever saw anyone earning'. There *was* a witness, a stranger, who, according to the defendant, had in fact been committing the offence, and had been prepared to give evidence that McD. had arrived *after* the event. He had pleaded guilty, but recognized McD. was not and gave a statement to that effect to the lawyer. Summoning him was left to the defendant's mother. Neither she nor the witness had a phone. She sent her 7-year-old son with a note. The witness's father took it at the door. She never knew if the witness himself received it. He certainly did not turn up. In court, the defence lawyer merely noted 'I had hoped to have some supporting evidence but unfortunately for one reason or another it is not available.' The magistrate, not surprisingly, saw 'no reason why I should doubt the evidence given by the policeman'. And the family even less surprisingly concluded: 'People like us don't have rights.'

Comments on the lawyers in my observed cases must necessarily be scant and maybe unrepresentative. This was a qualitative study of a relatively small number of cases and the number of lawyers was in the nature of things—and particularly in the nature of legal aid—few. There are other snippets of information that may lend support though: for example, Darbyshire's study of justices' clerks and her description of the courts as dominated by a handful of solicitors usually engaged on several cases at once, and always holding things up, or by inexperienced young barristers who 'hadn't a clue'. She assessed the level of advocacy she observed in action as generally 'mediocre' and 'appalling' with little legal argument,

and with (to her) obvious defences either not put at all or put as mitigation which if accepted would amount to a complete defence (Darbyshire
1978: 239). There is also the criticism of the level of advocacy in the
magistrates' courts made to the Royal Commission on Legal Services by
the Association of Magisterial Officers. My concern, however, is less with
assessing the level of performance and attitude of lawyers *per se* than with
teasing out what that demonstrates about the professional lawyer's ideology of the lower courts. On that score, the reply by the Law Association
is as telling as the criticism. First, the magisterial officers are themselves
derided for both their menial status and their lack of law since they 'for
the most part probably entirely lack legal qualification and were formerly
called the National Association of Justices' Clerks' Assistants'. Then the
offenders and offences and work of the court in general is discussed as
'relative trivia' and 'the dross of the criminal courts'. The suggestion by
the officers that such offenders and offences need specialists to deal with
them is noted as showing 'how divorced from reality their comments
must be' and as 'the best indication of the unreliability of this evidence
and the lack of thought which appears to have preceded it' (*The Times*, 23
August 1977). What these comments suggest is that the profession too is
imbued with the dominant images of the lower courts as neither serious
enough nor legally relevant enough to need lawyers. To simply prescribe
lawyers on tap for the lower courts as a solution to the defendant's
dilemma is thus to ignore the much more fundamental structural and
ideological realities which lie behind the courtroom situation.

The accomplishments

These images of the court are not just ideological accomplishments; they
also accomplish ideological functions themselves. Carlen points to the
marginality of the offences, the lack of ceremony and lack of lawyers in
the lower courts, as a problem for the magistrate in presenting the
court's work as justice (Carlen 1976: 38). But the situational problem is in
fact resolved structurally. The very same factors are transformed into
images of the court as trivial and non-legal: and the effect of those images
is that the court never actually has to account for its work anyway. The
magistrate may have an existential problem in portraying his work as
justice but he rarely has a social problem. For the magistrates' court is a
theatre without an audience.

Legal policy has established two tiers of justice. One, the higher courts,
is for public consumption, the arena where the ideology of justice is put

on display. The other, the lower courts, deliberately structured in defiance of the ideology of justice, is concerned less with subtle ideological messages than with direct control. The latter is closeted from the public eye by the ideology of triviality, so the higher courts alone feed into the public image of what the law does and how it operates. But the higher courts deal with only 2 per cent of the cases that pass through the criminal courts. Almost all criminal law is acted out in the lower courts *without* traditional due process. But of course what happens in the lower courts is not only trivial, it is not really law. So the position is turned on its head. The 98 per cent becomes the exception to the rule of 'real law' and the working of the law comes to be *typified not* by its routine nature, but by its *atypical*, indeed *exceptional*, High Court form. Between them the ideologies of triviality and legal irrelevance accomplish the remarkable feats of defining 98 per cent of court cases not only as exceptions to the rule of due process, but also as of no public interest whatsoever. The traditional ideology of justice can thus survive the contradiction that the summary courts blatantly ignore it every day—and that they were set up precisely for that purpose.

Notes

1. In England this refers to the magistrates' courts. In Scotland 'non-jury' trials and guilty pleas are dealt with not just by lay magistrates (indeed lay magistrates operate only on the fringes of criminal justice) and stipendiary magistrates but also by sheriffs sitting without a jury who deal with half of non-indictment prosecutions (Walker, 1976, p. 238). In England, though not in Scotland, the defendant can choose whether to be tried by jury or by magistrates for a range of offences, though there are systematic pressures towards 'opting' for summary justice, just as there are towards 'opting' for a guilty plea. For a start there is a much lower maximum penalty, six months' imprisonment or £1,000 fine (raised from three months and £500 by the Criminal Law Act 1977); second, the defendant cannot be committed to the Crown Court for sentence. These are described by Smith and Hogan (1977) as 'bonuses', though of course one could as readily interpret them as inducements.
2. That is, for law and justice. They *do* fill other ideological roles, e.g. on the virtues of employment and family life.
3. Extended to the lower courts only in the 1975 reorganization, or at least renaming, of the district courts.
4. The report retains discretion in the award of legal aid in cases triable only by magistrates, changing the emphasis from the need to find grounds to award it to the need to find grounds to deny it, but employing the same basic criteria.
5. James Report, 1975, Appendix.

6. See Rouse Jones, 1953, p. 6.
7. See Thompson, 1950.
8. Arguile, 1969; Lords Debate on the Magistrates' Courts, Hansard, 1952; Walker, 1976.
9. The *Weekly News*.
10. See Brogden, 1979.
11. See earlier in this Chapter.
12. Less so in Scotland; see note 1.

References

Arguile, R., *Criminal Procedure* (Butterworths, 1969).

Bottoms, A. E. and J. D. McClean, *Defendants in the Criminal Process* (Routledge & Kegan Paul, 1976).

Brogden, M.. 'All police is cunning bastards.' Paper presented at the BSA Conference on Law and Society (1970).

Carlen, P., *Magistrates' Justice* (Martin Robertson, 1976).

Coull, J. W. and E. W. Merry, *Principles and Practice of Scots Law* (Butterworths, 1971).

Darbyshire, P., *'The role of the justices' clerk and the court clerk'*. Ph.D. Thesis, Faculty of Law, Birmingham University (1978).

Dell, S., *Silence In Court*. Occasional Papers on Social Administration, 42 (Bell, 1971).

Hay, D., 'Property, authority and the law', in Hay *et al.* (eds.), *Albion's Fatal Tree* (Allen Lane, 1975).

Hetzler, A. N. and C. H. Kanter, 'Informality and the court', in S. F. Sylvester and E. Sagarin (eds.), *Politics and Crime* (Praeger, 1974).

James Report, Cmnd. 6323 (Home Office, Lord Chancellor's Office, 1975).

Mungham, G. and P. Thomas, 'Advocacy and the Solicitor-Advocate in magistrates' courts in England and Wales', *International Journal of the Sociology of Law* (May 1979).

Price, J. P., *The English Legal System* (M and E Handbooks, 1979).

Renton, R. W. and H. H. Brown, *Criminal Procedure According to the Law of Scotland*, 4th edn. (Green, 1972).

Rouse Jones, L., *Magistrates Courts*, (Sweet and Maxwell, 1953).

Royal Commission on Legal Services, Report (HMSO, Cmnd. 7648, 1979).

Smith, J. C. and B. Hogan, *Criminal Law*, 4th edn. (Butterworths, 1977).

Thompson, F., *Magna Carta*, (University of Minnesota Press, 1950).

Widgery, Report of the Departmental Committee on Legal Aid in Criminal Court Proceedings (Home Office, Cmnd. 2934, 1966).

Criminal Justice and Deserved Sentences

ANDREW ASHWORTH

Across the common law world and elsewhere, new sentencing systems are being introduced or recommended. For example, Sweden,[1] the United States federal jurisdiction[2] and several American states[3] have already begun to operate new sentencing schemes, and there are important proposals on the table in Canada,[4] the State of Victoria[5] and the Australian federal jurisdiction.[6] These systems differ on many points of detail, but they all involve a new set of general principles or general guidelines, as distinct from the sporadic and piecemeal efforts to guide sentencers which take place in England. In planning a new system it is necessary to think seriously about the purposes of sentencing, and it is at this stage that the 'just deserts' approach has been influential in many of the jurisdictions mentioned. This article offers a brief assessment of the 'just deserts' approach within a wider context of criminal justice policy. Many of the arguments can and should be taken much further than is possible here, but it is hoped that brevity will have some advantages.

The aims of sentencing

A preliminary task is to stake out the terrain. The aims of sentencing are clearly not identical with the aims of the criminal law itself. Sentencing is the stage after the imposition of criminal liability, and may be characterized as a public, judicial judgment of the degree to which the offender may rightly be ordered to suffer legal punishment.[7] The conviction establishes that the offender may be subjected to judicial sentencing, within the applicable limits, and so sentencing decisions are concerned with the *degree* of condemnation and with the form of the sentence. Any examination of the aims of sentencing should therefore focus on criteria for determining the quantum of punishment for the various offences and offenders, and on the form of the sentences. Any such justifications will inevitably be connected with the justifications for having a system of

criminal law and judicial sentencing at all, but there will be other considerations too.

The limits of sentencing

There is sometimes a tendency to discuss sentencing as if it were society's
major defence against lawbreaking, and the State's most propitious
opportunity to influence the frequency and patterns of crime. Many of
those who regard 'the protection of the public' as the chief aim of sentencing make this assumption.[8] It is a false assumption, and we must
have a firm understanding of why this is so.

The point is that the courts deal with only a tiny proportion of the
offences committed each year. Many crimes go unreported, and there are
various estimates of the proportion of crimes which actually find their
way into the official records.[9] Let us start with the ultra-cautious assumption that half of all notifiable offences are reported to and recorded by the
police. In England and Wales only about 35 per cent of notifiable offences
recorded by the police are 'cleared up': this represents some 18 per cent
of all offences actually committed on the estimations here (i.e. 35 per
cent of the 50 per cent of offences which are recorded). Of these offences
which are 'cleared up', just over half result in the conviction or formal
cautioning[10] of the offender—so we are down to 10 per cent of the total.
If one subtracts formal cautions from this figure, the offences for which
the courts pass sentence represent only 7 per cent of all offences committed in a given year. The Canadian Sentencing Commission also adopted
this style of analysis, starting from less cautious and more realistic
assumptions, and concluded that the courts probably deal with no more
than 3 per cent of all offences committed each year.[11] Of course the proportion will be higher for the more serious offences against the person,
where the detection rate is also higher; but the proportion will be considerably lower for run-of-the-mill property and other 'ordinary' crimes.

None of this is to suggest that public protection, in the sense of reducing
the risk of criminal offences occurring, is an unimportant aim. It is fundamental to the well-being of most members of society—particularly the disadvantaged sections of the community, as the 'left realist' movement in
criminology has recognized.[12] But public protection requires public policies
aimed specifically at crime prevention and aimed generally at reducing
criminogenic circumstances. By contrast with this broader approach to
criminal justice, the potentiality of sentencing for altering the frequency
and pattern of offending in society is severely handicapped by the fact that

such a small proportion of offences come before the courts, and then only after they have been committed. Of course sentencing fulfils an indispensable public function: without judicial sentencing, and the panoply of police, penal agents, and courts, there would undoubtedly be more crime.[13] But it is a perilous journey from this proposition, that judicial sentencing exerts an underlying deterrent influence on social behaviour, to the proposition that by increasing and decreasing their sentencing levels within tolerable limits, the courts can bring about substantial changes in rates of offending. Only in rare and unusual circumstances is this likely to happen: most of the evidence goes the other way.[14] We should conclude that public protection and crime prevention are more appropriate and more realizable as aims of the criminal justice system than as aims of sentencing.

The 'just deserts' approach to sentencing

The recent prominence of the 'just deserts' approach may be attributed not just to the clarity and persuasiveness of its protagonists[15] but also to background changes in penology and political philosophy. Briefly put, there has been (*a*) a sudden and perhaps over-dramatic loss of faith in the rehabilitative effects of sentences, stemming largely from Martinson's survey and the popularized conclusion that 'nothing works';[16] (*b*) a growing awareness of the limits to the individual deterrent and (as we have seen) the general deterrent effects of sentences—though some judges remain attached to anecdotes about exemplary sentences which worked,[17] the conditions under which general deterrent effects can be achieved through either a legislative or a judicial increase in sentence levels are complex and rare.[18] Both these changes have been propelled by criminological research and its interpretation, but simultaneously there has been increasing concern for the fairness of such sentencing policies and the 'rights' of persons subjected to them. Thus (*c*) developments in liberal political philosophy have argued for recognition of the right of each individual, as a rational and autonomous member of society, to be treated with equal concern and respect.[19] Despite the possibility that conflicts of rights may occasionally result in sacrifices being made,[20] there can be no doubt that in its overall orientation this strand of contemporary philosophy pushes in the same direction as 'just deserts', towards principled and proportionate sentencing.

What, then, are the main elements of the approach which has become so prominent in academic and official statements on sentencing in common law countries and in Scandinavia?[21] A point which is often overlooked is that the first element in the 'just deserts' approach relies heavily on general prevention. One of the justifications for judicial sentencing is that, without State punishment, 'it seems likely that victimising conduct would become so prevalent as to make life nasty and brutish, indeed'.[22] This empirical observation is taken to supply an instrumental justification for the institution of judicial sentencing. The other fundamental justification offered by von Hirsch is that a response to crime which 'fails to condemn the actor scarcely seems morally adequate'.[23] This seems to be advanced as a natural or conventional phenomenon—desert is 'an integral part of everyday judgments involving praise and blame'—which gives rise to a distinct purpose of sentencing, which is to censure offenders or, instrumentally, 'to express disapprobation of the conduct and its perpetrators'.[24]

The second main element brings us to the core of sentencing as a judgment of the degree of disapprobation: the principle of proportionality of sentence to crime. Here we meet an important distinction which is too frequently overlooked. Within the general idea of proportionality there are two distinct sets of concepts. One is ordinal proportionality. This concerns 'how a crime should be punished compared to similar criminal acts, and compared to other crimes of a more or less serious nature'.[25] Thus, once judicial sentencing has been established as a condemnatory institution to respond to criminal acts, its sentences ought to reflect the relative reprehensibleness of those acts.[26] That, in turn, is determined by the harm done or risked by the criminal act and by the culpability of the offender.[27] So ordinal proportionality is concerned with preserving a correspondence between relative seriousness of behaviour and relative severity of sentence, on which various moral and political judgments must be brought to bear.

This is to be contrasted with cardinal proportionality, which requires that the absolute level of the penalty scale, both maximum penalties and actual sentence ranges, be not disproportionate to the magnitude of the offending behaviour. This is a much looser notion of proportionality, often linked to what is current in the thought-patterns of a particular country at a particular phase in its history.[28] Fixing the level of the penalty scale afresh would require complex social and political judgments.

Some disadvantages associated with 'just deserts'

Having set out the key elements of the approach, the task now is to reflect upon some of the disadvantages and advantages associated with 'just deserts'—using the words 'associated with' advisedly, since some of the so-called disadvantages do not necessarily derive from 'just deserts' theory. For discussion here I select six possible lines of criticism.

(i) A cardinal weakness

It will be recalled that the 'just deserts' approach insists on both the cardinal and the ordinal proportionality of sentences of offences. There is, however, no clear notion of how to set the overall level of penalties so as to achieve cardinal proportionality: von Hirsch accepts that 'commensurate deserts is a limiting but not a defining principle when cardinal magnitudes are concerned',[29] and that social convention and general policy factors have much to do with it.[30] It is true that von Hirsch has argued strongly in favour of a reduction in the severity of penal sanctions and has always presented this as part of his desert approach.[31] However, that is surely a policy question on which different kinds of justification should be brought to bear, and there is no inevitable connection between the philosophy of 'just deserts' and policies such as reducing the use of custody or scaling down penalty levels. They are not incompatible, but neither are 'just deserts' and a policy of increasing the severity of sentences. It is well known that some United States sentencing reforms which have proclaimed 'just deserts' have been accompanied by a greater use of custodial sentences.[32] The attack on positions of this kind cannot be mounted satisfactorily from within 'just deserts'. It must be founded on a number of criminological and moral-social arguments, starting with findings that different levels of sanction severity have little discernible effect on crime rates[33] and moving to the proposition that it is morally unjustified to set cardinal proportionality at a given level when the balance of evidence suggests that a lower level would achieve a similar effect in terms of crime prevention. Proponents of 'just deserts' might claim this as part of their theory, since it is closely related to the underlying general preventive aim of this approach[34] which recognizes the necessary but limited function of the sentencing system. My reply would be that the policy arguments in favour of a reduced use of custodial sentences need to be articulated separately and vigorously, since they have been too readily overlooked by some of those wishing to trade upon the 'just deserts' brand name. Otherwise, it will remain a cardinal weakness that a liberal-inspired approach can be deployed so as to produce illiberal results.

(ii) Inordinate claims

How secure are the criteria upon which judgments of ordinal proportionality are founded? How can we determine whether robberies of a given kind should be regarded as more or less serious than certain forms of rape or certain forms of drug importation? There are some who would maintain that these are largely uncontroversial matters, since most members of most societies rank most offences in a similar order of relative gravity.[35] On this view there is a bedrock of shared values which can be used as a basis for constructing the rungs of ordinal proportionality.[36] Critics would assail this cosy, consensus view from various angles. First, there is no agreement on whether the scale of ordinal proportionality should take account of resulting harm, or should focus upon the harm intended or risked by the offender even if it does not occur.[37] Secondly, there have long been debates about the notion of culpability, and the extent to which it is theoretically sound or practically possible to hold an individual responsible for an offence and to distinguish degrees of responsibility.[38] Third, quantifying harms is both a complex and a changing enterprise. To regard it as self-evident or uncontroversial is to overlook its close relationship with the values of dominant social groups and with evolving social attitudes, such as the changing status of women and the resultant challenge to male-orientated values, and the complex changes in attitudes to intoxicants and the consequent rejection of drink-driving and hard drugs. How can the 'just deserts' approach lay down firm criteria for ordinal proportionality in such conditions of social flux? One response to this challenge would be to follow von Hirsch in seeking an overarching framework for the ranking of interests in society, which could then be adapted as a parameter for rating crimes.[39] This is an important line of enquiry, but it is necessarily at a high level of generality and needs to be supplemented by a more culturally specific examination of the values implicit in existing offence-ratings. Even in pluralist societies there are probably some shared values which are relevant to crime-seriousness,[40] and the task should be to build outwards from those shared values (or to propose some change) and to demonstrate the various implications of regarding certain crimes as more serious than others. This is a field in which social philosophers and criminologists must press forward with their work, not only developing critiques of the existing system but also constructing practical principles for alternative approaches.[41] Otherwise, judgments of ordinal proportionality will continue to be shaped by *ad hoc* political decisions and by the ideologies of dominant groups. The 'just deserts' approach has not yet travelled far enough in its elaboration of ordinal proportionality, but this is a general deficiency in theories of State punishment.[42]

(iii) A persistent problem

The effect of previous convictions on sentence remains an unsettled issue in the 'just deserts' approach. Does it require the sentence to be based on the current offence alone, or is it proper to take some account of previous convictions (reducing sentence for the first offender), and should all convictions count equally?[43] There is the consequential question, which straddles ordinal and cardinal proportionality, of the extent to which prior record should enhance the sentence where it is taken into account. How steeply should the sentence increase as the previous convictions multiply? Arguing that social disapproval of a first offence should be more muted than for second and subsequent offences, von Hirsch maintains that there should be 'primary but not exclusive emphasis on the current offence', so as to retain clear differentials between minor and serious crimes.[44] Nevertheless, the questions of how much of a reduction should be given for the first offence and what enhancements for subsequent offences do raise issues of cardinal proportionality, on which policy arguments come into play. One argument which is related to, but not necessarily integral to, the 'just deserts' approach is that non-minor offences of sex and violence should be placed higher than almost all property offences, even to the extent of ensuring that repeated property offenders are generally penalized on a lower scale than isolated crimes of sex and violence.[45] Another policy approach might be based on the findings of criminological research on the social effects of 'incapacitating' selected persistent offenders by imposing longer sentences on them. It has been claimed that policies of selective incapacitation may yield sufficient predictive validity and preventive efficacy to justify their pursuit, and some have argued for modifications of the 'just deserts' approach to allow limited departures which would capture some high-risk high-danger groups of offenders.[46] Departures of this kind challenge the philosophical underpinnings of 'just deserts', raising acute moral problems about relying on imperfect predictions which inevitably involve the subjection of some offenders to longer sentences without any social benefit by way of prevention. None the less, the prospect of some overall gains in crime prevention continues to lead some desert theorists to concede a limited role to incapacitative strategies.[47]

(iv) Unclear prescriptions about community sanctions

The supposed disadvantages of 'just deserts' so far discussed have been concerned with the severity levels of sanctions. In the same vein is the criticism that the practical application of 'just deserts' in some sentencing systems has led to a concentration of discussion on levels and bands of custodial sentences, with a relative neglect of non-custodial sentences. Neither this, nor the dearth of writings about a 'just deserts' approach to community sanctions, chimes well with the liberal refrain about reducing the severity of sentencing systems: there has been a failure to point the way for legislatures, sentencing commissions and judges. A significant step has now been taken by Wasik and von Hirsch in tackling the questions of justice and proportionality in non-custodial penalties—by discussing the ranking of these penalties in order of severity, examining the idea of grouping crimes in bands and allowing a limited choice among non-custodial measures within each band, and considering the various types of community sanction and the overall effect on the use of custody.[48] In this way the Achilles' heel of 'just deserts' in relation to the majority of sentencing dispositions (which are non-custodial) might be repaired.

(v) Non-sentencing and diversion

The 'just deserts' approach suggests that offenders should receive the proportionate sentence, no more and no less. Indeed, a lesser sentence might depreciate the seriousness with which the crime is viewed. Is this approach compatible with the growing use of selective non-prosecution in some countries?[49] Is diversion from prosecution, in the form of cautioning or other schemes, unjustifiable by reference to 'just deserts'? There is no necessary conflict between the practice and the theory. Formal cautioning and many other forms of diversion may be regarded as condemnatory to a degree, and they can be incorporated into a 'just deserts' approach by regarding them as proportionate responses to minor forms of lawbreaking or to offences of certain kinds by persons of low culpability. This requires clear and principled criteria for diversion, no less than for sentencing decisions.[50] So long as they form part of a system which reflects ordinal proportionality, diversion schemes can be regarded as a manifestation of a lowering (or at least a bifurcation) of cardinal proportionality.[51] The justifications for that policy, as mentioned under (i) above, can be found in penological arguments and not necessarily in 'just deserts' itself.

(vi) Neglect of the state's duty to care

Beneath some of the criticisms of the 'just deserts' approach to non-custodial penalties and to non-prosecution lies the deeper allegation that it is an uncaring approach towards offenders. It is charged with ignoring the causes of crime and with showing little interest in constructive ways of tackling crime. As a general line of criticism this somewhat misses the target: 'just deserts' is an approach to sentencing and not a set of prescriptions for the criminal justice system as a whole. It may be true that enthusiasm for 'just deserts' may have distracted attention from these wider and deeper issues, but that is a question of rectifying the balance of public discussion. The more specific line of criticism is that 'just deserts' has been at best equivocal about sentences which aim to treat the particular needs of certain offenders, such as probation orders. In fact, probation is not excluded from a 'just deserts' approach so long as it also constitutes a set of conditions and constraints imposed upon the offender for a stated duration. Indeed, in Wasik and von Hirsch's new model for non-custodial penalties the probation order would be an alternative measure for certain levels of offence, which could be invoked where there was 'particular reason to believe that this type of offender is potentially responsive'.[52] Thus the restrictions imposed on the sentencer and the conditions imposed on the probationer ensure that the former excesses of the rehabilitative approach to sentencing are avoided, whilst the actual selection of the measure and its real content may be distinctly oriented towards rehabilitation. Correctional agencies may continue their endeavour to devise effective treatment programmes for particular types of offender, thereby leaving some scope for those who support a revival of rehabilitation on the ground that it was condemned without ever having been properly tried.[53] It may be concluded, therefore, that treatment-oriented measures like probation *may* form part of a 'just deserts' sentencing system *if* there are sufficiently strong penological and social arguments in favour of them. One such argument may be connected with a humanitarian or paternalistic conception of the State as offering[54] treatment facilities to those who need and want them. Beyond that, there are empirical questions of the efficacy of the programmes, and the general constraints of proportionality imposed by a 'just deserts' approach.

Some advantages associated with 'just deserts'

In discussing some of the alleged disadvantages associated with the 'just deserts' approach it has been argued that the approach is concerned with the sentencing function and does not purport to supply a complete theory of criminal justice. It may therefore take its place in varying criminal justice systems, for it is an approach which does not of itself contain definite and integral arguments on cardinal proportionality, repeat offenders, crime prevention, and rehabilitation. Keeping in mind the elements of the theory set out in section 3 above, what are the advantages associated with the 'just deserts' approach in practice?

Coherence in the sentencing system

One of the benefits of the detailed discussions of sentencing which have taken place as part of the 'just deserts' movement is that the rules and principles of sentencing have been considered as a whole and as a system. Only where this has not taken place does one still find statements of sentencing objectives in the following mould—'there are four aims of sentencing: retribution, deterrence, reform, and incapacitation'—and usually recounted as if this is stating the obvious and needs no further discussion. In other words, the choice of aim is left largely to the sentencer in each case, and the choice of sentence is likely to vary accordingly.[55] This is sometimes referred to as the 'cafeteria' or 'smorgasbord' approach to sentencing, allowing the court to choose fairly freely among the available options. It is, of course, a prescription for sentencing anarchy. The claim of coherence cannot, however, be exclusive to the 'just deserts' approach. There could just as well be a coherent system based on deterrence. But the rise of 'just deserts' has undoubtedly served to focus attention on systematic structuring as an integral part of sentencing.

Consistent and principled sentencing

A sentencing system whose leading aim is 'just deserts' will promote certainty and consistency in the imposition of criminal penalties, features which not only recognize the right of each offender to equal concern and respect but also tend to enhance the public acceptability of a sentencing system (as compared with one which appears to be lottery, with no clear parameters). However, certainty and consistency can be bought at too high a price, and it may be argued that those sentencing systems which make the penalties mandatory or which confine courts narrowly succeed only in treating unequal cases equally. There is a need for some flexibility and discretion, but the discretion should be structured so that it is exercised in a principled manner. It is right that sentences should be chosen according to the seriousness of the offence and the record of the offender, but it is wrong that sentences should be chosen according to the personal predilections of the judge. It is right that sentencers should give effect to certain mitigating and aggravating factors, but it is wrong that they should be free to do so in a discriminatory way (e.g. on grounds of race, colour, religion, marital status, etc.).

Sentencing systems which allow wide discretion, without clear principles or an effective appellate system, permit both kinds of approach—the right and the wrong. One way of removing the wrong is to remove discretion entirely, but that also removes the right. As the mandatory and quasi-mandatory sentencing structures show, purging one form of injustice may lead to the creation of another. The solution is to structure the sentencing discretion according to stated standards, thereby ensuring that discretion is exercised according to legal principle while retaining judicial flexibility for cases whose combinations of facts do not fall within the guidelines or guiding principles.[56] By these means, judicial accountability is heightened and 'rule of law' values promoted. This is not to say that a sentencing system based on general deterrence could not achieve a similar structuring of discretion: it is merely that the theoretical framework of 'just deserts' and its close association with liberal 'rights' theories tend to guarantee the values of certainty, consistency, and accountability according to legal principle.

Public acceptability and comprehensibility

There is some evidence that a proportionality based sentencing system is more likely to meet public expectations: in a recent survey of public attitudes the most popular aim of sentencing was 'to give the offender what he deserves' (44 per cent of respondents). The same survey revealed widespread ignorance of the effect of parole on prison sentences.[57] Without suggesting that the function of judicial sentencing is to mirror public attitudes, it may be argued that there is likely to be greater public support for and confidence in a sentencing system which has clear benchmarks and which means what it says.[58] Thus the spread of 'just deserts' has been associated with the decline of parole and moves towards 'real time' sentencing, developments which may be regarded as natural concomitant of an approach whereby the proportionate sentence is calculated at the outset, not to be subverted by decisions taken at later stages which alter the effective sentence length.[59] However, it may be argued that parole is not necessarily excluded by adherence to a 'just deserts' approach, since it could be allowed to operate within overall proportionality constraints if the penological arguments were thought to be strong enough.

The development of hybrid systems

Despite the increased emphasis on the coherence of sentencing aims, some recent reforms have ducked the issue. The United States Sentencing

Commission constructed its guidelines from past sentencing practice (with modifications) and failed to indicate a priority of aims which might guide judges in exercising their discretion and thereby restrain them from pursuing personal preferences.[60] The Commission stated that 'in most sentencing decisions both philosophies [*viz.* 'just deserts' and crime control] may prove consistent with the same result.'[61] Some would wish to argue against this, others would question whether 'most' is enough in the context of thoroughgoing sentencing reform. But the undercurrents, here and elsewhere, are probably that many people involved in sentencing reform are conscious of the need to satisfy both political and judicial constituencies, and wish to 'hedge their bets' by allowing various aims of sentencing to play a part in shaping a new system. The key difference lies between an orderly plurality of sentencing aims on the one hand, and the kind of sentencing anarchy which is encouraged by statements in the form of 'there are four aims of sentencing . . .' on the other hand.

What is meant by an orderly plurality of sentencing aims?[62] In practice, it means that a number of different sentencing aims can be accommodated by adopting one of two methods. The first method is to declare a primary aim and then to delineate other classes of case in which different aims may prevail. An example of this might be the new Swedish sentencing law, which proclaims 'just deserts' as its leading aim but allows the pursuit of other aims for certain offences and for certain offenders, as defined in the law.[63] A second method is to stipulate a rank order of sentencing aims, giving clear guidance to courts in cases where the aims conflict. Recent years have seen a growing interest among scholars in the construction of coherent 'hybrid' models of sentencing, notably that of Paul Robinson.[64] Exploratory work of this kind indicates that those who accept the arguments of the 'just deserts' approach for the general orientation of the sentencing system, but feel that there are spheres in which either incapacitative or rehabilitative principles should be allowed to take precedence (usually, only where the empirical evidence is strong enough to justify them), should not regard it as necessary to argue against the values of certainty, consistency, and accountability which are embodied in the 'just deserts' approach. Those values can still be secured through a hybrid system, at least to a high degree.

Sentencing and criminal justice policy

We have seen that there are both procedural and substantive merits in each sentencing system having a coherent set of aims. It remains to consider sentencing in the wider context of criminal justice and society's response to lawbreaking. It was argued earlier[65] that so few of the offences committed each year result in a court sentence that sentencing has a severely limited capacity for influencing crime rates, even if it were thought proper to allow such preventive considerations to enter into calculations of sentence (which it is not, on a 'just deserts' approach, save in the sense of underlying deterrence). But sentencing is by no means the only opportunity which the State has for influencing the frequency and patterns of crime. Moreover, there are strong arguments for maintaining that the State has a duty to prevent crime and a duty to provide proper assistance for the victims of crime. The latter duty is receiving increasing recognition: for example, the European Convention on the Compensation of Victims of Violent Crimes (1984) establishes (within limits) a State duty to provide compensation to the victims of violent crime. Among the possible arguments for such a State duty is the theory 'that the State is bound to compensate the victim because it has failed to prevent the crime by means of effective criminal policy, or it introduced criminal policy measures which failed, or, having prohibited personal vengeance, it is bound to appease the victim or his dependants'.[66] One does not need to accept the whole of this 'principle of State responsibility for crime' in order to support the duty to provide compensation and support.[67] But there is an important distinction between proper support, services and compensation for crime victims, which have been neglected for too long as the responsibilities of the State, and the involvement of victims in decisions on prosecution and sentence, which ignores the 'public' element in the criminal law and sentencing and which would re-introduce into sentencing a fresh course of inconsistency in aims and practice.[68] Victims should indeed make their views known when the decisions on ordinal and cardinal proportionality are being taken in relation to a sentencing system, as should all sections of the community. But the views of a particular victim should have no special status in relation to the prosecution or sentencing of a particular person.

When one considers the policies necessary to carry through the State's duty to provide proper support and services for victims, the question of the State's role in the prevention of crime soon arises. It would be absurd for a government to provide support and compensation for victims without giving serious consideration to strategies for crime prevention, which could be expected to reduce the number of persons who become victims (and, of course, the number who become offenders). Crime prevention has received a great deal of criminological attention in recent years, particularly at the request of governments, and it is too large and politically volatile a subject to treat adequately here. There are, for example, various initiatives in situational crime prevention which attempt to limit the opportunities for offending or successful offending by the design of buildings and vehicles, by target-hardening, by increased surveillance, etc.[69] There are also initiatives in social crime prevention, such as that led by the French *Conseil National de Prévention de la Délinquance*, which attempt to provide wider social programmes aimed at groups likely to become lawbreakers.[70] The political implications of social crime prevention run deep, especially for those who reject the idea that the policies of a government on housing, employment, and public amenities have an influence on the volume of crime. However, if policies are available which suggest that fewer persons need become victims and fewer need become offenders, there is surely a heavy burden on a government to give serious consideration to such policies.[71] Thus, one answer to those who complain that it is impossible to propound a 'just deserts' approach to sentencing in the context of a fundamentally unjust society is that they misunderstand the function of sentencing. It should not be, and cannot be, a primary instrument of social reform. Sentencing is a public quantification of the individual offender's blameworthiness, determined according to acceptable standards of proportionality.[72] Sentencing should avoid discrimination on grounds of race, colour, wealth, employment status, and so on; but even criminal justice policy as a whole cannot be expected to bring about social reforms, although it can contribute to them. The remedy for an unjust society lies in social and economic policy; the criminal justice system can pursue more specific policies with concordant aims; and sentencing, with its symbolic condemnatory function and its limited instrumental capacity, should be designed to achieve fairness and proportionality within the given social value structure.[73]

Closely connected with this is another criticism of 'just deserts', already adumbrated above.[74] It is that the ideology of 'just deserts' has been used by some to legitimize repressive sentencing policies which focus on high sentences as the means to prevent crime and neglect other preventive and social approaches.[75] This is not necessarily a criticism of the 'just deserts' approach to sentencing: the argument against repressive sentencing policies is a penological and political one,[76] and the argument about the limited preventive scope of sentencing is criminological.[77] Those who are liberals and who embrace 'just deserts' must therefore give greater prominence to these other arguments if they are to prevent their formal principles being held 'guilty by association' with repressive forces in criminal justice.

Conclusions

This article has touched briefly on a wide range of issues, from which three main points emerge.

First, crime prevention and public protection neither should be nor can be regarded as aims of the sentencing system, except in the sense that the existence of the institution of judicial sentencing serves as an underlying general deterrent. Crime prevention should be accepted as a responsibility of the State, to be pursued through criminal justice policies (in accordance with wider social policy) rather than through sentencing. In dealing with individual offenders, the sentencing system should concentrate on proportionality and fairness.

Secondly, the 'just deserts' approach cannot provide and does not purport to provide answers to all the key issues which a sentencing system must determine. At various points it is necessary to resort to criminological, penological, and other policy arguments on questions relating to cardinal proportionality (e.g. setting the overall penalty levels, deciding on the place of non-prosecution and diversion, and determining the treatment of prior record), and there is also more work to be done on criteria for ordinal proportionality. In general, however, the 'just deserts' approach provides a fairly clear framework within which the allocation of sentences can be decided consistently and comprehensibly, with due regard for the rights of all members of society, including the offender.

Thirdly, even where a system pursues a plurality of aims rather than a single aim, it is essential that the various aims be either ranked in order of priority or confined to distinct spheres of application. Any system which allows courts to choose among sentencing aims without clear guidance will produce disorganization, with scant respect for consistency, accountability, or rights.

Notes

An earlier version was delivered at the conference of the Society for the Reform of Criminal Law, on 'Sentencing, Parole and Early Release', Ottawa, August 1988.

1. See Andrew von Hirsch and Nils Jareborg, 'Sweden's Sentencing Statute Enacted', [1989] Crim. L.R. 275.
2. United States Sentencing Commission, *Sentencing Guidelines and Police Statements* (3 April 1987); for a summary, see [1978] Crim. L.R. 593.
3. See the review by Michael Tonry in ch. 2 of *The Sentencing Commission and its Guidelines*, by A. von Hirsch, K. Knapp, and M. Tonry (Northeastern UP, 1987).

4. Canadian Sentencing Commission, *Sentencing Reform: A Canadian Approach* (1987); for a summary, see [1987] Crim. L.R. 353.

5. Report of the Victorian Sentencing Committee, *Sentencing* (Attorney-General's Department, Melbourne, 1988); for a summary, see [1988] Crim. L.R. 785.

6. Law Reform Commission of Australia, *Sentencing*, Report no. 44 (Canberra, 1988); for a summary, see [1988] Crim. L.R. 786.

7. Cf. Canadian Sentencing Commission (1987), 108–17, preferring to avoid the word 'punishment' and highlighting the question of the *degree* of censure.

8. The Canadian Sentencing Commission were rightly sceptical of this concept of 'public protection': op. cit. 148.

9. For an excellent discussion in the English context, see M. Hough and P. Mayhew, *Taking Account of Crime: Key Findings from the 1984 British Crime Survey*, Home Office Research Study No. 85 (HMSO 1985), 1–18.

10. A formal caution is administered by the police as an alternative to prosecution. The practice has no statutory basis, but the greater use of formal cautions was encouraged by a Home Office circular to chief officers of police in 1985 (HOC No. 14/85). The result has been an increase in the cautioning rate (i.e. the proportion of all persons cautioned or prosecuted who were cautioned) from 55 to 66 per cent of male juvenile offenders and from 5 to 12 per cent of male offenders aged 17 and over, between 1984 and 1987: *Criminal Statistics, England and Wales 1987* (Cm. 498 of 1988), Table 5.5.

11. Canadian Sentencing Commission (1987), 119, citing Ashworth, 'Criminal Justice, Rights and Sentencing: A Review of Sentencing Policy and Problems', in *Sentencing in Australia*, I. Potas (ed.) (Australian Institute of Criminology, Proceedings No. 12, Canberra, 1987).

12. See, for example, J. Lea and J. Young, *What is to be Done about Law and Order?* (Penguin, 1984), and T. Jones, B. Maclean, and J. Young, *The Islington Crime Survey* (Gower, 1986).

13. See n. 21 below and accompanying text.

14. See generally F. Zimring and G. Hawkins, *Deterrence: The Legal Threat in Crime Control* (Chicago, 1973) and D. Beyleveld, *A Bibliography on General Deterrence Research* (Saxon House, 1980); cf. the resurgence of deterrent arguments as part of 'optimal penalty theory' among economists.

15. Notably Andrew von Hirsch in *Doing Justice* (Hill and Wang, 1976), *Past or Future Crimes* (Rutgers University Press 1985, Manchester University Press 1986), and 'Deservedness and Dangerousness in Sentencing Policy', [1986] Crim. L.R. 79.

16. R. Martinson, 'What Works? Questions and Answers about Prison Reform' (1974), *Public Interest*, Spring, 22 f. For some reconsideration, see R. Martinson, 'New Findings, New Views' (1979) 7 *Hofstra Law Review* 243, and F. Cullen and K. Gilbert, *Reaffirming Rehabilitation* (Anderson 1982), 112 and 171–8.

17. The favourite judicial anecdote in England is still the 'exemplary sentences' passed on certain participants in the 1958 Notting Hill race riots, despite the doubts raised about 'cause and effect' in this case (see e.g. Ashworth, *Sentencing and Penal Policy* (1983), 344–5), and despite the evident ineffectiveness of similar 'exemplary sentences' in Birmingham in 1973 (see R. Baxter and C. Nuttall, 'Severe Sentences: No Deterrent to Crime?' (1975), *New Society*, 11–13).

18. See n. 14 above; for particular studies, see L. Ross, *Deterring the Drinking Driver: Legal Policy and Social Control* (Lexington, 1982) and D. Riley, 'Drinking Drivers: the Limits to Deterrence'' (1985) 24 *Howard Journal of Criminal Justice*, 241–56.

19. Notably R. Dworkin, *Taking Rights Seriously* (Duckworth, 1977), applied to criminal justice by D. A. J. Richards, 'Rights, Utility and Crime' in *Crime and Justice: An Annual Review* (M. Tonry and N. Morris (eds.), Chicago, 1981).

20. See A. E. Bottoms and R. Brownsword, 'Dangerousness and Rights' in J. Hinton (ed.), *Dangerousness: Problems of Assessment and Prediction* (Allen and Unwin, 1983).

21. For a Swedish discussion written in English, see Nils Jareborg's 'The Coherence of the Penal System' and 'Disparity in Sentencing' in his *Essays in Criminal Law* (Iustus Forlag, Uppsala, 1988).

22. von Hirsch (1985), 48.

23. Ibid. 49 and 52.

24. Ibid. 52. Compare the scepticism of Nicola Lacey, *State Punishment: Political Principles and Community Values* (Routledge, 1988), arguing against the 'mystery' of retributivism on the grounds, e.g. that 'a judgment that someone has behaved wrongly does not involve or justify the further judgment that they should be punished' (p. 21), with the defence by Michael S. Moore, 'The Moral Worth of Retribution', in *Responsibility, Character and the Emotions* (F. Schoeman (ed.), Cambridge, 1987), arguing, e.g. that the rendering of justice can itself be the good which justifies punishment (pp. 186–7).

25. von Hirsch (1985), 40.

26. Ibid. 36.

27. Ibid. 64 and generally chap. 6.

28. Ibid. 43–6. In this country sentence levels are now much higher than they were earlier in the century, whereas in the Netherlands sentence levels have been substantially lowered since the 1950s: see David Downes, *Contrasts in Tolerance* (Oxford, 1988).

29. von Hirsh (1985), 44.

30. Ibid, chap. 8.

31. See, for example, ibid. 11.

32. See M. Tonry, *Sentencing Reform Impacts* (National Institute of Justice, Washington, 1987), 4 and *passim*.

33. See, e.g. A. Blumstein, J. Cohen, and D. Nagin, *Deterrence and Incapacitation*, National Academy of Sciences, 1978, and above, n. 14.

34. See above, n. 22 and accompanying text.

35. Cf. the introduction to the 1978 edition of T. Sellin and M. Wolfgang, *The Measurement of Delinquency*, and the work of Rossi and associates, of which a recent example is 'Beyond Crime Seriousness: Fitting the Punishment to the Crime' (1985), *J. Quantitative Criminology*, 59.

36. von Hirsh reports that judgments of ordinal proportionality caused no controversy during the introduction of new sentencing guidelines in various American states: op. cit. (1985), 64.

37. Compare the report of the Road Traffic Law Review (HMSO, 1988), chap. 6, which takes some account of resulting harm, with Ashworth, 'Criminal Attempts and the Role of Resulting Harm under the Code and in the Common Law' (1988) 19 Rutgers L.J. 725–72.

38. For references, see Ashworth, *Sentencing and Penal Policy* (1983), 173–81.

39. von Hirsch (1985), chap. 6.

40. P. Rock, 'The Sociology of Deviancy and Conceptions of Moral Order,' (1974) 14 B.J. Crim. 139–51.

41. It would be a field for what Nicola Lacey terms 'the principle of consistent pluralism': *State Punishment*, 117–18.

42. Cf. the conclusions of Nicola Lacey, ibid. 193–8.

43. Compare von Hirsch (1985), chap. 7 with G. P. Fletcher, *Rethinking Criminal Law* (Boston, 1978), 460–6 and R. Singer, *Just Deserts: Sentencing Based on Equality and Desert* (Ballinger, 1979). Cf. M. Wasik, 'Guidance, Guidelines and Criminal Record', in *Sentencing Reform* (eds. K. Pease and M. Wasik, 1987).

44. von Hirsch (1985), 78 and 86–7.

45. See chap. 5 of A. von Hirsch, K. Knapp, and M. Tonry, *The Sentencing Commission and its Guidelines* (Northeastern, 1987), discussing the Minnesota choice of this approach.

46. For two different attempts to develop modified models of this kind, see J. Monahan, 'The Case for Prediction in the Modified Desert Model of Sentencing' (1982) 5 Int. J. Law and Psychiatry 103–13, and N. Morris and M. Miller, 'Predictions of Dangerousness' in *Crime and Justice: An Annual Review*, 6 (Chicago, 1986).

47. See the discussion of selective incapacitation by von Hirsch (1985), chaps. 9–12. In chap. 13 he expresses a willingness to permit 'categorial incapacitation' within the limits set by ordinal proportionality.

48. M. Wasik and A. von Hirsch, 'Non-Custodial Penalties and the Principles of Desert', [1988] Crim. L.R. 555; cf. also A. Freiberg and R. Fox, 'Sentencing Structures and Sanction Hierarchies', in *Sentencing in Australia* (Canberra, 1987).

49. In England and Wales, for example, the proportionate use of formal police cautions has increased (see n. 10, above). See, generally, P. Tak, *The Legal Scope of Non-Prosecution in Europe* (Helsinki Institute for Crime Prevention and Control, 1986).

50. See D. J. Galligan, 'Regulating Pre-Trial Decisions', in *Criminal Law and Criminal Justice*, I. Dennis (ed.) (Sweet & Maxwell, 1987); A. Ashworth, 'The "Public Interest" Element in Prosecutions' [1987] Crim. L.R. 595–607.

51. By 'bifurcation' I refer to the tendency to increase the severity of penalties for the most serious crimes whilst lowering severity for the least serious: the notion was given currency by A. E. Bottoms as part of his argument in 'Reflections on the Renaissance of Dangerousness' (1977) XVI *Howard Journal*, at 88.

52. [1988] Crim. L.R. at 569.

53. For this and other revivalist arguments, see F. Cullen and K. Gilbert (above, n. 16).

54. To compel treatment would be incompatible with the 'rights' philosophies associated with the 'just deserts' approach: treatment facilities should therefore be offered, in addition to the compulsory requirements of the sentence: see A. Bottoms and W. McWilliams, 'A Non-Treatment Paradigm for Probation' (1979), *British Journal of Social Work*, 159, and Nicola Lacey (above, n. 22), 30–2.

55. Little better than this are those common law cases on sentencing which refer to 'balancing' the various aims or achieving an 'instinctive synthesis' of them in each case, whilst articulating no clear priorities; e.g. the Australian case of *Williscroft* [1975] V.R. 292, at 299–300.

56. For a valuable recent study, see Galligan, *Discretionary Powers* (Oxford, 1986).

57. Nigel Walker and Mike Hough, *Public Attitudes to Sentencing* (Gower 1988), 185–6—a carefully constructed survey with carefully circumscribed results.

58. This is a major theme of the parole reforms proposed by the Parole System Review (chairman, Lord Carlisle), Cm. 532 of 1988, summarized at [1989] Crim. L.R. 81.

59. See A. von Hirsch and K. Hanrahan, *The Question of Parole: Retention, Reform or Abolition?* (Ballinger 1979), and Canadian Sentencing Commission (1987), 242–5.

60. One might argue that, within limits, it is no less inconsistent with 'just deserts' than the modifications for 'categorial incapacitation' discussed by von Hirsch (1985, chap. 13), and for probation as discussed by Wasik and von Hirsch (1988). However, parole decision-making would have to be fair and open.

61. United States Sentencing Commission, *Sentencing Guidelines and Policy Statements* (13 Apr. 1987), 1.4. For a critique see A. von Hirsch, *Federal Sentencing Guidelines: The United States and Canadian Schemes Compared*, Center for Research in Crime and Justice, New York University School of Law, Occasional Paper IV (1988).

62. See the valuable early discussion by Galligan, [1981] Crim. L.R. 297–311.

63. For example, the new s.30(7) and 30(8) of the Swedish Penal Code allow individualization and rehabilitation as aims when deciding, in a limited group of

cases, between probation and conditional discharge: see [1989] Crim. L.R. 280–1.

64. Paul H. Robinson, 'Hybrid Principles for the Distribution of Criminal Sanctions', (1987) 82 Northwestern U.L.R. 19–42, with commentaries by A. Blumstein, S. Stier, A. von Hirsch, and F. Zimring. See also the articles in n. 46 and M. Tonry, 'Prediction and Classification: Legal and Ethical Issues' in *Crime and Justice: An Annual Review* (Chicago, 1987), 367–413.

65. See n. 11 above, and associated text.

66. Council of Europe, *Explanatory report on the European Convention on the Compensation of Victims of Violent Crimes* (Strasbourg, 1984), 8–9.

67. Cf. Ashworth, 'Punishment and Compensation: Victims, Offenders and the State,' (1986) 6 Oxford J.L.S., 86–122. The text here is not to imply that *only* the state should undertake victim support.

68. Nils Christie, 'Conflicts as Property' (1977) 27 B.J. Crim. 1–15, criticized by Ashworth (above, n. 67). The issue of 'victim impact statements' hovers on the borderline.

69. For an excellent discussion, see Ronald V. Clarke, 'Situational Crime Prevention: its Theoretical Basis and Practical Scope', *Crime and Justice: An Annual Review* (1983, Chicago), 225–56.

70. See Michael King, *How to make Social Crime Prevention work: The French Experience* (NACRO, London, 1988), and comment at [1988] Crim. L.R. 197.

71. The full argument here would point out the need to consider conflicting social policies and needs, and to examine the crime rate in relation to (for example) accident rates.

72. On which see sections (i) and (ii) above.

73. Cf. the powerful argument for integrating sentencing and criminal justice into wider social programmes in Lacey, *State Punishment*, chap. 8.

74. In section (i), at n. 32.

75. e.g. Barbara Hudson, *Justice through Punishment: A Critique of the 'Justice' Model of Corrections* (Macmillan, 1987), 164.

76. See nn. 33 and 34 above, and associated text.

77. See n. 11 above, and associated text.

Criminal Justice Ideologies and Practices in Different Voices: Some Feminist Questions about Justice

KATHLEEN DALY

Introduction

This is what I mean by two voices, two ways of speaking. One voice speaks about equality, reciprocity, fairness, rights; one voice speaks about connection, not hurting, care, and response. My point is that these voices are in tension with each other. In my work I have attempted to ask, 'What does it mean to include both voices in defining the domain of morality, of humanity, and so forth?' (Gilligan in Marcus *et al*. 1985: 44).

Carol Gilligan's different voice construct has been influential in rethinking legal education, theory, and practice (see, for example: Marcus *et al.* 1985; Menkel-Meadow 1985; Finley 1986; West 1988). Feminist legal scholars argue that the voice of law and legal practice is 'male', although this voice is construed as representing a gender-neutral stance. In the male voice, moral problems are defined as problems of inequality, and these problems are resolved using justice reasoning, which contains values of individual rights, autonomy, and impartiality. The alternative, or 'female voice', sees the male values of detachment and objectivity in justice reasoning as the moral problem, and gives more emphasis to the values of care, responsibility, and connection in resolving moral dilemmas. In this essay, I analyse how the 'logic of justice' and 'ethic of care', which Gilligan associates with the male and female voices, respectively, apply to ideologies and practices in the US and other criminal justice systems.[1]

Although Gilligan asks, 'What would it mean to include both voices in defining the domain of morality?', I suggest that these voices have been in tension and have defined the domain of morality as it has been constructed in criminal law and applied to those accused and convicted of criminal wrongdoing. My argument advances two points. First, Gilligan's

An earlier version of this paper was presented at the American Society of Criminology Annual Meeting, Montreal, November 1987.

formulation offers yet another way to contrast two modes of responding to crime: (*a*) a depersonalized response based on a wrongdoer's harm to others and culpability (the logic of justice), and (*b*) a personalized response based on a wrongdoer's potential for reform and integration into a community (the ethic of care). The former is concerned with fair punishment, defined as a response in proportion to different degrees of harm and victimization suffered by others; uniformity and consistency are valued in a system of justice where 'like crimes' are punished the same. The latter is concerned with changing or reforming individuals; thus, an individualized response to their needs and potential necessitates a system of justice where 'like crimes' are punished differently. In short, Gilligan's formulation recapitulates debates in criminology and legal philosophy over the aims and purposes of punishment, e.g. deterrence and retribution versus rehabilitation, punishment as deprivation versus treatment, and the respective emphases of classical jurisprudence and positive criminology.

My second point is that, although the voice construct can be used to contrast ideologies of punishment, it fails to portray the ways in which criminal law is interpreted and applied. The relational, contextual, and concrete reasoning which Gilligan associates with the female voice *is* the voice of criminal justice practices. When court officials define crime and impose sanctions, they use relational reasoning and an ethic of care towards defendants in these ways: not criminalizing some offences and not wanting to impose a sentence that punishes others who are tied to the defendant. This female voice may not contain the same relational concerns that women (or feminists) desire, but that is different from saying that men's form of legal reasoning does not contain relational, caretaking, or responsibility concerns. Thus, the problem in criminal-court practices is not that the female voice is absent, but that certain relations are presupposed, maintained, and reproduced.

The impetus for this essay stems from several concerns. First, I want to challenge the association of justice reasoning as male or masculine and care reasoning as female or feminine in the context of criminal law and practice. Not only is this gender-linked association inaccurate, it misleads us to think a ready alternative to men's forms of criminal law and justice practices can be found by adding women's voice or econstituting the system along the lines of an ethic of care. Second, feminist critiques of criminal law and justice practices have paid much greater attention to women victims than women defendants; consequently, questions of justice from a victim's standpoint have been raised more

often than questions of justice for women (or men) accused and convicted of crime. Both must be considered; otherwise, a repressive agenda
will result. Finally, in canvassing feminist scholarship for ways to rethink
the problem of justice for men and women accused of crime, I find little
guidance. However, I draw from Harris (1987), Heidensohn (1986),
Lahey (1985), and Olsen (1984) in speculating about possibilities.

My essay is organized in three parts. In the first, I outline Gilligan's
thesis, give a flavour of its impact on the US academy, and offer a re-reading germane to my argument. The second part traces shifts in penal philosophy and current efforts to implement sentencing reform. The last
part considers problems in outlining a feminist conception of justice, and
cautions against a naïve embrace with an ethic of care.

Gilligan's ideas and the Gilligan phenomenon

Gilligan's book *In a Different Voice* was published in 1982; the volume of
response it received in many academic fields, as well as in the media,
show that she touched a raw cultural nerve. Special issues of journals,
books, fora, commentary, and critique followed (e.g. Nails *et al.* 1983;
Auerbach *et al.* 1985; Marcus *et al.* 1985; Kerber *et al.* 1986; Kittay and
Meyers 1987), together with empirical tests [see literature reviews in
Tronto (1987) and Furby (1987)]. What did Gilligan say that sparked such
interest and attention? She made two related claims. First, she argued
that Lawrence Kohlberg's theory of moral development—a major theory
in psychology—contained a masculinist bias. Struck by empirical findings
that girls were apparently arrested at a lower stage of moral development
than boys, as measured by Kohlberg's six-stage theory of cognitive development, Gilligan found that women's moral reasoning was not inferior,
but rather guided by different considerations not tapped in Kohlberg's
scheme. Second, she described the elements of this different moral
voice—terming it an ethic of care—and distinguished it from an ethic of
justice, which stood at the top of Kohlberg's hierarchy of moral development. The former centres on moral concepts of responsibility and relationship; it is a concrete and active morality. The latter centres on moral
concepts of rights and rules; it is a formal, universalizing and abstract
morality. Gilligan argued that the moral domain should include care and
justice, but because these moral orientations were gender linked,
women's voice was drowned out or misheard as morally inferior or
immature in comparison to men's.

Critiques of Gilligan's thesis have focused on whether these two moral orientations are in fact gender linked, whether the voice construct offers anything new for moral psychology and philosophy, and whether the ethic of care is a moral viewpoint articulated by subordinate groups, not just women; critics also pointed to methodological and interpretive weaknesses, and the lack of historical and cultural perspective (in addition to the contributors in the works cited above, see Lugones and Spelman (1983) and MacKinnon (1987)). However, Gilligan's ideas remain influential. This can be explained, in part, by a historical moment in US feminist thought and popular culture: difference discourse is in the air, and women apparently have something men do not—not simply a different, but perhaps superior, moral orientation. Other elements explaining the Gilligan phenomenon include the ambiguity of her argument (she simultaneously suggests that 'the different voice is characterized not by gender but theme' (Gilligan 1982: 2), but argues that women's moral development follows a different path than men's), her accessible prose (she uses myths, stories, and is herself a good storyteller), her critique of androcentric theory, and a set of arguments and empirical materials open to many readings depending on one's disciplinary interests. I shall consider the examples she gives of the logic of justice and the ethic of care from the perspective of criminal law and justice practices.

Jake and Amy

The most frequently cited illustration of the different voice construct is Gilligan's (1982: 24–39) analysis of how two 11-year-olds, Jake and Amy, reacted to the Heinz dilemma. The Heinz dilemma poses this situation: Heinz is a man whose wife is dying, but he is without the necessary money to purchase medicine for his wife that could save her life, and the druggist will not lower the price of the medicine. The question is: 'Should Heinz steal the drug?'[2] Jake's response is that Heinz should steal; even if he is caught, 'the judge will probably think it was the right thing to do' and 'the judge should give Heinz the lightest possible sentence'. Amy is more uncertain about what Heinz should do because, as Menkel-Meadow (1985: 46) says, she acts like a 'bad' law student and 'fights the hypo'. Amy is troubled by the druggist's failure to respond to the wife's need for the drug, and tries to resolve the dilemma by saying the druggist should understand the consequences of refusing to give the drug to Heinz.

Gilligan interprets Jake's resolution to the moral dilemma as reflecting the logic of justice in which life takes priority over property, and conflict over competing claims of individuals can be mediated through systems of law and logic. She interprets Amy's resolution as reflecting an ethic of care in which the maintenance of a network of relationships is central and the different needs (rather than rights) of individuals can be accommodated through communication and negotiation. Although Gilligan believes that Amy's response is as mature as Jake's, the Kohlberg scoring system would have placed Jake at a higher level of moral maturity.

I pause to consider Gilligan's justice and care terminology because it can be confusing. Justice is used in a broad sense to encompass matters of law and legal practice, which by inference do not embrace the care domain; but it is also used in a narrow sense to mean a particular set of justice standards, i.e. principles of objective and impartial treatment (see Furby 1987: 170; Cohen 1987). But this confusion reveals a core assumption in Gilligan's identification of a justice or care response to moral dilemmas (whether real or artificial). She invokes justice reasoning to describe those who think it necessary or acceptable to seek a third party (e.g. a legal or other authority) to settle a dispute, but she invokes care reasoning for those who try to resolve disputes between the parties without recourse to another (perhaps more impartial) third-party authority.

A re-reading of Jake's and Amy's response to the Heinz dilemma suggests that while Jake assumes that the judge will not view the theft as criminal because the motivation for the theft was to sustain life, Amy is uncertain of what will happen in court. She distrusts the judge and the legal process, and therefore seeks a solution that avoids the need for Heinz to break the law and consequently to be subject to criminal proceedings and perhaps unfair punishment. Jake's surmise of how the judge will interpret Heinz's act—not a criminal act, and thus with compassion and leniency—is probably how a judge would respond to the case. Thus, unlike Amy, Jake assumes that the judge will consider Heinz's responsibilities to his wife, as well as the context and motive that spawned Heinz's act—a reasoning pattern not in the male, but female voice. Amy's response reveals distrust and *naïveté* about law and legal processes, though a more radical reading is possible. If the world were ordered on Amy's terms, perhaps the need or desire to steal would be reduced, or perhaps the druggist (not Heinz) would be seen to be in the wrong. But in the current economic order, criminal law is not founded on this view of property.

Gilligan's reformulation of care and justice

In a more recent essay, Gilligan (1987: 24) attempts to clarify 'care as understood . . . within a justice framework and care as a framework or perspective on moral orientation', by suggesting that

Within the justice construction, care becomes the mercy that tempers justice . . . a decision to modulate the strict demands of justice by considering equity or show-ing forgiveness . . . [But] these interpretations of care leave the basic assumptions of a justice framework intact. . . . As a moral perspective, care is less well elabo-rated, and there is no ready vocabulary in moral theory to describe its terms.

She continues by saying that 'justice in [the context of a care perspective] becomes understood as respect for people on their own terms' rather than assuming 'one set of terms' (p. 25). What then does Gilligan make of criminal law and justice practices? Like Amy, Gilligan is distrustful and uncertain. The one set of rules may not allow for alternative interpreta-tions; and although a person detached from a conflict (e.g. a judge or other third party) can 'weigh evidence in an even-handed manner' and seek grounds for agreement, such 'detachment is *the* moral problem' from a care perspective (p. 31).

TABLE 1. *Justice and care in the state response to crime*

	Ethic of care	Logic of justice
Aims of punishment	Rehabilitation, special deterrence	Retribution, general deterrence
Decision criterion	Forward-looking (based on a prediction of future behaviour)	Backward looking (based on the offence committed)
Ideological elements	Equity, fairness, rationality (formal and substantive equality)	Equality, fairness, rationality (formal equality)
Prescriptive practices	Tailor the sentence to the crime and to offender characteristics; personalize sentencing	Equal treatment for those convicted of the same offence; depersonalize sentencing
Social unit of punishment	Family based; a person in relation to others	Individual based; a person not connected to others
Consequence	Variable punishment of individuals depending on their potential for reform	Equal punishment of individuals based on the crime charged and prior record
Concept of justice	Procedural and substantive equality, though greater emphasis on the latter	Emphasis on procedural equality
Sentencing scheme	Individualized	Just deserts

Drawing from Glaspell's (1917) classic short story, *A Jury of Her Peers*, Gilligan (p. 31) offers this interpretation of Mrs Hale's and Mrs Peters's decision to hide evidence that would convict Minnie Foster for the mur-der of her husband:

[T]he women solve the crime by attachment—by joining together. . . . In [removing the evidence], they separate themselves from a legal system in which they have no voice but also no way of voicing what they have come to understand. In choosing to connect themselves with one another and with Minnie, they separate themselves from the law that would use their understanding and their knowledge as grounds for further separation and killing.

Although Gilligan's (and Glaspell's) point is that law fashioned and interpreted by men cannot understand women's experience and knowledge, Gilligan implies here and elsewhere that *any* system of rules (even perhaps those fashioned and interpreted by women?) to settle disputes or to censure or punish harms to others will, by definition, fall in the justice domain. The ethic of care appears to have no place in law and legal practice, except as Gilligan suggests above, as subsumed within a justice framework.

Justice and care in the state response to crime

I lift the restrictions Gilligan imposes on justice and care as residing in the public and private domains, respectively. I want to recast justice and care as models by which the state responds to wrongdoing through the criminal law, the adjudication of crime, and the sanctioning process. The elements associated with each are shown in Table 1. Although this contrast is developed from the US criminal justice system, it is not peculiar to that system, as I discuss later. Obviously, these models are caricatures because neither exists (or has existed) in pure form. Depending on the case, judge, and court jurisdiction, more or less emphasis will be given to the elements associated with each. However, these models encapsulate different criminal justice ideologies, or what Garland (1985: 26) terms the 'official representation of penality'.

In the care model, the response to wrongdoing emphasizes varying sanctions by the particulars of an incident and the defendant's relations to others, though like crimes and persons may be punished the same; the rehabilitative aim is concerned with helping the defendant by strengthening his or her commitment to law-abiding behaviour and by maintaining ties to others. In the justice model, the response to wrongdoing is backward-looking, its guiding principle is that crime should not go unpunished; retribution (or censure) for crime is tied to a general deterrence aim of punishment (that is, putting others on notice that crime will not go unpunished may deter crime); little attention is given to the defendant's personal circumstances, ties to other, or potential for reform because the aim is to punish like crimes the same. While the justice model is concerned with aggregate and depersonalized justice, the care model is concerned with individualized and personalized justice.

The justice and care models can be associated with the 'just deserts' and 'individualized' sentencing schemes, respectively. Although common to each are values of fairness and rationality, there is an in-built contradiction in the care model which the justice model attempts to remove. Specifically, in an individualized sentencing scheme, like crimes and persons may be punished the same (procedural equality) or like crimes and persons may be punished differently (outcome or substantive equality), even if the latter is more pronounced. In a just-deserts sentencing scheme, however, fairness is predicated on punishing like crimes the same and in proportion to their harm.[3]

Criminal justice ideologies in historical perspective

I apply the justice-care schematic to shifts in penal philosophy in the US and England, although in broad outlines, it resonates with shifts in other western nations (see e.g. Radzinowicz and Hood 1979: 1327). In the last quarter of the nineteenth century in the US, a new penology emerged which sought to individualize punishment by introducing indeterminate sentences. The theory was that persons could be rehabilitated in prison, or under the guidance of a probation officer outside a prison setting, but that the time frame for rehabilitation should vary depending on a person's 'own exertions' (Walker 1980: 86). Associated with the rise of the new penology was the development of different institutions and programmes for men and women, and for adults and juveniles, together with sex- and age-based sentencing schemes and legal jurisdictions (e.g. a separate juvenile and criminal justice system, and separate courts for women). A strong version of the rehabilitative ideal was the juvenile court, which was characterized by informal procedures, a parental judicial role, and a strong emphasis on personalizing and individualizing each case. Although saving, helping, and treating persons were stated goals, the rehabilitation ethic was often coercive in practice (Platt 1969; Schlossman and Wallach 1982; Rafter, 1985).

As von Hirsch (1985: 5–6) suggests, the rehabilitative ethic had great appeal because it 'offered both therapy and restraint'. Those diagnosed as 'redeemable' could be treated, perhaps outside an incarceral setting, but those who showed little chance of improvement could be restrained. Reformers could therefore 'have it both ways'—care for the community (crime control) and care for the individual (treatment).

Garland's (1985) study of the transformation of penality in England from the Victorian to the modern period also reveals a shift from a justice to a care model. With respect to sentencing systems, he notes a change from 'a calibrated, hierarchical structure . . . into which offenders were inserted according to the severity of their offense, to an extended grid of non-equivalent and diverse dispositions', a shift that reflected a fundamental change in logic and philosophy: 'it became a respectable and established policy to disregard the formal equality of legal subjects and instead take account of their peculiarities as specific individuals' (p. 28). In summarizing the contours of the new penality, which he associated with a shift from the 'ideal Liberal State' to what would later be termed the 'Welfare State', Garland (p. 31) identifies these changes in relations among the state, the offender, and censure: the reconstruction of 'the offender' from a free and rational subject to a specific 'individual', whose needs and character are unknown and require diagnosis: and a change in the state's censuring role from 'a contractual obligation to punish' to an active effort to reform and help the individual. The state's relationship to the individual thus becomes one of 'benefactor . . . its power legitimated not in contractual terms, but in terms of a natural ascendancy marked by its resources and knowledge, *its ability to care*' (emphasis added).

For about a century, the care model reigned, at least ideologically, in the US and England, but today a shift back to the justice model is apparent. The historical circumstances in the US giving rise to a felt need for sentencing reform, together with the means by reform is to be accomplished, differ from those in other western nations. However, disillusionment with the rehabilitative ideal, concern with sentencing disparity, and a 'get tough' stance are not confined to the US (see e.g. Brants and Kok 1986; Ashworth 1987).

In the UK several factors converged in the late 1960s that challenged the individualized sentencing system, the authority of parole boards, and the rehabilitative ideal. Through a series of Supreme Court decisions in the 1960s, federal constitutional protections were extended to individuals adjudicated in state criminal and juvenile courts, and the discretion of state authorities (especially police powers) was curtailed. Meanwhile, sentencing practices were assailed for lacking a standard (Frankel 1972), there was major concern for racial disparities, and Martinson's (1974) study of correctional programmes suggested that rehabilitation did not work. Sentencing reform emerged in the mid-1970s, its principles appealing to a spectrum of political constituencies—radicals, liberals and conservatives (see Greenberg and Humphries 1980; von Hirsch 1985: 3–16).

The primary aim of sentencing reform is to reduce sentencing disparities by curtailing judicial discretion. The flexible, personalized, and highly discretionary features of the individualized sentencing system were found wanting because they led to abuses of discretionary authority and the appearance of too much inequality. A just-deserts sentencing system is seen as a way to solve this problem. By developing a set of standardized, prescriptive guidelines based on the crime (and typically, the defendant's prior criminal history) and a backward-looking approach to punishment, it is hoped that the sanctioning of wrongdoing can be more fair, rational, and equal. Sentencing reform in the US is not of a whole piece; different strategies are in place or proposed in the fifty states and the federal system (Blumstein *et al*. 1983; Shane-DuBow *et al*. 1985; Tonry 1987; US Sentencing Commission 1987).[4]

However, a broad shift from a care to a justice model is unmistakable. 'Just punishment' is now construed as equal punishment for like offences as reformers seek a principled basis for punishment. Von Hirsch's (1985: 27) commentary is one example of what reformers find principled in a justice model but unprincipled in a care model. The former, which von Hirsh advocates, is based on the one principle of desert, i.e. punishment for past crimes based on a penalty structure that is proportionate to the gravity of a person's conduct. The latter, however, tries to have it both ways, making judgments on the past and future conduct of a person. Under the surface of von Hirsch's concern that two conflicting sentencing principles will spawn incoherence lies a more fundamental concern: a desire to separate the crime from the person.

This search for coherent principles reveals the political nature of sentencing reform and problems of state legitimation. In part, sentencing reform reflects a short-term, reactive law and order stance towards crime control, a reaction against a widely held public perception that the law is more on the side of those accused than those victimized by crime. But it also affirms a cherished legal value in the US that individuals should be afforded equal treatment before the law. A more rationalized, orderly, and fair, but depersonalized sentencing system offers a way to quell the tide of crime and to implement the value of equality to a faceless criminal element. The question begs itself: is such a system possible or desirable?

Criminal justice practices

It is hard to argue against the idea that reducing sentencing disparity is a good thing. But it is equally hard to imagine that the activity of applying a just-deserts sentencing scheme will differ from its predecessor. The stated principles might shift from a care to a justice model (or some amalgam), but the practices will not. By 'practices' I am not referring simply to sentences received for like crimes, which may well become less varied. I refer instead to the activity of 'doing justice', of applying a sentencing scheme, no matter how well-scaled or fine tuned, to those accused and convicted of crime. I term this activity the female voice, not because it describes something women do more than men, but because it is consistent with those elements Gilligan associates with it, contextual and relational reasoning. From studies of criminal court decision-making by myself and others, it is clear that court officials' responses to crime are based on (i) a relational view of victims and offenders in defining crime, and (ii) a view of defendants in relation to others in sanctioning crime. In short, court officials take a more social and relational view of how best to respond to those accused and convicted of crime than that imagined by legislators, sentencing commissions, or the public, or that set forth in criminal codes.

I focus on two features of doing justice in the female voice. They reveal the impossibility of aligning an abstract standard of equal treatment with court practices.[5] The first is a gap between crime events as they are described in criminal statutes and crime as it occurs in a social context. The second is a gap between the social unit of punishment in sentencing statutes (individual based) and that used in sentencing practices (family based). Both reflect a problem of law: criminal statutes are written without social relationships and context in mind, but they can only be interpreted and applied with reference to social relationships and context.

Defining crime.   Criminal statutes define crime without regard to victim–offender relations (exceptions include statutory rape, rape, sodomy, offences between adults and minors). But it is well known that police and court officials define real or serious crime based on the nature of victim–offender relations (see e.g. Reiss 1971; Vera Institute of Justice 1977; Stanko 1982). In general, crime between those who know each other is viewed as less serious or not real crime in comparison to crime between victims and offenders who are strangers. This is not a novel insight (see e.g., Black (1976) on relational distance), but it shows that punishment schemes which are based on identifying gradations of harm or crime seriousness are abstractions. Furthermore, as Alschuler (1988: 852) notes, 'If we wrote explicitly that stranger crime shall automatically be punished more severely than nonstranger crime, we might recoil.'

Such schemes are apparently premised, however, on the idea that the crime in question occurred between persons unknown to each other. It could be argued that this is a correct premise, crime seriousness should not be based on victim–offender relations, but this warrants a closer look.

The role of victim–offender relations in adjudicating crime is most vividly seen in the Vera Institute of Justice (1977) study of New York City's courts. A significant proportion of cases (40 per cent and higher) in the criminal courts involved victims and offenders who knew each other, the authors concluding, 'We found an obvious but often overlooked reality: criminal conduct is often the explosive spillover from ruptured personal relations among neighbors, friends, and former spouses' (p. 135). These cases (burglaries, robberies, as well as assaults and rapes) had high dismissal rates because complainants were unwilling to press charges: and even when prior-relationship cases survived dismissal, they received more lenient sentences than cases involving people who did not know each other.

It seems that an ethic of care is operating, however passive in form or problematic in its implications. By not prosecuting prior-relationship crimes or by sentencing those convicted of such crimes more leniently, justice in the eyes of court officials is served by not severing relationships and by not penalizing personal grievances and grudges too heavily. This reaction is passive in that it may not mend relationships between victims and offenders who know each other (although mediation, restitution, or other conditions for dismissal might be established); but neither does it render conduct criminal. What is troubling is how, for some types of crimes and particular victim–offender relations (e.g. familial or intimate violence, rape), this ethic of care may be expressed by not hurting offenders, which can lead to continued harm and danger for victims. Moreover, it presupposes that there are acceptable levels of violence between acquaintances, lovers, and spouses (see e.g. Stanko 1982; Russell 1984; LaFree *et al.* 1985).

These issues are central for feminists in challenging the criminal justice response to men who batter and rape women because such incidents are not defined as real crime by police and court officials. I make an observation about these practices, and then raise some questions. I suggest that crime is defined using the female voice because it is contingent on the relations between victims and offenders and the different degrees of harm and culpability that are associated with these relations. But it is clear that certain relations can be assumed and ratified that are not in women's interests. Maintaining a web of connection can be harmful and coercive to women, a phenomenon which Olsen (1984: 393) terms 'forced community'. Several questions flow from this observation. Should the response to crime be based on the character of victim–offender relations? If the answer is yes, which relations should be preserved? What sorts of social fractures should be mended without making them a matter of the state's power to condemn and punish?

Defining punishment. A core assumption in the sentencing literature is that the individual defendant is the social unit of punishment. After all, so it is thought, an individual was found to have done something wrong, hence the individual is the legal subject of criminal sanctions. Research on gender differences in sentencing by Carlen (1983), Eaton (1983, 1985, 1986), Farrington and Morris (1983), Kruttschnitt (1982, 1984), and Daly (1987a–c) leads me to think this is not borne out in practice. Sentencing is more often family based than individual based. It is possible that when gender disparities in sentencing are a research focus, family is suddenly more visible. However, studies with a presumptive male as the defendant also reveal a family-based logic (Hogarth 1971; Gaylin 1974; Feeley 1979; Mann *et al.* 1980; Maynard 1982). In my interviews with court officials (Daly 1987a), I learned that they confront a dilemma of justice when men and women who have responsibilities for the care or economic welfare of others are convicted of crime. They may be obliged to punish the defendant, but they do not want to punish those who depend on the defendant because punishing 'the innocent' is a miscarriage of justice. Implied in their reasoning is a concern for the consequences of punishment, and more specifically, for the social harm that arises in imposing equal punishment on defendants who are and are not members of familial social groups. Thus, whether defendants have dependants or not, as well as the indispensability of their care-taking labour for others, are salient to court officials.[6]

How defendants' familial relations are used by court officials to diagnose character and potential for reform can take many forms. I offer one example of a female defendant with young children; for this woman, the subject of the court's sanctions is not the woman alone, but the woman and her children, and the consequences of punishment for this social unit. I use this example because some believe that if a woman with children is less likely to be jailed than a woman without children, the family based sentencing logic discriminates against women who are not 'committed to conventional female roles' (Carlen 1985: 4). However, if the same logic is applied to men, is structured by a concern to maintain affective and economic ties to others, and may mean that some men and women will less likely be subject to jail sentences, then it is hard to see that this leads to greater injustice for women than men. Certainly, there can be redounding effects for women (and men) when this family based logic is used, but it is essential that this problem be framed in comparative terms, i.e. whether family- or individual-based sentencing is preferable. In the criminal justice system, should sentencing judgments ignore familial relations, children, or other dependants?

Some feminist questions about criminal justice

It is easier to know what is unjust than what is just. That the state's power to accuse and punish wrongdoing is disproportionately visited on economically marginalized and ethnic minority men and women reveals injustice. That there exists harsh or punitive responses to some offences, such as prostitution or petty property offences, reveals injustice to some defendants, and that there is an overly lenient or lack of response to other offences, such as assaults or sexual violence between those who know each other, reveals injustice to some victims. That incarceration is thought to be a just response to crime is questionable for many men and women who are currently imprisoned. But what then is a just, or perhaps a caring, response to wrongdoing? What purposes and aims should a criminal justice system have? What should be the standards, values, and decision criteria?

TABLE 2.   *Heidensohn's models of justice (from her Table 1, p. 293)*

	Portia model	Persephone model
Values and characteristics	Masculine, rationality, individualism	Feminine, caring and personal
System	Civil rights, rule of law	Networks, informal
Concept of justice	Legal, equality, procedural	Responsibility, cooperation
Features	Norm is male	Norm is female

I raise these questions to push a feminist critique of criminal law and justice practices a step further. If history is a guide, our forms of justice need to consider: (i) the competing, but legitimate claims of procedural and substantive equality: (ii) what standards should be used in an individualized response; (iii) the legitimate and illegitimate sources of disparity and how much disparity is acceptable; (iv) the purposes and aims of redressing harms; and (v) how or whether legal ideologies (or values?) and practices can be aligned.

As feminists seek a larger role for the state in protecting women and children from abusive men, we should ask, what role is desirable? We might also see the danger in reconstructing criminal law and justice practices from the standpoint of victims alone. A victim-centred strategy can easily lead to a feminist law and order stance, and we should be wary of this for several reasons. It can spill over to a more punitive treatment of women defendants, and it can have especially harsh consequences for ethnic minority men.

I am unsure whether Gilligan thinks that the ethic of care cannot, by definition, reside in the domain of law, the state, or political life, or whether she thinks this is currently so. Feminist legal scholars infer the latter, arguing, for example, that 'we need to show that community, nurturance, responsibility, and the ethic of care are values at least as worthy of protection as autonomy, self-reliance, and individualism' (West 1988: 66). If so, then we need to take a careful look at what it means to institutionalize an ethic of care through law and in public life. I am not asking for a blueprint, but rather some historical perspective on previous efforts, their limitations and problems, and the place of rules and procedures in institution building. However, my more immediate concern with a feminist embrace of the ethic of care is that many think that abstract, formal, and rights-based reasoning is the voice of criminal law in action. On the contrary: there is a lot of female voice. It needs to be documented, understood, and analysed.

I turn to two scholars who have drawn from Gilligan in imagining alternatives to criminal law and justice practices. Heidensohn (1986) compares a Portia model of justice, which she thinks is operating in the courts today, with her proposed more women-centred alternative, the Persephone model (Table 2).

Several problems are seen with Heidensohn's contrast. First, criminal court practices today are in fact a blend of the Portia and Persephone models. In applying Gilligan's justice–care distinction, Heidensohn mistakenly assumes that criminal justice ideologies and practices are aligned in the male voice. Second, the sorts of problems that she sees arising from the Persephone model, 'welfare-based and individualized', are precisely those that the ideological shift from the care to the justice model is attempting to correct.

Harris (1987) suggests a radical break from conventional approaches to criminal justice reform, the centrepiece for her proposed alternative being a 'care/response' orientation. Like West, she argues that 'there is a need for a massive infusion of the values associated with the care/response mode of reasoning', although she also points out that 'it would be a mistake to try to simply substitute a care/response orientation for one focused on justice and rights', given existing power differentials (p. 32). Again, I wonder, how might these values be instituted? Or instituted differently from what has been tried in the past? Her piece raises several important questions, however. In discussing the paradox of protection and defence, she asks, 'How can we respond effectively to people who inflict injury and hardship on others without employing the same script and the same means that they do?' (p. 34). Linking change in criminal justice to movements for social justice and global peace, Harris envisions a range of 'compassionate, constructive, and caring arrangements' (p. 36) instead of incarceral institutions and a punitive response.

Others have imagined revisioning procedures and elements of law. For example, Lahey (1985: 535) poses this scenario:

Instead of formalized adversarial processes mediated by certified experts, dispute resolution would proceed on the assumption that all of the participants are 'correct', and that issues of power and oppression should be used as guidelines to discover the least oppressive resolution. In such an inquiry, each person's construction of what happened, or of its consequences, would be taken as valid; however, irreconcilable differences would be negotiated around the necessity of dismantling whatever accumulations of power seem to be responsible for the conflict in the first place.

Although an alternative to civil disputes, Lahey's scenario suggests a method of re-ordering the criteria for a substantive equality approach to the response to crime. Highly individualized and based on the particular 'accumulations of power' differentials between victims and offenders, the approach would be to reduce inequalities among them and to find the 'least oppressive' resolution. Where the state comes in, if at all, is uncertain; and how 'issues of power and oppression' might be applied across a range of harms and social relations stretches the imagination.

In seeking to retain the protective aspects of statutory rape laws but to remove coercive state controls and empower women, Olsen suggests the following 'startling proposal' as a heuristic device. Although all women (minor-aged or not) are free to engage in sexual intercourse, their characterizations of the sexual encounter as voluntary intercourse or rape would determine what transpired. Such an approach would 'reverse [the] conventional power-shift [and] would increase the power of women in their sexual relations with men' (Olsen 1984: 408). Unlike Lahey's assumption that all the participants are 'correct', Olsen's proposal suggests that for some crimes, this is not desirable. However, Lahey and Olsen envision a form of criminal justice which is based on redressing power relations between men and women.

Such an approach has potential for changing how crimes of violence by men against women are dealt with, and perhaps for challenging the criminal status of some offences (e.g. prostitution). In the criminal court, however, issues of power and state control also reflect class and race relations among men and women. Is there a way to include these power relations too? Or, does this dilute and dissipate feminist analyses and activism on behalf of women? I would like to see a feminist conception of criminal justice which maintains a focus on women's lives and on redressing harms to women, but which does not ignore those men who have been crippled by patriarchal, class, and race relations. Men's forms of criminal justice have not been able to sort these issues out, and perhaps there is no solution to the justice puzzle. But, with all its contradictions, a feminist vision of and struggle for something different is the more essential task today.

Notes

1. Many concepts used in this essay (ethic of care, logic of justice, male or female voice, equal treatment, like crimes, among others) could have quotation marks placed around them. However, I have adopted a minimalist approach of using quotation marks sparingly, and for some concepts, only for their first appearance in the text.
2. See Friedman (1987: 197) for the original full version of the Heinz dilemma, and for an interesting discussion of different readings when the gender of the characters is switched or greater detail is given.
3. For my purposes, I define these equality concepts in the following way: procedural or formal equality means equal treatment (or equal punishment) for like crimes; substantive or outcome equality means unequal treatment (or different punishment) for like crimes and like or unalike persons. The latter yields substantive equality because a different response is intended to yield a similar outcome, e.g. the same deterrent or rehabilitation effect may be accomplished by applying different sanctions to persons (see Daly 1987a: 286).
4. Several aspects of US sentencing reform bear note. First, simultaneous with the backward-looking emphasis on punishing the crime has been the proposed policy of selective incapacitation, which is based on identifying high-risk offenders by predicting their future behaviour (Greenwood 1982). Some argue that this policy is at odds with the just-deserts scheme (e.g. von Hirsch 1985). Second, although states vary in how sentencing reform is defined, for most states, elements of the

just-deserts sentencing scheme are serving to correct the highly discretionary individualized scheme, rather than to replace the latter entirely. Third, one searches in vain for any indication that sentencing commissions or legislators have considered women offenders; this raises questions for how the equal punishment ethos will affect the sentencing of women offenders, but there is every indication that more women will be jailed in the name of equality.

5. For the sake of simplicity, I confine my discussion to common crime.
6. Maureen Cain called my attention to the restrictive sense in which family is used in court discourse, precluding a variety of other equally strong emotional bonds. She is exactly right. As I suggest elsewhere (Daly, 1987a), familial ideology is applied restrictively because it is keyed to wage-earning and care-taking labour for others, not simply social bonds.

References

Alschuler, A. (1988), 'Comment, Conference Discussion Five', *Rutgers Law Journal*, 19: 849–53.

Ashworth, A. (1987), *Techniques for Reducing Subjective Sentencing Disparity in Sentencing*. Eighth Criminological Colloquim: Council of Europe.

Auerbach, J., Blum, L., Smith, V., and Williams, C. (1985), 'Commentary on Gilligan's *In a Different Voice*, *Feminist Studies*, 11: 149–61.

Black, D. (1976), *The Behavior of Law*. Academic Press: New York.

Blumstein, A., Cohen, J., Martin, S., and Tonry, M. (eds.) (1983), *Research on Sentencing: The Search for Reform*, vols. i and ii, National Academy Press: Washington, DC.

Brants, C. and Kok, E. (1986), 'Penal sanctions as a feminist strategy: a contradiction in terms? Pornography and criminal law in the Netherlands', *International Journal of the Sociology of Law*, 14: 269–86.

Carlen, P. (1983), *Women's Imprisonment*, Routledge & Kegan Paul: Boston, Massachusetts.

Carlen, P. (ed.) (1985), *Criminal Women*, Polity Press: Cambridge, England.

Cohen, R. (ed.) (1987), *Justice: Views from the Social Sciences*, Plenum: New York.

Daly, K. (1987a), 'Structure and practice of familial-based justice in a criminal court', *Law and Society Review*, 21: 267–90.

—— (1987b), 'Discrimination in the criminal courts: family, gender, and the problem of equal treatment', *Social Forces*, 66: 152–75.

—— (1987c), 'Rethinking judicial paternalism: gender, work–family relations, and sentencing', *Gender & Society*, 1987.

Eaton, M. (1983), 'Mitigating circumstances: Familiar rhetoric', *International Journal of the Sociology of Law*, 11: 385–400.

—— (1985), 'Documenting the defendant: placing women in social inquiry reports', in *Women in Law* (Brophy, J. and Smart, C., eds), 117–39, Routledge and Kegan Paul: Boston, Massachusetts.

Eaton, M. (1986), *Justice for Women?*, Milton Keynes: Philadelphia, Pennsylvania.

Farrington, D. and Morris, A. (1983), 'Sex, sentencing, and reconviction', *British Journal of Sociology*, 23: 229–48.

Feeley, M. (1979), *The Process is the Punishment*, Russell Sage: New York.

Finley, L. (1986), 'Transcending equality theory: a way out of the maternity and work-place debate', *Columbia Law Review*, 86: 1118–82.

Frankel, M. (1972), *Criminal Sentences*, Hill and Wang: New York.

Friedman, M. (1987), 'Care and context in moral reasoning', in *Women and Moral Theory* (Kittay, E. and Meyers, D., (eds.), 190–204. Rowman & Littlefield: Totowa, New Jersey.

Furby, L. (1987), 'Psychology and justice' in *Justice: Views from the Social Sciences* (Cohen, R., ed.), 153–203, Plenum: New York.

Garland, D. (1985), *Punishment and Welfare*, Gower: Hants, England.

Gaylin, W. (1974), *Partial Justice*, Knopf: New York.

Gilligan, C. (1982), *In a Different Voice*, Harvard University Press: Cambridge, Massachusetts.

—— (1987), 'Moral orientation and moral development', in *Women and Moral Theory* (Kittay, E. and Meyers, D., eds.), 19–33, Rowman & Littlefield: Totowa, New Jersey.

Glaspell, S. (1973), 'A jury of her peers', in *American Voices, American Women* (Edwards, L. and Diamond, A., eds.), 359–81. Avon Books: New York. (First published in *Everyweek*, 5 Mar. 1917.)

Greenberg, D. and Humphries, D. (1980), 'The cooptation of fixed sentencing reform', *Crime and Delinquency* (April), 206–23.

Greenwood, P. (1982), *Selective Incapitation*, The Rand Corporation: Santa Monica, California.

Harris, M. K. (1987), 'Moving into the new millenium: toward a feminist vision of justice', *The Prison Journal*, 67: 27–38.

Heidensohn, F. (1986), 'Models of justice: Portia or Persephone? Some thoughts on equality, fairness and gender in the field of criminal justice', *International Journal of the Sociology of Law*, 14: 287–98.

Hogarth, J. (1971), *Sentencing as a Human Process*, University of Toronto Press: Toronto, Ontario.

Kerber, L., Greeno, C., Maccoby, E., Luria, Z., Stack, C. and Gilligan, C. (1986), 'On *In a Different Voice*: An interdisciplinary forum', *Signs: Journal of Women in Culture in Society*, 11: 304–33.

Kittay, E. and Meyers, D. (eds.) (1987), *Women and Moral Theory*, Rowman & Littlefield: Totowa, New Jersey.

Kruttschnitt, C. (1982), 'Women, crime, and dependency', *Criminology*, 19: 495–513.

—— (1984), 'Sex and criminal court dispositions: the unresolved controversy', *Journal of Research in Crime and Delinquency*, 21: 213–32.

LaFree, G., Reskin, B., and Fisher, C. (1985), 'Jurors' responses to victims' behavior and legal issues in sexual assault trials', *Social Problems*, 32: 389–407.

Lahey, K. (1985), '. . . Until women themselves have told all that they have to tell . . .', *Osgood Hall Law Journal*, 23: 519–41.

Lugones, M. and Spelman, E. (1983), 'Have we got a theory for you! Feminist theory, cultural imperialism, and the demand for "the woman's voice"', *Women's Studies International Forum*, 6: 573–81.

MacKinnon, C. (1987), *Feminism Unmodified*, Harvard University Press: Cambridge, Massachusetts.

Mann, K., Wheeler, S., and Sarat, A. (1980), 'Sentencing the white-collar offender', *American Criminal Law Review*, 17: 479–500.

Marcus, I., Spiegelman, P., DuBois, E., Dunlap, M., Gilligan, C., MacKinnon, C., and Menkel-Meadow, C. (1985), 'Feminist discourse, moral values, and the law—a conversation', *Buffalo Law Review*, 34: 11–87.

Martinson, R. (1974), 'What works? Questions and answers about prison reform', *The Public Interest*, 35: 22–54.

Maynard, D. (1982), 'Defendant attributes in plea bargaining: notes on the modeling of sentencing decisions', *Social Problems*, 29: 347–60.

Menkel-Meadow, C. (1985), 'Portia in a different voice: speculations on a women's lawyering process', *Berkeley Women's Law Journal*, 39–63.

Nails, D., O'Loughlin, M. A., and Walker, J. (eds.) (1983), *Social Research*, 50(3).

Olsen, F. (1984), 'Statutory rape: A feminist critique of rights analysis', *Texas Law Review*, 63: 387–432.

Platt, A. (1969), *The Child Savers*, University of Chicago Press: Chicago, Illinois.

Radzinowicz, L. and Hood, R. (1979), 'Judicial discretion and sentencing standards: Victorian attempts to solve a perennial problem', *University of Pennsylvania Law Review*, 127: 1288–349.

Rafter, N. (1985), *Partial Justice*, Northeastern University Press: Boston, Massachusetts.

Reiss, A. J. (1971), *The Police and the Public*, Yale University Press: New Haven, Connecticut.

Russell, D. (1984), *Sexual Exploitation*, Sage: Newbury Park, California.

Schlossman, S. and Wallach, S. (1982), 'The crime of precocious sexuality: female juvenile delinquency and the Progressive Era', in *Women and the Law*, vol. 1 (Weisberg, D. K., ed.), 45–84. Schenkman Publishing: Cambridge, Massachusetts.

Shane-DuBow, S., Brown, A., and Olsen, R. (1985), *Sentencing Reform in the United States: History, Content, and Effect*, US Department of Justice, National Institute of Justice. US Government Printing Office: Washington, DC.

Stanko, E. (1982), 'Would you believe this woman? Prosecutorial screening for "credible" witnesses and a problem of justice', in *Judge, Lawyer, Victim. Thief* (Stanko, E. and Rafter, N., eds.), 63–82. Northeastern University Press: Boston, Massachusetts.

Tonry, M. (1987), *Sentencing Reform Impact*, US Department of Justice, National Institute of Justice. US Government Printing Office: Washington, DC.

Tronto, J. (1987), 'Beyond gender difference to a theory of care', *Signs: Journal of Women in Culture and Society*, 12: 644–63.

Vera Institute of Justice (1977), *Felony Arrests: Their Prosecution and Disposition in New York City's Courts*, Vera Institute of Justice: New York.

U.S. Sentencing Commission (1987), *Guidelines Manual*, Sentencing Commission, 1331 Pennsylvania Avenue, NW: Washington, DC.

von Hirsch, A. (1985), *Past or Future Crimes*, Rutgers University Press: New Brunswick, New Jersey.

Walker, S. (1980), *Popular Justice*, Oxford University Press: New York.

West, R. (1988), 'Jurisprudence and gender', *The University of Chicago Law Review*, 55: 1–72.

Community Involvement in Crime Control[1]

DAVID NELKEN

Does community involvement represent a new approach to helping solve the problem of crime and how should we assess its significance? To answer this question we need to explore what is meant by involving the 'community'.[2] Then we must examine how this call for involvement relates to the existing criminal justice system. Finally we shall need to reconsider the special place of community action in modern societies. In short, we need to be clear what proposals we are talking about, how they fit in with the official responses to crime, and whether such initiatives are plausible. For there is obviously no point in placing responsibilities on the community which it is unable to shoulder.

It has rightly been said that 'writers who call on community often expound a cause when they should have attempted to explore a meaning'.[3] And this comment is even more applicable to politicians. There is a crucial and central ambiguity in the arguments of many of those who recommend further community involvement in the control of crime. It is left unclear (perhaps deliberately) whether community is being proposed as a means to an end, i.e. as a new resource for tackling the problem of crime, or whether the creation of better community feeling is itself the end which is being pursued—and concern about crime merely the means of achieving this end. Put bluntly, are we after reduced crime or increased community? Most advocates of greater community involvement would probably stress that they cherish *both* goals—indeed that they are in some sense inseparable. But, as we shall see, this fudges the very difficult choices that have to be made in organizing strategies for increasing community involvement.[4] It conceals the political gulf between those on 'the right' who wish to draw on public support to help the forces of law and order and those on 'the left' who seek rather to empower the disenfranchised so that they can confront existing institutions and hierarchies. But above all, this reply begs all the important questions. If there already exists some identifiable sense of community to draw upon, what is its nature and potential? Where community spirit is lacking, what sort of community will be generated by a focus on crime? The fallacy here may be illustrated by an analogy. I once saw a speaker at Hyde Park Corner attempting to persuade passers-by with a placard around his neck which read 'UTOPIA could help to solve some of your problems. PLEASE LET ME EXPLAIN'.[5] Some advocates of community, we may think, similarly confuse ends with means.

It is especially important to define what we mean by community because it is a word which is never used in an unfavourable way or given any positive opposing or distinguishing term.[6] But it follows that if people agree about the need for more community involvement but otherwise hold different views and values, they must be agreeing about different things.[7] Which is not to say, as will be shown, that particular proposals for community action, or community-based programmes already in practice, have not had their critics. On the contrary, much recent American commentary has been predominantly hostile.[8] Yet somehow the promise of community retains its magic.[9]

Types of community involvement

Most discussions of community involvement are as fragmented, compartmentalized, and inconclusive as the programmes they purport to analyse. The first task in classifying what is being proposed in the name of community involvement is to attempt a typology of the various programmes which exist. What, if anything, is there in common between community policing; diversion schemes; neighbourhood justice centres; community service, or the use of community carers in place of children's homes? I shall suggest three possible classifications which distinguish schemes by the stages of the criminal process to which they relate or by the goals or sources of the community involvement they represent.

The most straightforward way of organizing the data on community involvement programmes is to show their contribution to different *stages* of the criminal process. On this view, community policing comes in at the enforcement stage and neighbourhood justice centres at the adjudication stage, whilst community service and community carers belong at the disposal stage.[10] All of these innovations can then be compared and contrasted with the existing input from the community at each of these stages: the part played by complainants and victims in police enforcement; by witnesses and juries at court; by volunteers in after-care, and so on. This way of organizing the data also draws attention to the interdependence of moves to increase community involvement at different stages of the criminal process.[11] For example, if neighbourhood justice centres take on some of the case load of traditional courts this will have implications for the way in which cases are brought to their attention and consequences for the way such cases are disposed of.

Often these linkages go unnoticed or disregarded by enthusiasts for particular innovations. This happens because in different countries the slogan of community involvement comes to be adopted for only certain stages of the criminal process. In Britain and Canada, for example, the emphasis is on community policing and neighbourhood crime prevention; in the United States more attention is given to experiments in community mediation. All three countries are simultaneously also trying to close down residential institutions in favour of community care or supervision, but the connection to other methods of involving the community is not always made. At other times the wider implications of particular initiatives are actually resisted because of the 'single-issue' nature of some campaigns for criminal justice reform. This is well illustrated by the response to a recent speech which the Home Secretary gave to the National Association of Victims Support Schemes. He linked their work to the possibility of encouraging the idea of community mediation forums and foresaw the emergence of 'a facility for reaching agreement between offenders and victims'.[12] The organizers of victims support schemes, however, immediately cast doubt on this attempt, as they saw it, to divert attention away from the needs of victims and back to the problems of the criminal justice system.[13]

Whatever uses this classification may serve, however, it provides little insight into the different *goals*[14] of community involvement and hence fails to clarify the various issues which are raised by these proposals.[15] To examine these matters it is more helpful to introduce three categories into which to divide recommendations for community involvement. Communities can be the *agents*, *locus*, or *beneficiaries* of crime control. To capture these distinctions in a phrase, we may distinguish control of crime *by* the community, control of crime *in* the community, and control of crime *for* the community: each of these categories may be relevant to any or all of the stages of the criminal process. Under the first of these headings, control *by* the community, we may group those initiatives which aim to give communities a greater role or say in the control of the criminal behaviour which affects them. Police liaison committees or neighbourhood justice centres are each, in their own way, examples of such efforts. Control *in* the community, on the other hand, means just that. It does *not* necessarily involve ordinary members of the community in any aspect of crime control, but represents rather a concern to keep offenders and others out of residential institutions if at all possible. Halfway Houses, probation hostels, diversion schemes, various forms of supervision on licence and community care programmes of temporary foster-care all illustrate this longstanding but recently much escalated effort to avoid residential care or control. Control *for* the community is again a different proposition. The idea here is to give greater recognition to the victims of crime, both as individuals and as members of the community at large. The most striking innovation here has been the introduction of community service as a new mode of punishment, but increasing interest in compensation and restitution orders also underlines this trend. As these latter penalties demonstrate, control *for* the community need not take place *in* the community and still less need it be administered *by* the community.

Whatever these trends may have in common, these three concerns do reflect somewhat different conceptions of crime and the way it should be controlled. Those interested in furthering control *by* the community focus on crime and criminality as anti-social conduct by individuals which it is part of the community's political and social responsibility to define and reduce. The approach inherent in the move to control *in* the community is the need to maintain and repair social relationships whose breakdown give rise to the disputes or alienation which lie behind criminal behaviour. Those who argue for more control *for* the community see crime as a social and environmental problem which impairs the quality of life of communities and the individuals who compose them. The first concern challenges the adequacy of the legal solution to the question of who should exercise social control. The second extends the welfare perspective on the causes of crime. The third, perhaps most distinctive theme, tries to design-out crime and mobilizes crime control as an aspect of social defence.

It would be unwise to belabour the message that prepositions can alter propositions, especially as programmes of community involvement on the ground often embrace more than one of these concerns. But unless we take the trouble to be clear about the point of any initiative it will not be possible either to assess its success or to appreciate its significance. If, as is likely, any coherence possessed by the move towards community involvement derives from political and practical pressures rather than from overall criminal policy considerations, we should not be too surprised if different schemes fail to reinforce or even contradict each other.

A third way of thinking about community involvement, which will be discussed further later in my argument, is in terms of the sources of community feeling which the initiative is designed to express. To anticipate later discussion, I shall argue that community solidarity, in this context, is assumed to derive *either* from sharing a neighbourhood, hence the stress on locality, *or* is conceived of as a kind of social relationship and concern. In the latter case, it is seen as a *non-localized* disposition to altruistic involvement with others, the way in which individuals find true fulfilment. Many schemes of community involvement, of course, attempt to draw on both these sources of community. But as Table 1 indicates, this is not always possible and some community initiatives seem to have no basis in either conception of community.[16]

TABLE 1 *Sources of Community Involvement*

Community as Location

		Yes	No
Community as Altruism	Yes	Neighbourhood Justice Centres	Community Carers Victim Support Schemes
	No	Neighbourhood Watch Schemes Community Policing	Diversion Schemes Community Service

Community justice and official justice

In so far as community involvement in crime control fits into an already functioning criminal justice system, anyone advocating more such involvement is duty bound to consider the relationship of such proposals to the existing system. We need to ask: is the initiative being advanced because of the failings of some part of the current system or because of the supposed intrinsic advantages of community involvement? Even when a problem has been identified we can still query whether more community involvement is the only remedy or even an appropriate one. Similarly those who oppose the move towards community involvement can either defend the success or virtues of the current system or point to the inherent drawbacks of involving the community.

But the main reason why we need to consider the relationship between official and community justice is that it represents the chief issue dividing the rival political views of those who advocate more community involvement. We may see this better if we examine the ways in which community involvement can impinge on the official system. We can assume, for these purposes, that such initiatives may be designed to assist, supplement, monitor, or replace official provisions for dealing with crime.[17] It is easy to think of existing examples of each of these roles for community involvement. *Assistance* to the police is provided by neighbourhood watch schemes; community mediation facilities *supplement* the task of courts; police consultative committees, and court-watching schemes in America, *monitor* the workings of the official system. Finally, the community-based system of Children's Hearings in Scotland provides an example of the admittedly least common role for community involvement by *replacing* the previous system of legally administered juvenile justice.

Not surprisingly, official sponsorship of community involvement concentrates on the part it can play either in assisting or supplementing the work of official agencies. Given the rising crime rate, say police spokesmen, there will need to be either an inordinately high level of policing or else the community must get more involved. If policing in sensitive multiracial areas is not to cause more problems than it solves, suggests Lord Scarman, it will need to take fuller account of the wishes and needs of those being policed. Likewise it is the spectre of overloaded courts being clogged up with cases that stimulates efforts to introduce community mediation, and the scandal of overcrowded prisons which forces consideration of alternative penalties.[18] The difficulty with these justifications, in terms of the questions raised earlier, is that they do not make clear the positive contribution which community-based measures are expected to make. Nor do they consider the possible conflict with existing provisions or processes which the introduction of such schemes may entail. They rarely explain why community involvement should be the response to the difficulties of the official systems, because, rather than examine what may be going wrong with existing agencies and institutions the problem is assumed to lie in their being asked to do too much and their need of more support. One is left with the suspicion that the major virtue of community alternatives is that they are thought to save money whilst usefully diverting attention from the failings of existing agencies.

In fairness to such officially sponsored or approved schemes it is proper to consider in more detail the claims which they themselves make. So I will take two examples of the most popular type of such initiatives, those geared to *community crime prevention*. For the past two years Canada has run a nationwide campaign, sponsored by its Solicitor General, aimed at involving the community in the prevention and reporting of crime.[19] Its goal was said to be 'to heighten awareness, broaden the crime prevention partnership and stimulate community-based crime prevention'.[20] It was explained that this had 'become popular in the face of the rising social and economic costs of crime and to have proven effective in helping reduce crime, reduce fear of crime and contribute to the development of more closely-knit communities'.[21] The strategies used, which involved co-operation between businessmen, voluntary organizations, lawyers and other professionals, as well as ordinary citizens, were aimed primarily at reducing burglary and vandalism in selected neighbourhoods. People were encouraged to take part in a wide variety of related activities: to learn about crime rates in their areas; to report suspicious occurrences; to participate in Garbathons (marathon pick-ups of litter!); even to lend their home for police radar traps to be set up to catch dangerously speeding drivers! In addition special awards were given to businesses which had helped promote crime prevention and individuals who had worked in various volunteer centres dealing with problems as diverse as battered wives, drug addicts, or delinquent teenagers. The picture which is conjured up by all this activity is in some ways more positive than I have been suggesting. Yet there is still something a bit strange about the hope for renewed community which supposedly underpins these efforts, an ambivalence well captured perhaps in the closing exhortation of the information handout which declared: 'Secure your own home but recognise that security also comes from a closely knit community.'[22]

A somewhat different method of reaching the same objective is represented by the NACRO crime prevention schemes operating in a number of high density housing-schemes in Britain.[23] Their threefold plan is to improve the physical fabric of the estates, obtain a more responsive attitude on the part of local authority housing officers to problems identified by the tenants, and involve a multitude of agencies in consultation with members of the estate in an attempt to reduce burglary, vandalism, and the fear of crime. All this is important *community work* (even if not always *community action*) but it remains questionable how far it can restore a sense of community. This is especially ironic in view of the fact that it was the creation of these estates in the first place which dispersed the community spirit which had previously existed in the slum districts from which the tenants were drawn.

On the other hand proponents of both of these schemes would probably be well satisfied with outcomes which fell far short of the renewal of a shared community life: some improvement in living conditions and reduction in crime would constitute real gains. And the opponents of officially sponsored schemes, for their part, have more serious criticisms than the comparatively minor sin of taking the name of community in vain.[24] Many of those on the political left argue that the role of community involvement must be limited to that of *monitoring* or *replacing* the official criminal justice system. They worry that, otherwise, officially sponsored community involvement will only be invited and tolerated as long as it furthers the aims of the official system. Rather than community involvement leading to more control of crime *by* the community, *in* the community, or even *for* the community, all that will be achieved is more control *of* the community.[25] Instead of decentralizing or devolving crime control, it will operate, they fear, as a method of dispersing the existing system, merely delegating (whether explicitly or not) its current concerns and priorities.[26] Officially sponsored community involvement amounts in practice, it is claimed, to a covert extension of the criminal justice system. More offenders are pulled into the net, often for less serious offences, at least some offenders are dealt with more severely than before, and the line between those inside and outside the criminal justice system and its agencies and institutions becomes dangerously blurred. When we seek to empty the prisons we get instead what Stan Cohen has called 'the punitive city'.[27]

The differences between the official and the critics' versions of community involvement are extreme. Where the official approach reflects a 'top-down' vision of community involvement, the critics will only accept a 'bottom-up' model of community justice, a movement arising from an existing network of community life. Significantly, where the official approach concentrates on community as a means to the end of crime control, the alternative strategy is dedicated to the achievement of community empowerment as an end in itself. And, for some of the critics of the official approach, even the achievement of a form of community self-government is not the ultimate goal. They look forward to the formation of community structures with a built-in oppositional commitment to confront existing agencies and undermine the hierarchies they serve to maintain.[28]

It is impossible to bridge such politically divergent visions of community justice and unprofitable even to attempt to do so. But even those who are unattracted both by official enthusiasms and by radical eschatology must take seriously the radical critiques of officially encouraged community schemes because they alert us to their hidden dangers and show the limitations of such exercises. In particular, four serious consequences are seen to flow from an uncritical acceptance of the official mobilization of community action.

The first problem which arises is that where community initiatives or institutions are subordinate to official goals, this can have deleterious effects on the kinds of case they are asked to handle. American experiments with mediation as an alternative to prosecution have found not only that the mediation service comes to depend almost entirely on cases referred to it from the official system but also that the cases referred tend to be those which officials prefer not to deal with themselves rather than those for which mediation is necessarily the appropriate method of processing.[29] Even worse, some institutions which were created to serve poorer groups in the community have ended up making victims of their intended beneficiaries.[30] The clearest example of this is the way in which some small claims courts, intended to provide a cheap and speedy form of justice, turned into debt-collection agencies for finance houses, public utilities, and the like. The critics point out that, whilst the talk now is of designing community alternatives to existing legal institutions, only 10 to 15 years ago the watchword was the need to provide more access for individuals to the official legal system so that they could vindicate their rights. This was thought essential both in dealing with business and bureaucracies and to protect the fragile 'new property rights' derived from the operations of the welfare state. By contrast, community institutions represent exit routes from the official legal system rather than opportunities for access to it. The goals of 'bringing law to the people'[31] and 'bringing the people into the law' may seem interchangeable but they are in fact radically different. If the official legal system remains the arena in which the important battles over liberties and rights have to be fought then it is that, claim the critics, which needs to be reformed rather than by-passed.

The second objection to the dependence of community initiatives on the requirements of the overall criminal justice system is that it falsifies any claim they make to being non-coercive alternatives to the official system.[32] The presence of official sanctions even as a possibility colours the meaning and alters the significance of community programmes. Diversion schemes typically proceed against the background of the threat of prosecution.[33] Community mediation is predicated on the continued agreement of the parties to attend and co-operate with the mediator or else the case is returned to the court system.[34] Non-residential alternatives for handling juvenile offenders may incorporate arbitrary and excessive resort to institutional treatment where this is thought to be required to maintain the programme's survival.[35] In all these cases the impression that the community measures are voluntary, or outside the criminal justice system proper, allows them to be imposed without the application of the usual safeguards.

Thirdly, even where such initiatives represent genuine and constructive alternatives to existing provisions they can still be used to legitimize more severe penalties for cases dealt with in the old way. All too frequently, the official system draws an over-sharp distinction between 'hard-core' offenders for whom retributive or deterrent sentences are deemed appropriate and other more deserving cases for which alternative ways may be tried.[36] In the area of juvenile justice, for example, the expansion of intermediate treatment goes hand in hand with the building of more detention centres.

The final and perhaps most controversial charge is that unless efforts are made to ensure that community alternatives actually *replace* existing institutions and agencies they will only add to the net amount of 'social control' in the society. Instead of encouraging the role of communities they enlarge the scope of 'the state' and the *intrusiveness* of its control mechanisms. The introduction of community initiatives from above leads, then, to the erosion of informal norms and communal understandings; this path can only eventuate in the 'legalization of community' rather than achieve the goal of generating constructive alternatives to official justice.[37]

There is considerable truth in these criticisms both as observations on existing initiatives and warnings concerning the likely outcomes of future community programmes. But it is important not to exaggerate their force. In the first place it must be over-simple to talk of 'the official system' as if it were monolithic when what is in fact being referred to is a set of institutions and agencies with different interests, values, and goals. Rather than merely being subordinated, community initiatives could further the goals of some of these agencies as opposed to others and even play on their internal disagreements.[38] As many of the critics would admit, criminal justice is neither a 'system' nor a pre-determined 'process', but rather an arena of struggle over purposes and outcomes which the introduction of new elements must be able to affect. Even on the view that 'the system' does in fact have a guiding structural logic,[39] or that there is what may be termed 'coherence without conspiracy',[40] there is no reason why the growth of community programmes should not upset this coherence—for better or worse. Some of the critics also reveal an uncharacteristic admiration for existing legal processes.[41] Whilst they may be right to assert that 'compromise amongst unequals produces inequality' they themselves have often demonstrated how the outcome of struggle in formal rule-bound systems is that 'the haves come out ahead'.[42] More cautious critics rightly admit that they would have to examine the conditions under which either type of forum and process offered greater advantages for the groups whose causes they favour.[43]

There are other important countervailing arguments. Whatever the very real dangers of co-option, the evidence to date from most American studies of community mediation schemes is that without the sponsorship of the existing court system the referral rate is so low that such initiatives have the greatest difficulty in getting off the ground.[44] The choice then is between semi-autonomy or failure. The claim that officially-approved community schemes merely extend the role of the state is also a difficult one to tie down. How do you measure the total amount of social control in a society, especially when, as here, you are asked to compare incommensurable *qualitative* changes in forms of social control?[45] Tony Bottoms, in a wide-ranging overview of penal changes in relation to Cohen's 'punitive city' thesis, points out that the fine is the penal sanction which has grown fastest, relative to other measures, and this is also one of the least intrusive penalties.[46] By contrast, probation and community service, penalties administered in the community, between them still take only a small proportion of offenders. Moreover, he also reminds us that the interweaving of government and private initiative is inescapable in a welfare state, being found in areas as diverse as health, education, and pensions and he suggests that it does not necessarily pose any greater danger here than elsewhere. In terms of future developments, however, a lot depends on how far community involvement comes to be allied to the now suspect panacea of the treatment ideology in crime control or whether its latent anti-professionalism helps the further decline of that ideology.

The importance of the debate between Cohen (and others) and Bottoms over the intrusiveness of community involvement justifies a slight excursus at this point which may help to clarify the issues that divide them. We may start by assuming that whether community involvement is proposed as an alternative or even as an addition to existing provisions its significance must lie in its *relationship* to what it is replacing or supplementing. We therefore need to contrast what is represented by community involvement with its competitors and to do this we must construct some necessarily oversimplified ideal types of the various alternative discourses which justify intervention in the criminal justice field.[47] A comparison of the discourses associated with the 'community', 'welfare', and 'justice'[48] approaches to the criminal process does, I think, lead to the conclusion that the approach represented by 'community involvement' could legitimate greater intrusiveness in the exercise of social control. This is largely but not exclusively because of what the approach shares in common with the welfare discourse, despite its potential for disagreement with it.[49]

(1) Like the welfare, but unlike the justice model, the community approach focuses on the offender rather than the offence, with all that this entails in terms of the extent of scrutiny and intervention which may be found relevant. But the community approach goes even further by also bringing into consideration the circumstances and needs of the victim and the community.

(2) Both the welfare and the community approach are committed to achieving substantive justice. This again legitimates greater scope for intervention, as compared to the stress of the justice approach on formal justice produced by the application of general rules which are consistent, predictable, and reviewable.[50] Again, however, the community approach is the most wide-ranging in its search for substantive justice, since its concern extends to the needs of the whole community.[51]

(3) In dealing with individual cases the welfare and community approaches are both forward-looking, whereas the justice model

mainly addresses its attention to past events. But the community approach, unlike the welfare approach, also takes into account the past history of disputes in so far as this may be relevant to their resolution. Again, all this justifies greater intervention.

(4) In trying to anticipate criminal events, both the welfare and community approaches place great emphasis on the preventing and designing-out of crime, whilst the justice approach tends to rely simply on deterrence.

(5) Neither the welfare nor the community approach have much use for the distinction between civil and criminal processes. Only the justice model stresses the special safeguards and requirements of the criminal process, which alone is seen as providing the framework for the legitimate exercise of violence by the state.[52]

(6) The different basis for criticizing departures from the ideal in each of these approaches also demonstrates the tendency to intrusiveness in the community approach. The 'process values' of the justice approach have to do with accountability, consistency, and fidelity to law; those of welfare systems, on the other hand, make reference to the expertise and skill of professionals. Unlike these self-referring criteria, the values of the community approach focus on participation and agreement. In short, the justice process stands to be corrected by better legal judgment, the welfare process by better professional training but the community process requires even more community involvement. Whilst the justice approach claims to deal with the problem of discretion by introducing checks and balances, the welfare approach does so by trusting professionals: the community approach however, denies the adequacy of these solutions and insists that it is necessary and possible to trust ordinary citizens.[53]

It is clear, then, that the community approach *can* license greater intrusiveness. But Bottoms and Cohen disagree not so much over the potential as over the current significance of community-based schemes of social control; on this there is more to be said on both sides. The common ground here is that Bottoms admits the growth of surveillance techniques, especially those in public places and those aimed at categories of suspected groups. He also notes the growing army of private security police. But the significance of community involvement is less clear-cut. Surveillance techniques can make it possible to dispense with the assistance or consent of the community or at least attempt to do so. On the other hand, computerized techniques of data collection and analysis allow information derived from the community to be collated on a scale never before attempted. Bottoms does not see much evidence of increasing resort to 'disciplinary' training as a mode of punishment, on the contrary, there is increasing evidence of withdrawal from state involvement in some areas. To this argument Cohen replies that the state does not need to act as parent or educator when parents and schools do this on the state's behalf. In his view it is important not to take the *scope* of state expansion as a measure of its intrusiveness. Yet Bottoms could argue that the trend by which the state usurped the role of lesser institutions such as the family does appear to have faltered. We have still to face the fact that what is distinctive about current populist politics is its method of undermining lesser agencies such as the local state by appealing over their heads to the individuals whom they serve.[54] Also, in so far as this ideological trend is the result of a fiscal crisis, it must follow that it may not always be feasible to exercise greater and more intrusive social control and at the same time save money. Hence the call to community and the ambiguous possibilities inherent in how the community responds.

So much for the lessons to be learned from the critics' attack on official sponsorship of community involvement. For their part, those who insist that such schemes remain independent must show why they are prepared to dispense with the advantages and safeguards offered by co-operating with the official system of criminal justice. For example, one of the early advocates of community involvement was quite explicit that the subordinate role he envisaged for community justice derived from the need to identify what was best done by the official system and hive off only those tasks which could be better done by community-based institutions and agencies.[55] Those who advocate community justice 'from below' have to meet the question whether they are really prepared to abandon the procedural protections of the official system, at least as a court of appeal. What if neighbourhood watch schemes become vigilante groups or community moots turn into kangaroo courts?[56] In less alarmist language, they must make clear where they stand on the limits of community action. Are they prepared to ask communities to organize both local police forces and local prisons? In sum, how can community initiatives in the short to medium term be organized except in full awareness of their links to the official justice system? And if that is true the problem must be to determine the conditions of such interdependence rather than simply welcome or reject it.

To avoid the somewhat over-simplified views of community involvement discussed so far the positive way forward would seem to lie in trying to determine the appropriate role for each form and forum of justice. We may take, for illustrative purposes, the competing virtues of official courts as compared to community mediation. In these terms there are three ways of structuring the relationship between official and community justice which repay further consideration; and I shall comment in turn on methods of allocating cases on the basis of pragmatism, appropriateness, and jurisdiction.

The first and most common criterion is pragmatism. The usual division of labour reflecting this is the distinction between serious and trivial offences, the latter being allocated to community courts, possibly on analogy with the lowest level of official courts.[57] However, the adoption of such obviously pragmatic reasons of convenience and economy in the allocation of cases is exactly what gives the impression that any special goals of community justice are being subordinated to the need of the official system. For if serious cases require and benefit from careful legal consideration, why is this not also true for trivial cases? On the other hand, if community mediation has something valuable to offer why should this not apply also to serious cases?

A more promising approach is to look instead for the types of case which each forum is best suited to handle. For example, a contrast is sometimes drawn between the 'family' approach to dispute-resolution in which people in continuing relationships are reconciled, or at least conciliated, and the 'battle' approach, represented by adversarial proceedings, which is best suited to dealing with situations where the parties do not have a prior or continuing close relationship.[58] The variety amongst types of dispute and closeness of the relationship can of course be broken down still further but this distinction broadly captures the point of having at least two systems.[59] A division of labour based on this criterion is invoked in many of the American experiments in neighbourhood justice and is gaining ground also in Britain. It does not necessarily produce the same allocation of cases as the first distinction: serious assaults, for example, will often rightly go to the community court whereas petty shoplifting would fall to be dealt with, if at all, by the usual adversarial proceedings.[60]

However, it should be noted that a number of problems still arise when using this approach even if none of them constitute fatal objections. It is not self-evident that there is anything *intrinsic* about cases which place them into one or other of these categories. To a large extent the processing of a dispute itself *transforms* it into suitable subject-matter by picking out what it chooses to treat as the salient features of the case for its purposes.[61] Nor should it be assumed that allocating cases to the appropriate forum will necessarily be associated with a better 'success rate' in resolving any underlying problem or reducing the likelihood of repetition.[62] Mediation, for example, is only marginally more successful, if at all, in dealing with disputants involved in continuing relationships than in satisfying those in fleeting relationships because disputes arising from continuing relationships are both particularly deep-lying and easily re-kindled. The underlying logic of the distinction appears to be that because adversarial proceedings tend to be backward-looking they are most tolerable where the parties do not have to continue in a relationship. Where they do need to do so, the greater flexibility and future-orientation of a mediation process constitutes a distinct advantage. But this underestimates the way adversarial proceedings can help parties to plan future dealings and overestimates the ability of mediation approaches to get away from the necessary task of clarifying past rights and wrongs, which it has to do without the benefit of legal proceedings. The more basic point in the present context is the question whether all this has anything to do with the aim of involving the community. The community is affected by all types of crime and is interested in the resolution, rather than merely the adjudication, of all disputes, those between relative strangers as well as those between familiars: all are members of the community with past and future obligations to it. Conversely, the choice between mediation and adjudication seems a different concern from that of the assertion or involvement of the community because, as many schemes have found, skills at mediation can be almost as rare and specialized as those deriving from legal training. It has never been suggested that the growth of arbitration has anything to do with the re-creation of community; it is surprising therefore to find that moving one further step down the dispute-processing continuum should hold such different significance.[63]

Another suggestion for dividing up cases comes nearer to meeting this point. Here the recommendation is that local courts should handle cases of local interest, whilst problems which transcend local concerns and which involve, as Danzig puts it, either local decisions which will produce 'externalities' or which concern external sources of control over the community, should be dealt with in official courts.[64] But any attempt to use this approach in practice soon succeeds in highlighting the difficulties of separating local and national concerns. Because so many of the conflicts and crimes in any area are linked to the operations of business, local authorities, or the state, what is left, when these are removed, are domestic and neighbour disputes or localized incidents of vandalism and theft. As with the previous recommendation, this may indeed produce a steady stream of cases for mediation programmes but it will also bypass many issues of vital community concern.

The question which all this raises, therefore, is the inherent *plausibility* of community initiative in modern society. Indeed, the discussion so far may have unwittingly underemphasized this problem by concentrating on the issues dividing official sponsors of community schemes from their more radical critics.[65] Both sides to *this* debate know what *they* mean by community even if they do mean different things and aspire to different goals. But by far the most common reaction to proposals for more community involvement is incredulity and suspicion of who and what will be taken to represent the community. Those who come forward to 'represent' the community are typically appointed or self-selected rather than democratically selected and are unrepresentative simply by virtue of their willingness to become involved. In any case, it is far from clear how they could or should represent their communities. We are reminded that a special risk of community action or assertion is the loss of protection for minorities, especially unpopular minorities. Some may also consider that existing institutions and agencies already represent the community, at least as far as that is either practical or desirable. The evidence is wanting which would establish that ordinary people actually want more community involvement, rather than, say, better services from existing agencies. For example, the low rate of self-referral to community mediation schemes hardly suggests a pressing need for such institutions. So where is the pressure coming from? In all these ways proposals for community involvement can be contrasted with the form in which modern complex societies and their legal systems are organized and, not surprisingly, such proposals are often found irrelevant or even dangerous. To find out if there is still any potential for community assertion in modern complex societies we must look more closely at the nature of community consciousness in such societies.

Community solidarity in modern society

We saw earlier that current proposals for greater community involvement in criminal justice tend to view community either in terms of shared locality or as a particular type of shared concern which transcends the confines of neighbourhood (see Table 1). Both manifestations of community may reinforce each other although they are assumed to be distinctive in their origins. We may now notice that each of these supposed sources of community rests on a somewhat doubtful diagnosis of the nature of community solidarity in modern society. The first view of community starts from the suspect premise that mere *proximity* generates shared concern, the second uses the label of community somewhat inaccurately, because it describes the operation of individual acts of *altruism*. The first approach appears to take the existence of communities as given and seeks to harness their potential to the task of crime control. Community here is seen as a useful resource, a means to an end. The second hopes that the combination of individual acts of caring for others will help to constitute or reconstitute a sense of community; here community is very much the end to be pursued. On closer inspection however, the positions are reversed. Initiatives which attempt to build up local activities, such as neighbourhood watch schemes, often appeal explicitly to *individual* self interest. In so far as these schemes have any ambitions beyond the mobilization of mutual self-interest, the idea is to use neighbourhood concerns as a launching pad for creating community concern. By contrast, encouragement of more individualistic seeming efforts, such as the foster work done by community carers, is inconceivable without the belief that there already exists a pre-disposition towards community concern.

The confusion which obscures these different strategies of community involvement may be clarified a little by distinguishing two sorts of community: a community of interests and a community of feelings which alone is properly described as solidarity. Community of interests exists where those involved have specific shared objectives and require mutual collaboration in order to achieve them. Solidarity, on the other hand, represents a sense of shared identity and common engagement. The roots of solidarity may derive from a shared awareness of local, national, ethnic, religious, or professional identity; from shared traditions or values; or, in general, from anything which helps the individual to see herself as part of a large entity or enterprise. With a community of interest the community is united only with reference to the shared interest and only so long as it subsists. It is otherwise with solidarity which both precedes and succeeds the pursuit of interest and for which interest may often have to be sacrificed. At its highest, the aim of involving the community in crime control is the attempt to transform what may begin as a community of interests into a community of feelings and solidarity. This is perhaps the correct resolution of the puzzling ambiguity about community involvement proposals with which I began, for it explains how community can figure simultaneously both as a means and as an end.

The crux question may therefore be reformulated as follows: can schemes of community involvement aspire to the creation or restoration of solidarity or must they be content with underlining the existence of an important community of interests? If solidarity is a real possibility what special form must it take in a pluralist complex society such as our own? For the past 200 years or so, since its birth as a subject, sociological writing has been largely devoted to telling us how and why we have lost the older forms of communal solidarity—explaining why we find ourselves instead living in a *society of strangers*. It is highly unlikely that *all* their arguments will be disproven by any amount of success in achieving more community involvement in crime control. We might rather argue that the reduction of crime is the last, least, and lowest common denominator in a society of strangers. It represents, we might say, the interest of everyone, or almost everyone, excepting criminals, criminologists, and locksmiths!

A variety of explanations for the loss of community were put forward by the classical sociologists. They pointed to the growth of the division of labour, industrialization, class divisions, and the attendant ethic of competitive individualism. They showed how the increase of instrumental rationality, secularization, and moral pluralism helped the decline of shared values and traditions. Some argued that the rise of the state and of national and international markets had helped to destroy local institutions and intermediate associations such as the Guild and the extended household by robbing them of their former functions and consequently also of their authority.[66] Others stressed the emergence of large towns and the regular movement of individuals in search of a better life, both of which reinforced the atomization and anonymity of life in modern society.

But the problem goes further than the lack of any current economic or institutional rationale for the maintenance of communities. The loss of community is a value as well as a fact. The political and legal structures of liberal societies enshrine the principle that individuals are the best judges of their interests. The charter of these institutions encourages them to create a framework in which individuals can pursue their *distinctive* visions of the good life without undue interference from others. In sum, the working assumption of liberal capitalist societies is, or was, that it is unwise to entrust your fate to others—especially if they exercise power over you. Our institutions have as their task the protection of individuals *from* the community *not* the promotion of their absorption into it. This founds the belief that 'law begins where community ends'.[67] The Catch-22 of community justice is that as long as community-based schemes are seen as marginal supplements to official institutions they may just about be tolerated, but as soon as they begin to wield real power the pressure to subject them to rules becomes irresistible. The nearest equivalent to community will which is given authoritative recognition in liberal societies is the collective national will embedded in representative government. Yet it is precisely these governments which now purport to abdicate some of their responsibility for internal crime control in favour of the community; all this at the same time as they continue to weaken the authority of those intermediary associations with any real competing power base such as local authorities and unions.

We can conclude from this that if there is in fact no power vacuum we should not expect community institutions to achieve either power or legitimacy. How is shared locality expected to overcome this? It is illogical to extrapolate from the historical connection between proximity and solidarity to modern day conditions. People who live closely together nowadays do not depend on each other for the performance of significant political and economic functions; they rely far more on the wider political and economic order, on the division of labour, on politicians, on professionals, and on the media.[68] If anything they may have more to fear than to gain from their neighbours, as is particularly evident on some housing estates. None of the neighbourhood schemes of community prevention confront this fact. The Conservative approach to neighbourhood responsibility stresses the obligation of all citizens to play their part in reducing crime, in reporting suspicious occurrences, in watching over their children. Community responsibility is here conceived as *individual* responsibility in the aggregate; in practice, community is merely the term used to describe the general public, anybody in fact other than state officials. The Fabian view, as exemplified in the NACRO projects on housing estates which were described earlier, does demand government responsiveness to the need for better conditions as the price for community self-help. But it too has only a vision of an assumed community of interests, established through market research into the consensus of community opinion.[69] Likewise the Canadian crime prevention schemes have as their strategy for creating a solidarity going beyond that of interests the hope that shared pride will be produced by the community pulling together and defeating the problem of crime. But once the goal of reducing crime is being achieved—the criminals moved on and the internal enemy no more—presumably the neighbourhood will return to the quiet pursuit of contented suburban competitive individualism! We return full circle. Proposals for community involvement are anchored either in locality or altruism because there is only limited scope for discovering discreet communities with their own identity and goals. Indeed real efforts to develop community in that direction would rightly be seen as a threat to the unity and integrity of the state. But this in turn means that those who seek to represent the community in deciding which crimes should be tackled most vigorously, or how cases should be dealt with, are unable to refer to any overarching sense of community requirements or mission which alone could sustain their authority. *A community of interests* can never amount to the same as *the community's interest*.

All this confirms the opinions of those who find talk of community in modern society implausible. But it also suggests that we may be failing to recognize the significance of moves towards community involvement because we are taking its rhetoric at face value. Like most social trends these moves are a result of pressures both from above and from below.[70] From a critical perspective we are now beginning to understand that official sponsorship of community action may have the effect not of restoring the dignity of intermediate associations or community structures but of unsettling and disaggregating solidarity associations by appealing to individually defined interests. But there is also another aspect of this trend in terms of the pressure from below. No society can exist without having some shared solidarity which goes beyond that of interests. One way of viewing the developments I have been discussing is to see them as an index of the changing nature of modern solidarity.[71] Some have argued that changes in responses to crime can indeed be seen to *anticipate* larger changes in social solidarity.[72] Seen in this way both of the conceptions of community which are used in calls for community involvement tell us something about the changing sensibilities of members of modern societies. On the one hand, for many people the shared experience of locality and neighbourhood have now become more of a curse than a blessing. Vulnerability to others leads to increasing concern about how to reassert control over their neighbourhood and how far to trust people. On the other hand, and almost in dialectical opposition to this, the increasing experience of impersonality and anonymity characteristic of life in modern society leads many people to want to take action which will bring them closer to others.

Some schemes of community involvement appear to bring these disparate concerns together in unexpected ways. A nice illustration is provided by the work of the National Association of Victims Support Schemes (NAVSS), which is now the fastest growing voluntary movement in Britain. Their fourth annual report tells us that their work falls into two main categories. Most of their work, about 75 per cent of cases, involves burglary victims, whilst an important sub-group of 10 per cent involves helping victims of violence. Each type of crime and response has its own characteristic features. The psychological shock of undergoing burglary has much to do with the way it brings home (literally) the experience of vulnerability. People are frightened of repetition because of the loss of anonymity which otherwise protects them in a society of strangers. The NAVSS response to this problem is *not* to pretend that the victim is in fact part of an identifiable community to which the helper belongs. Instead the volunteer presents herself as 'a stranger prepared to listen'.[73] To quote the insightful words of the report, 'the actions of the unknown burglar are offset by the help from unknown strangers offering much needed items (so that) confidence in others may not be permanently impaired'.[74] If burglary shows that the actions of unknown strangers can be at least partly offset by the generosity of other strangers, the opposite problem is faced by victims of violence. Here victims usually know their assailants and often such violence occurs in domestic settings. But volunteers are able to offer the reassurance that belonging to a society of strangers, unlike membership of a traditional community, means that ties are not limited to those of family and intimacy and that even where these fail, this sort of society offers the possibility of new life and new ties. In both types of situation no pretence is made that this type of community involvement will do anything to rekindle community spirit, yet its more modest expression of the solidarity of social ties in complex societies may be significant for all that.[75]

It is difficult to provide a neat conclusion to this survey of community involvement in crime control, partly because the comparative recency of the trend means that it is not easy to tell whether it represents a passing fashion or a permanent change. I have suggested, however, the need to clarify the diverse goals which lie behind these programmes, and discussed some of the choices which have to be made both between alternative visions of what they are designed to achieve and in terms of their relationship with the official provisions which already exist. One last point should be mentioned. Nothing I have said should be taken to dissent from any of the important values, such as accountability, participation, or reconciliation, which may lie behind the call for community involvement. What I am saying is that it is often not possible to pursue all these values simultaneously and that such lofty ideals should not mislead us as to the less attractive reasons for calling for more community involvement. Nor will these efforts do much to recreate traditional communities although it is just possible that in some cases they may be the harbingers of new forms of social solidarity.

Notes

1. This paper was first delivered as an invited lecture on the subject of 'The Community Response to Crime' given to the Second Annual Howard League Conference at Pembroke College, Oxford on 13 September, 1984. It was also presented at a seminar at the Home Office Research and Planning Unit on 30 January, 1985. I am grateful to both audiences for their valuable comments and I would also like to thank Mrs Mary McIsaac of Edinburgh University who first suggested to me the range of community involvement programmes and introduced me to relevant reports.

2. For the sake of simplicity I have avoided putting 'community' in quotation marks for the rest of the article. But it should be clear from my argument that I am far from assuming that the word has either a constant or a definite meaning. Some have suggested that the word should be avoided to be replaced for example by neighbourhood or by informal justice. Others would prefer to talk of the general public or laymen rather than community. But these expedients will not do because the initiatives considered here can involve any or all of these various shadings of meaning. Already by the time of Johnson's dictionary, community had acquired three of its central, but not necessarily consistent, meanings: things held in common; neighbourhoods; and the body politic as opposed to the state.

3. R. Plant, *Community and Ideology* (1974). Because community is such 'a contested concept' discussions of its meaning, including this one, are engaged in the business of persuasive definition.

4. The apparently abstract problem of whether community is being proposed as a means or as an end in fact carries the most practical of implications. Consider for example the comments of W. Felstiner and L. Williams, 'Community Mediation in Dorchester, Massachusetts' in R. Tomasic and M. Feeley (eds.), *Neighbourhood Justice: Assessment of an Emerging Idea* (1982), 123: 'if the basic concern is particular disputants and the failure of the criminal justice system to meet their needs then mediation services ought to be provided by a small number of experienced, highly motivated and closely supervised mediators. If, on the other hand, mediation is seen as an aspect of a community's struggle to settle its own quarrels, to take responsibility for its own social control and its own fate, then the base of mediators must be broad, even at the cost of less effective individual mediations.' They go on to describe how the less skilful mediators tended to get edged out as this programme was developed. A parallel example is found in the Scottish Children's Hearing System which recruits its panel of community representatives by applying the two, sometimes inconsistent, criteria of skill

at communication and breadth of representativeness. The resulting mixture confused some critics of the system, and, to a lesser extent, those of us who served in it.

5. Cf. E. Kamenka (ed.), *Community* (1980), 5, who compares the idea of community to that of Utopia. But if the tendency of Utopian experiments is to go sour, the fate of community initiatives is to become institutionalized.

6. R. Williams, *Keywords* (1973).

7. Writers on 'the left' tend to emphasize the mobilization of community as a means of increasing accountability and participation and returning the control of conflicts to those to whom they 'belong'. See for example N. Christie 'Conflicts as Property' (1977) 17, *British Journal of Criminology*, 1–15, and P. Carlen 'On Rights and Powers: Some notes on penal politics' in D. Garland and P. Young, *The Power to Punish* (1983), 203–17. Those on 'the right', such as J. Q. Wilson in *Thinking about Crime* (1975) stress the responsibilities of citizenship and emphasize the needs of the victim.

8. See, for example, the stimulating collection of essays in R. Abel (ed.), *The Politics of Informal Justice* (2 vols.) (1982), and J. Auerbach, *Justice without Law* (1983).

9. Cf. J. Auerbach, ibid., 'Law is crippled by its success, delegalisation survives its failures.'

10. We should also not lose sight of the part that is or should be played by the community in the all-important prior stage of rule making. See for example R. Unger 'The Critical Legal Studies Movement' (1983), 96 Harv. L. Rev. 563.

11. The vital role of the public in reporting and helping to convict criminals is at odds with the trend towards police professionalism, computer wizardry, and centralized direction. See R. Baldwin and R. Kinsey, *Police Powers and Politics* (1982). This is just one example of trends which cut against that of community involvement. We might think also of the selective nature of attacks on the lay elements in the trial: heavy criticism of the jury running alongside continued acceptance in official quarters of a lay magistracy.

12. *NAVSS Fourth Annual Report* (1983–4), 25. These remarks are interesting because they are one of the first signs of official endorsement in this country of the community mediation idea so popular in the USA. There is also evidence of approval if not financial support for conciliation schemes in a number of areas. If the past history of penal reform is any guide, interest in neighbourhood justice schemes in this country will really take off once it is discredited in the United States.

13. Ibid. 19–20: 'reparation by offenders—a new distraction.'

14. A different approach to identifying the goals of community involvement may be found in R. Tomasic, 'Mediation as an alternative to Adjudication: Rhetoric and Reality in the Neighbourhood Justice Movement' in R. Tomasic and M. Feeley (eds.), op. cit. *supra*, 215–49, and D. McGillis, 'Minor Dispute Processing: A Review of Recent Developments' in Tomasic and Feeley (eds.),

ibid. 60–78. I have not followed the approach used in these articles of listing the goals put forward by those advocating community involvement because that leads to difficulties in distinguishing rhetoric from reality even in the claims being made in the first place. Moreover since so many of these claims are inconsistent it is no surprise that these authors are able to show how far they are from being achieved. Their listing of goals tends to be specific and normative whereas the distinctions suggested in the text are intended to be more general and descriptive and offer an analytic framework that can be superimposed on the goals put forward for the various schemes.

15. For example, the issues raised by moves to increase control of crime *by* the community include the requirements of professionalism, such as operational decision-making, in competition with the needs of accountability and participation. Moves to control *in* the community relate to concern over growing public surveillance and paradoxically also its opposite, the fear of neglect of those presently in institutions once they are put into the community. Questions concerning control *for* the community turn on whether the victim or the wider community should benefit and whether the offender is in this way reintegrated into the community or instead used, as Durkheim would have suggested, to integrate the community itself. Some of these issues will be taken further in Section 2 in so far as they enter into the debate between official proponents and radical critics of community justice.

16. There is room for disagreement over the correct categorization of all of these programmes, for example whether or not neighbourhood watch schemes or community policing should also count as altruism. It should be remembered that I am also in the business of persuasive definition!

17. For other purposes it would be important to consider other effects of community involvement, the most important perhaps being its legitimation function.

18. But a number of recent studies have suggested that 'overload' is a product of the practices of legal officials and court staff even more than it is a result of objective increases in case load. It is also difficult to define what is meant by 'overload' and hard to decide when the appropriate response is to build more courts or more prisons to meet the demand. In short, relieving overload is not the simple concept it first appears.

19. *Partners in Preventing Crime* and *Good Neighbours Report*; Programmes Branch Ministry of the Solicitor General, Ottawa, Ontario, Canada; 1 March 1984.

20. Ibid.

21. Ibid.

22. Ibid.

23. NACRO, *Briefing: Neighbourhood Approaches to Crime Prevention* (1984).

24. In the text I have been obliged to simplify what is in fact a rather more complicated debate which includes: those who favour both official and independent types of community involvement scheme (e.g. Warhaftig, *supra*, note

44); those who advocate such schemes as long as they are not officially sponsored (e.g. Bankowski and Mungham, see *infra*, note 26); proponents of officially sponsored schemes but not independent schemes (e.g. Danzig, see *infra*, note 55) and opponents of all schemes (e.g. Auerbach, see *supra*, note 8).

25. Note the interesting ambiguity of the term 'community policing' which can be taken to mean both the exercise of greater self-policing *by* the community as in the phrase 'community control' or alternatively more policing *of* a community as in 'community education'.

26. Z. K. Bankowski and G. Mungham, 'Lay people and law people in the administration of the lower courts' (1981), 9 *International Journal of Sociology of Law*, 85–100.

27. S. Cohen, 'The Punitive City: Notes on the dispersal of social control' in (1979), 3 *Contemporary Crises*, 339–63, and T. Mathiesen, 'The future of control systems—the case of Norway' (1980), 8 *International Journal of Sociology of Law*, 149–64.

28. R. Abel, 'Conservative conflict and the reproduction of capitalism: the role of informal justice' (1981), 9 *International Journal of Sociology of Law*, 245–67. M. Cain 'Beyond Informal Justice', SEUI Working Paper 84/129 (1985).

29. See W. Felstiner and L. Williams, in R. Tomasic and M. Feeley, op. cit. *supra*, note 4, at p. 149.

30. See for example M. Lazerson, 'In the corridors of justice: the only justice is in the halls' in R. Abel (ed.), *The Politics of Informal Justice*, op. cit. i. 119–50.

31. See especially, A. Podgorecki *et al.*, *Knowledge and Opinion about Law* (1973).

32. See R. Abel, 'The contradictions of informal justice' in R. Abel (ed.), *The Politics of Informal Justice*, op. cit. *supra*, i. 267–310.

33. See the effort given to avoiding the problems this creates in the report of the Stewart Committee on alternatives to prosecution in Scotland: *Keeping offenders out of court: further alternatives to prosecution* (1982), Cmnd. 8958.

34. See W. Felstiner and L. Williams, loc. cit. *supra*, note 4.

35. See P. Lerman, *Community Treatment and Social Control* (1975).

36. See S. Cohen, 'The *Punitive City*', op. cit. *supra*, note 27; B. De Sousa Santos in R. Abel (ed.), op. cit. *supra*, note 30.

37. See R. Abel, 'The contradictions of informal justice', loc. cit. *supra*, note 28.

38. See T. Mathiesen, *The Politics of Abolition* (1974) for the best account of how such a strategy could be pursued whilst avoiding the dangers of co-option.

39. See D. McBarnet, *Conviction* (1981).

40. See D. Nelken, *The Limits of the Legal Process: a Study of Landlords Law and Crime* (1983), chap. 7.

41. This is particularly true of American radical commentators who share their culture's 'rights' consciousness.

42. M. Galanter, 'Why the Haves come out Ahead: Speculations on the Limits of Legal Change' (1974), 9 *Law and Society Review*, 95–160.

43. R. Abel, 'The contradictions of informal justice', loc. cit. *supra*, note 30.

44. P. Waharftig, 'An Overview of Community-Orientated Citizen Dispute Resolution Programmes in the U.S.A.', in R. Abel, *The Politics of Informal Justice*, ii. 75–99, is one of the few studies to provide evidence of flourishing self-help community mediation schemes in modern American cities. He makes a useful distinction between 'agency' and 'community' schemes of community mediation but admits that special conditions need to exist before self-help community schemes may be considered viable.

45. A controversial attempt at such an exercise may be found in D. Black, *The Behaviour of Law* (1976), but even he has difficulty in translating qualitative into quantitative changes. From a methodological viewpoint it is also possible that the influence of the work of Foucault, whose conception of state and power is itself intrusive and micro-political, may have influenced radical critics to perceive greater intrusiveness partly as a result of their new theoretical framework.

46. A. Bottoms, 'Some neglected features of contemporary penal systems', D. Garland and P. Young, op. cit. *supra*, note 7, 166–203.

47. These ideal types differ from those put forward by E. Kamenka and A. E.-S. Tay in their influential typology set out in 'Beyond Bourgeois Individualism; The Contemporary Crisis in Law and Legal Ideology', in E. Kamenka and R. S. Neale (eds.), *Feudalism, Capitalism and Beyond* (1975). Such heuristic devices are always created for particular purposes so that the divergence between these ideal types should not be necessarily taken as evidence of material disagreement. My typology goes some way towards showing what 'Gemeinschaft' discourse is like under modern conditions incorporating, as it does, some of the elements of what Kamenka and Tay refer to as 'bureaucratic-administrative law'. For the community approach to crime control combines elements of the traditional Gemeinschaft emphasis on 'the whole man' and concern with reconciliation and harmony with new methods for the prevention and regulation of criminal *activity* divorced from its human actors, as with bureaucratic-administrative law. However, unlike Kamenka and Tay, I see the juxtaposition of different forms of discourse as typically offering mutual reinforcement rather than as constituting a 'crisis'. See D. Nelken 'Is there a Crisis in Law and Legal Ideology?', in [1982] 9 *Journal of Law and Society*, 177-92.

48. Discussions of the justice and welfare approaches to the criminal process have been developed mainly in the debate over juvenile justice, see A. Morris and M. McIsaac, *Juvenile Justice?* (1978), and S. Asquith, *Children and Justice* (1983). The justice approach has of course appropriated or misappropriated the term to mean *formal* justice.

49. I prefer to talk of discourses rather than institutions and processes because it is difficult to know how much a change in discourse reflects or obscures real change. See S. Cohen, 'Telling stories about correctional change' in D. Garland and P. Young (eds.), op. cit. *supra*, note 7, 101–30.

50. But it is a sign of the continued strength of the justice approach that laymen tend to be criticized for *being insufficiently legal* in their decision making (see Z. Bankowski and J. McManus's study of District Court Lay Judges in Scotland; unpublished report for the Scottish Office 1983) whilst they are more likely to be criticized for *failing to stand up to* welfare professionals; see S. Asquith, 'Relevance and lay participation in juvenile justice' (1977), 4 *British Journal of Law and Society,* 61–76.

51. It is not always sufficiently noted that welfare systems change their significance at a time of financial cutbacks. When funds are no longer so freely available, instead of licensing excessive intervention, welfare systems can become a back-door method for allowing continuing concern with matters of substantive justice which the hardship of cutbacks tends to make even more relevant. Ideally, therefore, there should be some scope for combining the strengths of both the welfare and the justice approach. For attempts to defend such a combination in the context of the (community based) Scottish Children's Hearing System see D. Nelken, 'Children's Hearings—the Way Forward' *SCOLAG* (1980), 144–9 and 'The courage of whose convictions?' in *Journal of the Law Society of Scotland,* May 1983.

52. There is a growing and important literature which attempts to integrate the goal of community involvement without sacrificing the protections offered by the justice model. See, e.g. R. Unger, *Knowledge and Politics* (1975) and *Law in Modern Society* (1976); P. Selznick and P. Nonet, *Law and Society in Transition* (1978); G. Teubner, 'Substantive and Reflexive Elements in Modern Law' in (1982), 17 *Law and Society Review,* 239; S. Henry, *Private Justice* (1983), T. O'Hagan, *The End of Law?* (1984).

53. See Z, Bankowski and D. Nelken, 'Discretion as a Social Problem' in M. Adler and S. Asquith (eds.), *Discretion and Welfare* (1982), 247–69.

54. See M. Adler and D. Nelken, *Social Legislation and the Changing Role of the State,* Report of a Nuffield Funded Conference 1982.

55. R. Danzig, whose 1974 article in the *Stanford Law Review* (26: 1–54) helped launch the idea of community mediation in America, entitled it 'Towards the creation of a *complementary,* decentralised system of criminal justice'. He argued quite explicitly 'those who support this plan should do so not because they want community control of the operation of the current system but rather because they want a new system which fills a need overlooked in urban America to date'.

56. But for a sympathetic treatment of community action during the Portuguese Socialist Revolution which comes close to meeting this description see B. De Sousa Santos, 'Popular Justice, Dual Power and Socialist Strategy' in B. Fine *et al., Capitalism and the Rule of Law* (1979), 151–64; cf. D. Nelken, 'Capitalism and the Rule of Law' [1980], *International Journal of the Sociology of Law,* 193–200.

57. See D. McBarnet, *Conviction* (1981), chap. 7, for an acute discussion of the 'ideology of triviality'.

58. See J. Griffiths, 'Ideology in Criminal Procedures or A Third Model of Criminal Process' (1979), 88 Yale L.J. 359–417.
59. See the stimulating discussion in W. Felstiner and L. Williams, loc. cit. *supra*, note 4, at pp. 116–21, where they distinguish enduring relationships which involve only sporadic encounters (such as those between landlord and tenant) from enduring relationships which supposedly involve intimacy (such as marriage). They also challenge the assumption that the closeness of a relationship is measured by the extent of its harmony. Note also the work of J. Comaroff and S. Roberts in *Rules and Processes* (1983), 115–16 *et seq.*, who contrast conflicts which take place *within* an enduring relationship from those where the conflict is *about* the relationship itself.
60. Some of the neighbourhood justice centres in American cities handle cases of rape and serious assault.
61. See, for example, D. Nelken, op. cit. *supra*, note 40, chaps. 4–6, on the ways in which landlord and tenant disputes are first framed in terms appropriate for conciliation and then selectively transformed for handling by adjudication once the case reaches court.
62. See W. Felsteiner and L. Williams, loc. cit. *supra*, note 4, at pp. 123–9.
63. The supposed connection is that both mediation and the community approach are concerned with harmony. But this again confuses means and ends. Communities can achieve harmony in so far as they can appeal to values which guide disputants to sink their differences. Trying to achieve the same goal in the absence of shared ideals is a different matter.
64. Danzig, loc. cit. *supra*, note 55. Danzig's overall argument is that the official courts must continue to deal with 'true crime' because: they involve 'danger'; the need for professional training; dispassionate commitment; due process considerations, and the problem of 'externalities which cannot be satisfactorily dealt with in any local community'. In addition, official courts should process cases which call for the *isolation* of the offender leaving community courts to specialize in cases which require the individual's *reintegration* into society. But this is hardly a coherent basis for distinguishing the two systems. It is hard to see what holds together the motley collection of reasons for handling cases in official courts. Moreover the arguments are often question begging. Is it really the aim of all official processing to *isolate* offenders from the community? And this approach would exactly fulfil the fears of those who argue that community involvement can only lead to bifurcation of sanctions and greater severity for those dealt with in the old way. Having said all this, Danzig's article remains an essential starting-point for any attempt to work towards a semi-autonomous system of community justice.
65. This debate also ignores many other important and relevant connections between crime and community. There has been too little attempt to bring together the criminological literature with the more recent work on dispute-processing. Community support—in the form of youth sub-cultures or ethnic

identity—can be seen as a force which frustrates efforts at crime control quite as much as a resource for achieving control. Some crimes, such as vandalism, are more likely to express group assertiveness than others, such as burglary, which are more individual and instrumental. The response to these two crimes, which are the typical targets of community crime control, might need to be correspondingly different otherwise the predictable gain in community cohesiveness might easily be counter-balanced by gain in the cohesiveness of the groups being controlled. Similarly, some crimes can be attributed to the absence of ties to the community whereas others may be the result of over-eagerness to fulfil community-approved goals or to conform to groups with different expectations. In general, criminologists seem to be moving closer to an acceptance of the rights of communities (however they be defined) to exercise some greater control over the crime which affects them even if this tends to make for greater inconsistency between communities. See, for mainstream criminology, K. Bottomley, *Criminology in Focus* (1979), 116–18, and for left-wing criminologists, J. Lea and J. Young, *What is to be Done About Law and Order?* (1984), 234–5.

66. See R. A. Nisbet, *The Quest for Community* (1958).

67. J. Auerbach, op. cit.

68. See W. Felstiner, 'The Influence of Social Organisation on Dispute Processing' (1974), 9 *Law and Society Review*, 63–94 for an illuminating analysis of the nature of relationships in technologically complex and technologically simple societies with reference to the types of dispute processing in each society. Felstiner stresses the possibilities of 'avoidance' in more complex societies.

69. Tönnies saw consensus as the key to association rather than community. See F. Tönnies, *Community and Association* (1974).

70. No attempt has been made to provide any sort of comprehensive account of the sources of this trend, which in any case vary from country to country. Amongst the different explanations advanced have been: (1) the fiscal crisis and the need for cutbacks in non-productive state activities; (2) growing pressures on the official court system; (3) attacks on professionals in general and the rise of consumerism; (4) the breakdown of policing by consent. See, for further discussion, A. Scull, *Decarceration* (1976), and R. Abel (ed.), *The Politics of Informal Justice*, op. cit. *supra*, note 8.

71. Most interpretations of these changes employed by radical critics of community involvement have tended to draw on neo-Marxist themes but each of the classical sociologists would have something to contribute to their explanation. Thus some have also drawn on Weber's cyclical theory of formal and substantive justice (see Rheinstein (ed.), *Max Weber on Law and Economy in Society* (1954), chap. 11). A more challenging task would be to show how the current rise of community involvement under the conditions which Durkheim called organic solidarity, manages to combine elements of both

repressive and restitutive sanctions. In the text I have chosen instead to draw out one implication of Simmel's notion of the special role of the stranger in modern society. See K. Woolf (ed.), *The Sociology of George Simmel* (1950).

72. See D. Garland, 'The Birth of the Welfare Sanction', 8 *Brit. J. Law and Soc.*, 29–47, who shows how penal changes prefigured the growth of the welfare state.

73. *NAVSS 4th Annual Report*, p. 32.

74. Ibid. at p. 30.

75. One response to this discussion might be to dismiss such voluntary work as mere 'do-gooding' although it would be more difficult to do the same to the simultaneous growth of *self*-help groups. My argument is that the open admission that the person offering help is a stranger united only by actual or imaginative experience of a similar crisis is one way of undercutting the dangers inherent in this role. Interestingly, a probation officer in my audience felt that this approach made more sense for him than the statutory talk of befriending offenders. It is also relevant to note that Felstiner changed his views about the possibility of strangers acting as successful mediators from his a priori assumption in his 1974 article that this constituted a basic objection to community mediation to his view by his later study of the Dorchester experiment that strangers could be successful mediators.

Inside the System

STANLEY COHEN

Imagine a complete cultural dummy—the Martian anthropologist or the historian of centuries to come—picking up a textbook on community corrections, a directory of community agencies, an evaluation study, an annual report. How would he or she make sense of this whole frenzied business, this *mélange* of words?

There are those agencies, places, ideas, services, organizations, and arrangements which all sound a little alike, but surely must be different:

- pre-trial diversion and post-trial diversion;
- all sorts of 'releases'—pre-trial, weekend, partial, supervised, semi-supervised, work and study;
- pre-sentence investigation units and post-adjudication investigation units;
- community-based residential facilities and community residential centres;
- all sorts of 'homes'—community, foster, small group, large group, or just group;
- all sorts of 'houses'—half-way, quarter-way, and three-quarter-way;
- forestry camps, wilderness, and outward-bound projects;
- many kinds of 'centres'; attendance, day, training, community, drop-in, walk-in, and store-front;
- hostels, shelters, and boarding schools;
- weekend detention, semi-detention, and semi-freedom;
- youth service bureaux and something called 'intermediate treatment';
- community services orders, reparation projects, and reconciliation schemes;
- citizen-alert programmes, hot-line listening posts, community radio watches, and citizen block watches;
- hundreds of tests, scales, diagnostic, and screening devices . . . and much, much, much, more.[1]

All these words at least give us a clue about what is happening.[2] But what of:

GUIDE (Girls Unit for Intensive Daytime Education);
TARGET (Treatment for Adolescents Requiring Guidance and Educational Training);
ARD (Accelerated Rehabilitative Dispositions);
PACE (Public Action in Correctional Effort);
RODEO (Reduction of Delinquency through Economic Opportunity);
PREP (Preparation Through Responsive Educational Programs);
PICA (Programming Interpersonal Curricula for Adolescents);
CPI (Critical Period Intervention);
CREST (Clinical Regional Support Team);
VISTO (Volunteers in Service to Offenders); not to mention
READY (Reaching Effectively Acting Out Delinquent Youths);
START (Short Term Adolescent Residential Training); and
STAY (Short Term Aid to Youth)

Then who are all those busy *people* and what might they be doing? Therapists, correctional counsellors, group workers, social workers, psychologists, testers, psychiatrists, systems analysts, trackers, probation officers, parole officers, arbitrators, and dispute-mediation experts? And the para-professionals, semi-professionals, volunteers, and co-counsellors? And clinical supervisors, field-work supervisors, researchers, consultants, liaison staff, diagnostic staff, screening staff, and evaluation staff? And what are these parents, teachers, friends, professors, graduate students, and neighbours doing in the system and why are they called 'community crime control resources'? To find our way through all this, let us begin with an over-elaborate, somewhat arch and even, occasionally, quite misleading metaphor.

Imagine that the entrance to the deviancy control system is something like a gigantic fishing net. Strange and complex in its appearance and movements, the net is cast by an army of different fishermen and fisherwomen working all day and even into the night according to more or less known rules and routines, subject to more or less authority and control from above, knowing more or less what the other is doing. Society is the ocean—vast, troubled and full of uncharted currents, rocks and other hazards. Deviants are the fish.

But unlike real fish, and this is where the metaphor already starts to break down, deviants are not caught, sorted out, cleaned, packed, purchased, cooked, and eaten. The system which receives the freshly caught deviants has some other aims in mind. After the sorting-out stage, the deviants are in fact kept alive (freeze-dried) and processed (shall we say punished, treated, corrected?) in all sorts of quite extraordinary ways. Then those who are 'ready' are thrown back in the sea (leaving behind only the few who die or who are put to death in the system). Back in the ocean (often with tags and labels which they may find quite difficult to shake off), the returned fish might swim around in a free state for the rest of their lives. Or, more frequently, they might be swept up into the net again. This might happen over and over. Some wretched creatures spend their whole lives being endlessly cycled and recycled, caught, processed, and thrown back.

Our interest is in the operation of this net and the parent recycling industry which controls it: the whole process, system, machine, apparatus or, as Foucault prefers, the 'capillary network' or 'carceral archipelago'. The whole business can be studied in a number of quite different ways. The fishermen themselves, their production-line colleagues, and their managers profess to be interested in only one matter: how to make the whole process *work better*. They want to be sure, they say, that they are catching 'enough' fish and the 'right' fish (whatever those words might mean); that they are processing them in the 'best' way (that the same fish should not keep coming back?); that the whole operation is being carried out as cheaply and (perhaps) as humanely as possible. Other observers, though, especially those given the privileged positions of intellectuals, might want to ask some altogether different questions.

First, there are matters of *quantity*: size, capacity, scope, reach, density, intensity. Just how wide are the nets being cast? Over a period of time, do they get extended to new sites, or is there a contraction—waters which are no longer fished? Do changes in one part of the industry affect the capacity of another part? And just how strong is the mesh or how large are its holes, how intensive is the recycling process? Are there trends in turnover? For example, are the same fish being processed quicker or more new ones being caught?

Second, there are questions about *identity*. Just how clearly can the net and the rest of the apparatus be seen? Is it always visible as a net? Or is it sometimes masked, disguised, or camouflaged? Who is operating it? How sure are we about what exactly is being done in all the component parts of the machine?

Third, there is the *ripple* problem. What effect does all this activity—casting the nets, pulling them in, processing the fish—have on the rest of the sea? Do other non-fish objects inadvertently get caught up in the net? Are other patterns disturbed: coral formations, tides, mineral deposits?

Time to switch metaphors to something less elaborate, but more abstract. The deviancy control system occupies a space in any society—both a real space (buildings, technology, staff, clients)—and a social space (ideas, influences, effects). Of any physical object in a space, we may ask questions of *size and density* (how much space is being taken up?); *identity and visibility* (what does the object look like and where are its boundaries?) and *penetration* (how might the object—by magnetism, gravitational pull, radiation, or whatever—affect its surrounding space?). These are the three sets of problems which this chapter will address. Whether or not visions of fishing nets and objects in space help very much, my task is to describe the new patterns of crime control established over the last decades. Again, the focus will be on the ideal of community control.

Size and density

By definition, the destructuring movements were aimed at decreasing the size, scope, and intensity of the formal deviancy control system. All the visions were abolitionist, destructive, or at least reductive: decreasing reliance on the treatment ideology, limiting the scope of the criminal law, ending or radically decreasing incarceration, restricting the full force of the criminal justice system, minimizing formal system intervention whenever possible, screening out offenders into less intrusive alternatives. To return to the net analogy: the size and reach of the net should be decreased and so should the strength of its mesh.

I focus here on the two most established and popular strategies to achieve these ends: deinstitutionalization/community alternatives and diversion. Leaving aside for the moment questions about causality, consequence, and failure, the size and density questions can be answered quite simply:

1. there is an increase in the total number of deviants getting into the system in the first place and many of these are new deviants who would not have been processed previously (wider nets);
2. there is an increase in the overall intensity of intervention, with old and new deviants being subject to levels of intervention (including traditional institutionalization) which they might not have previously received (denser nets);
3. new agencies and services are supplementing rather than replacing the original set of control mechanisms (different nets).

No one who has listened to the historical tales of the last chapter, particularly about the results of earlier alternatives and innovations such as probation, parole, and the juvenile court,[3] should be altogether surprised at any of this. But these patterns need careful scrutiny, are not always self-evident, and are never easy to explain.

The old institutions remain

Let us start with the (apparently) simple question of whether the decarceration strategy has worked in reducing the rates of juvenile and adult offenders sent to custodial institutions. The obvious index of success is not simply the proliferation of new programmes, but whether custodial institutions are being replaced, phased out, or at least are beginning to receive fewer offenders overall. The statistical evidence here is by no means easy to decipher and there are complicated methodological problems in picking out even the crudest of changes. But all evidence here indicates failure—that in Britain, Canada, and the USA rates of incarceration are not at all declining and in some spheres are even increasing. Community control has supplemented rather than replaced traditional methods. We may approach this data in a number of ways.[4]

First, by using official national statistics, we might simply look at overall rates of custody. The picture here is quite clear. In none of the countries we are considering, has there been any appreciable decline in the number of adult or juvenile offenders in traditional, closed custodial institutions. These numbers have either been constant or more often, have increased either steadily or dramatically. Each standard index of imprisonment—numbers of inmates in custody at any one time, rates of custody per 100,000 of the population, numbers or rates of annual admissions, length of time in custody, building programmes, custodial budgets, or staff numbers—shows a slightly different pattern, but the overall picture is indisputable: the continuation or expansion of the custodial institution. Here is a crude summary and a few examples from the mass of statistics covering the period from the late 1960s to the present.[5]

Britain   For adults, with the exception of a slight decline in 1974, there has been a steady upward spiral in the number and rates of imprisonment. In 1982 the average daily prison population was 43,700: 11,000 of these were crowded into two per cell and 3,600 into three per cell. This was the ninth successive year in which more adults were received under sentence of immediate imprisonment. Average sentence length has increased. An estimated £80 million was spent that year on a prison building programme, not enough to accommodate the estimated number of 49,000 prisoners expected by 1991. The prison population nearly doubled over the 'decarceration' period and, by 1982, according to the Home Office Minister of State, the country was 'in the middle of the biggest prison building programme for a century'.

For juveniles, where the anti-institution and pro-community rhetoric was stronger, the increased use of custody during this period has been even larger and more dramatic than for adults. This included even the hardest and most traditional forms of custody—young adults in prisons (under-21s constituted 30 per cent of the custodial population in 1982), Borstal (up by 136 per cent between 1969 and 1977) and detention centres (up by 158 per cent during this period)—as well as the softer, more welfare-oriented institutions. Overall, a massive increase in custodial sentences to juveniles throughout this period.

USA   For adults, the pattern is quite clear—a slight drop in incarceration rates from the mid-1960s to the early 1970s (102 prisoners per 100,000 of the population in 1968 to 93 in 1972), then a dramatic increase over the 1970s (a 54 per cent increase in number between 1972–9) and continually rising. By 1982, the rate of imprisonment per 100,000 of the population was 153 and by 1982, some 175. The rise (on an annual basis) in the first half of 1982 was 14.3 per cent—the highest rate ever recorded since 1926. In 1982 alone, the net annual gain in inmates admitted to State and Federal Prison was 37,309—nearly 90 per cent of the total gain from 1977 to 1980. At this rate of increase, there will be 500,000 prisoners by 1985. During this period there has been an incremental increase in corrections expenditure, reaching 6,361 billion dollars in 1979. Custodial staff similarly increased (more than the inmate rate, thus giving a more intensive staff : inmate ratio).

For juveniles, there was some reduction over this period of numbers of residents in public (state and local government) facilities, and incarceration rates for categories such as status offenders decreased. Much of this overall decrease however, has been offset by the increase in the number of state or privately run welfare and psychiatric establishments. Even in the conventional sector, from 1971–9, the cost of juvenile detention facilities rose from $92.1 million to $228.8 million—an increase of 148.5 per cent. The budgets of training schools increased by 60 per cent in this period. And, at the hard end, locking up juveniles in adult jails had not declined; by the end of the 1970s at least 500,000 juveniles were still processed in this way.

Canada   After a slight drop in the early 1970s, incarceration rates began to climb back to the late 1960s level and, by 1982, rates (in Federal and provincial prisons) were showing an all-time high, both in the standing population and those flowing through the system. Correctional service personnel increased by 84 per cent between 1966 and 1979 (as with the USA, an increase that exceeded the number of inmates).

These data are extremely complex and there are all sorts of internal variations which need explaining, for example: changes according to different types of offences, the differences between Britain and the USA, the dramatic success of other reasonably similar countries (such as Holland)[6] in cutting incarceration rates. It is important also to note that, although overall imprisonment rates are not declining, there has been in most places a proportionate decline in the use of imprisonment as a percentage of all sentences. In other words—to take the British example—although more identified offenders are being sent to prison each year, fewer of the total being sentenced (a decline of about 25 per cent in 1965 to 15 per cent in 1980) are being sent to prison. Only in this respect can decarceration be said to have 'worked'—a slight decline in the reliance on imprisonment in the overall sentencing repertoire. Yet even here there are doubts because many of these alternative sentences are ways of deferring or suspending imprisonment. In every other sense, though, there has been an exponential rise in the use of imprisonment: prison populations in the USA and Britain have roughly doubled since 1950.

A second empirical strategy in looking at net size, is not to use global rates, but to compare systems with differing degrees of commitment to the community ideology. This is logically the most useful research strategy but for obvious reasons the most difficult. This sort of comparison between different states in the USA clearly shows that increased reliance on community programmes is not accompanied by a corresponding decrease in the use of institutional programmes. The reverse is true: the states which score high on use of community programmes, also have an above-average use of institutions.[7]

A third strategy—a refinement of the simple reliance on official statistics—is a detailed follow-through of the overall dispositional patterns of one correctional system over time. Exemplary work of this kind is Hylton's time-series analysis of trends in the Sasketchewan province of Canada from 1962–79. At the end of the 1950s, the province adopted a clearly articulated philosophy of community control, there was a massive investment in the new programmes and a clear belief that they would replace institutions.

The results showed no reduction at all in reliance on custody, whether measured by numbers and rates of admission or number and rates incarcerated on any given day. The average daily inmate count per 100,000 of the population increased from 55.23 in 1962 to 84.87 in 1979—a 54 per cent increase in incarceration rates on any given day over 18 years. The rate of admissions rose over this same 18-year period by 58 per cent. Institutions now process more offenders than at any time in the province's history and all trends indicate that this expansion is increasing. Again, decarceration has worked only in the sense that the relative reliance on custody compared to other dispositions has decreased—from about two-thirds of all sentences in 1962 to about a quarter in 1979. Some potential inmates are syphoned off but the institution remains and expands.

A final research approach is to narrow down even further to case studies of particular legislative acts, projects, or programmes. The most publicized (and evaluated) series of programmes in the USA have been the Massachusetts reform, the California Probation Subsidy programmes, DSO (Deinstitutionalization of State Offenders), and Community Corrections Acts in states such as Minnesota. These are mainly variations on the strategy of providing economic incentives (bribes) to local authorities to switch from custody to community. There have been some notable successes here, for example the DSO programme in certain states and the well-known and dramatic Massachusetts strategy of closing down all juvenile training schools.[8] Although there are important reservations, which I will consider later, about the nature of the alternatives, it is clear that traditional custody has declined in these cases. These exceptions are important for social policy. Overall assessment of other programmes, however, suggests far more negative or equivocal results.

In California, for example, initial reported decreases in commitments to the Youth Authority have been interpreted differently by later research and do not seem to have been sustained.[9] While the programme shifted control of juveniles destined for state institutions to local jurisdiction, this did not reduce the state's overall reliance on custody. That is to say, the form and location of confinement changed and these new forms of commitment 'compensated' for any reductions in conventional admissions. Commitments shifted to local county levels, there was more detention by the police, and (as we shall see) the notion of 'intensive treatment in the community' actually glossed over a degree of hidden custody within the community programmes themselves. Overall, offenders ended up spending more time in institutions.

Little research of equivalent sophistication is available in Britain, but the Intermediate Treatment (IT) experience certainly fits this general pattern.[10] Implemented from the beginning of 1971, this is a system of intensive supervision in the community designed to provide care and control for a whole range of juvenile offenders and 'children in trouble' who would otherwise have been sent to 'residential care' (the English euphemism for custody). Quite the opposite has happened. As the national data suggest, there has been a massive increase in custodial sentences for juveniles from 1968 to the present. The greater the IT provision, the larger become the institutional populations.

From all these sources then—with isolated exceptions—the story is of stable or increasing institutional populations over the last twenty years. As one analyst of the British evidence notes, the institution has not only survived the ethos of the 'era of decarceration' but has actually become stronger.[11]

Overall the system expands

If the use of community control is increasing and if traditional custody is either increasing or only remaining constant, an inescapable conclusion suggests itself—that the system overall is getting larger. This, in fact, is the trend reported from all research.

Again, we might approach the problem by examining global statistical trends or by trying to isolate specific effects of community strategies. The total correctional caseload in the USA (adults and juveniles incarcerated or under supervision) increased from 1,281,801 (661.3 per 100,000 of the population) in 1965 to 1,981,229 (921.4 per 100,000) in 1976. This was an absolute increase of 54.6 per cent and a rate increase of 39.3 per cent. By 1983, it was estimated that some 2.4 million persons were under some form of correctional care, custody or supervision—a rate of 1,043 per 100,000 of the population (leaving out allied forms of welfare and psychiatric tracking). Three-quarters of these were somehow 'in the community'. Twenty years after 1965, the overall system will have nearly doubled its reach.

Other indices from the USA, Britain, and Canada also show overall increases in rates 'under correctional sanction or supervision'. Hylton's data on one province in Canada are a microcosm of the trend to expand in systems committed to community control. The rate per 100,000 of the population under supervision of the Saskatchewan correctional system increased from 85.46 in 1962 to 321.99 in 1979—277 per cent in 18 years. The admissions rate increased in these years by 179 per cent—a rate of increase each year of about 44 per cent. In simpler terms, the rate of persons under supervision by the correctional system on any given day more or less tripled during these 18 years.

This type of finding is duplicated throughout the research literature. The system overall expands relentlessly while the relative proportions sent to prison rather than community programmes declines (in that Canadian case, from two-thirds down to one-quarter over 18 years). The obvious inference then, strongly supported by correlational evidence, is that the use of community alternatives actually causes an overall system expansion which might not otherwise have occurred. The correlational logic is simple enough: if community programmes were *replacing* institutions, then systems high in community places would show a less-than-average use of institutions. But if community was *supplementing* institutions, then systems high in community would also have an above-average use of institutions and this is just what seems to be happening. Such tricky statistics aside, how does all this happen?

New deviants are drawn in and intervention intensifies on the same old ones

The simplest way of visualizing the non-reduction of incarceration rates and the concomitant expansion of the whole system, is to argue that the 'wrong' populations are being swept into the new parts of the net. 'Wrong' in the sense of being inappropriate, 'inappropriate' in the sense of not being the populations for whom the original reforms were meant—in other words, not the populations who would otherwise have been incarcerated if the new programmes did not exist.

Clearly, of course, some of the new 'clients' *are* being kept out of institutions; the changes in relative disposition rates show this. But large proportions of these populations—the literature sometimes shows between a half and two-thirds—are 'shallow-end' or soft delinquents,[12] minor or first offenders whose chances of incarceration would otherwise have been slight. As long as the strategy is not being used for genuine 'deep-end' offenders and as long as institutions are not literally closed down or phased out, incarceration will tend to increase, the system will be more interventionist overall, and a substantial number of community clients— perhaps a majority—will be subjected to a degree of intervention higher than they would have received under previous non-custodial options such as fines, conditional discharge, and ordinary probation or parole.

There are considerable research problems in showing all this and especially in estimating the shallow-end : deep-end ratio. Macro-research on how the system changes overall will not necessarily produce the same results as micro-research trying to show that particular offenders on a new 'alternative' programme would not have been sent to an institution anyway. And as Klein suggests in regard to status offences, the total confusion about the original definition of such terms makes it almost impossible to know whether the right clients have been 'targeted'.[13] Nevertheless, there is overwhelming consensus that a considerable number of community clients, perhaps the majority, are shallow-enders. To mix these aquatic metaphors: the old nets keep on catching most of the original deep-end fish, while the new nets take up the remainder but mostly catch the original shallow-enders (the minnows).

All these spatial trends can be observed even more clearly in regard to diversion. Because the idea itself is more radical than deinstitutionalization—deflection from the whole system and not merely its deep custodial recesses—studies of the diversion strategy demonstrate failure even more radically.[14] Diversion was hailed as the most radical form of destructuring short of complete non-intervention or decriminalization. At the height of the diversion 'fad' (as it is now being called) official estimates and hopes were that as many as 70 per cent of juveniles passing through the formal system could be diverted away into less intrusive options. (The figure 70 per cent seems to have a magically radical ring. At the crest of the decarceration wave, this was the figure most often quoted as the proportion of inmates who do not 'need' to be locked up.) The grand rationale is to restrict the full force of the criminal justice system to more serious offences and either to eliminate or substantially minimize penetration for all others. By diverting people at the 'front end' of the system, it is hoped that more reductions can take place at later stages. The strategy has been most systematically adopted for juveniles (a remarkable development, as the central agency from which offenders were to be diverted, the juvenile court, was itself the product of the Progressive's reform movement aimed at 'diversion').

Clearly all justice systems, particularly juvenile ones, have always operated with a substantial amount of diversion. Real diversion has always occurred in the sense that by far the majority of delinquent acts noticed by parents, teachers, social workers, neighbours, employers, and casual observers are simply not acted on in any way at all. And at the earliest formal part of the system's front end, police discretion has always been widely used to divert juveniles: either right out of the system (by dropping charges, informally reprimanding, or cautioning) or by informal referral to social service agencies. Most research routinely quotes figures as high as 70 per cent for this type of police diversion.

What has now happened, is that these discretionary and screening powers have been formalized and extended and, in the process, quite transformed. Diversion is no longer something that just 'happens': it takes the form of a massive infrastructure of programmes and agencies: throughout the 1970s, the US Federal Government, through the Law Enforcement Assistance Administration (LEAA), funded over 1,200 adult and juvenile diversion programmes, at a cost of $120 million.

It is this infrastructure which calls for the distinction between *traditional* or *true* diversion—removing the juvenile from the system altogether by screening out (no further treatment, no service, no follow-up) —and *new* diversion which means screening plus programme (formal penetration is minimized by referral to programmes in the system or related to it). Only traditional diversion is true diversion in the sense of diverting *from*. The new diversion diverts—for better or worse—*into* the system. Cressey and McDermott's laconic conclusion from their evaluation of one such set of programmes might apply more generally:

> If 'true' diversion occurs, the juvenile is safely out of the official realm of the juvenile justice system and he is immune from incurring the delinquent label or any of its variations—pre-delinquent, delinquent tendencies, bad guy, hard core, unreachable. Further, when he walks out of the door from the person diverting him, he is technically free to tell the diverter to go to hell. We found very little 'true' diversion in the communities studied.[15]

In other words, to return to the example of police discretion, where the police used to have two options—screen right out (the route for the majority of encounters) or process formally—they now have the third option of diversion into a programme. It is this possibility which allows for net extension and strengthening. For what happens is that diversion is used as an alternative to screening out and not as an alternative to processing. The system thus expands to include those who, if the programme had not been available, would not have been processed at all (genuine new fish). Or if the diversion programme is located at a later stage of the machine, the clients are those who would otherwise have received less obtrusive options like fines, conditional discharge, suspended sentence, or traditional probation (old shallow-enders). Both phases are examples of what the literature now calls 'accelerated penetration'.

In either case, diversion simply has not occurred: 'diversion means to turn away from and one cannot turn someone away from something toward which he was not already heading'.[16] As with community 'alternatives', the exact proportions of such wrong clients (their 'transitional probability rating', to use the approved term) are difficult to estimate. Such averages hide massive variations from one programme to another, but the research consensus is that at least half the divertees are what American police sometimes call 'cream puff' cases—young people who would otherwise have been 'counselled and released' by the police or would never have been inserted this far into the system. Compared to other offenders, they tend to be younger, have committed less serious offences or status offences (which might include matters such as 'incorrigibility', running away, and truancy), have a less serious (or no) past record, and are more likely to be female.

Moreover—an even more radical form of net extension—these diversion clients might not have committed any offence at all. The ideology of early intervention and treatment and the use of psychological or social-work selection criteria, allows diversion to be incorporated into wider preventive strategies. Legal definitions and due process give way to low visibility, 'discretionary decision making' by administrative or professional agencies. The drift is to work with parts of the population not previously reached, variously defined as young people 'in trouble', 'at risk', or 'in legal jeopardy', 'pre-delinquents' or 'potential delinquents'. These trends are not primarily a widening of social control into 'empty' spaces, but an intensification and formalization of previous methods. Populations who once slipped quickly through the net are now retained much longer; many innovative alternatives become adjuncts to established sanctions such as probation and fines.[17]

We arrive then at something close to a total reversal of all the supposedly radical justifications on which the original diversion strategy was based: reduction of stigma and labelling, non-intervention, decreased emphasis on individual treatment, more justice, and reduction of system load. Instead, intervention comes earlier, it sweeps in more deviants, is extended to those not yet formally adjudicated, and it becomes more intensive. And all this takes place in agencies co-opted into the criminal justice system (but less subject to judicial scrutiny), dependent on system personnel for referrals and using (as we shall see) more or less traditional treatment methods.

The whole topic of net space and density is altogether fascinating and complex. I have given only a glimpse of the intricate ways in which the system grows, renews itself, and mutates, and how all this might be studied. Note, for example, what we can learn from the characteristics of the new clients of these community and diversion programmes. These clients are not simply mistakes who enter the system because screening has been relaxed. Quite the contrary. It is only because screening is so careful and successful that the shallow-enders and cream puffs are pulled further in. They come from precisely those backgrounds—fewer previous arrests, minor or no offences, good employment record, better education, younger, female—which all research suggests to be overall indicators of greater success. The point is to find as clients for community services those who have the strongest community ties and commitments in the first place. Behind the elaborate ritual of psychological testing and diagnoses, this is, in fact, how selection takes place. Many agencies, such as various pre-trial bail release schemes, simply use a crude points system which guarantees acceptance on to the programme to those who score best on length of residence in one place and employment record. This, presumably, goes according to the old principle of giving more to those that have more.

Of course, as the statistics indicate, some bad risks (the 'real' target clients) do get in. Certain programmes do give the offender a genuine choice about entry and there is pressure to make the programme look impressive by really rescuing offenders from the deep end. In these cases, some of the old losers—who probably prefer anything to returning to the traditional system—will enter the programme.[18] But too many of them will make the programme look bad and lead to pressure for a clampdown. If there is little room for such self-selection (the normal state of affairs) then only the shallow-enders will be let in—those who will make the programme less risky. This process repeats itself at all the increasing stages in the system: each level creaming off the clients it wants—those who are amenable, treatable, easy to work with, the good prospects. The rest are 'diverted' to the next level up.

All this ensures a steady clientele. And the more benign, attractive, and successful the programme becomes defined, the more it will be used, the more staff and budgets will be needed, and the wider it will cast its net (nearly everyone could do with a little 'help'). Police will divert because this is less risky than outright release and much less trouble than fighting the case through the courts (especially as the courts become more legalistic and therefore make it difficult to secure a conviction). Judges are attracted to the new programmes because this avoids unnecessary incarceration, while at the same time ensuring that 'something constructive' is done.

To use yet another metaphor (fishing nets? objects in space?), we have here a benevolent kind of suction machine, driven by the principle of *incremental eligibility*. Each stage retains its own eligible material, leaving another body—in a deeper or shallower part of the system—to operate its own eligibility criteria. Of course things might not always run so smoothly. Agencies within the criminal justice system might compete over the same potential clientele, or clients might be tracked and retracked between crime, welfare, and psychiatric systems. These moves in the game of relabelling and moral passage then might be formalized in administrative or legal changes.

A typical example would be status offenders. They can be relabelled 'downwards' as being in need of care, treatment, or resocialization and thus the property of welfare or treatment agencies. But just as likely, youths previously defined as status offenders and hence eligible for decarceration, diversion, or even decriminalization, can now be relabelled upwards as real delinquents. The police might push up the arrest rates of such offenders in order to compensate for the loss of the status offender market. As Lemert says, they are simply doing what comes naturally and easily to them: dipping into the reservoir of youths who might otherwise have gone free.[19] And this dipping does not occur randomly. Research evidence is mounting, for example, that *girls* with little prior system contact are a particularly vulnerable group for further processing by the new programmes.[20]

The suction principle is even more complicated by the fact that as the system changes, so all its component parts adjust themselves, in good cybernetic fashion, to take into account the new feedback. The disposition received by an offender arriving at a particular level is now affected by the knowledge that he was 'diverted' at an earlier level. The most severe punishments go not just to the worst offenders in legalistic terms, but to those who foul up at their previous level. In 1981, for example, about one out of every five admissions to prison in the USA were for conditional release violations rather than as direct sentences from the court.

Sometimes, with radical system changes, whole stages might be skipped. This appears to be one of the effects of Intermediate Treatment in Britain. Some previous shallow-enders (who might have received probation, fines, or conditional discharges) become defined as unsuitable for the new programmes and are sucked straight into the custodial end of the system. The new 'care order' (a custodial sentence based on welfare rather than legalistic criteria) permits some marginal delinquents to go to custody while the new system prefers to take others who might not have committed offences at all but come from 'deprived backgrounds'. Many of the care orders which fail to demonstrate the supposedly objective criteria for care (one study found as many as 89 per cent were in this category)[21] are renewed not because of further offences, but because the client fouls up in the system (by being uncooperative or by absconding).

In summary, net expansion occurs through a series of what Illich nicely called 'iatrogenic feedback loops'. The juvenile court diverted from the adult system; diversion agencies divert from the juvenile courts; new diversion agencies divert from the diversion agencies. Each stage creates the deviant it wants and constructs its programmes accordingly. These organizational loops thus do more than enlarge the capacity of the system, they also change its character. For example, as the community rhetoric becomes accepted (even if it is not what it might seem) traditional agencies change their operating principles. Prisons now become defined in more negative terms: warehouses for the incorrigibles, hard cases, those which the soft end of the system has been unable to reach. They have been given their chance in the community, now they have reached the bottom of the barrel.[22]

There are also such feedback loops to networks of deviancy control, care, and treatment right outside the criminal justice apparatus. As I will describe in the next section, boundaries between these systems are now less clearly defined and therefore gains and losses are virtually impossible to estimate. The flow occurs in both directions: former offender groups are retracked into the welfare or mental health system and previous patients (notably decarcerated mentally ill adults) come into the criminal justice system.

This is merely one example of the technical complexity of describing changes in the size and density of the control network. But the broad outlines are clear—the older and discredited parts of the system (particularly traditional custodial institutions) remain. Overall, the system enlarges itself and some, at least, of this enlargement is due to the proliferation of the newer community alternatives. I will raise later the obvious question of the relationship between this expansion and increasing crime rates. It is enough to say here that in every case system expansion is larger than crime expansion.

Visibility, ownership, and identity

Most forms of net widening are perceived as largely unintended consequences of destructuring reforms. Or at least, as the notion of 'unintended consequences' already implies a particular theory, these effects could not be predicted in any simple way from the ideology. I turn now to three properties of the machine: the visibility of its boundaries; its ownership or sponsorship; and the identity of its operations. The first two of these could certainly have been predicted and understood from the ideology.

The segregated and insulated nineteenth-century institutions made the actual business of deviancy control invisible, but its boundaries visible. That is to say, what went on inside these places was supposed to be unknown. Institutions like prisons gradually became wrapped with an impenetrable veil of secrecy.[23] Segregation came to mean insulation and invisibility. This was the transition which Foucault charted—from the visible, public spectacle (torture, execution, humiliation) to the more discreet form of penitentiary discipline. The public trial remained the only visible part of the system.

But a condition for internal invisibility was to have the boundaries of the punitive system more visible and obvious. We should not see or know what went on behind the walls of the prison, but we should definitely know that these were walls. Whether prisons were built in the middle of cities, out in the remote countryside, or on deserted islands, they had clear spatial boundaries to mark off the normal from the deviant. And these spatial boundaries were reinforced by ceremonies of social exclusion: prisoners were sent away or sent down, their 'bodies' were symbolically received at the prison gate, then—stripped, washed, and numbered—they entered another world. Those on the outside would wonder what went on behind the walls, those inside could try to imagine the 'outside world'. Inside/outside, guilty/innocent, freedom/captivity, imprisoned/released—these were all distinctions that made sense.

In the new world of community corrections, these boundaries are no longer nearly as simple. The way *into* an institution is not clear (it is just as likely to be via a post-adjudication diagnostic centre as a police car) the way *out* is even less clear (graduated release or partial release is just as likely as full freedom) nor is it clear what or where *is* the institution. There is, we are told, a 'correctional continuum' or a 'correctional spectrum': criminals and delinquents might be found anywhere in these spaces. And so fine, and at the same time so indistinct, are the gradations along the continuum, that it is by no means easy to know where the prison ends and the community begins or just why any deviant is to be found at any particular point. Even the most dedicated spokesmen for community treatment have some difficulty in specifying just what 'the community' is; one early report confessed that the term community treatment 'has lost all descriptive usefulness except as a code word with connotations of "advanced correctional thinking" and implied value judgements against the "locking up" and isolation of offenders.'[24]

Even the most cursory examination of the new programmes reveals that many varieties of the more or less intensive and structured 'alternatives' are virtually indistinguishable from the real thing. A great deal of energy and ingenuity is being devoted to this problem of definition: just how isolated and confining does an institution have to be before it is a prison rather than, say, a 'residential community facility'? Luckily for us all, criminologists have got this matter well in hand and are spending a great deal of time and money on such questions. They have devised quantitative measures of internal control, degree of community linkage, normalization (harmony with neighbourhood, type of building, name of programme), and the like. There are now any number of standardized scales for assigning programmes along the 'institutionalization–normalization continuum' or awarding them PASS (Program Analysis of Service Systems) or MEAP (Multiphasic Environmental Assessment Procedure) scores.[25]

But these are not just untidy loose ends which scientific research will one day tie up. Community control is a project explicitly devoted to changing traditional ideas about punishment. The ideology of the new movement quite deliberately demands that boundaries should not be made too clear: the metaphor of 'crumbling walls' implies an undifferentiated open space. The main British prison reform group, the Howard League, once called for steps to 'restore the prison to the community and the community to the prison'. Less rhetorically, here was an early enthusiast for a model 'community correction centre': 'the line between being "locked up" and "free" is purposely indistinct because it must be drawn differently for each individual. Once the client is out of Phase I, where all clients enter and where they are all under essentially custodial control, he may be "free" for some activities but still "locked up" for others.'[26]

There is no irony intended in using inverted commas for such words as 'free' and 'locked up' or in using such euphemisms as 'essentially custodial control'. This sort of blurring—deliberate or unintentional—may be found throughout the complicated networks of 'diversion' and 'alternatives' which are now being set up.

The half-way house might serve as a good example. These agencies—called variously, 'residential treatment centres', 'restitution shelters', 'rehabilitation residences', 'guidance centres', 'reintegration centres', 'community training residence programmes', or (with the less flowery language preferred in Britain) simply 'hostels'—invariably become special institutional domains themselves. They might be located in a whole range of odd settings—private houses, converted motels, the grounds of hospitals, YMCAs, beach clubs, the dormitories of university campuses, or even within the walls of prisons themselves. Their programmes turn out to reproduce regimes and sets of rules very close to the institutions themselves: about security, curfew, passes, drugs, alcohol, permitted visitors, required behaviour, and surveillance.[27] Indeed it becomes difficult to distinguish a very 'open' prison, with liberal provisions for work release, home release, and outside educational programmes, from a very 'closed' half-way house.

Any number of half-way houses, for example, can be found to be more 'institutional' than the Vienna Correctional Centre, a minimum security institution in Illinois which counts as a prison.[28] Here, inmates:

- are trained as emergency technicians and operate radio-directed ambulances;
- learn fire fighting and constitute the local fire department;
- serve as umpires on a Little League baseball field;
- make up a band to entertain at concerts and high school games;
- meet local residents who come to fish in the prison lake, play basketball in its gym, or join in its adult education centre or vocational training programme.

The prison, we are told, looks like a suburb or college campus, paths lead to separate 'neighbourhoods', and prisoners have the key to their own rooms. Many hostels 'in the community' are more restrictive and artificial than this sounds.

To confuse matters further: half-way houses may be half-way *in* for those too serious to be left at home, but not serious enough for the institution—and hence are a form of 'diversion'—or half-way *out* for those who can be released from the institution but are not yet 'ready' for the open community—and hence are a form of 'after care'. To make life more difficult the same centre is sometimes used for both these purposes, with different rules for the half-way in inmates and the half-way out inmates.

Even this degree of blurring and confusion is not enough: one advocate draws attention to the advantages of *quarter-way* houses and *three-quarter-way* houses.[29] These 'concepts', we are told, are already being used in the mental-health field, but are not labelled as such in corrections. The quarter-way house deals with people who need supervision on a near permanent basis, while the three-quarter-way house is designed to care for persons in an 'acute temporary crisis needing short-term residential care and little supervision'. Then, taking the opposite tack from devising finer and finer classification schemes, other innovators argue for a 'multi-purpose' centre. Some half-way houses already serve as a parolee residence, a drop-in centre, a drug-treatment programme, and a non-residential walk-in centre for after care. And in the absence of a handy multi-purpose centre in the neighbourhood, a package deal is worked out around the offender himself, shuttling him from probation, a day training centre, a hostel, a service for alcoholics, and a job creation programme.[30]

Behind all this administrative surrealism, this manic activity, some more significant forms of blurring are happening. For many of these 'multi-purpose' centres, bureaux, services, and agencies are directed not just at convicted offenders, but are preventive, diagnostic, or screening enterprises aimed at potential, pre-delinquent or 'at risk' populations. The ideology of community treatment and the preventive thrust of the diversion strategy allows for an altogether facile evasion of the delinquent/non-delinquent distinction.

A good example of this evasion is the British system of Intermediate Treatment (IT). This is not just an intermediate possibility between sending a child away from home and leaving him in his normal home environment, but also a new way 'to make use of facilities available to children who have not been before the courts, and so to secure the treatment of "children in trouble" in the company of other children through the sharing of activities and experiences within the community'.[31] Note the wording of these accounts of IT projects: 'a provision for young people at risk of institutionalization, unemployment, homelessness, family breakup, and lack of work skills'; 'community based provision for adolescents and children who are deprived or who are more at risk of getting into trouble than their contemporaries'; 'a continuum of care . . . with intensity increasing according to the degree of deviancy or perceived needs'.

There is a deliberate attempt here to evade the question of whether a rule has actually been broken. 'Illegal behaviour' (degree of deviancy?), we are assured, 'merges almost imperceptibly with behaviour which does not contravene the law' (perceived needs?). The 'deprived' are not very different from the 'depraved'. The point is to devise a service flexible enough to deal with both—a service which is simultaneously a response to delinquency and to other 'crises' (family breakdown, deviant leisure styles, school problems, unemployment) in the 'normal life cycle'.[32]

This type of definitional 'flexibility' is ensured by the tendency of the new agencies to operate in a closed circuit free from legal scrutiny. While the traditional screening mechanisms of the criminal justice system have always been influenced to a greater or lesser degree by non-offence related criteria (race, class, demeanour) the offence was at least considered. Except in the case of wrongful conviction, some law must have been broken. This is no longer clear: a delinquent may find himself in custody ('short-term intensive treatment') either because of welfare/treatment criteria (at risk, deprived) or by programme failure (violating the norms of some other agency in the continuum, for example by non-attendance at a therapy group or 'acting out'). By 1981, through a classic form of net widening, at least 45 per cent of participants on all IT programmes were not subject to any court order at all.

The definitional blurring which occurs in regard to individual judgements (referral, diagnosis, screening, eligibility) is reproduced at the organizational and personnel level. Agency names like 'Youth Service Bureau' or 'Intermediate Treatment Centre' and staff titles such as 'counsellor' or 'supervisor' are interchangeable and they might just as easily be managed by the educational, welfare, or health sectors as by criminal justice authorities. All this again is intentional: 'as institutional walls disintegrate, figuratively speaking, the boundaries between the various human service areas will disappear as well—and correctional problems will come to be the problem of a range of professionals serving communities'.[33] Crime and delinquency nets thus not only become blurred in themselves but get tangled up with other welfare, treatment, and control nets. In Britain, social workers are the most powerful human service professionals operating in these waters, while in the USA the mental-health net is more important.

For adults, the mental health/crime interchange has been reported from two quite opposite directions. With the successful decarceration of the mentally ill ('successful' because whatever the damaging criticism of the end result, average daily mental hospital populations in the USA declined dramatically from 600,000 in 1955 to 100,000 in 1980) and the development of more stringent civil liberty requirements, many offenders with records of mental illness get into hospitals. This is because the crime-like notion of 'dangerousness' is increasingly being used to decide on commitment standards. Commitment is thus used in lieu of arrest. From the opposite direction, however, many recently decarcerated mental patients who do not seem dangerous, but certainly are troublesome and bizarre, might be arrested on minor public order charges (like loitering) because the police can think of nothing else to do with them.[34]

For juveniles, there are even more intricate patterns of retracking, between delinquency, mental illness, and welfare systems. Besides hybrid services such as intermediate treatment, the most significant development is a hidden correctional system (largely, as we will see in the next section, privately owned) which operates along psychiatric lines. There is a network of agencies—in-patient psychiatric settings, residential treatment centres, out-patient clinics—that redefine delinquency in terms such as 'disruptive behaviour', 'acting out', 'adjustment reaction', or 'runaway reaction by adolescents'. Lerman has described in detail the various levels of relabelling now taking place in the juvenile system in America: how terms such as 'voluntary admissions', 'other non-offenders', or 'dependency' are used to retrack petty offenders from the old training schools into 'community treatment' in a private facility; how child welfare and social service workers use psychiatric rather than juvenile court labels to justify removal of the child from family; and how the child welfare, mental health, and juvenile correctional systems are drawing on overlapping populations.[35]

These forms of de- and re-labelling are extremely difficult to demonstrate empirically. It is already clear, however, that a probable outcome of this blurring (especially with regard to juveniles) is the creation of a hidden custodial system, under welfare or psychiatric sponsorship, which official delinquency statistics simply ignore. This is what is meant by the accurate (if clumsy) term 'transinstitutionalism'.

But leaving aside these intricate overlaps between the crime, mental illness, and welfare nets, it is evident that even within the criminal justice system itself, we are witness to something more than just the proliferation of agencies and services, finely calibrated in terms of degree of coerciveness or intrusion or unpleasantness. The uncertainties are more profound than this: voluntary or coercive, formal or informal, locked-up or free, guilty or innocent. Those apparently absurd administrative and research questions—When is a prison a prison or a community a community? Is the alternative an alternative? Who is half-way in and who is three-quarter-way out?—beckon to a future when it will be impossible to determine who exactly is enmeshed in the formal control system, and hence subject to its jurisdiction and surveillance, at any one time.

Public merges with private

The notion that the state should be solely responsible for crime control only developed in Britain and the USA in the nineteenth century. The key changes then—the removal of prisons from private to public control and the creation of a uniformed public police force—are taken as the beginning of the continued and voracious absorption of deviancy control into the centralized apparatus of the state. And this process indeed seems endless: increasing state control in the form of more laws, regulations, administrative and enforcement agencies.

In parts of the system, though, there are important developments which are moving in a different direction. Particularly with regard to the police, some observers have claimed that 'the spheres of public and private have actually become progressively less distinct', that there has been a 'privatization of social control'.[36] This interpenetration between public and private is even seen as going back full circle to the link between crime control and other forms of profit-making at the end of the seventeenth century. Today's forms of 'privatization' are obviously not quite the same as those of that earlier era, nor can they ever be in the rationalized, centralized state. It is apparent, though, that along with the other types of blurring, there has been some merging of the obviously public and formal apparatus of control with the private and less formal. The ideology of community control implies this: on the one hand, the repressive, interventionist reach of the state should be blunted, on the other, the 'community' should become more involved in the day-to-day business of prevention and control.

At the macro-political level, particularly in the USA and under the influence of monetarist economic policy, the increasing attempt to shuffle social services from the public to the private sector is transparent enough. Indeed, as we shall see, the impetus for the whole decarceration movement itself has been attributed by theorists like Scull to the 'fiscal crisis' in which the state divests itself of expensive crime-control functions allowing private enterprise to process deviant populations for profit.

In the case of mental illness, the trend to privatization is now beyond dispute. Those chronic mental patients whose previous fate was to be assigned to the back wards, are now (if they are not in the back alleys) commodities to be exploited as a source of income. As Scull suggests, this commodification (or rather re-commodification) of social junk marks a sharp break with the pattern of state responsibility for the mentally ill, even the beginning of a 'new trade in lunacy'.[37] Today's network of private clinics, nursing homes, and welfare hotels, run on a direct private basis or under contract from the state, is the twentieth-century equivalent of the madhouse—that profitable business in eighteenth- and early nineteenth-century *laissez faire* capitalism.

The retracking of some forms of delinquency into the mental-health system gives an additional boost to the entrepreneurial boom in private mental hospitals for adolescents—'transinstitutionalism'. Overall, however, privatization is a much more complicated business for crime control than for mental illness. Strictly speaking, 'privatization' means that the state ceases to supply a particular service and it is supplied instead by private enterprises which are directly paid by the public as customers. With the important exception of the private security industry (to which I will return) there is not much room for this form of privatization in the crime-control system. The recipients of the 'service' are, to say the least, somewhat unwilling customers.

But there is far more room for the weaker form of privatization where the state contracts out certain services to private enterprise, retaining some measure of control. There is now considerable evidence on how this type of arrangement is taking place. Helped by fiscal changes at the local,[38] state, and federal levels, commercial entrepreneurship has now joined the more traditional forms of moral entrepreneurship.[39] A significant proportion of community agencies and diversion projects are financed and contracted in this way. Lerman in fact argues that through shifts in federal and state budgeting, the entire policy of community alternatives has been made possible by the increasing dominance of the private sector.[40] The public sector takes up the more secure (hard-end) facilities while the private sector moves into the less restrictive facilities such as special schools, ranches, group homes, and foster homes.

By the end of the 1970s, one-third of all delinquents, even in the official custodial system, were in privately owned facilities. And in the private sector overall, the majority of youth were either status offenders or fell into categories such as 'voluntary admissions', 'dependency', or 'other non-offenders'—euphemistic labels for petty delinquency. These traditional soft-enders (younger and more often girls) have become the major clients for the private sector. There is a new division of labour then— public funding of a profitable private business in 'community control'. In Massachusetts, for example, the sudden 'decarceration' led to a near monopoly by the private sector. Spending on 'privately purchased human services' increased from $25 million in 1979 to $300 million in 1981 (the number of separate facilities increasing from 9 to 164 over this period). Over 90 per cent of residential programmes for 'court-involved youth' (mainly for CHINS—children in need of supervision) are now privately run.[41] And this is genuine commodification—not 'Little House on the Prairie' families looking after deprived children, but large corporations, experienced contract lawyers, and organized lobbying of the state legislature.

Indirect privatization of this type ('third-party funding') is likely to develop in other parts of the American system as a result of the massive post-1979 cutback in LEAA budgets. Not only did individual agencies go private, but so did coordinating and planning projects such as the NCCJPA (National Clearing House for Criminal Justice Planning and Architecture). Between 1969 and 1978 this body was involved in interpreting and writing LEAA standards for some 1500 adult and juvenile correctional projects. Now, in the form of a private corporation, 'Centre for Justice Planning Incorporated', it advertises for business like any other private enterprise. There are also new groups of criminal justice professionals, calling themselves 'clinical' or 'forensic' criminologists, who prepare private pre-sentence reports for defence attorneys. Claiming to do a better job than a probation service reduced by budgetary cuts, such private organizations as 'Criminological Diagnostic Consultants Inc.' in California, are now employed as hired guns (like private psychiatrists), charging fees of up to $2000 for a pre-sentence court report.[42]

There is no shortage of such schemes for moving other services into the private sector, even going back to pure Benthamite utilitarianism by negotiating contracts with payment conditional on some agreed measure of success. Private agencies would receive bonus payments for each recidivism-free client or (in true monetarist terms) offenders could be given 'treatment vouchers' to spend where they want, thus driving out unsuccessful treatment from the 'market'.[43]

The fate of most private agencies though, especially if they prove successful, is not to remain very 'private' but to be co-opted and absorbed into the formal state apparatus. This has happened even to some radical self-help organizations which originated in an antagonistic relationship to the system. In the case of diversion, the ideal non-legal agency (free from system control, client-oriented, with voluntary participation, independent of sponsor's pressure) often becomes like the various 'para-legal' agencies closely connected to the system and dependent on it for space, referrals, accountability, and sponsorship.[44] Various compromises on procedure are made as temporary tactics to deflect suspicion and criticism, but are then institutionalized. The private agency might expand by asking for public funding and in turn changes its screening criteria to fit the demands of the official system. It becomes increasingly difficult to assign the status of private or public to these agencies.

The recruitment of volunteers is another rapidly growing form of privatization. Whatever the reasons for this growth—filling service gaps created by budget cuts, the ideology of community involvement, the perception that volunteers are often as effective as paid professional staff— volunteers are to be found in every part of the control system.

Ex-offenders treat offenders; indigenous community residents are recruited as probation 'aides' or to voluntary 'big brother' schemes; family members and teachers are used in behavioural contracting programmes, and university students take on counselling functions to obtain credits for their course work.

There is obviously very little new in the voluntarism principle itself. Probation, prison visiting, and other such schemes often originated as volunteer efforts. But the combination of an expanding community network and declining social services budgets ensures an even greater future role for volunteers. The community setting, with its emphasis on the supposed 'naturalness' and 'normality' of the intervention process is particularly suitable for volunteer workers. As with private agencies themselves, the potential for volunteers to be absorbed into the official system is high. Often the volunteers are retrained or formalized into para-professional or professional status, either in fact or else by giving a new name to what they were already doing. This last practice is nicely illustrated by calling jailhouse lawyers 'para-legals'.[45]

All this, though, is fairly far removed from pre-nineteenth-century forms of privatization. The parallels, however, are closer in the area of policing, where four developments are worth singling out: (i) the private police industry, (ii) pro-active policing, (iii) community police relations; and (iv) citizen policing.

In all Western societies, private policing has become a massive growth industry. Already by 1975, in the USA and Canada, private police began to outnumber their counterparts in the public sector. This growth is usually attributed to the increasing involvement of the ordinary police with 'non-crime' work: peacekeeping, traffic control, disguised social work, social sanitation, and various other forms of human-services dirty work.[46] This leaves large corporations dependent on the private sector for all sorts of protective and investigative operations, both of the 'hard' and visible type (security forces, personal bodyguards, etc.) and for less visible work (employee pilferage, industrial espionage, computer fraud investigations, security checks, and credit card scrutiny).

All this might not be quite the same as seventeenth-century thief catching by piecework, but it certainly represents a massive transfer of costly crime-control functions to the profit-making private sector. Far from being an 'adjunct', a mere 'junior partner' to the criminal justice system, the private security system operates in its own realm of justice. The implications of this may be quite profound. As Shearing and Stenning note, the enormous growth of contract security has taken place in public rather than purely private places. There has been an increase in what they call 'mass private property' (shopping centres, residential estates, campuses, airports) where the maintenance of public order as well as the protection of private property is at issue. Huge areas of public life previously under state control are now in the hands of private corporations. The result, this analysis suggests, is 'an unobtrusive but significant restructuring of our institutions for the maintenance of order, and a substantial erosion by the private sector of the state's assumed monopoly over policing and, by implication, justice'.[47]

At the same time as these forms of privatization are taking place, certain changes in ordinary public policing might be leading to directions with other curious historical parallels—to the time when the dividing lines between the civilian population and a uniformed, centralized police force were not at all clear. There has been an increasing emphasis on proactive rather than reactive policing, that is operations aimed at anticipating and preventing crimes not yet committed, particularly through the use of informers, secret agents, undercover work, *agents provocateurs*, decoys, and entrapment. Besides the particular (and traditional) practice of the infiltration of social movements by informers and *agents provocateurs*,[48] observers of undercover work[49] note a more fundamental switch in police strategy. The move is not to decrease illegal opportunity structures (by patrolling etc.) or target hardening, but actually to *increase* the opportunity structure for crime.

These techniques go beyond 'anticipation' towards actually trying to facilitate the controlled commission of crime. Routine forms of undercover work include cooperation with others in illegal activities, secretly creating opportunities, and generating motives for crime. Standard methods range from buying or selling illegal goods and services (police posing as prostitutes seeking customers, as customers seeking prostitutes, buying or selling drugs, setting up fencing operations, running pornographic book shops); using decoys to draw street crime (posing as elderly citizens, physically handicapped, derelicts) and various forms of intelligence gathering and 'morality testing'. (A much publicized recent example was the FBI 'Sting' operation designed to expose corrupt judges. This included the use of false defendants, false attorneys, the invention of crimes, and the bugging of Judges' chambers.)

All this is not so much privatization as a form of boundary blurring through the deliberate use of deception. As Gary Marx suggests, the move (for pragmatic rather than ideological reasons) is from coercive to deceptive forms of social control—not only making the police look more like citizens, but to make citizens believe that any one of their fellow citizens could be a police officer in disguise.

But while these parts of police work are becoming more underground and secretive, others are reaching out more openly into the wider community. Movements to strengthen community police relationships, to improve the public image of the police, and to develop schemes for 'community-based preventive policing' have become standard. Community relations officers, juvenile liaison bureaux, school-linked officers are all trying to establish closer links with the community, humanize the face of police work, and encourage early reporting. Policemen are now 'friends' (who help neighbourhood kids with sports activities and take them on weekend hikes) or social workers who are trained in 'human relationships'.

Besides general image building, all this is directed to obtaining greater citizen cooperation in the form of reporting and informal surveillance. In the USA especially, a much more formalized type of enlistment of private citizens into police work has been taking place. Volunteer work such as driving cars, traffic control, and escort services is provided to overloaded police forces, but more particularly there has been a formalization of neighbourhood surveillance and reporting systems: crime-stoppers groups, neighbourhood patrols, citizen crime-reporting projects, whistle-alert neighbourhoods, citizen-band radio reporting, block-watch projects.[50] More dramatically (and certainly closer to early forms of privatization) there has been the growth of various forms of local 'auxiliary justice'. With overload on the formal criminal justice system and the perception among victims and potential victims that the state is 'letting them down', new forms of private and vigilante justice—fanned by racialism and community tensions—have developed.[51] Whether they see themselves as 'by-passing' or as 'helping' the police, these activities are easily blurred with the formal system.

All these forms of policing appeal to the same community involvement vision which informs the destructuring movement as a whole. Once again though, new structures are being created rather than old ones being replaced. Nor can attempts to reproduce pre-urban systems of mutual responsibility, peacekeeping, and good neighbourliness be very successful. Citizens of today's suburbia or inner-city slum cannot through an effort of will recreate the conditions of an eighteenth-century rural parish. Closed-circuit television, two-way radios, vigilante patrols, private security companies, and police decoys hardly simulate life in a pre-industrial village. This is not for want of trying. In some large stores, private security police are posing as employees. They conspicuously steal and are then conspicuously 'discovered' by the management and ceremonially disciplined, thus deterring the real employees. They then presumably move on to stage somewhere else another such Durkheimian ceremony of social control.

But Durkheimian theory notes the functions of social control in clarifying and strengthening boundaries. All our examples in this section point to the increasing *invisibility* of the net's boundaries.

Inside, the same old things are being done

If I were being processed by the machine ('my own actual person, me myself') few of the matters contemplated so far would be of very great interest: not how big the net might be, nor what it is called, nor what it looks like, nor who runs it. Only one thing matters: what is actually going on inside all these 'offices'?

The promise was a form of intervention that would be less intrusive, onerous, coercive, stigmatizing, artificial, and bureaucratic; more humane, just, fair, helpful, natural, and informal. What are we to make of these good intentions? Is the new system subject to the same commonplace of those historical tales about the old system—that the most benign innovations come to mask the most coercive of practices and consequences?

At first sight, the benevolence of the new agencies seems obvious. The very language of the community and diversion movements speaks of good things happening. And without doubt, the end results are often humane, compassionate, and helpful. Some 'clients', at least, are kept out of the harsher recesses of the system, many are offered a wider range of services than they would have received before, and almost all would prefer the new variety of agencies to the stark alternative of the prison.

But the word 'alternative' should alert us to the immediate problem of the new nets. The claim to be doing more good (or less harm) is somewhat less valid if the alternatives are not real alternatives at all, but supplements. The size and density evidence shows that many offenders are exposed to the new system *in addition* to traditional processing or else instead of not being processed at all. The mystifying nature of the idea of alternatives may be nicely illustrated by the curious justification of agencies like half-way houses: being just as successful in preventing recidivism as direct release into the community. As Greenberg notes, when participation in such programmes is a condition of release from prison, 'the contrast between the brutality of the prison and the alleged humanitarianism of community corrections is besides the point, because the community institution is not used to replace the prison; instead the offender is exposed to both the prison and the community "alternatives" '.[52]

Even when the notion of 'alternative' is not phoney, the idea of 'preference' or 'choice' most often is. At the deep end of the system, choice is seldom offered while at the shallow end, the generation of new treatment criteria and the pervasiveness of the social welfare and preventive rhetorics, often ensure an erosion of traditional rights and liberties. In a system of low visibility and accountability, where a high degree of discretion is given to administrative and professional bodies (in the name of 'flexibility') there is often less room for such niceties as due process and legal rights. Police diversion programmes are the most notable examples here: juveniles usually proceed through the various filters on the assumption or admission of guilt. As one critic of such programmes comments: 'to force a youngster to participate in a diversion program under the threat of adjudication, has most of the elements of the formal justice system save due process'.[53]

Making future status contingent on programme participation is only one form of hidden coercion. Overall, the rhetoric of welfare and treatment allows all sorts of invisible discretion about referral, recall, resentencing, reallocation, and so on. Lerman's often-quoted research on Californian community projects showed that offenders in the experimental (community) groups, spent much more time in traditional custody than was generally believed, and could be locked up for reasons quite unrelated to their legal offence: violating treatment expectations, administrative convenience, missing a group meeting, sassing a teacher, the threat of 'emotional explosion' or 'acting out', community pressure, or even diagnostic purposes. As Messinger comments on this research:

When subjects failed to comply with the norms of the intensive treatment regime, or even when a program agent believes subjects might fail to comply, then, as they say in the intensive treatment circles, detention may be indicated. Both these features, and the extensive use of home placements as well, suggest that the term 'community' like the term 'intensive treatment' may come to have a very special meaning in programs designed to deliver 'intensive treatment in the community'.[54]

Phoney choice, problems of legal rights, and hidden custody aside, we might still want to ask whether most bona fide forms of community programmes are not, after all, experienced as more humane and helpful by the offender. There is little evidence either way on this, beyond the rather bland common-sense assumption that most offenders would prefer not to be 'locked up'. What tends to happen is that deep-end projects—those that are genuine alternatives to incarceration—make a trade-off between treatment goals (which favour an integrated community setting) and security goals which favour isolation. The trade-off under these conditions, especially given widespread community reluctance to open its arms to the joyous project of reintegration, will invariably favour security. The result is programmes which simply recreate the institutional domains under a different name, regimes which simulate or mimic the very custodial features they set out to replace. Even when the security trade-off is less important, community treatment is often just 'semantic trivia' for traditional programmes whose physical location in an urban area is the sole basis for identifying the programme as community-based.[55]

This is certainly the case with the many half-way house programmes which contain stringent security conditions, compulsory therapy, intensive observation and surveillance, and continual requirements to 'avoid undesirable behaviour sequences' and to 'develop and display positive attitudes'.[56]

Let me give a specific example of a 'community correctional facility' which is part of a wider community corrections programme. This is Fort Des Moines, a 50-bed non-secure unit, meant for adult offenders not stable enough to be granted probation, but not dangerous enough to be sent to a traditional locked institution.[57] The unit is housed in the converted barracks of an ex-army base, the clients work in ordinary jobs in the community, and there is only minimal physical security such as bars and fences. The security trade-offs, however, result in an intensity of intervention at least as high as that in most maximum-security prisons. The following are some examples.

1. The low 'client–counsellor' ratio of one staff person for every two clients allows for intensive 'informal observation' of the clients for security purposes. A 'staff desk person' signs clients in and out, recording their attitudes and activities. And a 'floating staff person' circulates throughout the institution, observing client behaviour, taking a count of all clients each hour (called the 'eye check'), and recording the count in the log. The staff have total discretion in granting furloughs, visits, searching for contraband, and administering a urine analysis or breath test at any time.

2. The client has to 'contract' to behave well and participate actively in his rehabilitation and the sanction of being returned to prison is always present. From the beginning of his stay (when he has to sign a waiver

of privacy granting the programme access to information in confidential agency files) he is closely scrutinized. Besides obvious offences like using drugs, fighting, or trying to escape, the failure to maintain 'a significant level of performance' is one of the most serious offences a client can commit and results in immediate return to jail.

3. The court retains jurisdiction over the client, receiving detailed rosters and programme reports and having to authorize internal requests for work, schooling, or furloughs. In addition, the local police and sheriffs' departments receive weekly listings of the residents, indicating where each has to be at specified hours of each day. This information is available to patrol officers who may see inmates in the community.

Every item of behaviour and attitude is recorded on the Behaviour Observation Report. It is this panopticon principle, together with the commitment to a compulsory programme of behaviourist conditioning, which casts the most doubt on the humanity and non-intrusiveness of the new programmes. This is true even when the project is more genuinely 'in the community' than the unfortunately named Fort Des Moines. Let us consider a few examples of this kind, community projects genuinely not anchored in a custodial base.

One well-described example is the Urbana Champaign Adolescent Diversion Project (ADP). Juveniles considered as 'beyond lecture and release and clearly headed for court' are referred by the police to a programme of behavioural contracting organized by a university psychology department. The volunteer staff monitor and mediate contractual agreements between the youth and his parents and teachers—privileges in return for his compliance with the curfew, doing house chores, and maintaining his personal appearance. Here are extracts from a typical day in the life of Joe, a 16-year-old who had come to the attention of the juvenile division for possession of marijuana and violation of the municipal curfew laws:

Joe agrees to	*Joe's parents agree to*
1. Call home by 4.00 p.m. each afternoon and tell his parents his whereabouts and return home by 5.00 p.m.	1. Allow Joe to go out from 7.30 to 9.30, Monday through Thursday, evenings and ask about his companions without negative comments.
2. Return home by 12.00 midnight on weekend nights.	2. Allow Joe to go out the subsequent weekend nights.
3. Make his bed and clean his room daily (spread neat; clothes hung up).	3. Check his room each day and pay him 75 cents when cleaned.

| 4. Set table for dinner daily. | 4. Deposit 75 cents per day in a savings account for Joe. |

Bonus

If Joe performs at 80% or above ##1 through ##4 above his parents will deposit an additional 3 dollars in his account for each consecutive seven-day period.

Sanction

If Joe falls below 60% in ##1 and ##2 above in any consecutive seven-day period, he will cut two inches off his hair.[58]

Variations of the two main elements in this project—close surveillance and behavioural contracting—are being used throughout the USA, Canada, and Britain. The Intensive Probation Program in Georgia includes regular contacts with the officer, an 8.00 p.m. curfew, community service, and registration on the state computer system (for which service the offender pays a monthly fee!).[59] In Florida, community control takes the form of residential house arrest: armed community officers, equipped with urine analysis kits and surveillance devices, are empowered to enter the offender's home at any time.

In Britain, the favoured solution for 'heavy-end' offenders deflected from custody has become Intensive Intermediate Treatment (IIT). Directly exporting the techniques (and terminology) from the system developed in Massachusetts, projects such as PACE (Project for Alternative Community Experience) are using a complex system of 'tracking'.[60] An infinite number of IIT permutations have already appeared: 'full-time IT', 'IT Plus', 'short-term holding', 'long-term holding', 'intensive tracking', and 'booster tracking'. But the basic model is something like this: the 'trackee' starts off in a carefully graded 'residential component'; he or she passes through close supervision in a residential unit, then 'supervised and monitored outside contact', and then 'increasingly unsupervised but still monitored outside contacts' (with curfew, spot checks, regular phone reports). The amount of time in each phase depends on progress made.

This is followed by the 'community/intensive supervision' or tracking component (some projects only start at this stage). This again entails decreasing levels of intensity according to progress. The 'young person' is linked to a tracker who knows where he is at all times, ensures that he follows a structured and approved routine, teaches him social skills, advises him about work, school, and family and generally monitors his behaviour. As in the ADP model, offenders have to agree to a written behavioural contract and this usually calls for direct involvement by the family. Breaking any clause in the contract (in one project this includes filling in a log book for each hour of the day between 9 a.m. and 11 p.m. and 'acting like an adult in arguments'), can result in a series of graded sanctions, including more intensive tracking, return to the court, or recall to a 'short-term residential experience'. One project describes how a trackee's 'persistent acting-out behaviour' could lead to a weekend in the 'residential flat' in the company of his tracker. Supervision is gradually decreased until the 'lad' can function on his own. The programme might end, as it did for 'John' on the Coventry PACE project, with a staged incident in a local community setting (a pub). Now, the interactionally skilled and properly socialized offender does not explode into uncontrollable rage.

It should be absolutely clear that whatever else these community programmes might be and, as we move along, we will see all sorts of justifications for them, they are not examples of normal, integrated community life. Moreover, because of the increasing dominance of the just-deserts rhetoric for allocating punishment, these programmes are required to look to the courts as credible alternatives to custody. That is, they must be controlling and intrusive enough to be a response in good faith to the judicial demand for sentences that do actually punish and restrict. The uncomfortable policy dilemma is that it is very difficult to think of a 'credible capacity to incapacitate' besides imprisonment.[61]

Meanwhile, there is no problem in finding criminologists, psychologists, social workers, and others who will justify all these community alternatives as humane, kindly, and even 'therapeutic'—as they have historically justified anything that could be called treatment. This is the particularly wondrous advantage of those programmes which use the explicit rationale of behaviourism.[62] But leaving such considerations aside, the most fundamental fact about what is going on in the new agencies is that it is much the same as what went on and is still going on in the old system. The new 'service delivery modalities'—as the evaluation pros call them—are dominated by the same forms of individual or group treatment used in custodial institutions or traditional one-to-one encounters such as probation. Whether it is individual counselling, vocational guidance, encounter groups, role playing, or behaviour contracting, it is one person doing something to another person or group of persons. And however normal, banal, and everyday the activity might be (in other words, however close it might come to what happens in real communities) it is justified with the old (and supposedly discredited) rhetoric of treatment.

This is the real, awful secret of community control. Not the old closely guarded secrets of the penitentiary (the brutality, the chain gangs, solitary confinement). These things cannot occur in the community—and this is, by any measure, progress. The secret is a much less melodramatic one: that the same old experts have moved office to the community and are doing the same old things they have always done. Once again, we do not know *what* they are doing, not because they are hidden behind walls but because they are camouflaged as being just ordinary members of the community.

Picture a lake on which a duck tranquilly floats. On the grass edge sits a happy pre-adolescent boy chatting to a laid-back, bejeaned, student-looking young man. Brothers? Friends? No, this is just one of the activities of CREST—the Clinical Regional Support Team in Gainesville, Florida. The older boy is a 'volunteer' graduate psychology student, gaining some course credits by counselling a young probationer on this community programme. What are they doing by the lake? The caption on the photo tells all: 'A relaxed comfortable environment sets the stage for meaningful counsellor—client dialogue.'[63]

Penetration and absorption

With that happy image of the dialogue by the lake, we arrive at the third and last of the inquiries I posed about the machine: the extent and nature of its penetration beyond the known space it occupies. For Foucault, it was precisely the redistribution of the penal power into a wider social space that marked the great disciplinary projects of the nineteenth century. It was not just that disciplinary establishments increased, but that 'their mechanisms have a certain tendency to become "de-institutionalized", to re-emerge from the closed fortresses in which they once functioned and to circulate in a "free" state: the massive compact disciplines are broken down into flexible methods of control which may be transferred and adapted'.[64]

For the ideologists of today's control system, not a glimmer of this history is visible. Theirs is a classic story of progress: the gradual dawning of the light in the mid-twentieth century. The magic word is 'reintegration'—the new 'R' in the history of corrections. This was the ritually quoted sequence: we are in the middle of a third revolution in corrections: the first from Revenge to Restraint (in the first part of the nineteenth century), the second from Restraint to Reformation (from the late nineteenth to the early twentieth century), and now from Reformation to Reintegration.[65]

Although, as history, this story is quite absurd, as ideology it does proclaim a preferred change quite profound and radical. What is being proposed is a greater direct involvement of the family, the school, and various community agencies in the day-to-day business of prevention, treatment, and resocialization. But this means something more than simply recruiting more volunteers, improving communication with schools, or encouraging citizens to report more crime. It implies some sort of reversal of the presumption in positivist criminology that the delinquent is a different and alien being. Deviance rather is with us, woven into the fabric of social life and it must be 'brought back home'. Parents, peers, schools, the neighbourhood, even the police should dedicate themselves to keeping the deviant out of the formal system. Together they should constitute a gigantic shield of diversion: deflecting, absorbing, integrating the deviant back into the community where he belongs.

This master notion also informs the many other 'Rs' of contemporary corrections—reparation, restitution, repayment, reconciliation. If crime results from the estrangement of the individual from meaningful community contacts, imprisonment can only make this worse. These new modes of control allow the offender to undo the damage he caused (thus responding to the demands of justice) while, at the same time, integrating himself by working in and for the community.

The ideology of reintegration (buttressed usually by some variant of labelling theory) signifies, as my later chapters will show, a move more portentous than 'operational changes in the correctional system'. The vision was of an inclusionary rather than an exclusionary mode of social control. The asylum represented not just isolation and confinement, like quarantining the infected, but a ritual of physical exclusion. Without the possibility of actual banishment to another society, the asylum had to serve the classic social function of creating a scapegoat: the animal driven into the wilderness, bearing away the sins of the community.

In the new ideology of corrections, there is no real or symbolic wilderness, just the omnipresent community into which the deviant has to be unobtrusively 'integrated' or 'reintegrated'. Boundary blurring implies both the deeper penetration of social control into the social body and the easing of any measures of exclusion and stigmatization. Deviants must remain in their own natural society as long as possible.

In operational terms—as they say—what all this means is that the overburdened, inefficient, and inhumane formal system (doing things it should not be doing) must shift its load to the primary institutions of society. They (schools, family, neighbourhood) and not the experts and professionals must take responsibility for deviancy control. Instead of depriving them of their potential, they should be strengthened and used as natural resources in the war against crime. They should prevent the deviant from getting into the machine, they should substitute for the machine, they should look after him when he gets out of it.

So much for the vision. The reality does not look quite the same. Far from *avoiding* the touch of the formal system, the primary institutions have, in various metaphors, been invaded, penetrated, besieged, or colonized by the formal system. Far from there being any less reliance on experts, these same experts are simply working within the primary institutions. If there has been any 'absorption' it is not that the deviant has been absorbed by community institutions, but that the community institutions have been absorbed by the formal control system. The spaces surrounding the net—to return to my old metaphor—are increasingly drawn into its orbit.[66]

The historical sequence, then, is a little different from the story of the four Rs. First, there is control in the community; second, control is concentrated in the prison—an isolated, specially constructed model of what the good community should look like; third, prisons are reformed (this is what the Progressives visualized) to make them less artificial and more like ordinary communities—the community is brought into the prison; then, fourth, the modality of the prison is dispersed and exported back into the community.

Here, I want to give a more limited idea of how the new network is making itself felt in its surrounding space, using family, school, and neighbourhood as examples.

Family

The role supposedly being reallocated to the family is, perhaps, the clearest example of the integration and inclusion ideology at work. As part of a wider movement of the rediscovery of the family in social policy, this is a variation on the standard theme that the 'lost' functions of the family should be restored. The family is not only a natural way of preventing and containing the deviance of its own members, but is an obvious resource for treating the deviance of others.

Thus recent years have seen the extension of established methods of community treatment such as foster care, substitute homes, and family placements. One enthusiast even looked forward to 'the day when middle class American families actually wanted in large numbers to bring juvenile and pre-delinquent youths into their homes as a service commitment'.[67] The family having a delinquent living with them is seen as a 'remarkable correctional resource' for the future. In Britain and Scandinavia a number of alternative systems of family placement besides salaried foster parents have been tried, for example 'together at home'— the system of intensive help in Sweden in which social workers spend hours sharing the family's life and tasks. Other programmes require selected adults to act as parent models or surrogates. Once these parents are trained, children with 'behavioural problems' are placed in their model homes.

The delinquent's own family is also used in this way. This is standard practice in various behavioural contract programmes. Joe's family, in the ADP programme, becomes a 'correctional resource' and under the watchful eye of the university psychologist, it learns the correct behavioural sequences and reinforcement schedules. In Intensive IT and other tracking or befriending programmes, parents and siblings are parties to the behavioural contract and are expected to play an active role in retraining their errant child. In the regions of the system not influenced by behaviourist psychology, the fashion is for family sensitivity groups, weekend marathon family encounters, conjoint family therapy, PET (Parent Effectiveness Training), and the like. One must assume that a family with a member under house arrest is also a 'treatment resource'.

But the purposeful use of families in this way is less significant— statistically and socially—than the overall senses in which the contemporary family has become a site for expert invasion and penetration. As Lasch argues, the same market forces which undermined the traditional functions of the family are now—far from restoring these functions— undermining them still further.[68] The increasing array of guidance, instruction, therapy, counselling, and advice now being offered to the family strengthens the process of its 'proletarianization', which started well before the era of 'reintegration'.

School

The discovery by reintegrationists that most children go to school as well as live in families, coincided with the emergence in the 1970s of the school as a major site where crime, delinquency, and violence actually took place. This has meant that the penetration of the school has taken both a soft and a hard edge. The soft, liberal, thrust comes from the community-integration ideology and takes the form of incorporating the school as a preventive, diagnostic, screening, or diversion agency. The hard thrust, provoked by concern over violence, disruption, vandalism, unruliness, or indiscipline in school, takes the form of target hardening, drug or behaviourist controls, and increasing segregation of troublemakers. As these movements often share common technologies, such as behaviourism and early prediction techniques, it is not always easy to keep them apart in practice.[69] The discovery of hyperkinesis nicely illustrates the convergence of the benevolent treatment rhetoric with the need for a technology of pacification.[70]

At the soft edge, an increasing array of professionals, paraprofessionals, counsellors, social workers, psychologists, and experts of all sorts have attached themselves to the school. Their task is to 'pick up' deviancy problems at their source and, where possible, contain them without formal referral to the system. The fact that these personnel are themselves part of the machine is not usually seen as a contradiction, despite the increasing formalization of their methods, for example, the use of diagnostic rating scales to weed out the potential delinquents, the inclusion of schools in behaviour-contract agreements with criminal justice agencies, and the incorporation of token economy programmes into the routine of the classroom.

At the hard edge, the legendary vision of the blackboard jungle has dominated social control policy. In Britain, the strategy has been exclusion and isolation—the setting up over the seventies of special units for the segregation of disruptive pupils.[71] From 1947–77 alone, the number of these units (on or off the site of the school) increased from 40 to 239. The model is the classic one of individual pathology. The benevolent rationale was to 'help young people who find it difficult to adjust to schooling' while at the same time saving the rest of the class from being disturbed by these troublemakers. Referral takes place on the vaguest of diagnostic criteria (including restlessness, 'potentially disruptive behaviour', answering back, irritability, not wearing uniform, or 'difficulty in making relationships') and pupils might spend anything from a month to a few years in the segregation unit before being returned to the ordinary school or the outside world. The units are given names such as sanctuaries, withdrawal groups, and even pastoral care units.

The harder forms of school 'controlization' in the USA have little room for such euphemisms. From the 1978 'Safe School Study' onwards, the entrepreneurial direction has been towards a massive investment in hardware and preventive technology: video surveillance, ultrasonic detectors, hot lines to the police, redesigning buildings into clusters of manageable space. Problems such as bomb threats, arson, vandalism, violence, drug pushing, 'mass disruption', and 'rumour control' are stressed, the object of the exercise being a safe, secure school. Parts of the relevant literature read like blueprint for converting the school into a closed-security prison. This is the message of 'involvement' directed at school administrators by such private agencies as the Institute for the Reduction of Crime.[72]

Compared with the family, the school is obviously more of a 'public' institution and its connections to the state are more direct. This will allow an even greater degree of penetration, soft or hard, in the future.

Neighbourhood

The ideology of reintegration and the strategies of community and diversion demand a physical relocation of the business of deviancy control: not the wilderness and not the closed fortress, but the immediate physical space in which ordinary people live and go about their business. So the growing network of new agencies enters the city and tries to normalize its presence there. A conscious attempt is made to locate half-way houses, hostels, or day centres in the most inconspicuous and normal environments, on the assumption that this will reduce stigma and social distance. The local 'community' is not always so enthusiastic about these encounters and legal action, media pressure and restrictive zoning regulations often force the new agencies back into the social badlands of the city. Despite these counter forces though, this kind of physical penetration is slowly taking place.

There are, in addition, some less visible forms of penetration—like that relaxed counselling session next to the lake. Anxious to avoid the stigma of the office, the agency corridors, and the waiting room, the new professionals and their aides increasingly try out more normal community settings for their encounters. Detached youth workers and street corner workers have, of course, traditionally used such 'reaching out' methods. The literature now is full of stories of clients being encountered or contacted in bars, cafes, parks, cars, and even rock concerts. Least visible of all are the *linkers* (local leaders used to break down mistrust between the community worker and the neighbourhood deviant sub-culture) and the *befrienders*, *trackers*, and *shadows*—workers in high-intensity community programmes who attach themselves to individual clients and make sure they get out of bed in time, get to work, and attend their therapy sessions.

Outside the city, who knows whether that happy group of kids hiking up a mountain, building a campfire, or swimming in a river are not taking part in a delinquency programme such as ACTION (Accepting Challenge Through Interaction with Others and Nature)?[73] The only way to tell that these are not, after all, boy scouts, would be to know that the participants had been pre-tested and then, after coming back from the wilderness, would be post-tested about their self-concepts, their relationship with their peers, and their perception of the role of authority figures.

Back in the city, there are other forms of treatment such as community-service orders which offer further opportunity for the normalized presence of the offender. Satisfying the aims of both integration and reparative justice, offenders on such schemes are sentenced to useful (usually supervised) work in the community: helping in geriatric wards, driving disabled people around, painting and decorating the houses of various handicapped groups, building children's playgrounds.

These are all the softer forms of the reintegration strategy at work, and are directed at the individual offender *after* his apprehension and conviction. Other forms of neighbourhood penetration are not only 'harder', but move from the individual offender to preventive and proactive strategies directed at whole groups or environments (a move which, as we shall see, some observers consider the most significant of all changes in social control).

Obvious examples come from the new forms of community and preventive policing I reviewed earlier. In addition to the now-routine technologies of prevention, detection, deterrence, and surveillance in public and private space (stores, airports, shopping malls), the reintegration ideology demands a more active form of participation. Citizens are urged to provide neighbourhood centres for potential delinquents, organize all sorts of surveillance and early reporting schemes, take part in 'court-watching programmes', and conduct crime prevention seminars in their homes.[74] Through programmes such as CAPTURE (Citizens Active Participation Through Utilization of Relevant Education) and national organizations such as the National Centre for Community Crime Prevention, neighbourhoods are absorbed into general crime-prevention strategies. Some projects call for collective surveillance and reporting (block clubs, neighbourhood watch, radio-alert networks, tenant patrols, secret-witness programmes) while others teach personal survival and protective techniques (though seminars and booklets with such titles as 'Safe Passage in City Streets' or 'Mugging Avoidance Techniques'). The neighbourhood now becomes an 'untapped human resource for delinquency prevention'.[75]

The police on their side are also more actively 'reaching out', by joining neighbourhood organizations, serving on local committees, and helping in school and youth groups. Increasingly, urban design and planning decisions (about shops, streets, housing estates, parking areas) are made with reference to crime-control needs. Planners routinely use the rhetoric of defensible space, target hardening, or illegal-opportunity structure. And we must add to all this the activities of private security companies, as well as the possibility that the beggar on the pavement, the old lady crossing the street, a client in the local massage parlour, and your friendly neighbourhood dope dealer might all be policemen in disguise. The city streets take on a different look.

Let me summarize this section on 'penetration and absorption' by drawing the lines a little bit more sharply than the reality. The system penetrates the space of the family, the school, and the neighbourhood; it tries to buttress their existing control processes by exporting the modes of discipline and control which characterize its 'own' spaces; it rationalizes all this by appealing to a vision of what the real family, school, or community looked like once or should look like now—and these institutions are then changed further rather than restored to their pristine state.

Conclusion: the emerging patterns

Let us now forget fishing nets, suction machines, and objects in space. Forget also the question of whether or not what is happening is what was intended. We have arrived at a point where this long chapter needs to be summarized: can today's master patterns of social control be picked out in the same way as those of the early nineteenth century? Any answer must be highly qualified and tentative. Some of the patterns I described are indeed clear enough, some are highly contradictory and ambiguous, yet others are merely hints of what might come.

But these are the main outlines: a gradual expansion and intensification of the system; a dispersal of its mechanisms from more closed to more open sites, and a consequent increase in the invisibility of social control and the degree of its penetration into the social body. My selection of examples to arrive at even this crude outline are obviously open to dispute. On the one hand, for instance, I might have overplayed the element of novelty. A reading of correctional stories gives an exaggerated notion of how much innovation there has been: novel alternatives such as tracking or house arrest involve only a minority of offenders. Many such programmes started in the heyday of the community movement have now closed through lack of funding and most offenders under supervision receive traditional forms of probation and parole. And, most important of all, it is the continued persistence of the prison, as well as the 'dispersal' of its mechanisms which has to be explained.

On the other hand, certain critics of the 'dispersal of discipline' thesis would pick out a quite different set of changes.[76] To them, the *proportionate* decline in the use of imprisonment is a noteworthy achievement as well as its replacement by modes of punishment (such as fines, suspended sentences, victim compensation and support schemes) which are not 'disciplinary' in the sense of demanding continuous supervision and attempting to change behaviour.

But it seems to me that beyond all the complex empirical problems, historical comparisons, and implied value judgements which terms such as 'discipline' and 'dispersal' might hide, there is the over-riding fact of proliferation, elaboration, and diversification. No one, least of all that proverbial Martian anthropologist with whom this chapter started, cannot but be impressed by all this bustling, frenzied activity, all these busy people doing so many things in so many places to so many others.

While it may be difficult to know which of these activities are old or new, vague or definite, there is no doubt that the logic of these master patterns, as opposed to their particular current forms, is not at all new. Their antecedents can be traced, though, not to their supposed model—the idyllic pre-industrial rural community—but to the very same patterns of punishment and classification laid down in the nineteenth century.

Foucault, we remember, reconstructed (or rather fantasized) the vision of the eighteenth-century judicial philosophers: power dispersed throughout the 'punitive city'—not the vengeful and arbitrary power of the sovereign, concentrated in the spectacle of torture, but a discreet dispersal of social control through 'hundreds of tiny theatres of punishment', each a perfect arithmetical representation of the bourgeois social contract. A right and just arithmetic of punishment, no more and no less. The juridical project, however, was never fully realized. It was replaced, or rather overlaid, with the carceral or disciplinary vision. The offender is observed, judged, normalized—something is done to him. He is returned to society, if at all, not as the requalified subject of the social contract, but the retrained, obedient subject.

But where was this new disciplinary project to be put into practice? Here, Foucault confuses us. On the one hand there was concentration: punishment becomes concentrated in the coercive institution of the prison—a single uniform penalty varied only according to length. On the other hand, there was dispersal—not of judicial semiotics but of projects of docility. The same microphysics of power reproduces itself in the prison and the community: hierarchical surveillance, continuous registration, perpetual assessment, partitioning and repartitioning, discipline, and resocialization. 'The prison transformed the punitive procedure into a penitentiary technique; the carceral archipelago transported this technique from the penal institution to the wider social body.'[77]

To describe today's system as simply a continuation of the disciplinary society—nothing more and nothing less—is mistaken. This would be to ignore the real differences outlined in this and later chapters. The attack on positivism, for example, in the name of 'neo-classicism' or 'back to justice' (the early 'judicial' vision) certainly does not fit Foucault's history of the present. Nor do all those innovations in policing and crime prevention which denote a move from the individual offender to opportunity structures and the control of whole populations.

But every one of the major patterns I have described in this chapter—expansion, dispersal, invisibility, penetration—is indeed continuous with those original transformations. The prison remains—a stubborn continuous presence, seemingly impervious to all attacks—and in its shadow lies 'community control'. Together, they make up what appears in Foucault as the 'carceral archipelago' or (to list all his images), 'net', 'continuum', 'city', 'circle', and 'pyramid'. The creation of all those new agencies and services surrounding the court and the prison, the generation of new systems of knowledge, classification, and professional interests is little more than a widening and diversification of the last century's archipelago, made possible by resources, investment, ingenuity, technology, and vested interest on a scale that befits 'post-industrial society'.

All these agencies—legal and quasi-legal, diversionary and alternative, administrative and professional—are marking out their own territories of jurisdiction, competence, and referral. Each set of experts produces its own 'scientific' knowledge: screening devices, diagnostic tests, treatment modalities, evaluation scales. And all this creates new categories and the typifications which fill them. Where there was once talk about the 'typical' prisoner, first offender or hardened recidivist, now there are typical 'clients' of half-way houses or community correctional centres, typical divertees, trackees, or pre-delinquents. These creatures are then fleshed out—in papers, research proposals, official reports—with sub-systems of knowledge and new vocabularies. Locking up becomes 'intensive placement', dossiers become 'anecdotal records', rewards and punishments become 'behavioural contracts'.

The enterprise, I will argue, justifies itself: there is hardly any point in asking about 'success', this is not the object of the exercise. Research is done on the classification system *itself*—working out a 'continuum of community basedness', prediction tables, or screening devices.

This is not to say that the classification is in any sense random. From the foundation of the control system, a single principle has governed every form of classification, screening, selection, diagnosis, prediction, typology, and policy. This is the structural principle of binary opposition: how to sort out the good from the bad, the elect from the damned, the sheep from the goats, the amenable from the non-amenable, the treatable from the non-treatable, the good risks from the bad risks, the high prediction scorers from the low prediction scorers; how to know who belongs in the deep end, who in the shallow end, who is hard and who is soft.[78]

Each individual decision in the system—who shall be chosen?— represents and creates this fundamental principle of bifurcation. The particular binary judgements which have come to dominate the present system—who shall be sent away from the custodial institution and who shall remain in it, who shall be diverted and who shall be inserted—are but instances of this deep structure at work.

Notes

1. One early textbook, Vernon Fox, *Community Based Corrections*, (Englewood Cliffs, NJ: Prentice Hall, 1977), listed 142 types of 'service'. And a three-year follow-up study of 570 juveniles moving through the Massachusetts Departmental Youth Service showed that, collectively, they experienced 132 different programmes: R. B. Coates et al., *Diversity in a Youth Correctional System: Handling Delinquents in Massachusetts* (Cambridge, Mass.: Ballinger, 1978).
2. Our bewildered cultural dummy might also be helped by the *Criminal Justice Thesaurus* published regularly by the National Institute of Justice.
3. Note, for example, Rothman's comments about the early twentieth-century impact of the psychiatric ideology on the criminal justice system: 'rationales and practices that initially promised to be less onerous nevertheless served to encourage the extension of state authority. The impact of the ideology was to expand intervention, not to restrict it.' David T. Rothman, 'Behaviour Modification in Total Institutions: A Historical Overview', *Hastings Centre Report*, 5 (February 1975), p. 19.
4. Here, as throughout this chapter, I draw on the following excellent evaluations of deinstitutionalization and community control: James Austin and Barry Krisberg, 'Wider, Stronger and Different Nets: The Dialectics of Criminal Justice Reform', *Journal of Research in Crime and Delinquency*, 18, 1, (January 1981), pp. 165–96, and 'The Unmet Promise of Alternatives to

Incarceration', *Crime and Delinquency*, 28, 3 (July 1982), pp. 374–409; John Hylton, 'The Growth of Punishment: Imprisonment and Community Corrections in Canada', *Crime and Social Justice*, 15 (1981), pp. 18–28, *Reintegrating the Offender: Assessing the Impact of Community Corrections* (Washington DC: University Press of America, 1981), 'Community Corrections and Social Control: The Case of Saskatchewan, Canada', *Contemporary Crises*, 5, 2 (April 1981), pp. 193–215, and 'Rhetoric and Reality: A Critical Appraisal of Community Correctional Programs', *Crime and Delinquency*, 28, 3 (July 1982), pp. 341–73, Paul Lerman, 'Trends and Issues in the De-Institutionalization of Youths in Trouble', *Crime and Delinquency*, 26, 3 (July 1980), pp. 281–98; Andrew Rutherford and Osman Bengur, *Community Based Alternatives to Juvenile Incarceration* (Washington DC, NILECJ, October 1976); Malcolm W. Klein, 'Deinstitutionalization and Diversion of Juvenile Offenders: A Litany of Impediments', in N. Morris and M. Tonry (eds), *Crime and Justice: An Annual Review of Research* (Chicago: University of Chicago Press, 1979), vol. 1, pp. 145–201.

5. Unless otherwise stated all these statistics are drawn from the following sources. For England: Annual Reports of the Work of the Prison Department; 'Digests' and 'Briefings' published by NACRO (National Association for the Care and Resettlement of Offenders), 1979–83. For the USA: T. Flanagan and M. McCleod (eds), *Sourcebook of Criminal Justice Statistics 1982* (Washington DC: Bureau of Justice Statistics, 1983), *Report to the Nation on Crime and Justice: The Data* (Washington DC: Bureau of Justice Statistics, 1982); K. Carlson et al., *American Prisons and Jails, Population Trends and Projections* (Washington DC: National Institute of Justice, 1980), vol. II, and Barry Krisberg and Ira Schwarz, *Rethinking Juvenile Justice* (Unpublished MS. National Council of Research on Crime and Delinquency, 1982). For Canada, Janet B. L. Chan and Richard V. Ericson, *Decarceration and the Economy of Penal Reform* (Centre of Criminology, University of Toronto, 1981). All these sources contain detailed information on recent patterns of imprisonment.

6. See David Downes, 'The Origins and Consequences of Dutch Penal Policy Since 1945', *British Journal of Criminology*, 22 (October 1982), 325–57.

7. Robert Vintner et al. (eds), *Time Out: A National Study of Juvenile Correctional Programs* (Ann Arbor, Mich.: National Assessment of Juvenile Corrections, University of Michigan, 1976).

8. For a series of detailed case studies of the effects of the DSO programme, see Joel F. Handler and Julie Zatz (eds), *Neither Angels Nor Thieves: Studies in the Deinstitutionalization of Status Offenders* (Washington DC: National Academy Press, 1982).

9. The classic study of the California projects is Paul Lerman's *Community Treatment and Social Control: A Critical Analysis of Juvenile Correctional Policy* (Chicago: University of Chicago Press, 1975). See also Sheldon Messinger, 'Confinement in the Community: A Selective Assessment of Paul Lerman's

"Community Treatment and Social Control"', *Journal of Research in Crime and Delinquency*, 13, 1 (1976), pp. 82–92; and E. M. Lemert and F. Dill, *Offenders in the Community: The Probation Subsidy in California* (Lexington: D. C. Heath & Co., 1978).

10. David H. Thorpe et al., *Out of Care: The Community Support of Juvenile Offenders* (London: George Allen and Unwin, 1980). For further analysis, see Andrew Rutherford, *A Statute Backfires: The Escalation of Youth Incarceration in England During the 1970's* (London: Justice for Children, 1980).

11. Barbara Hudson, 'Against The Ethos: Incarceration in the Era of De-carceration' (Unpublished Paper, International Symposium on the Impact of Criminal Justice Reform, San Francisco, 1983).

12. This shallow-end/deep-end argument was nicely used by Rutherford and Bengur in *Community Based Alternatives*.

13. Klein, 'Deinstitutionalization and Diversion', pp. 162–6.

14. The deinstitutionalization and diversion strategies usually overlap. But, in addition to the general literature on community control cited in note 4, I have relied on the following evaluations of diversion: Thomas Blomberg, 'Diversion and Accelerated Social Control', *Journal of Criminal Law and Criminology*, 68, 2 (June 1977), pp. 274–82, 'Diversion from Juvenile Court: A Review of the Evidence', in F. Faust and P. Brantingham (eds), *Juvenile Justice Philosophy* (Minneapolis: West Publishing Co., 1978) and 'Widening the Net: An Anomaly in the Evaluation of Diversion Programmes', in Malcolm Klein and Katherine Teilmann (eds), *Handbook of Criminal Justice Evaluation* (Beverly Hills: Sage, 1980); Marvin Bohnstedt, 'Answers to Three Questions about Juvenile Diversion'. *Journal of Research in Crime and Delinquency*, 15, 1 (January 1978), pp. 109–23; Bruce Bullington et al., 'A Critique of Diversionary Juvenile Justice', *Crime and Delinquency*, 24, 1 (January 1978), pp. 59–71; Donald Cressey and Robert McDermott, *Diversion From the Juvenile Justice System* (Washington DC: NILECJ, 1974; Franklyn W. Dunford, 'Police Diversion—An Illusion?', *Criminology*, 15, 3 (November 1977), pp. 335–52; Malcolm Klein et al., 'The Explosion of Police Diversion Programs: Evaluating the Structural Dimensions of a Social Fad', in M. Klein (ed.), *The Juvenile Justice System* (Beverly Hills: Sage, 1976); Andrew Rutherford and Robert McDermott, *Juvenile Diversion* (Washington DC: NILECJ, 1976). On Britain, see Allison Morris, 'Diversion of Juvenile Offenders from the Criminal Justice System', in N. Tutt (ed.), *Alternative Strategies for Coping With Crime* (Oxford: Basil Blackwell, 1978), and Robert Adams and Jim Thomas et al. (eds), *A Measure of Diversion? Case Studies in Intermediate Treatment* (Leicester: National Youth Bureau, 1981).

15. Cressey and McDermott, *Diversion from the Juvenile Justice System*, pp. 3–4.

16. Klein, 'De-institutionalization and Diversion', p. 153.

17. Note here the literature on various forms of restitution and victim compensation schemes. For example, J. Hudson and B. Galaway (eds), *Victims, Offenders*

and Alternative Sanctions (Lexington, Mass.: Lexington Books, 1980). The British experience with such schemes shows a more genuine development of alternatives, the American a tendency to use them as supplements to other penalties.

18. D. C. McBride and S. G. Dalton, 'Criminal Justice—Diversion for whom?', in A. Cohn (ed.), *Criminal Justice Planning and Development* (Beverly Hills: Sage, 1977), pp. 103–16.

19. Lemert, 'Diversion in Juvenile Justice', p. 17.

20. In addition to the general literature, note particularly the fascinating system research on the Illinois Status Offender Services, see Irving A. Spergel et al., 'De-institutionalization of Status Offenders: Individual Outcome and System Effects', *Journal of Research in Crime and Delinquency*, 28 (January 1981), pp. 4–33 and 'Response of Organization and Community to a Deinstitutionalization Strategy', *Crime and Delinquency*, 28, 3 (July 1982), pp. 426–49. The research demonstrates clearly that females are now subject to more intense processing because of the new options. Spergel and his colleagues also suggest that the ISOS had the least effect in the most affluent communities and that in the poorer fragmented communities where it was most active, it actually *inhibited* the development of natural means of informal control in the community.

21. Quoted in Thorpe et al., *Out of Care*, p. 82.

22. For speculation on how the community strategy might feed back to the internal organization of the prison, see Stanley Cohen, 'Prisons and the Future of Control Systems: From Concentration to Dispersal', in M. Fitzgerald (ed.), *Welfare in Action* (London: Routledge, 1977).

23. See Stanley Cohen and Laurie Taylor, *Prison Secrets* (London: National Council of Civil Liberties, 1978).

24. National Institute of Mental Health, *Community Based Correctional Programs: Models and Practices* (Washington DC: US Government Printing Office, 1971), p. 1.

25. See Coates et al., *Diversity in a Youth Correctional System*; and Jean Ann Linney, 'Alternative Facilities for Youth in Trouble: Descriptive Analysis of a Strategically Selected Sample;' and Appendix C: 'Multicomponent Assessment for Residential Services for Youth', both in Handler and Zatz, *Neither Angels Nor Thieves*, pp. 127–75 and 740–79. Linney's research shows that average PASS ratings did indeed improve following 'deinstitutionalization', that is the institutions began to look more normal and comfortable. But it was also apparent that a secure, isolated facility could offer a 'normalizing' internal experience, while a group home, with its 'seeming openness and small size' could be restrictive and regimented internally.

26. H. B. Bradley, 'Community Based Treatment for Young Adult Offenders', *Crime and Delinquency*, 15, 3 (1969), p. 369.

27. For a survey, see R. P. Seiter et al., *Halfway Houses* (Washington DC: NILECJ, 1977).

28. Described in Charles Silverman, *Criminal Violence, Criminal Justice* (New York: Random House, 1978), pp. 417–23.

29. Fox, *Community Based Corrections*, pp. 62–3.

30. See Colin Thomas, 'Supervision in the Community', *Howard Journal of Criminology and Crime Prevention*, 18, 1 (1978), pp. 23-31.

31. N. Hinton, 'Intermediate Treatment', in L. Blom Cooper (ed.), *Progress in Penal Reform* (Oxford: Oxford University Press, 1974), p. 239. For other sources on the ideology of IT see Thorpe et al., *Out of Care*, Ray Jones and Andrew Kerslake, *Intermediate Treatment and Social Work* (London: Heinemann, 1979) and, in particular, the regular 'Aspects' and 'Briefings' on IT published between 1978 and 1983 by the Youth Social Work Unit, National Youth Bureau (Leicester).

32. J. A. Pratt, 'Intermediate Treatment and the Normalization Crisis', *Howard Journal*, 22, 1 (1983), pp. 19–37.

33. National Advisory Commission on Criminal Justice Standards, quoted in G. R. Perlstein and T. R. Phelps (eds), *Alternatives to Prison: Community Based Corrections* (California: Goodyear Publishing Co. 1975), p. 74.

34. For a sensitive account of the plight of the mentally ill tracked in this way—the 'forfeited' patients whom nobody wants—see Gary Whitmer, 'From Hospitals to Jails: The Fate of California's Deinstitutionalized Mentally Ill', *American Journal of Orthopsychiatry*, 50, 1 (January 1980), pp. 65–75.

35. Paul Lerman, 'Child Welfare, the Private Sector and Community Based Corrections', *Crime and Delinquency*, 30, 1 (January 1984), pp. 5–38.

36. Steven Spitzer and Andrew Scull, 'Social Control in Historical Perspective: From Private to Public Responses to Crime', in D. F. Greenberg (ed.), *Corrections and Punishment* (Beverly Hills: Sage, 1977), pp. 265–86 and 'Privatisation and Capitalist Development: The Case of the Private Police', *Social Problems*, 25, 1 (October 1977), pp. 18–29.

37. Andrew Scull, 'A New Trade in Lunacy: The Re-modification of the Mental Patient', *American Behavioral Scientist*, 24, 6 (July/August 1981), pp. 741–54.

38. Note here the series of Rand Corporation studies on the impact of fiscal cutbacks in the criminal justice system: W. E. Walker et al., *The Impact of Proposition 13 on Local Criminal Justice Agencies: Emerging Patterns* (Santa Monica: Rand Corporation, 1980), and J. M. Chaiken et al.. *Fiscal Limitation in California: Initial Effects on the Criminal Justice System* (Santa Monica: Rand Corporation, no date). As well as the degree of 'privatization', this research suggests that 'a leaner and smaller public sector may also turn out to be meaner and harsher'.

39. See Carol Warren, 'New Forms of Social Control: The Myth and Deinstitutionalization', *American Behavioral Scientist*, 24, 6 (July–August 1981), pp. 724–40.

40. Lerman, 'Child Welfare, the Private Sector'.

41. Joanne A. Arnaud and Timothy Mack, 'The Deinstitutionalization of Status

Offenders in Massachusetts: The Role of the Private Sector', in Handler and Zatz, *Neither Angels Nor Thieves*, pp. 335–71.

42. See Chester J. Kulis, 'Profit in the Presentence Report', *Federal Probation*, 47, 4 (December 1983), pp. 11–16. His melodramatic vision is of private operators 'rising phoenix-like' from a criminal justice system 'charred' by budget cuts and staff layoffs.

43. For references to these and similar bright ideas, see Charles A. Lindquist, 'The Private Sector in Corrections: Contracting Probation Services from Community Organizations', *Federal Probation*, 44, 1 (March 1980), pp. 58–63.

44. This process is well described in Rutherford and McDermott, *Juvenile Diversion*. 'Non legal' becomes 'para-legal', 'para-legal' becomes 'legal'.

45. See A. A. Cain et al., *Para legals—a Selected Bibliography* (Washington DC: NILECJ, 1979).

46. Spitzer and Scull, 'Privatization and Capitalist Development'. And see Clifford D. Shearing and Philip C. Stenning, 'Modern Private Security: its Growth and Implications', in M. Tonry and N. Morris (eds), *Crime and Justice: An Annual Review of Research* (Chicago: University of Chicago Press, 1981), vol. 3, pp. 193–245 and 'Private Security: Implications for Social Control', *Social Problems*, 30, 5 (June 1985), pp. 493–506.

47. Shearing and Stenning, 'Private Security', p. 496.

48. See Gary T. Marx, 'Thoughts on a Neglected Category of Social Movement Participant: The Agent Provocateur and the Informant', *American Journal of Sociology*, 80, 2 (September 1974), pp. 402–42.

49. Notably Gary Marx, whose various writings on the subject I rely upon here: 'The New Police Undercover Work', *Urban Life and Culture*, 8, 4 (1980), pp. 400–46, 'Who Really Gets Stung? Some Issues Raised by the New Police Undercover Work', *Crime and Delinquency*, 28 (April 1982), pp. 165–93 and *The Expansion and Changing Form of American Secret Police Practices*, unpublished MS. (Massachusetts Institute of Technology, 1982).

50. For approved examples of these new forms of policing, see L. Bickman, et al., *Citizen Crime Reporting Projects* (Washington, DC: NILECJ, 1977) and R. K. Yin et al., *Citizen Patrol Projects* (Washington DC: NILECJ, 1977).

51. On the problems of these developments (and an attempt to distinguish them from 'genuine' forms of popular justice) see James F. Brady, 'Towards a Popular Justice in the United States: The Dialectics of Community Action', *Contemporary Crises*, 5, 2 (April 1981), pp. 155–92.

52. Greenberg, 'Problems in Community Corrections', p. 8.

53. Dunford, 'Police Diversion', p. 350.

54. Messinger, 'Confinement in the Community', pp. 84–5.

55. See Rutherford and Bengur, 'Community Based Alternatives', p. 4. The (admittedly extreme) example they cite of something called 'community treatment', consisted of 25 full-time staff, 15 clients and was located on the fourth floor of a 1000-bed public hospital.

56. For examples of this sort of regime, see Seiter et al., *Halfway Houses*.

57. D. Brookman et al., *An Exemplary Project: Community Based Corrections in Des Moines* (Washington DC: NILECJ, 1976). For a more general impression of community correctional centres, see R. M. Carter et al., *Community Correctional Centers: Program Models* (Washington DC: National Institute of Justice, 1980).

58. R. Ku and C. Blew, *A University's Approach to Delinquency Prevention: The Adolescent Diversion Project* (Washington DC: NILECJ, 1977). Note that both my examples—Fort Des Moines and the ADP—were among the 20 'exemplary projects' selected by the LEEA for their effectiveness and adaptability.

59. This programme was hailed by John Conrad as 'News of the Future' in *Federal Probation*, 47, 4 (December 1983), pp. 54–5.

60. For general information, see *Intensive Intermediate Treatment* (Leicester: Youth Social Unit, National Youth Bureau, July 1983). On the Coventry PACE project, see Alistair Crine, 'A Lifeline For Young Offenders', *Community Care*, 10 February 1983.

61. Michael E. Smith, 'Will the Real Alternatives Please Stand Up' (Unpublished Paper, Colloquium on Prison Overcrowding Crisis, New York University Review of Law and Social Change, March 1983).

62. Lest it be thought that I am prejudiced against behaviourism (which I most certainly am) here is an example of another type of 'treatment modality in the community'. Three 'sociopathic' girls were taken from a corrective school and 'voluntarily committed' to a psychiatric hospital unit where they were administered minimal daily doses of insulin to instil hunger and anxiety. Each girl was then assigned to a 'selective maternal companion' with whom she 'interacted spontaneously' 5 hours daily for 6 months. 'Close dependent relationships developed, changes in identification took place and there was some suggestion that super ego changes are possible.' This is cited, without a hint of criticism or comment, by Marguerite Warren, *Correctional Treatment in Community Settings: A Report of Current Research* (Washington DC: National Institute of Mental Health, 1974).

63. *Project Crest: Counselling for Juveniles on Probation* (Washington: US Department of Justice, 1980).

64. Foucault, *Discipline and Punish*, p. 211.

65. Lamar T. Empey, *Alternatives to Incarceration* (Washington DC: US Government Printing Office, 1967).

66. I could, a little melodramatically, describe the system's effect on its surrounding space as 'prisonization', 'institutionalization' or—to invent an even more clumsy term—'controlization'. These processes are similar to Lindheim's notion of the 'hospitalization of space' (as used by Illich to describe the medical colonization of everyday areas of social life).

67. D. Skoler, 'Future Trends in Juvenile and Adult Community Based Corrections', in Perlstein and Phelps, *Alternatives to Prison*, p. 11.

68. Christopher Lasch, *Haven in a Heartless World: The Family Besieged* (New York: Basic Books, 1977).

69. The following references give some sense of the literature. In the USA: J. M. McPartland and F. L. McDill (eds), *Violence in Schools: Perspectives, Programs and Positions* (Lexington Mass: D. C. Heath and Co., 1977); Robert J. Rubel, *Unruly School: Disorders Disruptions and Crimes* (Lexington Mass: D. C. Heath and Co., 1977), and 'HEW's [Health Education and Welfare] Safe School Study—what it says and what it means for teachers and administrators' (Maryland, Institute for Reduction of Crime, 1978); Robert Rubel et al., *Crime and Disruption in Schools: A Selected Bibliography* (Washington DC: NILECH, 1969); S. D. Vestermark and P. D. Blauvelt, *Controlling Crime in the School—A Complete Security Handbook for Administrators* (West Nyack NY: Parker Publishing Co., 1978); National Institute of Education, *Violent Schools—Safe Schools: The Safe Schools Study*, Report to Congress (Washington DC: US Govt. Printing Office, 1978). In England: J. W. Docking, *Control and Discipline in Schools: Perspectives and Approaches* (London: Harper & Row Ltd., 1980) and Del Tatum, *Disruptive Pupils in School and Units* (Chichester: John Wiley, 1982).

70. See Peter Schrag and Diane Divoky, *The Myth of the Hyperactive Child* (New York: Pantheon, 1975).

71. Department of Education and Science, *Behavioural Units* and *Truancy and Behavioural Problems in Urban Schools* (London: DES, 1978).

72. Here are a few sample questions from an Institute publicity leaflet aimed at selling its security package to schools: 'Although you feel that the percentage of unruly children hasn't changed much over the years, you also feel that your control over them is slipping away;' 'Your usual administrative remedies such as suspension and detention, don't seem to work anymore, either with individuals or the overall group of unruly pupils;' 'Because courts are limiting how you can discipline students, you are now alienating your teaching staff as you are forced to return borderline students to their classrooms'.

73. See John Winterdyk and Ronald Roesch, 'A Wilderness Experiential Program as an Alternative for Probationers: An Evaluation', *Canadian Journal of Criminology*, 24 (January 1982), pp. 39–51.

74. See J. T. S. Duncan, *Citizen Crime Prevention Tactics: A Literature Review and Selected Bibliography* (Washington DC: National Criminal Justice Reference Service, 1980).

75. Anthony Sorrentino, *How to Organize the Neighbourhood for Delinquency Prevention* (New York: Human Sciences Press, 1979).

76. See Anthony F. Bottoms, 'Some Neglected Features of Modern Penal Systems', in D. Garland and P. Young (eds), *The Power to Punish* (London: Heinemann, 1983).

77. Foucault, *Discipline and Punish*, p. 113.

78. The term 'bifurcation' was used by Bottoms to refer to the split in modern

British penal policy towards adult offenders: new tough measures for the really serious or dangerous offender, a more lenient line towards the 'ordinary' offender. See Anthony Bottoms, 'Reflections on the Renaissance of Dangerousness', *Howard Journal of Penology and Crime Prevention*, 16, 2 (1977), especially pp. 88–91.

Papa's Discipline: Disciplinary Modes in the Scottish Women's Prison

PAT CARLEN

'We do not need to carry batons; we rely on talk.' (Comment by a female prison officer when I remarked on the fact that female officers, unlike their male colleagues, do not carry batons.)

A constant theme in feminist writings from Wollstonecraft to de Beauvoir and beyond concerns the debilitating contradictions which have been inherent in the social constructions of both femininity and female subjectivity. Much of contemporary feminist struggle is concerned with confronting and theorizing the contradictions which have atrophied women's abilities to make sense of themselves in a world publicly defined by men. Even today, after feminist writings and sustained campaigns have resulted in some significant legislative and ideological victories, the contradictory conditions within which individual women struggle for autonomy can still cause anguish and pain. For though women may nowadays be more aware of the ideological sources of these contradictory definitions—definitions both of legitimate womanhood and the conditions which engender such a state—they are, none the less, still constituted within them.

At the same time, of course, the very existence of the diffuse but ideologically powerful women's movement has enabled many women to confront successfully (and thereby change) the conditions of their own existences. The progressive effects of the women's movement have, however, been partial. There remain many women whose oppression is still made possible by a stubborn matrix of ideological and economic conditions. The women whose family life I described in Chapter Two [not reproduced in this edition] are a case in point. Brought up both in ignorance of, and yet dependent upon, male-related authority and domesticity, these women were, at an early age, quickly isolated in domestic conditions and family relationships over which they felt they had no control. It has been argued that it is this feeling of futility and powerlessness which has resulted in the mystery illnesses and often life-long depressions to which middle-class women have been perennially subject and which were particularly prevalent at the turn of the century (Ehrenreich and English, 1979). Depressed (or oppressed) working-class women, however, have not had the option of comfortable invalidity at home. For them the alternatives have been stark—either to put up with their lot or to reject it altogether. Rejection of family and domesticity has often led to the bottle or to the mental hospital. Even when it has led to neither, many women who have rejected maternal responsibilities have found themselves further isolated—as women out of place. If they then get into criminal trouble, their lack of maternal responsibilities, the fact that they are outwith domestic discipline, may go against them in the courts. If they go to prison they will yet again become victims of contradictory and debilitating definitions of womanhood.

In this chapter, therefore, I shall show how contradictory definitions both of legitimate womanhood and the conditions engendering it are dominant both in the penal discourses and the extra-discursive practices of the women's prison. I shall show how, together, they weave a fine web of penal control around women prisoners. Within the fractured and discontinuous elements of these discourses and institutional practices imprisoned women are again and again deconstructed and reconstructed to the point of debilitation. The features of the disciplinary regime which are specific to women's imprisonment elevate, fracture, and realign opposed ideological elements of the prisoners' subjective experience until they have been constructed as women both irrevocably within and irretrievably without adult female subjectivity. Women prisoners are contradictorily defined as being: both within and without sociability; both within and without femininity; and, concomitantly with the two previous conditions, both within and without adulthood.

Imprisoned—within and without sociability

The short-term prisoners in Cornton Vale's Papa Block, the main focus of this part of the study, feel that they are the most restricted prisoners within the prison. Many of them expressed a sense of injustice that this should be so. By and large their crimes have been less serious than those of the long-term prisoners; they have been moved to Papa Block because, through their behaviour whilst under observation, they have demonstrated that they can conduct themselves reasonably with less supervision than the women whose behaviour has caused them to be kept in Sierra, the secure block. Many of Papa's short-term prisoners have been in

Cornton Vale so frequently that they are well-known to the staff and are trusted by them. So why the severity of their treatment? It is because they are the ones for whom the disciplinary organization of the prison—and all general prisons—is devised. The prisoners doing Open University degrees, receiving specialist training, living in specially devised units are the exceptions, not the rule, within the prison system. None the less, it is likely that the women in Papa Block at Cornton Vale receive an even stricter and more coercive surveillance than do their counterparts in men's prisons.

According to the Governor of Cornton Vale the short-term prisoners in Sierra have to be allowed more latitude because they are the most difficult prisoners to contain. The longer term prisoners in Papa's open units are allowed 'association' (i.e. the freedom to sit in each other's rooms in the evenings and to watch television from 6.30 pm to 8.00 pm) as a privilege. The majority of prisoners, however, are serving much less than six months; they are locked into their rooms from 6.30 pm during the week and, unless they have a twenty-minute visit on a Saturday afternoon, from 1.30 pm until the next morning on Saturdays and Sundays. Several prisoners remarked on the fact that Cornton Vale's much publicized gardens are 'only for show', that the women prisoners are not allowed to exercise in them and are only occasionally allowed to sit outside in the fresh air. Lack of relaxing exercise (as opposed to hard physical labour working in the gardens or humping dustbins) was often complained about—and in this context, as in several others relating to recreational facilities, the women thought that they were much worse off than male prisoners, even the short-term male prisoners. Certainly at Saughton prison men are able to associate on two nights a week and during Saturday and Sunday afternoons after only two months' imprisonment. At such times male prisoners are allowed to play darts, cards, table-tennis, dominoes, etc. None of these activities were available to the women prisoners at Cornton Vale even to those allowed association. Thus, at the most elementary and physical level the women felt that they were more restricted than the general fact of their imprisonment warranted.

I'd do anything to pass the time, so when I came in I asked if they had a netball team and they said 'Oh no, nothing like that.' (Freda Franklin)

Likes of Sierra and Romeo have exercise, but we don't get nothing. If we were allowed out even for a game of football every now and then it would help—at least it would help me, because it would get rid of my excess energy. (Phyllis Prince)

Not all the women felt so energetic but many of them wanted to do more than just sit and watch television:

In the open units they have a record player—but we're not allowed one. In men's prisons they have table tennis; I've not even seen a pack of cards over here. (Hermione Hall)

Men's prisons are different from women's; they have cards and pool and table-tennis. (Kirsty King)

Though to this last Olive O'Brien added darkly, 'They wouldn't tolerate this carry-on in a men's prison.'

The majority of women prisoners at Cornton Vale are not in 'association' at all. When they are not at work, cleaning the unit, or eating their meals they are locked alone in their rooms. Apart from listening to their transistors they have little to do but churn over their problems. Reading does not come easy to most of the women at any time. In a prison cell many of them find it even more difficult. Some find it impossible:

You try to concentrate on a book but your thoughts go back to home. People who say they really concentrate on a book in here must be really good, they must be used to it. 'Cos it's very difficult. I read a fair amount outside, here I can't. I pick up a book, I read a bit and then my mind wanders—to home, my children, my father—are they all right? And then I start to worry. (Thelma Thompson)

Talk can relieve tension but the short-term prisoners at Cornton Vale get little time to talk to each other. Georgina Green was expressing a general opinion when she commented: 'I think we're locked up far too much. We don't get any time to sit and talk to other prisoners.' As a result of this enforced seclusion, when the prisoners do meet at mealtimes the talk can be frenetic and not have a cathartic effect at all. Ingrid Ingham described what often happens and why:

When I was in the closed unit it was hard, because you're always locked up. All day Saturday and Sunday you're locked up. You feel as if the walls are closing in on you. Then, when you all get out for tea or supper you're all squawking at the same time; talk, talk, talking because you've been locked up all that time. I don't think I ever really got a clear conversation with anybody because it was all stupid things we talked about; for the sake of talking when we got out. (Ingrid Ingham)

Thelma Thompson who had previously been in Holloway claimed that this isolation is peculiar to Cornton Vale:

In the English prison you have more free time to communicate more with the other inmates. So there, instead of bickering about small, silly things when you do get to meet them, you're getting to understand them. Taking away your freedom is a true word in every sense in Scotland.

The purpose of the 'family' concept of organization at Cornton Vale is, according to the Governor, that women 'should have their self-respect restored to them within a disciplined setting'. The women tell a different tale, a tale of isolation from each other and of self-estrangement.

The women who outside the prison are denied the legitimate pleasures of public conviviality and communality are yet again denied any real communicative experience once they get to prison. The division of the women into family units of seven allows for a rigid surveillance and control. Women from one unit are not allowed to communicate with women from another unit. Within each unit conversations between members are constantly monitored by officers, the permitted modes of conversations and the legitimacy of the topics discussed arbitrarily changing according to the dictates of the officers on duty. Further, the women are required to be sociable without being allowed to engage in the types of exchanges considered to be constitutive of sociability outside the prison. This constant emphasis on social behaviour outwith the normal channels of sociability makes the women tense in their relationships with each other and distrustful of their own ability to develop or maintain any sense of individual autonomy or self-direction. The major disciplinary effect of Cornton Vale's 'family unit' system is that the women prisoners are, both literally and symbolically, both physically and mentally, spaced-out.

Several women complained of the strict surveillance by officers over their movements within the blocks and of their confinement to the same small groups: 'If you go from one unit to another unit without asking permission you can get put on report for it.' (Thelma Thompson)

The lassies in the open units aren't really supposed to speak to the lassies in the closed units. For what reason I've no idea. I got into trouble for it one day, so I did. I went down to Unit 5 to take the milk jug and I put my head in to say 'Hello' to the lassies and I got called into the office and told that if I didn't want my privileges taken off me not to speak to prisoners in other units. (Freda Franklin)

Many prisoners just get fed-up with being with the same small group. After all, several of them, like Melissa Malcom, had decided to live out-with domesticity because, as they described themselves, they were 'loners'. Melissa in fact often went days without speaking to anyone other than to those officers who addressed her directly. Others said that they experienced a certain amount of strain from being forced into close company with people with whom they had nothing in common other than the fact of their incarceration. Phyllis Prince said, 'I'm not one for crowds, so this place just beats me', whilst Ann Archer felt disdain for the company she was being forced to keep:

There's a lot of people in here—no harm to them—I just don't like them. But I've got to put up with them. If you're in the same unit with somebody you don't like (say, you hate her) and she doesn't like you, you've just got to put up with each other and it causes a lot of tension. Tension builds up here.

However, even when women do get on with each other within the units, even when they wish to communicate with, and help, each other, there are many bars to sociability. The women in the closed units are not allowed to go into each other's rooms. The women in the open units are inhibited by the possibility that the intercom button in their rooms may be on, the officers thereby being able to listen-in on their conversations. Bernice Bradley described what could happen:

They've got these intercom things on the wall, and sometimes you can be sitting there and they can be listening to every word you're saying. While I was in the open unit we were all sitting talking one day and the officer just came belting out over this intercom thing. It was a good job it was an officer that was all right, but she'd heard every word we'd said.

In the closed units officers are always present when the women are talking:

You can't have a joke without them asking what you're laughing about. (June Jones)

You can't have a laugh and joke without them telling you to shut-up. Yet you cannot talk privately without them sticking their noses in. (Phyllis Prince)

Freda Franklin (along with others like Bernice Bradley and Phyllis Prince who had both at one time been in open units and found the artificiality of the enforced sociability too much of a strain) pointed out to me that I should not fall into the error of assuming that women in the open units had greater access to privacy than those in the closed:

Having a key means that you can open your own door. But the officers still come into your room when they want to, even if your key's on the other side of the door. It doesn't keep them out.

A more frequent complaint was that the officers even monitored meal-time talk and behaviour:

When you get your food in the sitting room an officer is there. She comes in and sits there. I don't call that freedom. I mean they're right outside in any case but they come in and sit just next to you. Why don't they leave you alone to your meals? The only time you feel you've got freedom is when they lock the doors when you're in your room. (Vivienne Vincent)

Thus one ironical result of the women's recognition that they are being forced into a coercively monitored sociability is that they are driven into even greater isolation, a debilitating isolation outwith both sociability and privacy. Yet several women thought that they *should* communicate more with other people, that keeping themselves to themselves was not a good thing (indeed it had been a part of the ethic of respectable female domesticity which they had earlier rejected), that lack of communication with others had been one of their problems in the past. Melissa admitted that she was often bad-tempered and 'hated' other people just because 'alone I have bad thoughts' while Thelma Thompson, continually told-off by officers for talking too much, knew quite well why she did it:

As I say, I talk a lot. Sometimes I'm rambling on and on and it's of no interest to anyone else, it's just relieving my tension. I *can* sit and have a reasonable discussion with anyone if they're willing to but before the discussion's closed you're back in your room. By the time you get back you've forgotten what you were discussing in the first place. So therefore you don't carry it on, you go on to something else and everything's one big mumbo-jumbo. You've no time to get anything off your chest. I am inclined to talk a lot, it's just my way of relieving my nerves. Some of them say 'Do you never get tired of speaking?' And it used to worry me, but why should it, if talking is helping me and saving me from cracking up? (Thelma Thompson)

Some women are *so* overburdened by their own problems that their inclination is to avoid engaging in the exchanges which would entail hearing about other people's troubles. The prison officers encourage this attitude of non-involvement in the affairs of other prisoners:

A lot of the women think 'Oh, I've got enough on my plate myself without bothering about anybody else' and in here it is sometimes better to be like that because if something does blow-up you're pulled into it. Then you're told that you shouldn't be talking to other people or that you shouldn't be finding out about each other, that it's an officer's job. (Clare Carlton)

Not only are the women discouraged from discussing their own affairs they are, in fact, actually forbidden to engage in many of the expected civilities of normal social life. June Jones was very indignant that she had had her lighter taken from her and that she had also been put on report for giving someone a light, 'I mean, if everyone's sitting round and somebody says "Give us a light", you're not going to say "No, you're not getting one".' She (amongst others) was also indignant that having been forced to live with a homeless woman in a 'family' unit she was then not allowed to give that same woman information that could help her upon liberation:

There's a woman in our unit who's got nowhere to go when she gets out. So I gave her my address and I got locked up for that. The officer just took the address off me and tore it up. (June Jones)

Sharing of privileges and skills is also forbidden:

If you get books sent in you must keep them to yourself and when you've finished those books they go right into your property. One lassie got five books sent in and she asked if she could put them in the library so the other lassies could go and get them. But no way. (Freda Franklin)

I've got City and Guilds. One of the girls who's going out says to me that she could get a job as a waitress, a living-in position, so that she wouldn't have to worry about where she's going to stay. But she says 'I'm not a good waitress'. I says 'Well, come on, get the knives and forks out and I'll show you' and I was saying 'Put this, this side and that, that side' and I got into serious trouble. The officer says to me 'You can't tell people what to do on the outside.' They don't like you to know anything. They'd rather think you're all dumb and stupid. (Melody McDuff)

Olive O'Brien summed up the general feeling of contempt for a disciplinary system which though purporting to engender a sense of social responsibility in those subject to it at the same time attempts to extinguish all signs of mutual self-help.

You cannot speak in private. We're not allowed to go into another lassie's room. We can't even borrow a paper off a lassie. You cannot give another lassie a smoke. Even a lassie who had come in from Dundee and didn't have any tobacco. Surely to God I could be allowed to give that lassie a fag. I've worked for it and it's my money. But you cannot do it, you're on report for that as well. It doesn't make sense, that. (Olive O'Brien)

Ann Archer agreed with Olive:

You're apt to get selfish in prison too. If you get tobacco or people's got sweets, they're not allowed to share it out with each other. Well I'm not like that outside and I don't see why I should be like that in here. So I don't think prison helps anybody, it just makes you more selfish and bitter.

And Kirsty King claimed that so much normal sociability and communication is suppressed at Cornton Vale that it is more like a hospital than a prison: 'It is more like a hospital, you know. You're all separated and you don't know half of what is going on. In the real prison you had much more social life.' Yet the real prisons of the nineteenth century also operated with the principle of 'divide and rule'. It is ironic, but not accidental, that features and effects of the nineteenth-century separate system should reappear in new form in the much-lauded 'family unit' system of Cornton Vale.

Some women, like Thelma Thompson, admitted to experiencing an extreme tension. Others said that they could keep a tight rein on their emotions, that in particular they would not allow officers to 'wind' them up. Olive O'Brien, Daphne Daniels, and Melody McDuff commented on this phenomenon, a common and sinister feature of institutions where the power of one group is both arbitrary and total:

They try to wind up some of those lassies until they are in a terrible state.' (Olive O'Brien)

Some of the officers, when they see a girl's nerves are kind of bad, they'll try and pick on her. (Daphne Daniels)

One girl said something to an officer which she didn't like and the officer says 'We can always make it a hundred times harder for you in a hundred different ways'. (Melody McDuff)

Melody is a photographic model by profession. She told me how the prison officers constantly goaded her about certain aspects of the job:

MELODY: When I came into reception they started making remarks like 'Oh, here she comes, here come Paris models now.' Then when they told me to strip and put this sheet round me, I went to turn my back and she says 'Turn round, you've shown it all before'.

PAT CARLEN: And did this continue?

MELODY: Yes. The other day I was down on my knees doing the floor and this officer comes along and says 'Oh, look, everyone, it's rear end we've got now, not topless'.

After this very conversation I myself was jokingly told, 'Oh, you interviewed the model this morning, didn't you?'

In a more serious context I witnessed what must surely count as an outstanding instance of 'winding-up'. It involved a woman in Sierra. This woman, let's call her Cleopatra, was by all accounts one of the most disturbed women in Cornton Vale. The following report is mainly of a conversation (which was noted down verbatim as it occurred) and of the circumstances in which it took place (which were noted down about ten minutes after the end of the episode). I was rather surprised that such an episode could occur in front of someone known to be an 'official' researcher sponsored by the Scottish Office.

Ms X, a prison officer, introduced me to Cleopatra. 'Cleopatra is our star. When she misbehaves she's horrible. Now don't go near Mrs Carlen because your breath stinks.' We sat down in the sitting-room together with a new inmate who had not as yet been given any work to do. The conversation turned to illness and Cleopatra said that she was scared of getting cancer. Ms X said to her, 'Perhaps Mrs Carlen would like to contribute to buying you a copy of *Exit* for Christmas.' Cleopatra said, 'What's that?' 'The book of the Euthanasia Society . . . you could go when you like then.' After some further desultory conversation Cleopatra announced that she was going to comb her hair and put on some make-up. Ms X responded with, 'Well, don't do those silly bunches you did the other day and don't make yourself up like a circus clown.' When in reply to these injunctions Cleopatra began to shout, Ms X caught hold of her by the lapels and shouted threateningly 'Are you starting up again?' Cleopatra cried, 'No, Miss, I'm not starting. It's just all this aggravation, all this antagonism.'

When Cleopatra had left the room an extremely thin woman came into the sitting room. (I was later told that she was suffering from anorexia.) Ms X now turned her attention to this lady and introduced her to me with 'Now, look at this one Mrs Carlen. Watch out for this one, she's a handful. Looks horrible, too, doesn't she? It's because she won't eat.'

Sierra Block is occupied mainly by the women who are said to have 'personality disorders' and whose behaviour can be very strange indeed. It also serves as an induction unit for all convicted prisoners over the age of 21, all of whom remain in Sierra for at least the first six weeks of their sentences. The reason for combining the initial observation unit with the secure unit for very disturbed offenders is punitive. The bizarre behaviour of some of the women in Sierra terrifies new prisoners and, as one officer said, 'it makes them realize they're in prison'. The Governor herself said that 'it is good for women to go into Sierra when they first come in as it makes them feel guilty. It makes them feel that they are in prison.' And other officers also expounded on the positive disciplinary advantages accruing from Cornton Vale's over-large proportion of severely disturbed offenders: 'All admissions have to go to Sierra and they think they are in a madhouse' (Prisoner Officer No. 4).

Being in Sierra can have a good effect on first offenders. Some get very frightened of people like Cleopatra. One woman was in with two who were worse than Cleopatra. They threatened to take her food and to beat her up. And we can't be there all the time. . . . At least it did frighten her. (Prison Officer No. 7)

The staff *want* Cornton Vale to be experienced as a prison.

It is good for them to realize they're in prison. One woman, an embezzler, told me that when she came into Sierra she cried all night because women were screaming and she was so frightened. She said she thought 'Oh my God! What have I let myself in for?' (Prison Officer No. 5)

In Sierra, too, new prisoners learn that all powers of definition are the officers'. The 'good' prisoner 'opens up' to the officers and doesn't think that she is any better than the other women. Camilla, for instance, was a new prisoner who had not yet learned this, as the following dialogue (held in the presence of a half-dozen prisoners) demonstrates:

PRISON OFFICER (*to Pat Carlen*: They're just like bairns. If you sit in here with five of them you've got five competing for your attention. Yesterday I was in here and they were all trying to talk to me at once.

CAMILLA: I wasn't, I didn't say a word.

PRISON OFFICER (*snaps*): And that's just as bad as the other way. You were keeping too much to yourself. You'd been here two days and it was only last night that you began to open up.

Once, however, the women have opened up, have made their private lives into public property, they are reprimanded if the officers think that they talk too much! Phyllis Prince summed up the double-bind in which many of the women found themselves: 'They tell you that you should be yourself, just be natural and be yourself. If I was myself in here I'd never be off report.'

There is resentment and suspicion of the women developing a private realm of consciousness, yet at the same time there are bars to sociability which prevent them developing a public realm of consciousness. Though, therefore, the women are *physically* locked into small family units which might appear to provide secure rehabilitative settings, the superimposed prison discipline ensures that they are mentally and emotionally straitjacketed into the same debilitating tension and isolation which they have already experienced in nuclear family situations outwith the prison. When many of the prisoners subsequently indicate that not only are they outwith the family physically but that emotionally and mentally too they are committed neither to family relationships nor to domesticity, the prison officers find it difficult to endow their charges with any kind of legitimate social being at all. The women who have stepped outside family and domesticity are also seen to be beyond femininity and without adulthood.

Imprisoned—within and without femininity

But she's not like a woman, is she?   Smelling like that! Ye canna say she's a woman. She's lovable enough—more like a bairn, but she's never a woman. (Prison Officer No. 6 talking to me about Kirsty King)

You're not allowed razors or Immac for your arms nor tweezers for your eye-brows. It's most uncomfortable when you've been used to it. Some of the officers would be willing to bring in their old make-up but they're not allowed. I mean, why can't they bring in their old make-up and put it into a box so that the lassies can use it? It would make the women feel better, and make morale better any-way. There's nothing worse than feeling down in the dumps. Even at home if you're feeling a bit down—you go and have a bath, do your hair, and put make-up on. There are lassies in here that are good at putting make-up on and good at hairdressing. And I think they should be encouraged to do that kind of thing. Still . . . maybe they like to see you walking about like something from the Dark Ages.'[1] (Clare Carlton)

Familiness is one dominant conceptual axis along which women's imprison-ment is conceived by the Scottish judicial and penal authorities. Femininity is another. Together with the insistence that deviant women should be interpellated as members of a family and reconstructed as life-long candidates for domesticity is the insistence that, because prisoners in Cornton Vale are treated as women, they should behave accordingly. Sometimes when the officers contended that 'at least they're treated as women' they were merely referring to the fact that Cornton Vale has standards of sanitation far superior to most British prisons. At other times they were making reference to some innate female 'need' for familiness catered for by the small 'family' units. On other occasions again they were referring to the higher standards of cleanliness and decorum expected of women. At the same time, however, officers continually pointed out to me that few of the women had acquired the ordinary 'female' accomplishments of baking and sewing, whilst the women them-selves complained that the prison authorities denied to them most of the sartorial and cosmetic props to femininity which they were accustomed to enjoying outside the prison. Lest, however, it is thought that talk of femininity exhausted the discursive parameters within which the women themselves talked of their bodily and psychological confinement, it must be noted that the women were equally concerned about the generally degrading aspects of the prison regime, aspects common to most British prisons and stubbornly and surprisingly (or not) retained even in a mod-ern institution such as Cornton Vale. For, despite the reiterated claims of the officers that women are not degraded at Cornton Vale it has to be remembered that at any one time about a third of the adult women there may be accommodated in closed units, thereby being forced to use the hated chamber-pots whenever they are locked up, whether it be during the day or at night. Netta Nelson thought that the system was both generally degrading and particularly distressing to women:

It's degrading, women of our age having to use a chanty. And a lot of people here have got diarrhoea too. There's a girl in my unit she's got piles and she's got these tablets off the doctor but she's scared to take them in case they make her go to the toilet after lock-up time. Hardly anyone uses the chanties, most of them just hold it in. And when you've got your periods, some people are heavy, you know, there's no way you can get out to change the towel or anything.

Several of the women spontaneously made the point that prisoners received little sympathy regarding pre-menstrual tension and even less recognition of their need for increased access to washing facilities during menstruation.

I took my periods one day on a Monday. I had bled a lot and I asked if I could go over and get changed and get washed. I was told 'No'. And that was me from early afternoon to quarter to five when I had to come over and take a bath. (Ingrid Ingham)

Further (and despite the sheriff's belief in the quality of the medical provision at Cornton Vale) one of the greatest complaints of the women concerned their lack of unmonitored access to the doctor. Ten of the women spontaneously complained about the system whereby all requests to see the doctor have to go through a person with no medical qualifications at all, i.e. a prison officer. That the initial diagnosis of their complaint was made by a lay person was, however, the least of their worries. What the prisoners were more concerned about was, first, the lack of privacy in which they had to make their requests to see the doctor, and, second, that once the request had been made they sometimes did not see the doctor for a week or, in some cases, if the officer had so decided, not at all. Olive O'Brien was angry about this lack of privacy:

There was a lassie had piles up in her thingy. That's a sore thing, that. And the officer was asking her 'What do you want to see the doctor for?' And she didn't want to tell her 'cos everyone was sitting round the table. So the lassie said 'It's personal'. Well, she's never got to see the doctor yet.

And June Jones also pointed out that refusal to give a reason for requesting to see the doctor could result in not seeing him at all.

If you're requesting to see the doctor they'll say, 'What's it for?' So you say 'Well, it's personal'. Next thing you're in the office and the Principal Officer is asking what you want to see the doctor for. And if you don't tell her, you don't get to see him.'

The officers, for their part, justified this official screening of the women's requests to see the doctor by claiming that some women would always be seeing the doctor about trivial or even non-existent complaints if they had absolutely free access to him. Against this, both Melody McDuff and Bernice Bradley pointed out that if the doctor was so over-worked then it was surprising that 'when it suited them' the officers could invoke the doctor's authority for the granting or not of requests which need not have been seen as being medically related at all. Thus when Melody and Bernice separately requested an extra blanket for their beds on the grounds that their rooms were particularly draughty they both received the same reply; that they would have to make an appoint-ment to see the doctor to seek his authorization for the issue of an extra blanket on *medical* grounds! As neither of the women felt that she could make out a *medical* case for an extra blanket both of them went without.

In addition to the general complaints about degrading sanitary condi-tions and the denial of privacy in relation to medical matters, most of the women mentioned that they felt 'degraded' by the ill-fitting wrapover dresses which they were forced to wear for work. Further, they were lim-ited in the extent to which they could improve their appearance by make-up. Only three pieces of make-up are allowed to each woman and when it is used up they are not allowed to have any more sent in but, instead, have to replace it out of their weekly earnings of 82 pence. Prisoners are never allowed to wear their own clothes and the clothes issued for associ-ation and visits (and locked away after each occasion for which they've been issued) are often as ill-fitting as the wrapover dresses issued for work. Women are not even allowed to wear their own shoes! As for tights . . . 'Now', said Bernice Bradley, 'You know what ordinary tights are like—how they get holes? Here, you've to wear them sometimes until they're literally falling off!'

Regulation of dress has traditionally been a major mode of control in total institutions and particularly in girls' schools (see, for example, Oakely, 1978), but the rigid sartorial control of women prisoners at Cornton Vale is hardly conducive to repair of their already-fractured self-images. Once again, therefore, there is a bifurcation between the official and discursive claims that women are 'helped to regain their self-respect' and the extra-discursive institutional conditions wherein the self-respect is further battered and bruised, if not altogether destroyed.

Institutional control of the women's self-presentation does not stop at sartorial control. Although, as Freda Franklin said, prisoners are not allowed 'even the simplest of things that would help a woman feel more female' there is, at the same time a rigid control of the washing of their hair, their clothes, and their bodies. Clare Carlton, a woman in her late forties, gave an instance of the type of control which she and others found most humiliating.

CLARE   I don't think they should tell normal grown-up women that they've got to change their underwear every day. It's just a matter of course. I mean I wouldn't be putting on pants that I'd had on yesterday. Yet you get officers saying 'Now don't forget to wash your knickers'.

PAT CARLEN   To you? They've actually said that?

CLARE   Aye, oh aye, you get this a lot. And lassies just turn round and say 'Aye, I'll wash them', and walk away.

Clare had added that she could understand that women who had been 'skippering' might need to be told about such matters of cleanliness. However, Melissa, who had been skippering for over ten years, was equally annoyed about the indignity of being told when and how to wash, saying angrily, 'I've skippered, but I've always kept myself clean—always.' My continued scepticism about the claims that officers regulated *all* adult prisoners in this way was in fact destroyed by a prison officer who herself offered a spontaneous and sympathetic comment on the effects of such bodily control:

They have no independence here. And the majority do mind. They hate being told when to take a bath, when to wash their hair. I wouldn't like it myself, though of course I don't think about that when I have to do my job. (Prison Officer No. 6)

The accommodation of the women in small family units means that their every move is monitored. How they dress, how they eat, what they talk about, who they talk with, their mental and physical health—it is all screened by the prison officers for reasons of rehabilitation and security. Just as the women are denied sociability in the name of the social, just as the development of a public realm of communication is denied them in the name of the public good, so too in the name of femininity are they denied the physical and psychological props normally attendant upon the celebration of the feminine myth. Such concomitant celebration and denial of the myth causes confusion and bitterness. As Phyllis Chesler, writing of Goffman's *Asylums*, put it:

[Goffman] is primarily thinking of the debilitating effect—on men—of being treated like a woman. . . . But what about the effect of being treated like a woman when you are a woman? And perhaps a woman who is already ambivalent or angry about just such treatment? (Chesler, 1974)

'I'm awfully, awfully bitter' was indeed the one phrase most commonly used by the women to describe their feelings about life in general and their prison experience in particular. Yet their bitterness did not stem solely from the ways in which their femininity was engaged, played upon, and then denied. Their major complaint was that, in being treated like 'wee lassies' they were also being denied full adult status.

Imprisoned—within and without adulthood

I think of myself as a mother to inmates and officers. Down in that office, I'm the mother. (Prison Officer No. 10)

They're very childish. They're just like bairns. You wouldn't speak to a four-year-old how we have to speak to some of them, sometimes. (Prison Officer No. 9)

One effect of Scottish women's imprisonment is that it turns 'grown women into wee lassies'. Ann Archer summed up what happens when she claimed that 'they're awfully, awfully childish in here. See, when you come in you're grown up, but I feel I've got awfully childish since being in here.' Explanations for this phenomenon varied. It has of course been noted previously in descriptions of penal institutions. Bettelheim (1960) in particular has described how prisoners' infantile dependency was the dominant factor in the interaction between guards and prisoners in a concentration camp. Both officers and women at Cornton Vale could likewise give specific examples of the childishness which inseminated all aspects of prison life. Some of the officers thought that women prisoners *are essentially* childlike, that it is their lack of maturity, their inadequacy, etc. which has landed them in prison in the first place. The more analytical officers and women blamed the hierarchical organization of the prison itself for the childishness which permeated it. Other women thought that many of the prison's disciplinary and security measures were *actually designed* to induce feelings of infantile dependency in the prisoners.

That British prisons are hierarchically organized is well known (see for example, Thomas, 1972); that such hierarchical organization also permeates the whole system, having adverse effects on staff and prisoners alike, was borne out by both staff and women at Cornton Vale. When I remarked to one officer that the women complained that they were too often treated like children she replied:

We are treated like children, too. Why do you think we have such a turnover of staff? They come in at that gate and are out a few months later and people wonder why. I'll give you an example. I once phoned the Deputy Governor and asked if I could have an appointment with him sometime. Within half an hour my Principal Officer and Chief were on to me: 'How dare I contact the Deputy Governor without contacting them first, without telling them what it was about'. (Prison Officer No. 11)

The lack of lateral channels for the transmission of information was confirmed by both the prisoners and the Governor. The women complained about a system set up to ensure that all their requests to see the doctor, the social worker, the Governor and anyone else, had to go through a prison officer. They all complained that this inhibited form of communication was often, in practice, no form of communication at all. Only Melody McDuff, however, speculated about why prison officers themselves might favour such blocked forms of communication. Speaking of one principal officer in Papa Block, Melody said,

If she can deal with it herself, she will. Rather than say to the Governor 'There's five girls to see you this morning'. She'd rather say 'Nobody to see you'. So the Governor thinks 'Oh, it's all nice and quiet', whereas in fact the girls are getting refused everything right, left, and centre.

I myself asked the Governor if the women had any kind of forum where they could put forward requests and suggestions. She replied:

No, not as such, if you mean the type they have in certain Scandinavian countries and in Canada, an actual prisoners' committee. There's nothing like that. What you do find is that in the small units they often possibly have a spokesman who talks to the staff and that comes up through the principal officer. . . . But nothing formal.'

The Governor thought that from her point of view this hierarchical transmission of knowledge was successful: 'You have your chief officers and through them you get to know everything. They're often surprised at how much you do know.' A prison officer dissented—as people at the bottom end of an hierarchical structure often do! 'The Governor walks round with rose-coloured spectacles. All the information she gets is controlled by the chiefs. She hears only what they want her to hear.' (Prison Officer No. 13)

However, whether or not the hierarchical structure affects knowledge transmission within the prison, it certainly ensures that those at the very bottom—the prisoners—have no space in which to develop any positive forms of independence. Again and again when I asked prisoners if they knew *why* a certain procedure or rule was in operation I received replies like:

I don't know, I've never really asked them why. It's just one of the rules and I just do what I'm told. (Clare Carlton)

You get to the stage where you sort of don't bother to ask reasons because you never get a direct answer back anyway. (Bernice Bradley)

Clare Carlton claimed that the prison officers wanted the prisoners to react like 'automatons' and for her part a prison officer explained that she always had to let women know 'who is wearing the uniform' even when they were attempting to be totally helpful. Talking of Eliza Eastwood, Prison Officer No. 10 said:

She's no trouble, but she's just really funny sometimes. She says to me 'All right then, I'll do it for you, I'll do this, Hen, and then I'll do that'. And I have to say 'Wait a minute, who's wearing the uniform?' Then she says 'Oh! Sorry Miss'.

The instances discussed in this section so far are general to prisons and to other establishments where a hierarchical discipline is enforced. They are not peculiar to Cornton Vale. At Cornton Vale, however, the general features of the hierarchical discipline combine with the domestic work programme, with the denial to prisoners of sociability and adult woman-hood, and with the organization of the women into small family units, to ensure a mental and bodily surveillance which denudes the prisoners' daily life of all dignity and independence.

Several women were scathing about the type of work on offer to them. It is not surprising that Melody McDuff, who had had more formal education than the other women interviewed, should be most vocal on this score.

People who are bright get treated like wee girls. They don't want to know you've had an education. You can go to the canteen; you can go to the laundry; you can work the machines; you can go to the cookhouse; you can go round and empty the bins; or you can just stay here and clean the unit. But you're not going to get a job you could put your mind to.

Some of the prison officers were also of the opinion that there was no interesting work for the 'more intelligent' women, though both Melody McDuff and Thelma Thompson claimed that even access to education classes and discussion groups themselves was monitored too closely by the officers.

I'm treated like a 4-year-old. There's classes over there but before you can get that far you're taken into the office and it's, 'Now, are you sure you can manage this?' I mean, it's just like being a wee girl. (Melody McDuff)

Last night, for instance, I was at the Bible Class. The purpose was to have a discussion when the film finished. Myself and another girl spoke up and at the end of it, one of the officers says to me 'Give some of the other girls a chance'. I felt really bad about it and actually last night is the first night I've cried since I've been in here. (Thelma Thompson)

Yet, even when women had become resigned to the fact that imprisonment in Cornton Vale means a constant round of routine domestic and machine work interspersed with contrasting periods of isolation and enforced and monitored sociability, they still resented the enforcement of minor rules relating to forms of address, deportment, conversation, etiquette, and other forms of self-presentation in general. When they repeatedly made the point that 'men wouldn't put up with this carry-on, this rigmarole' they were more often than not referring to the type of discipline that is usually only enforced in schools, young people's training centres, or the armed services. But there are striking differences. When these modes of behaviour are enforced in the armed services the whole organizational edifice and ethos is consistently militaristic and impersonal. In Cornton Vale, by contrast, a dominant official discourse invokes the concepts of familiness, domesticity, and self-regulation, principles at odds with the elements of partly school-girlish, partly militaristic discipline actually imposed. One could also argue that *all* prisoners, male and female, suffer humiliation through the arbitrary enforcement of innumerable petty rules. Male prisoners, however, being less isolated one from another, are usually able to develop a mutually supportive counter-culture which militates against male prison officers regulating the minutiae of their charges' personal presentation and style to the same degree that women prison officers, imbued with notions of womanly propriety, regulate the minutest details of the women prisoners' self-presentation.

The prisoners address the officers as 'Miss'. This in itself is a hated reminder of schooldays.

We've got to say 'Yes, Miss', and 'No Miss', sort of 'three bags full, Miss', this sort of thing. (Thelma Thompson)

I work in Reception. If I want to go to the toilet, I have to say 'Please, Miss, can I go to the toilet, Miss?' (Ann Archer)

In their turn the officers monitor the women's deportment and personal cleanliness. At the age of 59 Mandy MacDonald was resentful of being told by a young officer that she must keep her hands out of her pockets; Clare Carlton felt that she did not need a young officer to tell her how to keep her cell clean and tidy:

We're all grown women in here. I'll be 47 on Saturday and when I get a young lassie of 21 telling me how to polish my floor, how to make my bed, it gets right up my nose. (Clare Carlton)

Women, like Clare, whose whole life has been steeped in the ethos of maternal responsibility, experience a very specific and painful loss of status when they themselves are treated as the children of a paternalistic regime which denies them their adulthood.

I think most grown women know how to keep themselves and their room clean. Perhaps it's different with men . . . or with very young girls, but I think that most women who've had a home and reared a family don't need to be told. (Clare Carlton)

Thelma Thompson thought that it was *because* she was treated like a child in prison that she had deteriorated into a 'rambling' chatterbox!

If they would treat us more like adults we would feel better. Sometimes it's hard to be an adult if you're getting treated like a child. . . . You know . . . going in twos, 'Take your hands out of your pockets'. You talk like that to children, you don't talk like that to married women with children, or grandchildren. (Thelma Thompson)

But is was the close surveillance of leisure and meal-times which the women particularly resented and which they felt would not be so docilely accepted by male prisoners. Altogether eleven women spontaneously claimed that although the women in Papa Block were supposed to be the more stable and responsible of all the adult prisoners, they were, in fact, 'treated like kids'. The following catalogue, made up of remarks made by a few of the women covers the main complaints which were repeatedly made as I talked with the prisoners. They are all concerned with the extreme degree of control which is exercised over the bodies of women prisoners.

Even if you want your toe-nails or your fingernails cut you've to go over to the Health Centre and ask to get them cut (Ingrid). You're never allowed to sit on the floor of the sitting room, you've always to sit on chairs (Melody). See, even if you don't want anything to eat you've still got to sit at the table until they say (June). They tell you what you're going to eat, when you're going to eat and how you're going to sit. They practically spoon-feed you. You're treated more like a kid than a grown woman. Bed at eight o'clock, told what to do all the time and when to do it. Even on a day when you don't want your jacket on you're made to put it on. We went to the pictures last night and it was 'Get into twos, hands out of pockets; first ten step forward, next ten'. Even if you go up to medication you're told to walk in twos, not to talk, to take your hands out of your pockets. (Phyllis Prince)

So much for the sheriffs' notion that Cornton Vale is not really a prison!

This article has provided a conventional picture of a conventional prison, a prison without the brutal physical conditions of the old Victorian prisons, but a prison none the less. This description of Cornton Vale should astonish no-one. The prisoners admitted that, just as the physical conditions are in themselves lacking in brutality, so too are the officers. Most of the women saw most of the officers as being 'pretty fair in the main', and as 'just doing a job'. The prisoners complained less about the officers, more about the 'system'. And their complaints were not just about the prison system but about the various 'systems' via which they had arrived at Cornton Vale. For the astonishing thing about Cornton Vale is the composition of its prison population.

It is often assumed that a reduction in the prison population will result in only the most 'dangerous' offenders, or maybe the most persistent of the serious offenders going to gaol. The concept of 'dangerousness' is a tricky one when applied to almost anything, particularly so when applied to offenders, but, on none of its possible definitions would the majority of women at Cornton Vale be seen as dangerous. Approximately a third of all adult women received at Cornton Vale under sentence in 1980 had been convicted of breach of the peace, and, altogether, 54 per cent had been convicted of Class VII miscellaneous offences. Another third had been convicted of crimes against property without violence. Half of all the women in prison were there because of failure to pay a fine. So why maintain an extremely secure, technologically complex establishment at a cost of approximately £100 per week for each woman for these few petty offenders? The reasons are many and complex—and are only obliquely connected with the punishment of crime.

Note

1. In fact, there was evidence that some officers attempted to help the women maintain attractive appearances. Several prisoners told me that officers had cut or permed their hair and one officer told me that she had brought in some of

her own cologne for one of the women about to be liberated. The women did not in the main complain about the prison officers; rather they complained about a system which appeared to be at best paternalistic and at worst deliberately obstructive of their own attempts to maintain individuality of expression.

References

Bettelheim, B. (1960) *The Informed Heart,* New York, Free Press.

Chesler, P. (1974) *Women and Madness,* London, Allen Lane.

Ehrenreich, B. and English, D. (1979) *For Her Own Good,* London, Pluto Press.

Okaely, J. (1978) 'Privileged, schooled and finished', in Ardener (1978).

Thomas, J. E. (1972) *The English Prison Officer Since 1850,* London, Routledge & Kegan Paul.

Tactics for Reduction

ANDREW RUTHERFORD

In introducing the reductionist alternative, this chapter presents case studies of three prison systems which have taken a reductionist direction. Some of the tactics and strategies described may be transferable to other jurisdictions, but of crucial significance is the demonstration that reductionist policy can be implemented successfully. In the late 1960s and early 1970s much use was made of the notion of decarceration. Articles were published and papers presented at seminars; but it was actual events in Massachusetts which were, around 1972, to gain most attention in and beyond the United States.[1] As Commissioner of the Department of Youth Services, Jerome Miller was able to show that huge reductions in institutional populations could be achieved and sustained. Although it was not possible to replicate the particular reductionist tactics used in Massachusetts, Miller's achievement gave an urgency to efforts elsewhere to cut back the scope of incarceration.[2]

The three case studies portray substantial reductions in prison population size which were sustained at the new low level. The first case study deals with the thirty-year period in England which ended with the Second World War. England's prison population rate, at about 30 per 100,000 inhabitants in the mid-1930s, had become one of the lowest in Europe. By comparison, in the Netherlands at this time, the prison population rate was 52 per 100,000, not very different from the rates of 56 and 61 achieved by France and Belgium respectively.[3]

The other two cases of reductionist tactics described in this chapter are the national prison systems of Japan and the Netherlands over the period 1950–75. It is instructive to compare the shifts in prison population size of these two prison systems with that of England over this period, shown in Table 1.

In considering these three reductionist case studies, it must be re-emphasized that the level of recorded crime is a most unreliable indicator of the direction of prison population size. Of paramount significance is the impact of various intervening strategies which shield the criminal justice process from the impact of crime. Recorded serious crime for Japan,

TABLE 1   *Prison population size 1950–75 (1950 = 100)*

	1950	1955	1960	1965	1970	1975
England	100	103	132	148	190	194
Japan	100	79	76	61	48	44
Netherlands	100	60	51	46	36	35

Source: cross-national study.

the Netherlands, and for England for the period 1950–78 is displayed alongside prison population rates, in Table 2.

In the concluding section of the chapter some general considerations arising from the case studies are discussed together with a brief review of the tactics used to generate and sustain reductionist policies.

TABLE 2   *Recorded serious crime and prison populations, shown as rates per 100,000 inhabitants, 1950–78, England, Japan, and the Netherlands*

	England		Japan		Netherlands	
	Crime	Prison popul.	Crime	Prison popul.	Crime	Prison popul.
1950	1,051	47	1,515	123	902	66
1955	952	48	1,457	91	826	38
1960	1,613	59	1,312	83	1,048	30
1965	2,397	64	1,216	64	1,277	25
1970	3,228	80	1,140	47	1,959	19
1975	4,297	81	1,040	40	3,270	17
1978	4,869	85	1,107	43	3,670	24
The same data are shown below expressed as 1950 = 100						
1950	100	100	100	100	100	100
1955	80	102	96	74	91	57
1960	153	125	87	67	116	45
1965	228	136	80	52	141	38
1970	307	170	75	38	217	29
1975	408	172	67	32	362	26
1978	453	180	73	325	406	36

Note: serious crime is defined as: Japan—non-traffic penal code offences; Netherlands—penal code offences; England—indictable offences.

Source: abstracted from cross-national study files.

England 1908–38

England experienced a remarkable drop in prison population size during the period of 1908-20 and sustained this lower level throughout the inter-war years. The English experience attracted attention overseas, exemplified in the United States in a detailed analysis by the American criminologist Edwin Sutherland who began his article: 'Prisons are being demolished and sold in England because the supply of prisoners is not large enough to fill them.' Sutherland described the events as being, 'part of a great social movement which has been underway in England and other countries for at least a century'.[4] During the fifteen-year period, 1908–23, the size of the English prison population was halved, falling to around 11,000. At a rate per 100,000 inhabitants, the decline over this period, as shown in Table 3, was from 62 to 30, and for the next fifteen years the rate remained one of the lowest in Europe.

TABLE 3   *Prison population and rate per 100,000 inhabitants, 1908–38*

	Total prison population	Rate per 100,000
1908	22,029	63
1913	18,155	50
1918	9,196	25
1923	11,148	29
1928	11,109	28
1933	12,986	32
1938	11,086	30

Source: based on figures abstracted from the annual *Reports of Prison Commissioners, England and Wales*.
Note: the years 1908 to 1923 refer to year beginning 1 April, above and in subsequent tables.

In 1908 the English prison system as a national entity had been in operation for thirty years, having been established by the Prison Act, 1877 which amalgamated the centralized convict prisons with jails which were the responsibility of local government. The size of the convict system had grown from 6,000 prisoners in 1850 to 10,000 prisoners housed in thirteen prisons by 1878. The Act of 1877, which took effect on 1 April, 1878, at a stroke added to the central government's prison system some

112 local prisons holding a little over 20,000 prisoners. The total prison population of almost 31,000 represented a rate of 118 per 100,000 inhabitants. Once the national prison system was established there followed a phase of considerable rationalization, achieved mostly by prison closures. In 1878, forty-four prisons were immediately closed, a further nine were closed by 1887, and six more prior to 1914. By 1888, the size of the prison population had declined to 21,200 and to 17,600 by 1898. However, over the next decade the prison population increased by 25 per cent and in 1908 stood at 22,000, only marginally below the certified capacity of the prison system. There was overcrowding in some local prisons and the Prison Commissioners referred to, 'a great strain on the cellular accommodation'.[5]

A principal feature of the English prison system in 1908 was the magnitude of throughput of prisoners, in excess, excluding remand prisoners, of 200,000 persons annually. The profile of prisoners received into the prison system in 1908 was one of very large numbers of petty offenders. Three out of every four prisoners received were either sentenced for a non-indictable offence or imprisoned as fine defaulters. Less than fifteen per cent of receptions had been sentenced for indictable offences. By 1910 there was a determination within the Home Office to effect a reductionist policy, and the principal initiative in setting this direction was taken by Winston Churchill during his brief tenure as Home Secretary between February 1910 and October 1911. Churchill displayed considerable scepticism as to what might be achieved through the prison system, and he quickly came to believe that imprisonment was greatly over-used. He corresponded with John Galsworthy on the need to reduce solitary confinement, he used his powers of executive clemency more frequently than was customary;[6] and, of most significance, he set about framing legislative proposals to reduce severely the number of persons entering the prison system.

In a memorandum to the Prime Minister in September 1910, Churchill described the main problem as being, 'the immense number of committals of petty offenders to prison on short sentences'. He noted that two-thirds of sentenced prisoners were sentenced to two weeks or less. He described the situation as being, 'a terrible and purposeless waste of public money and human character'. The concern led to specific proposals in order to 'break in upon this volume of petty sentences for trifling offences from several different directions with a view to effecting a substantial and permanent reduction in them'. Churchill listed four possible strategies:

- to extend the use of probation for young adult offenders;
- to abolish imprisonment for debt;
- to allow time for persons to pay fines;
- to give courts the powers to suspend sentences, for petty offences, of up to one month.

Churchill's target was to reduce the number of short prison sentences by 'at least a third, perhaps much more' and to achieve a reduction of 10 to 15 per cent in the average daily prison population. In his reply to Churchill, the Prime Minister, Herbert Asquith, himself a former Home Secretary, anticipated particular difficulties with respect to abolishing imprisonment for debt but none the less promised general support. Churchill redrafted his memorandum and submitted it as a confidential paper to Cabinet under the heading 'Abatement of Imprisonment'.[7] Twelve months later, Churchill was moved to the Admiralty but left behind a momentum for reforming legislation. The Prison Commissioners publicly stressed the need for legislative action, and in 1913 commented: 'Of the many social problems now demanding the attention of Parliament, we believe the question of unnecessary commitment to prison to be one of the most urgent, and we similarly trust that the Secretary of State will be able to press forward legislation with a view to dealing with this matter.'[8] Two important statutes were enacted immediately prior to the outbreak of war, aimed to divert mentally retarded persons from prison sentences, and requiring magistrates to allow time for the payment of fines unless there were exceptional reasons for not so doing.[9]

Winston Churchill played a crucial role in creating the political climate for change. Upon the accession of King George V, remission was granted to all convicted prisoners in England and Wales who, on 23 May, 1910, had still to serve more than one month of their prison sentence. The following formula was used:

One week remission: persons with one month or more to serve; one month remission: persons with one year or more to serve; two months remission: persons with three years or more to serve; three months remission: persons with five years or more to serve.[10]

In July 1910, shortly before dispatching his legislative proposals on reducing the scale of imprisonment, Churchill described to the House of Commons the action which had already been taken to reduce the prison population:

When His Majesty came to the Throne one of the very first wishes which he was pleased to express was the desire that at a time when all hearts were stirred, and when everyone felt anxious to lay aside old quarrels, the wretched prison population of the country should not stand outside that movement in the national mind.

On similar previous occasions the proposal has always been to release a certain number of prisoners indefinitely. I think we have found a much better way, and that is not to release individuals, but to make a general *pro rata* reduction of sentences over the whole area of the prison population. The remissions which were granted on this occasion affected 11,000 prisoners, and at a stroke struck 500 years of imprisonment and penal servitude from the prison population. I am glad to be able to tell the House that no evil results of any kind have followed from this. It is not at all true to say that a number of the men released have already returned to gaol.[11]

Churchill continued his speech with an eloquent summary of his penal philosophy:

We must not allow optimism or hope, or benevolence in these matters to carry us too far. We must not forget that when every material improvement has been effected in prisons, when the temperature has been rightly adjusted, when the proper food to maintain health and strength has been given, when the doctors, chaplain, and prison visitors have come and gone, the convict stands deprived of everything that a free man calls life. We must not forget that all these improvements, which are sometimes salves to our consciences, do not change that position. The mood and temper of the public in regard to the treatment of crime and criminals is one of the most unfailing tests of the civilization of any country. A calm and dispassionate recognition of the rights of the accused against the State, and even of convicted criminals against the State, a constant heart-searching by all charged with the duty of punishment, a desire and eagerness to rehabilitate in the world of industry all those who have paid their dues in the hard coinage of punishment, tireless efforts towards the discovery of curative and regenerating processes, and an unfaltering faith that there is a treasure, if you can only find it, in the heart of every man—these are the symbols which in the treatment of crime and criminals mark and measure the stored-up strength of a nation, and are the sign and proof of the living virtue in it.[12]

The new legislation of 1913–14, together with shifts in sentencing practice, arising from the new mood for change and the upheavals of the First World War, had immediate effects on the English prison population, both in terms of size and throughput. The drop in the number of fine defaulters entering prison was especially sharp, falling by 80 per cent between 1908 and 1923. In 1908 fine defaulters accounted for half of all sentenced receptions into prison compared with one-third in 1923. In their annual reports, the Prison Commissioners stressed that the downward trend of the prison population had preceded the War and was, 'due to many social causes operating in different directions, but due also to a very considerable degree, to the legislation of 1908 (Children Act, which excluded under 16-year-olds from prison) and 1914 (Criminal Justice Administration Act, which extended time to pay fines)'.[13] The Commissioners emphasized that the reduction was not the result of a decrease in crime but reflected a shift in sentencing practice.

Time to pay fines, new developments in probation, and the screening out of some mentally defective offenders were among the significant specific shifts of practice. However, Sir Evelyn Ruggles-Brise, head of the prison system, drew from the decline in prison population lessons for prison reform which he turned upon his critics, perhaps in particular, the Prison System Enquiry Committee which had been set up in 1919.

The real solution to the penal problem is to be found, not in fanciful suggestions and devices preferred by advocates of so-called prison reform, but by the great political considerations which determine trade and the consumption of alcohol.[14]

In the early post-war years the Commissioners, with an eye to the general economic situation, anticipated an increase in prison population size but concluded that this would be countered by unemployment benefits. By 1922 the prison population exceeded 12,000 but then, instead of increasing further as the Commissioners expected, it dropped to around 11,000. The Commissioners were quick to note that their forecast of increased prison population was misplaced, and took an early opportunity to pay tribute to the courts.

Unforeseen events may falsify any forecast, especially in prison matters, but present circumstances and the history of the past few years give us reason to hope that prison population will not only not increase in the near future; but will show a steady, if slow, decline. No general remarks on this subject would be complete without a tribute to the increasing care which is being shown by Courts of Justice in investigating the circumstances of offenders and avoiding unnecessary committals to prison.[15]

The prison population remained at around 12,000 prisoners until the early 1940s. The sceptical mood as to the efficacy of the prison system, which had been created by Churchill and others, was revived in the years immediately following the First World War. Two books published in 1922 as companion volumes helped consolidate the mood of scepticism about the prison system during the inter-war years. *English Prisons Under Local Government* by Sidney and Beatrice Webb, while dealing mainly with local prison administration prior to 1878, contained an epilogue sharply critical of several aspects of contemporary prison administration, especially its cloak of secrecy. While noting with approval the shift away from custody in sentencing practice, the Webbs maintained that magistrates, in particular, continued: 'almost recklessly to commit to prison offenders who would otherwise be spared this demoralising and dangerous experience'.[16] They noted geographic variations in sentencing practice and recommended the compilation of comparative court statistics so that central government could 'bring home to the minds of those judicial authorities who were making the most extravagant use of the device of imprisonment that they were falling behind the more enlightened of their colleagues'.[17] The Webbs concluded that the 'most practical of all prison reforms is to keep people out of prison altogether'.[18] *English Prisons Today*, edited by Stephen Hobhouse and Fenner Brockway, was addressed directly to the existing prison system.

The Prison System Enquiry Committee had been set up in 1919 by the Labour Party's research department but two years later broke its official association with the Labour Party. The committee included persons who, like Hobhouse and Brockway, had themselves been imprisoned as conscientious objectors during the war. It was this direct experience of the English prison system which prompted the study. The result was a carefully documented indictment of the Ruggles-Brise administration, concluding that, 'imprisonment actually creates or perpetuates rather than abates crime in those upon whom it is inflicted'.[19] Furthermore, despite the reductions in prison committals which had occurred over the previous decade, it was forcefully argued by Hobhouse and Brockway that fine defaulters were still being imprisoned unnecessarily, that probation was insufficiently used, and that restitution provisions made available in 1907 were largely ignored.[20]

The new scepticism did not permit the progress that had been achieved to stave off further criticism. In particular, Hobhouse and Brockway held that the Prison Commission was hidebound, lacking both 'an inside experience that has enthusiasm and initiative, and an outside enthusiasm that is based on correct knowledge'.[21] In 1921, the Howard Association became the Howard League for Penal Reform and quickly became identified with the need for alternatives to imprisonment.[22] The following year, a further significant event was the appointment of Alexander Paterson to the Prison Commission. Paterson served as a Prison Commissioner until retiring in 1946, and although he never became chairman his influence inside and beyond the English prison system was immense. In his writings, Paterson did not shirk from highlighting the negative aspects of imprisonment, although he firmly believed that rehabilitative results could be achieved under some circumstances. Paterson wrote:

What is easy is always dangerous. The Court has attached to it, as a ready hand-maid for its use, a state or provincial prison. Once guilt is ascertained, the easiest method for the disposal of the prisoner is a sentence of imprisonment. It may or may not be the best method of disposal on psychological grounds, or on those of economy and common sense.'[23]

The mood of doubt and scepticism about the prison system, initiated by Churchill and others in the years just prior to the First World War, was carried forward into the 1920s and beyond. It is against this background that sentencing practice for the period is considered.

TABLE 4   *Prison receptions (excluding remand prisoners) 1908–38*

	Civil prisoners	Fine defaulters	Prison sentences	Total receptions (1908 = 100)	
1908	20,315	95,686	89,215	205,216	100
1913	14,761	74,461	61,963	151,185	74
1918	1,903	5,264	20,786	27,953	14
1923	11,837	15,261	30,874	57,972	28
1928	13,562	13,260	27,189	54,011	26
1933	12,054	11,615	27,066	50,735	25
1938	8,205	7,936	24,289	40,430	20

Source: abstracted from annual reports of Prison Commissioners for England and Wales.

As can be seen from Table 4, there was a reduction in the number of persons received into the English prison system immediately prior to and during the First World War. In 1923 the number of receptions into English prisons was less than one-third of what it had been fifteen years before. This trend reflected a distinct shift in sentencing practice. In 1908, of all indictable offences dealt with by the courts, 49 per cent received imprisonment compared with 25 per cent in 1923 and 19 per cent in 1938. As is evident from Table 5, there was also much less use made of prison by the courts with respect to non-indictable offences. The movement away from custody by the courts occurred in the context of comparative stability followed by gradual growth in the number of guilt findings. In the period 1908–23, indictable guilt findings increased by an annual rate

TABLE 5   *Sentencing practice, 1908, 1923, and 1938*

	Total guilt findings	Prison	Juvenile institutions	Fine	Dismissal recognisance	Probation	Other
	Indictable offences Percentage of total guilt findings						
1908	59,052	49	3	16	17	7	8
1923	60.711	25	2	19	19	24	11
1938	78,463	19	4	18	24	31	4
	Non-Indictable Offences Percentage of total guilt findings						
1908	649,243	13	1	75	8	1	2
1923	520,790	3	—	83	11	1	1
1938	709,019	1	—	87	10	1	3

Source: based on figures abstracted from the relevant volume of *Criminal Statistics, England and Wales*.

of growth of 0.2 per cent, and non-indictable guilt findings had an average decline of 0.3 per cent. During the second fifteen-year period, 1923–38, there was an average annual growth in indictable guilt findings of 1.3 per cent and in non-indictable guilt findings of 2.4 per cent.

It is important to note that the reduction in prison population and subsequent stability took place against a background of a gradual increase in indictable offences recorded by the police. Table 6 sets out recorded crime, convictions for indictable offences, and prison population size. The gap between recorded offences and guilt findings widened very considerably over this period. As a later study of crime statistics pointed out,

TABLE 6   *Recorded crime, guilt findings, and persons received into the English prison system, 1908, 1923, and 1938*

	Indictable offences			Prison receptions		Average daily population
	Recorded by police	Guilt findings	Fine defaulters	Prison sentences		
				Non-indictable	Indictable	
1908	105,279	55,966	95,600	63,400	28,972	22,029
1923	110,200	60,711	15,261	16,758	15,092	11,148
1938	283,000	78,000	7,936	9,824	14,570	11,086

Source: based on figures abstracted from relevant volume of *Criminal Statistics, England and Wales*, and *Reports of Prison Commissioners*.

this was the consequence not of a declining conviction rate, but of the falling clear-up rate by the police over the period.[24]

The result was that the total number of persons found guilty for indictable offences was only 33 per cent more than it had been in 1908 despite an increase of about 160 per cent in the level of recorded indictable crime.

The data displayed in Table 6 underline the importance of the decline in persons sentenced to prison for non-indictable offences and, as noted earlier, received by the prison system in default of payment for fines. The pattern of receptions into the English prison system between 1908–38 is displayed in Table 7.

TABLE 7 *Receptions into the English prison system 1908, 1923, and 1938 (shown as percentage of total receptions)**

			Prison Sentences	
	Civil prisoners	Fine defaulters	Non-indictable	Indictable
1908	10	46	30	14
1923	20	26	28	26
1938	20	20	24	36

* *Note*: the totals on which these percentages are based exclude remand prisoners, and differ slightly from those in Table 6 for 1908 and 1923 due to use of financial year by Prison Commissioners and the calendar year for Criminal Statistics.

Source: based on figures abstracted from relevant volumes of *Criminal Statistics, England and Wales* and *Reports of Prison Commissioners*.

Edwin Sutherland, in his 1934 article on the decrease in the English prison population, drew particular attention to the decline in public intoxication and of the change in sentencing practice of persons convicted of drinking offences. He suggested that, 'a considerable part of the reduction in commitments to prison is due to the decrease in intoxication and this decrease has not been off-set by increases in other important types of non-indictable offences'.[25] Sutherland also noted that crime rates over this period, as measured by indictable offences recorded by the police, were not related to the trends in sentences to prison.

The estate and personnel of the prison system during this period showed no signs of growth. Indeed, between 1914 and 1929, twenty-five local prisons were closed. There was virtually no new capacity added to the system with the exception of borstal institutions. In 1930 the English prison system consisted of 22 prisons and seven borstals, two of which were part of adult prisons. Total capacity, as measured by certified normal accommodation, was 19,600.[26] The decline in capacity over the period 1878–1938 is shown in Table 8. In 1901 there were 2,993 officers in the prison system and by 1909 this number had increased to 3,330.[27] However, staff numbers substantially declined over the next fifteen years. In 1923 there were 2,144 staff of officer grade and a further 351 persons working in prisons and borstals.[28] There was no regional structure and the number of staff at headquarters over the period remained small.[29]

TABLE 8   *Capacity of the English prison system, 1878–1938*

1878	37,771
1908	22,872
1823	21,386
1938	15,778

Source: abstracted from relevant volumes of *Reports of the Prison Commissioners*.

The Criminal Justice Bill, introduced into Parliament in 1938, sought to consolidate the emphasis of policy away from the use of custody. In particular, the Bill had the intention of extending the use of probation and restricting the imprisonment of persons under the age of 21. New facilities to be introduced included attendance centres for persons aged 12–20 and residential hostels, to be known as Howard Houses, for persons aged between 16 and 20. The Bill was in Committee stage when war was declared, and in November 1939 it was abandoned. It was not until 1947 that criminal justice legislation was again considered, but by this time the mood of the country had hardened on law and order; and the prison population had already increased by almost 80 per cent over the pre-war level.

Japan, 1950–75

In recent years, Japan has attracted considerable attention as a result of a sharp decline in the level of recorded crime. Over the same period, prison population size was substantially reduced. The physical capacity of the prison system and the number of personnel remained stable. In 1935 there were some 55,000 sentenced prisoners in Japan,[30] representing a

rate of 56 per 100,000 inhabitants.[31] Ten years later, at the conclusion of
the Second World War, the total prison population was a little under
54,000. During the five-year period, 1945–50, the prison population in
Japan increased by 92 per cent.

As shown in Table 1, over the next two decades there was a period of
steady decline, and by 1968 the prison population had returned to its 1945
level. Between 1970 and 1975 the decline continued, although at a
reduced rate, and in 1975 the prison population rate per 100,000 inhabitants had fallen to 40, one of the lowest rates in the Western world. The
Japanese prison population rate in 1975 was half the size of the rate in
England and almost one-fifth of the rate in the United States.[32] The rate
of decline of sentenced and unsentenced prisoners over the period was
similar, with unsentenced prisoners remaining about 17 per cent of the
total. The declining prison population size was accompanied by a reduction in the number of persons received by the prison system on sentence,
as shown in Table 9.

TABLE 9   *Prison population and persons received on sentence, Japan 1950–75*

	Prison population		Persons received on sentence* (1950 = 100)	
	Total	Rate per 100,000 inhabitants		
1950	103,170	123	65,860	100
1955	81,868	91	68,153	104
1960	78,521	83	54,399	83
1965	63,515	64	48,299	73
1970	49,209	47	35,370	54
1975	45,690	40	34,133	52

* includes fine defaulters and all other receptions of sentenced prisoners.
Source: figures abstracted from cross-national study files.

The decline in serious crime recorded by the police between 1950 and
1975 is displayed in Table 2 alongside the prison population, as rates per
100,000 inhabitants. Between 1945 and 1950 recorded serious crime had
risen sharply and has been accounted for by Japanese commentators on
criminal justice in terms of the damaged economic system and the shattered social order brought about by the military defeat in 1945. Since the
mid-1950s most people in Japan have benefited from the rapid economic

growth, with average individual incomes rising fourfold in real terms between 1955 and 1978. During this period the number of more serious offences such as those involving violence declined.

An official statement on crime in Japan cites four explanatory factors as to why Japan has differed from other industrial nations with respect to its relatively lower level of recorded crime. These factors are first, the existence of informal social controls, strengthened by a homogeneity of culture, ethnic origin, and language; second, a fair and efficient criminal justice process which receives general public support, and whose goals are shared with non-criminal justice agencies; third, the efficient control of weapons and drugs; fourth, the relative affluence of Japanese citizens and the relatively equitable distribution of wealth across all social groups.[33] A possible fifth factor stressed by David Bayley, an authority on policing practice in Japan, is the natural deference displayed by the Japanese to authority.[34] Bayley places the Japanese recorded crime rates in a comparative context by noting that, taken overall with respect to serious crime, the rate per population in the United States is four times as great than in Japan, and for certain offences very much higher. The robbery rate, for example, is more than 100 times higher in the United States than in Japan.

Changes in the Japanese prison population size cannot simply be accounted for in terms of recorded levels of crime. As shown in Table 2, the prison population fell more sharply than the level of recorded serious crime between 1950 and 1975. It is important, therefore, to consider how criminal events and offenders were dealt with at the different stages of the criminal justice process.

Diversion by prosecutors

The police in Japan enjoy unusually high clear-up rates. In 1979 the overall clear-up rate for non-traffic penal code offences was 59 per cent. The clear-up rate for robbery was 88 per cent, for rape 89 per cent, and 55 per cent for theft. All criminal cases investigated by the police are referred to the public prosecutor, who exercises discretion as to whether or not to take the case to court in the light of personal circumstances or considerations with regards to the offence. Prosecutorial discretion to dismiss minor offences dates from 1885 and was formally authorized in the 1922 Code of Criminal Procedure. In 1978 43 per cent of adults found by public prosecutors to have committed non-traffic penal code offences were granted suspension of prosecution. The rate of prosecutorial suspension varies considerably between offences. For example, in 1978, 64 per cent of embezzlement cases were suspended, compared with nine per cent of robberies. An official Japanese statement refers to prosecutorial dismissals as contributing significantly

to the speedy disposition of vast numbers of criminal cases and a consequent reduction of criminal court dockets . . . prompt recognition can be given to expression of contrition even in relatively serious cases without exacting the price of a criminal conviction; restitution and expressions of apology to victims can be required without a necessity for extended criminal proceedings.[35]

Sentencing practice

Courts in Japan are able to exercise broad discretion in sentencing practice. Of particular importance are powers to suspend prison sentences which were introduced in 1905 and, subsequent to the 1922 Code of Criminal Procedure, suspended sentences accounted for some 10 per cent of all sentences of imprisonment. The Penal Code permits sentences of imprisonment of three years or less to be suspended for a period of one to five years. The revocation rate for suspended sentences of imprisonment in 1978 of persons sentenced in 1975 was 14 per cent, rather higher than earlier years for which data are available. It is, however, important to note that breach does not necessarily involve imprisonment; where there are extenuating circumstances and the suspension did not involve supervision, a new prison sentence, if not over one year in length, can again be suspended. Suspension of imprisonment varies by offence; and in 1978 the variation was from 57 per cent for theft, 44 per cent for fraud, 33 per cent for robbery involving violence, and 28 per cent for homicide.[36]

Powers to fine were much expanded in the 1907 Penal Code, and in 1978 fines accounted for about 85 per cent of all penal code sentences. Defaulting is quite unusual and such persons in 1978 made up less than 0.2 per cent of the total prison population. Defaults accounted for about 0.1 per cent of all persons fined.[37]

Probation supervision arises with respect to some sentences of imprisonment which have been suspended. The court has discretion regarding cases where no previous suspended sentence has been made, but must order probation supervision where a second suspended sentence is imposed. In 1978 some 8,500 persons were placed under probation supervision.

Prison population throughput

A striking feature of Japan's prison system is the relatively low throughput of prisoners. The length of sentences imposed in Japan are relatively

TABLE 10   *Length of prison sentences, Japan 1976*

	Number sentenced	Per cent of total
One year or less	15,309	53.4
Over one year to three years	10,731	37.4
Over three years to five years	1,815	6.3
Over five years to ten years	654	2.2
Over ten years	108	0.3
Life sentence	30	0.1
Total	28,647	100

Source: cross-national study.

long as can be seen in Table 10. Less than 20 per cent of those released in 1978 served under six months compared with over 65 per cent in England. Comparative data on time served by prisoners for the two countries are displayed in Table 11.

TABLE 11   *Time served (months) by releasees in England and Japan, 1978*

Months	under 6	6–11	12–23	24–47	48+	Total releasees
England	66.3	20.6	10.3	2.4	0.4	72,077
Japan	19.2	31.5	29.9	11.6	2.1	28,123

Source: cross-national study.

Regulation of prison population size

Parole availability in Japan for prisoners who have served one-third of a fixed term dates from the latter part of the nineteenth century, but for many years has been used sparingly, not exceeding about 10 per cent of all released prisoners. With the sharp increase in the size of the prison population after the Second World War, parole became an important instrument of reductionist policy. In 1949, 80 per cent of all releasees were paroled. As an official report put in, 'this reflected severe prison overcrowding brought about by the socio-economic chaos of the immediate post-war era'.[38] Without the pressures arising from prison overcrowding the parole rate fell and in 1978 was 51 per cent. During the first half of this century pardons were frequently used; and mass amnesties have been promulgated more than twenty times to mark national occasions, most recently in 1956 on the occasion of Japan joining the United Nations.[39]

Prison system capacity and personnel

The drop in prison population size in Japan between 1950 and 1975 has not matched a reduction in the physical capacity and numbers of prison system personnel. As shown in Table 12 total capacity has remained at around 60,000 since 1945, and since 1970 there has been a margin of about 20 per cent excess capacity.[40] Old prisons have been replaced by new construction without adding to total capacity, but there has been no attempt to reduce the prison system's overall physical estate. In 1980 the Japanese prison system consisted of 189 prisons.

TABLE 12   *Capacity of Japan's prison system and occupation factor, 1945–78*

	Capacity	Occupation factor
1945	60,483	0.88
1950	66,941	1.54
1955	66,056	1.22
1960	56,955	1.37
1965	62,220	1.02
1970	63,581	0.77
1975	62,273	0.73
1980	61,986	0.80

Source: abstracted from cross-national study files.

Similarly, total staff numbers remained fairly constant between 1950 and 1975. In 1975 there were 13,500 custodial staff and 1,100 administrative and clerical staff. Given the sharp drop in prison population the custodial officer-to-prisoner ratio increased from 1 : 7 to 1 : 3 over this period. It is important to recognize that despite the fact that prison population was more than halved and although capacity and personnel were held steady, total operating costs substantially increased. Between 1950 and 1978 operating costs increased in real terms by 260 per cent and on a per prisoner basis, given the fall in prison population size, by 430 per cent. The Japanese experience illustrates that even during a phase of prison population reduction there is a tendency for costs to escalate.

In 1975 the decline in Japan's prison population came to an end, and between 1975 and 1978 prison population increased by 9 per cent. This growth was due largely to an increase of 11 per cent in the number of sentenced prisoners entering the prison system over this period. Between 1970 and 1975 there had been a decline in guilt-findings for non-traffic penal code offences but a slight increase in the proportion receiving immediate prison sentences. Between 1975 and 1978 guilt-findings increased, but the proportion receiving immediate prison sentences declined. But for this shift in sentencing policy away from custody, the recent increase in the size of the Japanese prison population would have been greater. In part, the prison population growth is a result of an increase in convictions for drug offences from 8,200 to 18,000 between 1975 and 1978. In 1978 persons imprisoned for alcohol or drug offences constituted 15 per cent of the total sentenced prison population compared with 2 per cent in 1960. The Japanese prison system is geared for moderate expansion during the 1980s. The prison system has forecasted that the prison population will increase over the decade by between 3 and 10 per cent. This simple linear prediction is based upon recent trends in prisoner numbers, especially with respect to drug offences. In line with the projected increase in prison population the Japanese prison system is planning to increase physical capacity.

The Netherlands, 1950–75

Between 1950 and 1975 the prison population in the Netherlands fell from over 6,500 to under 2,500. In terms of the rate per 100,000 inhabitants, the reduction was from 66 to 17. The United Nations International survey of prison populations, prepared for the Fifth United Nations Congress on the Prevention of Crime and the Treatment of Offenders held in 1975, reported no other Western country with a rate under 30.[41] The reductionist policy, which has been successfully pursued in the Netherlands, has attracted extensive international attention.[42] The dramatic drop in the Netherlands prison population, unlike the situation in Japan over the same period, was accompanied by an increase in reported crime. The reduction in prison population is associated with the relative mildness of Dutch criminal justice, typified by measures which filter offenders out of the criminal justice process. The mildness of criminal justice in the Netherlands has long been commented upon by both Dutch and foreign observers. As early as 1750, the situation in the Netherlands was favourably contrasted with that in England in the following terms: 'more criminals are executed in London in a year than have been in all Holland for twenty years'.[43] Two centuries later, Herman Bianchi observed:

Any survey of radical success in the field of social control would probably show that the Netherlands has one of the least inhuman systems in the world.[44]

The decline in prison population size in the Netherlands since the end of the Second World War has been spectacular. On the last day of 1947 the prison population was 12,836, and this total was to drop by two thousand over each of the next two years. Table 13 sets out the subsequent decline which took place between 1950 and 1975.

TABLE 13   *Prison population in the Netherlands, 1950–75*

	Total	Rate per 100,000 inhabitants
1950	6,730	66
1955	4,075	38
1960	3,449	30
1965	3,105	25
1970	2,433	19
1975	2,356	17

Source: cross-national study.

The decline in the Dutch prison population, at least since 1955 for which more complete data are available, has been almost entirely with respect to sentenced prisoners. The number of remand prisoners in custody fluctuated over this period, with remand prisoners increasing as a proportion of the total prison population from 36 per cent in 1955 to 46 per cent in 1975 and rising further to 60 per cent by 1980. The proportion of remand prisoners in the Netherlands is very much higher than in most other national prison systems. In most other European countries, the remand population constitutes about one-fifth of the total. The details for the Netherlands are set out in Table 14.

Between 1955 and 1975 the remand population fell by 6 per cent compared with a drop of 51 per cent in sentenced population. Efforts to sustain a reduction in the remand population have not been successful. For

TABLE 14   *Remand and sentenced prison population, Netherlands, 1955–80*

	Remand	Sentenced	Total	Remand prisoners as percentage of total
1955	1,479	2,596	4,075	36
1960	1,510	1,939	3,449	43
1965	1,460	1,645	3,105	47
1970	1,350	1,083	2,435	55
1975	1,094	1,262	2,356	46
1980	1,921	1,282	3,203	60

Source: cross-national study.

example, an act of January 1974 had the purpose of reducing the extent to which powers of remand in custody were used. The act appears to have had an effect for some offences. For example, the remand in custody rate for burglary fell from 50 per cent in 1972 to 38 per cent in 1975, and to 32 per cent in 1977.[45] However, as noted above, the Dutch prison population increased between 1975 and 1980; and this growth is almost entirely accounted for by increases in the remand population, which rose by 75 per cent compared with virtually no change in the sentenced prison population.

The reason for the increase in the population of unconvicted prisoners has to do with an increase of numbers and not length of stay on remand. Average length of stay on remand remained throughout the 1970s at about 70 days. The details are set out in Table 15.

Average time in custody on remand is very much longer than time in custody after sentence. In 1977 the average time in custody for all prisoners, remand and sentenced, was 41 days; and Dato Steenhuis reports that the average number of days for remand prisoners was about 70 days.[46]

TABLE 15   *Time spent in custody on remand, Netherlands*

	Total remands in custody	Percentage of total			
		up to 42 days	43–103 days	103–192 days	192 days
1970	6,761	24	46	26	NIL
1974	6,452	34	41	20	NIL
1979	7,164	38	36	20	6

Source: cross-national study.

Calculating the balance for sentenced prisoners shows an average length of stay for sentenced prisoners of 33 days, less than half the average time spent in custody by unconvicted prisoners.[47]

The decline in prison population size between 1950 and 1975 was in large part the result of shielding the criminal justice process from rising levels of reported crime over this period, for which the annual rate of growth was 11 per cent, as detailed in Table 2. Shielding criminal justice from crime events can occur in a number of ways which may or may not represent intended policy. The following overview of practice in the Netherlands takes recorded crime as the starting-point and examines four stages in the criminal justice process where there is significant filtering of persons from deeper penetration into the criminal justice process. These stages are police investigation, prosecutorial screening, judicial sentencing, and the calling-up of prisoners by the prison system.

Detection of crime

The proportion of all offences detected by the Dutch police between 1970 and 1980 fell from 41 to 30 per cent.[48] The apparent decline in police efficiency may, as was suggested in a recent study, be related partly to the high dismissal rate by prosecutors.

The police undertake a certain preselection from economic considerations. The involvement of the machinery of criminal law is limited by them to cases which appear prosecutable in principle.[49]

Prosecutorial diversion

Since at least 1960 there has been an increasing tendency by public prosecutors to dismiss cases rather than to proceed with prosecution through the courts. In 1960, of all prosecutorial dismissals and guilt findings combined, 30 per cent were dismissed by prosecutors compared with 44 per cent in 1975.[50] The upward trend in dismissals of cases by public prosecutors is also evident with respect to certain more serious offences. Between 1960 and 1975, of all rape cases handled by public prosecutors, the percentage dismissed increased from 40 to 53 per cent. In the case of robbery and burglary offences, the increased dismissal rate was quite dramatic, up from 20 to 43 per cent and from 31 to 50 per cent respectively.[51] By 1978 the percentage dismissed by public prosecutors for rape, robbery, and burglary had further increased to 53, 48, and 59 per cent respectively.[52] The discretion exercised by public prosecutors in the Netherlands plays a crucial part in determining both the volume and composition of cases dealt with by the courts.

Sentencing practice

Despite the decline in clear-up rates and the increase in prosecutorial dismissals, the total number of persons found guilty by the courts between 1950 and 1975 increased by 54 per cent, as displayed in Table 16. Over the same period the proportion of offenders receiving immediate imprisonment (unconditional or partly conditional prison sentences) remained fairly constant, at between 27 and 29 per cent. In fact it was not until after 1975 that the use of immediate prison sentences, as a proportion of all guilt findings, began to decline.

TABLE 16   *Sentencing practice, 1938–79, shown as percentage of total sentenced*

	Total sentenced	Prison sentences				Fine	Other
		(i) Per cent suspended prison	(ii) Per cent partially suspended	(iii) Unconditional prison	(iv) Immediate prison (ii + iii)		
1938	23,329	14	3	29	32	42	12
1947	60,040	9	4	25	29	58	4
1950	35,129	10	5	22	27	58	6
1955	34,401	7	7	19	26	55	12
1960	36,550	6	10	17	27	59	7
1965	40,167	4	10	19	29	53	13
1970	45,334	4	10	18	28	64	3
1975	54,230	4	9	20	29	65	3
1979	69,497	4	8	13	21	72	4

Source: abstracted from relevant volumes of *Statistical Yearbook of the Netherlands*, 1951 to 1979.

The length of unconditional prison sentences increased during the 1970s. In 1979 8 per cent of unconditional prison sentences were for periods of one year or more compared with 3 per cent in 1970. Additionally, the percentage of unconditional prison sentences which were for periods of under six months fell from 90 to 86. This shift towards longer prison sentences, in part, was the consequence of a more severe approach to narcotics offences. In particular the Opium Act, 1975 increased prison terms of heroin dealing. On the other hand there was, as noted below, a shift from imprisonment to fines with respect to offences of drunken driving which contributed to the decline in the proportion of very short prison sentences.

Researchers in the Ministry of Justice have argued that it is instructive to compare penal practice in the Netherlands and elsewhere not only in terms of the prison population rate but also with respect to the extent to which imprisonment is used as a sanction. Dato Steenhuis and colleagues suggest that more use is made of imprisonment in the Netherlands than in Sweden and West Germany.[53] However, account has to be taken of differences in decision-making prior to the sentencing stage. The relatively lower level of prosecutorial diversion by prosecutors in West Germany is, as Steenhuis acknowledges, of crucial significance. Furthermore, it is possible that less resort is made to the criminal justice process in Holland across a wide spectrum of events. Any firm conclusion on prison usage across different countries would need to take account of these considerations. The Steenhuis study, however, usefully draws attention to total numbers of persons passing through the prison system, emphasizing that this measure is as important as prison population rate.

The main sentencing alternatives to custody in the Netherlands are suspended sentences and fines. Suspended sentencing powers were introduced in 1915 and were extended in 1929. Most forms of judicial sentence, including fines, can be suspended. Sentences can be fully or partially suspended, and since the mid-1950s courts have preferred the partially over the fully suspended sentence. Of particular importance, breach of a suspended sentence, as in Japan, is not usually dealt with by custody. This may explain why use of the suspended sentence in these two countries has not had the unintended consequence experienced in England of increasing pressure on the prison system. In the Netherlands it is a complicated process to invoke the suspended sentence, and the Commission on Alternative Sanctions has recommended that additional conditions be first satisfied. As a result the suspended sentence mainly has a symbolic function.

The fine is by far the most frequently used penal sanction. Courts were empowered to impose fines on a wide scale as alternatives to custody in 1925. Between 1950 and 1975 fines were used increasingly by the courts, rising from 58 per cent of all sentences in 1950 and 65 per cent in 1975. Between 1975 and 1979 the use of fines increased to 72 per cent. The Netherlands has not adopted the day fine approach of matching the fine to the offender's income, but the individual in practice sets the ceiling. The decline in the proportion of custodial sentences during these four years reflected this increased use of the fine. In the early 1980s the deliberations of the Commission on Property Sanctions appear to have had an important impact on prosecutorial and sentencing practice even though legislation still has to take effect. Reports of the Commission were widely distributed and these may have been especially influential with respect to drunken driving offences, where the use of fines increased from 16 to 80 per cent between 1968 and 1978. This shift away from custody in sentencing drunken driving offences was in part due to a campaign by the Coornhert League, an influential pressure group on criminal justice issues.

Probation agencies in the Netherlands date back to the 1820s. These agencies are non-governmental and, in the main, are organized by Protestant, Catholic, and non-religious organizations. The work of these agencies is largely at the pre-sentencing stage, with probation supervision being most often initiated as a consequence of a prosecutorial dismissal rather than a sentence of the court.[54] In fact, probation supervision as a court sentence has declined since 1965 when it was used in 2 per cent of cases. In 1975 it was used in only 1 per cent of cases and by 1979 even less frequently. Probation in the Netherlands has the task of helping to befriend the offender, but also has the broader purpose of influencing the criminal justice process and public opinion.

The Prison Waiting List

A customary aspect of Continental criminal procedure is to delay the start of a prison sentence where the offender was not remanded in custody up to the time of sentence.[55] In the Netherlands this procedure has been developed and manipulated by the prison system so as to reduce pressure of numbers on prison capacity. Table 17 shows the increase in the size of the waiting list for prison places, sometimes referred to as 'running sentences'.

The waiting list process has been described by the head of the Netherlands prison system as follows:

TABLE 17   *The prison waiting list, 1965–75, the Netherlands*

	Total immediate imprisonment	Waiting list	Total per cent waiting
1965	11,872	7,934	67
1970	12,954	9,261	71
1975	14,316	10,627	74

Source: see note 51.

An important measure, which underlines the independence of the inmate and moreover may stimulate his co-operative attitude, is the system of calling people up to serve their sentences. Persons sentenced to imprisonment are divided into two categories: those remanded in custody who have to serve their sentence following the remand in custody, who number about 6,000 a year, and those sentenced to imprisonment without being remanded in custody, of whom there are about 10,000 a year. The latter are not arrested at the trial but are sent a letter inviting them to report on a certain date at a specified prison. If a person responds to the call-up, security measures against escape are considered to be superfluous. Therefore, they serve their sentence in a semi-open institution, that is to say, one without walls or fences designed to prevent escape. Moreover, on the site of the institution these prisoners are allowed almost unlimited freedom of movement.[56]

The waiting-list arrangement is a centralized system to allocate prison space by deferring the start of a sentence, which is granted on reasonable grounds. Of those called up, usually about 40 per cent report immediately, and 40–5 per cent after requesting deferment; approximately 15 to 20 per cent do not answer and have to be arrested by the police.[57] Delays of a year or more may occur but the average waiting period is about three months.[58] A build-up in the waiting list resulted from a decline in capacity in 1971 and enactment of legislation which expanded indictments for driving under the influence of alcohol, together with an increase in drug-related convictions, many of which involve imprisonment. In 1975 an attempt was made to reduce the size of the waiting list by means of a mass pardon, especially for sentences of up to fourteen days. The relief provided by this measure was only brief, and a second mass pardon was rejected by the government which feared judicial opposition. During the late 1970s the Ministry of Justice reviewed the problem of reducing the waiting list which at that time amounted to some 11,000 cases. Of this number it was estimated that only 3,300 formed an avoidable backlog with the balance being persons whose cases were being processed.[59] The call-up process has the consequence of locating the pressure point outside rather than inside the prison system. Whereas in England and parts of the United States pressure from the courts has resulted in severely overcrowded prisons, in the Netherlands overcrowding has been avoided. The use of the waiting list and call-up process in the Netherlands complements the statutory prohibition on cell-sharing.

The prison system estate, personnel, and budget

The large-scale reduction in the size of the Dutch prison population was accompanied by some reduction in the physical capacity of the prison system estate, but also by a marked increase in personnel. The prison system's capacity hovered at around 4,300–4,500 between 1960 and 1967, then gradually declined to 3,100 by 1975. Since then it has increased slightly.

Sixteen prisons were closed between 1949 and 1973, but, as shown in Table 18, capacity began to increase in 1975, in part due to the opening of two new remand prisons. In 1975 the Maastricht local prison with 228 places was opened, followed in 1978 by the largest prison in the Netherlands, the Amsterdam local prison with 622 places. Louk Hulsman's observations on the background to this new prison construction are of considerable interest. He notes that the van Hattum Commission, reporting in 1977, recommended that contrary to the prison system's original plans further prison construction was not required. As a consequence of changes in the national economy, a number of projects conceived in the 1960s were reinstated including the Maastrict and Amsterdam institutions. Hulsman notes:

As the implementation of such construction plans did not fall under the principal jurisdiction of the Ministry of Justice, the Ministry and the Justice Committee of Parliament were not informed at first of the Amsterdam project. The outcry which greeted the news of the project's implementation caused Parliament to adopt a motion of opposition. The Ministry of Justice however, decided that the project was too far advanced to be stopped. Therefore, the Amsterdam project is still underway and the Maastricht project has been completed. Two of the most important projects conceived since the War are thus in contradiction to the principles of officially adopted criminal policy.[60]

After citing a study showing fairly constant prison capacity in the Netherlands since the 1840s, David Downes poses the crucial question as to why the Dutch should regard capacity as a constant.[61] Despite the two

TABLE 18   *Capacity of the Dutch prison system 1960–78*

	Capacity	Occupation factor
1960	4,546	0.75
1965	4,241	0.73
1970	3,770	0.77
1975	3,127	0.75
1978	3,555	0.94

Source: abstracted from cross-national files.

jails constructed in the 1970s, national policy has eschewed prison build-ing programmes. Furthermore, enshrined by statute since 1950, the one-prisoner-to-a-cell rule in the Netherlands has enabled existing capacity to impose a ceiling on prison population size.

As shown in Table 19, the number of prison system employees increased by 40 per cent between 1960 and 1978, and the custody staff-to-prisoner ratio in 1976 was 1:1.3 compared with 1:2.2 in 1960.

TABLE 19   *Prison employees, Netherlands, 1960–76*

	1960	1965	1970	1976
Custody staff	1,560	1,425	1,640	2,246
Total	2,826	2,973	3,293	3,964
Ratio of custody staff to prisoners	1:2.2	1:2.1	1:1.5	1:1.3

Source: abstracted from cross-national files.

A relatively high percentage, about 30 per cent, of prison system per-sonnel are involved in the provision of services.[62] Efforts are made by staff to keep prisoners in touch with the wider society. However, despite this heavy investment in staff and the strivings made to humanize the prison regime, the emphases of the prison system remain on the goals of security and control. Louk Hulsman claims that no real progress has been made in terms of improving the legal status of prisoners. Furthermore, Hulsman concludes that, overall, the quality of life within Dutch prisons worsened during the 1970s.[63]

Associated with the steady growth of manpower there has been a sub-stantial increase in the prison system's budget. Between 1960 and 1978, total operating costs rose in real terms by 360 per cent. Given the decline in the prison population over this period, operating costs per head increased even more sharply, rising by over 500 per cent. As in Japan over the same period, the financial costs of the prison system rose sharply despite the significant reductions in prison population size. That prison personnel should have risen so sharply is of interest given the low numbers in the Netherlands of criminal justice personnel generally. The ratio of police to population, for example, is relatively low at 178 per 100,000 inhabitants in 1980.[64] There are only 200 public prosecutors and 700 judges who also handle civil cases and some 600 social workers involved in the criminal justice process. As Louk Hulsman comments, the imposition of an immediate custodial sentence consumes more time of criminal justice officials than do other solutions. 'The system's reduced capacity in this sense results in a strong self-limiting tendency.'[65]

The reduction in prison population size in the Netherlands between 1950 and 1975 was less the result of articulated policy than a combination of factors within and beyond the criminal justice process. In addition to citing the relatively low capacity of the criminal justice process, Louk Hulsman points to the importance of a well-developed system of social security, the extensive network of social services which is less treatment oriented than is generally the case elsewhere, and the relatively mild and informal coverage of crime issues by the media. Although there has been some increase in the remand population since 1975 there are no indications that the prison system in the Netherlands is likely to depart from its reductionist course.

Conclusion

Three examples have been described of prison populations being reduced and sustained at a new low level. Two general conditions have emerged. In each of the three countries, key decision-makers shared a profound scepticism as to what benefits, if any, derive from imprisonment. This viewpoint is exemplified by an official statement of the Japanese government in 1980, which held that although imprisonment,

> may achieve the correctional aims advanced to justify it, the disadvantages suffered by those undergoing imprisonment must not be overlooked. Indeed, the adverse effects are not limited to loss of liberty during confinement; imprisonment affects prisoners' social life after release, an aftermath from which their families are not exempt. Moreover, incarceration, particularly over a long period of time, weakens the ability of offenders to adapt themselves to society following release and destroys the foundation of free community life experience indispensable to reintegration into society. This in turn strongly enhances the likelihood that they will recidivate. It should also be stressed that indiscriminate and widespread use of imprisonment as a sanction against criminal conduct that is not truly serious not only imposes an un-needed financial burden on the community, but also dilutes the deterrent impact of imprisonment generally in potential criminals and thus may promote rather than hinder the commission of heinous or serious offences.[66]

In the Netherlands widespread doubts as to the utility of prisons are expressed by many leading criminal justice practitioners who are well versed as to the negative research findings on imprisonment. One student of the Dutch penal scene has concluded:

the judiciary in the Netherlands have evolved a distinctive occupational culture, central to which is the strongly negative value placed upon imprisonment, which is viewed as at best a necessary evil, and at least as a process likely to inflict progressive damage on a person's capacity to re-enter the community.[67]

Likewise, in England between 1908 and 1938 there was considerable questioning of the prison system. This mood was set during the vigorous stewardship of the Home Office exercised by Winston Churchill between 1910 and 1911. In 1922, in the preface to the Webbs' *English Prisons Under Local Government*, George Bernard Shaw wrote: 'Imprisonment as it exists today . . . is a worse crime than any of those committed by its victims; for no single criminal can be as powerful for evil, or as unrestrained in its exercise, as an organised nation.'[68] The companion volume by Stephen Hobhouse and Fenner Brockway concluded:

our prison system, while it sometimes makes good prisoners, does almost nothing to make good citizens. It fails to restore the weak will or to encourage initiative; it reduces energy by the harshness of its routine and adds depression to the depressed . . . The influences of the prison system are, therefore, not only anti-individual but anti-social as well; in both directions it debases the currency of human feeling. That debasement is its fundamental defect; and in so far as this stands proved against it, it must necessarily be judged as a failure. And the more the system costs the community, the more highly it is organized, the more monumental must that failure be.[69]

The second general conclusion to emerge from the three case examples is that the crucial factor in understanding changes in prison population is less the level of recorded crime or known offenders but, more significant, the responses to crime by officials engaged throughout the criminal justice process. Of particular importance, in the Netherlands and Japan the criminal courts have been insulated from the impact of increasing numbers of offenders as a consequence of action taken by public prosecutors. Prosecutorial decisions to dismiss charges have been one of the most important mechanisms for achieving and sustaining reductions in prison population size. In England, during the inter-war period, total numbers of persons dealt with by the courts remained fairly stable, but this was due to fewer offences cleared up by the police rather than shifts in prosecutorial practice. The critical intervening tactic was the movement away from custody in sentencing practice by the courts. In 1908, of all offences, indictable and non-indictable combined, 16 per cent received prison sentences compared with 3 per cent in 1938.

A further crucial component of the sustained low level of imprisonment in the Netherlands and Japan is a profound intolerance of overcrowding in prisons. In the Netherlands, since 1950 there has been a statutory prohibition on more than one prisoner being placed in a cell designed for one person. Under these circumstances, capacity acts as a powerful constraint on prison population growth and, in the absence of new construction, places a ceiling on prison population size. In Japan in the late 1940s there was also revulsion at the level of overcrowding which then existed. Total capacity of the prison system in Japan remained constant during the subsequent period of prison population decline, and by the mid-1960s there was much excess capacity.

By contrast, in England during the inter-war years capacity declined alongside a reduction in prison population size. Average daily prison population fell from 22,000 to 11,100 between 1908 and 1938, and capacity declined from 22,600 to 15,700. There was virtually no prison construction during this period, and indeed some twenty-five prisons were closed. In the English case, however, it is doubtful that capacity would at that time have acted as a brake in population growth. There was overcrowding at various times during the nineteenth century and first decade of the twentieth century, and excess capacity in the period up to the Second World War. Once prison population expansion got underway soon after the Second World War, overcrowding quickly reappeared. The high tolerance for crowding in England played an important part in the expansionist phase which began after 1945. It is crucial to understand why tolerance for prison overcrowding should differ so markedly from one country to another.

The experiences of the three prison systems examined in this chapter demonstrate that although reductionist policies can be pursued successfully there remain powerful tendencies towards expansion. The thirty-year reductionist phase of the English prison system was followed by a phase of relentless expansion which has persisted for over forty years. As a rate per 100,000 inhabitants the prison population is rapidly approaching what it was at its earlier zenith of the mid-nineteenth century. The contrast of two phases of the English prison system, 1908–38 and the period since 1945, provides a sober reminder of the inherent problem of sustaining reductionist initiatives. Similarly, in the Netherlands and Japan, in the period since 1975 there have been pressures threatening to reverse reductionist gains made over the preceding twenty-five years. In the Netherlands the size of the prison estate has slightly increased along with the number of unsentenced prisoners. Despite these pressures there are no indications of a political willingness in the Netherlands to adopt an expansionist course. In Japan prison building plans exist which anticipate an increase in prison population during the 1980s. In both the Netherlands and Japan contemporary strains on the prison system in part reflect new criminal justice concerns such as the increased processing of drug-related offences. The availability of the prison system makes it especially vulnerable to new uses and serves to discourage inventive thinking as to alternative resolution. Policy and practice on the prison system dictates the scope and substance of alternatives to imprisonment.

Notes

1. For accounts of the events in Massachusetts see, Andrew Rutherford, *The Dissolution of the Training Schools in Massachusetts*, Columbus, Ohio: Academy for Contemporary Problems, 1974; and Lloyd Ohlin, Robert B. Coates and Allen D. Miller, 'Radical Correctional Reform: A Case Study of the Massachusetts Youth Correctional System.' *Harvard Educational Review,* **44** (1974), 74–111.

2. See e.g. *Report of Working Party on Children and Young Persons in Custody,* Chairman, Peter Jay (NACRO, Chichester and London: Barry Rose, 1977), 49–54.

3. Howard League for Penal Reform, *The Prisoner Population of the World* (London, 1936).

4. Edwin H. Sutherland, 'The Decreasing Prison Population of England', *Journal of Criminal Law and Criminology,* **24** (1934), 800.

5. *Report of Prison Commissioners, England and Wales for 1908–09,* Cd 4847 (1909).

6. For a description of Churchill as Home Secretary, with particular reference to the use of executive clemency, see Leon Radzinowicz and Roger Hood, 'Judicial Discretion and Sentencing Standards: Victorian attempts to solve a perennial problem', *University of Pennsylvania Law Review,* **127** (1979), 1288–349.

7. See, Memorandum from Winston S. Churchill to H. H. Asquith, 26 September 1910, included in Randolph S. Churchill, *Winston S. Churchill,* Volume 11, Companion, Part 2, 1907–1911 (London: Heinemann, 1969), 1198–203, and 1204. No action was taken at that time on civil prisoners. See generally, *Report of the Abatement of Imprisonment Committee,* a confidential Home Office document prepared in 1911 and setting out for Churchill the legislative options. PRO, HO 45/10613/194534.

8. *Report of the Prison Commissioners, England and Wales for 1911–12,* Cmnd 6406 (1913), 8. However, not all Home Office officials shared Churchill's views. In early 1911 the Criminal Statistics for 1909 were published with an introduction by H. B. Simpson of the Home Office (writing, as the Permanent Under-Secretary noted in the foreword, in a personal capacity). After making a

number of general observations on the rising trend of recorded crime since 1900, Simpson went on to note an increase in the proportion of fines which defaulted. Of all fines imposed, the percentage resulting in default had increased from 15 per cent in 1900 to 20 per cent in 1909. Simpson observed: 'It may be that prison is losing the terror it once had; that imprisonment is coming to be regarded more as a misfortune than a disgrace, and that, consequently, convicted offenders are less likely than once they were, to make pecuniary sacrifice in order to escape it.' *Introduction to Judicial Statistics of England and Wales, Part I, Criminal Statistics*, Cd 5473 (1911), 15.

Churchill retorted: 'the publication of the Criminal Statistics for 1909, including as they do, Mr Simpson's Memorandum, is exceedingly ill-timed, and will probably cause me embarrassment and trouble. I regret that none of those privy to my confidential plans of Prison Reform thought fit to consult me before making this inopportune and injudicious publication.' Memorandum by Winston S. Churchill, 3 February 1911, included in Randolph S. Churchill, op. cit., p. 1245, n. 7.

9. The Mental Deficiency Act of 1913 and the Criminal Justice Administration Act of 1914.

10. *Judicial Statistics, Part 1, Criminal Statistics 1910*. Cd 6071 (1912), 164. Although this royal amnesty did not result in the immediate release of a large number of prisoners, it did impact upon the numbers released on 'special grounds' as can be seen from the following data:

Prisoners discharged on special grounds for year ending:

1910	287
1911	1,128
1912	674
1913	296

Source: abstracted from the relevant annual reports of the Commissioners of Prisons and the Directors of Convict Prisons.

11. Home Office Supply (Report), H.C. Debates, 5th Series, vol. 19, cols. 1353–4, 20 July 1910.

12. Ibid., col. 1354.

13. *Report of the Prison Commissioners for 1916–1917*. Cd 8342, 19. The following year the Prison Commissioners speculated as to whether the 30 per cent depletion in the number of police officers, with the outbreak of war, might have been a factor in the prison population decline.

14. *Report of the Prison Commissioners for 1918–19*, Cmd 374 (1920), 6. In fact, the conclusions as to the declining prison population reached by the Prison System Enquiry committee were similar to those of the Commissioners. 'The great drop between 1914–18 was due principally to war conditions—to full employment, to liquor restrictions, and to the induction of a large proportion of the male population in the army.' Hobhouse and Brockway, op. cit., 3.

15. *Report of Prison Commissioners for 1923–24*, Cmd 2307 (1925), 6–7.

16. Sidney and Beatrice Webb, *English Prisons under Local Government* (London: Longmans, Green, 1922), 249.

17. Ibid. 250. This notion was developed half a century later by Radical Alternatives to Imprisonment, with the annual 'Ball and Chain Award' to the locality making most use of custodial sentences.

18. Ibid. 248.

19. Stephen Hobhouse and A. Fenner Brockway, *English Prisons Today, Being the Report of the Prison System Enquiry Committee* (London: Longmans, Green, 1922), 593.

20. Ibid. 49–51.

21. Ibid. 66.

22. See, Gordon Rose, *The Struggle for Penal Reform, the Howard League and its Predecessors* (London: Stevens & Sons, 1961), 113. In 1933, E. Roy and Theodora Calvert, who were closely associated with the Howard League, argued, on the basis of 1930 data, that total receptions, including remand prisoners, could be reduced by 60 per cent. E. Roy Calvert and Theodora Calvert, *The Lawbreaker* (London: George Routledge, 1933), 145.

23. Alexander Paterson, paper prepared in 1934, included in *Paterson on Prisons*, ed. S. K. Ruck (London: Frederick Muller, 1951), 157.

24. F. H. McClintock and N. Howard Avison, *Crime in England and Wales* (London: Heinemann, 1968), 149–52.

25. Sutherland, op. cit., p. 894, n. 4.
    The decline in convictions for drunkenness was indeed dramatic, as can be seen below:

1913	188,877
1923	77,094
1937	46,757

    Abstracted from Herman Mannheim, *Social Aspects of Crime Between the Wars* (London: George Allen and Unwin, 1940), 165.

26. *Report of the Prison Commissioners for 1930*, Cmnd 4151 (1932).

27. PRO HO 45/10606/191265.

28. *Report of the Committee Appointed to Inquire into the Pay and Conditions of Service at the Prisons and Borstals in England and Scotland and at Broadmoor Lunatic Asylum*, Chairman, The Earl of Stanhope, Cmd 1959 (London: HMSO, 1923).

29. The turnover in heads of the English prison system was greater during this period than it had been earlier. There were two chairmen of the Prison Commission during its first four decades, between 1878 and 1921. Over the next two decades, 1921–42 there were five chairmen.

30. It might be noted that in 1885 the prison population rate in Japan was 165 per 100,000.

31. Howard League for Penal Reform, *The Prisoner Population of the World* (1936).

32. In making cross-national comparisons, differences as to the age jurisdiction of the respective prison systems should be kept in mind. In Japan the age cut-off

point between adult and juvenile justice is the 20th birthday and it is unusual for juveniles to be held by the prison system. In 1978 there were 50 under-20-year-olds held by the prison system; there were some 3,270, however, held in training schools. If these training school juveniles are included in the total population of Japan's prison population, the rate per 100,000 inhabitants increases only marginally in 1978 from 43 to 46. However, in previous years when the training school population was larger, the contribution of juveniles to the national prison population rate would have been greater, for example, in 1960 up from 83 to 94, and in 1970 up from 47 to 52.

33. *Crime Prevention and the Quality of Life*, National Statement of Japan to the Sixth United Nations Congress on the Prevention of Crime and the Treatment of Offenders (Tokyo, 1980), 4.

34. David H. Bayley, *Forces of Order, Police Behaviour in Japan and the United States* (Los Angeles: University of California Press, 1976).

35. *Crime Prevention and the Quality of Life*, op. cit., pp. 12–13, n. 33.

36. Ibid. 65.

37. Ibid. 27.

38. Ibid. 28.

39. Ibid. 63.

40. An important consideration arising with reference to rated capacity in the Japanese prison system is whether the prisoner uses a Japanese style bed called 'Futon' (roll-away) or a Western-style bed. In the case of the former for single occupancy cells, 3.77 square metres (41 sq. ft.) is required compared with 5.52 (59 sq. ft.) for the latter. Where cells are shared, the requirements are 2.6 square metres (28 sq. ft.) and 4.2 square metres (45 sq. ft.) per person, respectively. These two types of bed provide prison administrators in Japan with some flexibility in determining capacity of the prison system.

41. Working paper prepared for the Secretariat, Fifth United Nations Congress on the Prevention of Crime and the Treatment of Offenders, A/CONF.56/5 (New York, 1975), 67.

42. See, for example, Polly D. Smith, 'It Can Happen Here: Reflections on the Dutch System', *Prison Journal*, **58** (1978), 31–7; David Downes, 'The Origins and Consequences of Dutch Penal Policy since 1945', *British Journal of Criminology*, **22** (1982), 325–62.

The May Committee briefly considered the reductionist path followed in the Netherlands, but did not draw any clear-cut conclusions for practice in the United Kingdom. See, *Report of the Inquiry into the United Kingdom Prison Services*, Cmnd 7673 (London: HMSO, 1979), 44–7.

43. *Gentleman's Magazine* (May 1750), 235.

44. Herman Bianchi, 'Social Control and Deviance in the Netherlands' in *Deviance and Control in Europe*, ed. H. Bianchi *et al* (London: Wiley, 1975), 51. See also, L. H. C. Hulsman, 'The relative mildness of the Dutch criminal justice system: an attempt at analysis', in *Introduction to Dutch Law for Foreign*

Lawyers, eds. D. C. Fokkema, W. Chorus, E. H. Hundius, *et al.* (Deventer: Kluwer, 1978), 373–7.

45. D. W. Steenhuis, unpublished paper for cross-national study.

46. Ibid.

47. A more detailed analysis would need to take account of time on remand which counts against the length of time served by sentenced prisoners.

48. This calculation is based upon data abstracted from Netherlands Central Bureau of Statistics, *Statistical Yearbook of the Netherlands, 1981* (The Hague, 1982), table 24; the declining detention rate appears to date from at least 1960 when Downes states it was 60 per cent. Downes, op. cit., p. 331, n. 42.

49. J. J. M. van Dijk and C. H. D. Steinmetz, *The ROC Victim Surveys, 1974–1979* (The Hague: Ministry of Justice, 1980), 68.

50. Derived from data abstracted from *Statistical Yearbook of the Netherlands* (for 1978 and 1979), and from cross-national study files. Cases may be dismissed by prosecutors for varying reasons, but the published statistics do not go much beyond the data given here.

51. David Downes, op. cit., p. 330, n. 42.

52. Ibid.

53. Dato W. Steenhuis, L. C. M. Tigges, and J. J. A. Essers, 'The Penal Climate in the Netherlands: Sunny or Cloudy', *British Journal of Criminology*, 23 (1983), 1–16.

54. However, a study of a new initiative in early intervention by a probation agency achieved its intention of reducing remands in custody to only a limited extent. See, E. G. M. Nuyten-Edelbroek and L. C. M. Tigges, 'Early Intervention by a Probation Agency: A Netherlands Experiment', *Howard Journal*, 1 (1980), 42–51.

55. For example, in Sweden the waiting time for persons sentenced to imprisonment, on bail at the time of sentence, is about four months. Ekhart Kuhlhorn, draft report for cross-national study.

56. Hans Tulkens, *Some Developments in Penal Policy and Practice in Holland* (London: NACRO, 1979), 9.

57. Ibid.

58. Downes, op. cit., p. 332, n. 42.

59. 'Policy problems in the penological scene', Discussion paper by the Minister of Justice, Houses of Parliament (The Hague, 1976–7).

60. L. H. C. Hulsman, 'The Evolution of Imprisonment in the Netherlands', *Revue de Droit pénal et de criminologie* (Belgium), 57 (1977), 48.

61. Downes, op. cit., pp. 337–9, n. 42.

62. Cross-national study data file.

63. Hulsman, op. cit., p. 52, n. 60.

64. *Statistical Yearbook of the Netherlands, 1981*, 378. It is of interest, however, to note that the number of police officers and prison personnel increased at the same rate between 1965 and 1976, by 33 per cent in both cases.

65. Hulsman, op. cit., p. 47, n. 60.
66. *Crime Prevention and the Quality of Life*, op. cit., p. 62, n. 33.
67. Downes, op. cit., p. 345, n. 44.
68. George Bernard Shaw, preface to Sidney and Beatrice Webb, op. cit., p. vii, n. 16.
69. Hobhouse and Brockway, op. cit., p. 585, n. 19.

Fiefs and Peasants: Accomplishing Change for Victims in the Criminal Justice System

JOANNA SHAPLAND

The results of research into victims' reactions to their victimization and subsequent treatment by the criminal justice system now read almost like a litany, so universal are the findings. The studies emphasize the need for support and help to get over the effects of the offence, and for information from and consultation with the agencies of the criminal justice system, notably the police and prosecution. It has been shown consistently that throughout the Anglo-American system of adversarial criminal justice—in England, Scotland, the United States and Canada—victims who are bewildered, angry, or fearful, turn to the police and other officials for comfort and guidance, only to find them operating according to different priorities which place concern for victims low on the list (Shapland *et al.*, 1985; Chambers and Millar 1983, 1986; Elias 1983*c*; Holstrom and Burgess 1978; Kelly 1982; Baril *et al.* 1984; Canadian Federal-Provincial Task Force 1983). There are fewer research findings concerning the more inquisitorial systems of continental Europe, but questionnaire returns from member states of the Council of Europe—on which the Council's proposals for reform are substantially based—show little difference there (Council of Europe 1983, 1985, 1987).

Ideas and strategies to alleviate the plight of victims have come thick and fast over the last few years and, in contrast to the consistent way the problem has been defined, the response presents a varied picture. Victimologists in the United States have largely followed a 'rights'-based strategy—encouraging the passing of state and federal legislation to allow victims greater participation in the criminal justice process (see, for example, NOVA 1985). Legislation is also in train in Canada (Waller 1986*b*), and here it has been accompanied by significant funding of pilot and demonstration programmes for victim assistance, based within various agencies of the criminal justice system (Bragg 1986). These initiatives have seemed slightly alien to European eyes. In Europe, by contrast, the emphasis has been on training and/or commanding parts of the criminal justice system to take on duties relating to the provision of victim services (for example, van Dijk 1986a; Council of Europe 1985). In Britain, official action has been particularly low-key, and has been based on a perceived need to persuade agencies to devise their own responses and actions on behalf of victims.

These differences are unsurprising. Where action on behalf of victims has to involve the criminal justice system, it will tend to follow the criminal justice tradition of that country. Indeed, victims themselves will expect action within their own tradition. In complete contrast, however, the provision of *victim support* varies relatively little between different countries. If one looks through the summary of questionnaire returns made by member states of the Council of Europe it is clear that the pattern of support and assistance is extremely similar throughout (Council of Europe 1987). State provision of social and medical services of course varies, but many countries also have generalist victim support services similar to those provided by VSS in the UK, as well as RCC and shelter homes for battered women.

The development of these services has been essentially a process of parallel evolution. Though there are personal and, on occasion, more formal links between those running services in different countries, these have tended to occur after the different services have become established. The trend towards cross-national associations, meetings, and conferences is growing in strength now, mainly because quite a few countries have formed the kinds of networks or formal associations which make it easier to take part.

Does this similarity of organization, then, repudiate the assertion above that criminal justice traditions will compel different solutions to victim needs? I think not. The interesting fact about these victim support and assistance programmes is that they seem everywhere to have developed outside the realm of government and largely outside the ambit of the criminal justice agencies. They have their roots in the community or in voluntary associations, and rely heavily on voluntary workers and support. Governments have been hastening to try to catch up with and understand these mushrooming and popular voluntary bodies, not helped by their localization and hence the lack of central information about them. The problems of the associations are those of the voluntary sector: underfunding, lack of publicity about their services, inconsistency of approach in different parts of the same country, untrained personnel, and shortage of specialist advice and support (see Maguire and Corbett 1987 for a comprehensive review of the position in England and Wales). The relative similarity of victims' services in different countries has resulted, I would argue, from their independence from criminal justice systems and governments.

The above exception is clearly of great importance and merits exploration elsewhere. However, in the remainder of this paper I shall concentrate upon those victim services which have had to involve the criminal justice system. The main task will be to use the experiences of different countries to assess the likely outcomes and relative success of different approaches to instituting change. This is problematic, given the lack of evaluation of initiatives in many countries, and it will be necessary to fall back on occasions upon theoretical analysis of the likely results of each approach.

Victim services involving the criminal justice system

Where the response to victim need has had to involve the criminal justice system, it has tended to be different in different countries. In North America, as mentioned above, it has often taken the form of legislated rights for individual victims, or the drawing up of charters of such rights. These are essentially expressions of opinion or statements of values as to what the position of victims should be in a particular jurisdiction. They derive their strength from the future developments they may produce in concrete practices—through individual victims claiming and using those rights, or from the inspiration that practitioners in the system may derive from those statements of values to change their own practices. There is, however, very little *coercion* on either victim or practitioner to improve the lot of victims.

This is the problem with the use of a rights strategy to accomplish change. Success depends crucially on the willingness of individuals to institute legal action which will lead to judgments that enforce change. It has proved relatively successful in the field of prisoners' rights in England, where cases taken to the European Court of Human Rights in Strasbourg have led to a few changes in practices in prisons (see Maguire *et al.* 1985). However, even these changes have been patchy: an approach to change based on individual action cannot accomplish a wide-ranging review of current assumptions and practices. Moreover, individuals are often only successful in such cases if they are supported by a dynamic pressure group of their fellows, entirely committed to that strategy. This was the case, for example, with the campaign based upon legal action taken by MIND in England to change the 1959 Mental Health Act (cf. Gostin 1977).

While the national association in North America, NOVA, strongly supports the passing of legislation improving victim rights, the same is not true of its English counterpart, NAVSS. In England and Wales until recently, the language of individual rights has generally been seen as alien to the historical tradition of the criminal justice system (though one exception has been the right of the offender not be unlawfully detained). In order to explore how change might be accomplished here, we need to digress in order to explore the nature of the English criminal justice system.

There has been considerable talk recently about interdependence and the benefits of cooperation among the various agencies of the criminal justice system (for example, Moxon 1985). By agencies, I am referring not only to those commonly seen as separate parts of the system—police, prosecution, judiciary, court administration, probation, prisons, and so on—but also to the various branches of the executive: the Home Office, the Lord Chancellor's Office, and, now, the Attorney General's Department. Despite the obvious links between the agencies in terms of the numbers of offenders passing through from one to the other, I feel it is more apt to characterize the agencies not as part of an interconnected system, but as independent 'fiefs' under a feudal system. Each fief retains power over its own jurisdiction and is jealous of its own workload and of its independence. It will not easily tolerate (or in some cases even permit) comments from other agencies about the way it conducts its business. This tendency is exacerbated and continued by the separate education and training of the professional workers for each fief, by their separate housing and by the hierarchical structure of promotion within fiefs, with little or no transfer between them. Negotiations between adjacent fiefs do occur over boundary disputes (for example, in the form of Court User Groups), but these tend to be confined to the agencies directly affected which see themselves as entering the negotiations as equally powerful parties (Feeney 1985). Nor is there any 'Round Table' (such as a sentencing commission—see Ashworth 1983; Shapland 1981).

It is interesting that the recent construction of a new system of prosecution was accomplished by the production of yet another separate fief in the form of the Crown Prosecution Service, whose workers, premises, and philosophy will again be separate from all the others, and which will be responsible to a different Minister (the Attorney General). This new fief, charged with producing a statement of its working practices, has responded naturally enough with one that concentrates almost entirely upon the central task—that of deciding upon prosecution. Its *Code of Conduct for Crown Prosecutors* appears to ignore the need to discuss and regulate relations with other fiefs and with those not represented by fiefs at all—victims and defendants (Crown Prosecution Service 1986).

This type of criminal justice system has the advantage that the necessary independence of its different parts is built into the structure. The structure does not need careful tending, since the natural tendencies of the fiefs will reinforce it in its current state. However, their separateness and pride in their independence are also likely to lead—and in my view have already led to a very great degree—to failures to perceive the need for control of the whole system and to an overall lack of consistency. The system breeds a reliance on individual decision-making and on discretion by the fief's workers, which has been elevated by some into an absolute virtue. There is no corresponding stress upon the needs of the consumers of the fief's services, whether other fiefs or individuals. When individuals seriously question what is happening, as those espousing the needs of victims have done, their challenge is likely to be taken as a challenge to the autonomy and authority of the fief, rather than as a comment on its ways of working.

Taking again the advent of the Crown Prosecution System as an example, the negotiations that have taken place on the needs of victims—for information, for consultation, and for the effective collection and presentation to the courts of information related to claims for compensation—seem to have been fraught with difficulty and demarcation disputes. The difficulty with victims is that their needs span several fiefs. For example, the police are the agency that will have both the most contact and the most ready contact with victims to ascertain losses and injuries; but with responsibility passing to the Crown Prosecution Service they can no longer ensure that this information is made available to the court. Again, as the police are now often not told the results of cases, they cannot notify victims of the outcome, even should they be willing to do so. In fact, the relatively simple and uncontroversial needs of victims in relation to the criminal justice system (advice, information, consultation, witness expenses, compensation—see Shapland *et al.* 1985) cannot be the subject of an instruction such as a Home Office Circular without negotiations taking place with at least six fiefs (three ministries and three other agencies).

The problem of producing change in such a system is one of either persuading an agency that its own view of its mandate and of the way it operates must change, or of imposing change from without. In other parts of Europe, the sectors of the criminal justice system are fewer in number and there is an acceptance that some are subordinate to others. For example, in the Netherlands, the police are under the direction of the prosecutors, who in turn are part of the Ministry of Justice. Changes in policy can be accomplished through convincing just one agency—the Ministry of Justice—of the need for them. For example, the Ministry has issued instructions to other agencies to support victim assistance schemes and to inform victims of the results of cases, and has affected sentencing levels by asking prosecutors to advocate different sentence lengths in court. Opposition from other, independent parts of the system, such as the judiciary, has been muted, owing partly to the similarity of outlook and frequency of communication between them. Another example is to be found in Scotland, where prosecutors have the power to influence police investigations and to talk directly to witnesses.

Even in these more co-ordinated systems, there are those who advocate a still greater degree of consistency and central co-ordination and communication (for example, Steenhuis 1986). In England and Wales, people have always railed at the criminal justice system for its inconsistencies and its diffusion of power. They have usually been answered with incantations about the need for independence of the various fiefs. It is not my purpose to advocate a centrally controlled, uniform system. Clearly, the separateness of its parts is one of its main strengths. On the other hand, there is also the danger that the checks and balances will become so 'perfectly' adjusted that stasis sets in. At that point, one which I think we have reached now, change becomes extremely difficult to produce without coercion (or popular revolt from those not enfranchised in a fief). Persuasion may not work because agencies see no need to change their current positions.

Legislation or persuasion?

There is little detailed information about how agencies in England and Wales have responded to the pressure for change to meet victims' needs. At the central government level, Rock (1987) has documented how the Home Office, in contrast to the relevant government agencies in Canada, has been slow to change its view. He shows how it has tended to follow belatedly, rather than produce policy to lead, on such issues as victim support. We still have no co-ordinated government policy on all matters affecting victims in the criminal justice system. Even where there have been relevant international documents, such as the Council of Europe Convention on state compensation for victims of violent crime (1983), these have not formed a central pivot of policy. Indeed, the Convention has not yet been ratified. This lack of a central policy lead for agencies, one suspects, partly reflects the division into fiefs at government, as well as at practitioner, level.

Nevertheless, certain agencies have become convinced of the need for change to take account of the problem of victims. Senior police officers have changed their attitudes markedly over the last ten years and, in certain cases, this has led to local initiatives to improve the lot of victims in practice. The most notable examples are the part played by the police in the rise of VSS (Maguire and Corbett 1987) and the provision of facilities for victims of sexual assault (Shapland and Cohen 1987). The police have not, however, been able to pass on this enthusiasm to other fiefs (and indeed would not see it as appropriate that they should exert such an influence).

We have already addressed the problems in respect of the Crown Prosecution Service. (In case it may be thought that this inactivity is an inevitable feature of the prosecutorial role, it is pertinent to mention initiatives involving prosecutors in other countries. These include the guidelines of South Australia (1985) promoted by the Attorney General and the right of victims in the Netherlands to appeal to an ombudsman— who may award damages—against the decision of the prosecutor.) Shapland and Cohen's (1987) survey also covered the administration of justice, in the form of justices' clerks from England and Wales. Here, it was apparent that a substantial minority of clerks were not only trying to improve the lot of victims, but did not agree that to do so was part of their job. In other words, it may be concluded that where there is no agreement within a fief that a particular task, such as providing for victims, is part of its mandate, then persuasion will not work. Nor will guidelines or other manifestations of the service model be produced from within the profession. Pressure from without can be resisted.

Would legislated rights for individual victims, on the American model, break the deadlock? The problem is that, in order to claim them, victims have to be acknowledged as parties to the criminal justice system. If they are not, then again pressure can be ignored. A potential right of this kind was embodied in the Criminal Justice Bill 1986, although it was not legislated because of the intervention of the general election. This was a proposed requirement upon sentencers to give reasons if they decided not to make a compensation order. It is interesting to compare this with the obligation put upon magistrates under the Criminal Justice Act 1982 to give reasons before passing a custodial sentence upon a young adult. Burney's (1985) finding, that as many as 14 per cent of custodial disposals were not accompanied by a statement of reasons, does not lead one to believe that all judges and magistrates would comply with the comparable obligation proposed in the Criminal Justice Bill. Furthermore, an important difference between the two measures is that, while young adult defendants have a definite right of appeal in such cases, the position of victims is less clear. Could victims appeal if no reasons were given? What would then happen to the sentence if any appeal was allowed— would the defendant be re-sentenced? Would the victim obtain damages (on the Dutch model)?

More pertinently, even if these kinds of difficulties could be overcome, it appears that few, if any, young adult defendants have exercised their right of appeal in connection with the provisions of the 1982 Criminal Justice Act. Would victims exercise any equivalent right of appeal?

As a means of imposing change, then, such legislative provisions do not seem to be very effective. (They may be stimulating changes in attitudes, of course, but that is a long-term and stealthy process, not susceptible to research.) Given the lack of acknowledgement of the legal status of victims and the lack of a legally-inclined pressure group for victims, it is unlikely that this path will produce much change in the short term.

This is not to decry the need for individual, justiciable rights in some circumstances for victims. I have argued elsewhere (Shapland and Cohen 1987) that procedural duties backed up by victims' rights of appeal may well need to be enacted, for example, to ensure that details of victim injuries are placed before the court at the time of sentence (to allow the court to consider a compensation order). The need for rights as remedies, however limited the circumstances in which they apply, is a token of the difficulty of producing change in an unwilling system—a system which is unwilling both because parts of it do not appreciate the need for change and because it is insufficiently coherent to be able to produce change between its separate fiefs. The difficulty is that rights, by themselves, will be insufficient—they will need backing up by training and by codes of practice which bridge the gaps between the fiefs involved.

In essence, a package of measures is required to accomplish the changes in the criminal justice system that are necessary to ensure that victims are informed and consulted and that information about their losses and injuries is placed before the court at the appropriate time. To be effective, this package will need to contain some justiciable rights for individual victims and/or some legally enforceable duties upon particular fiefs of the criminal justice system. That implies new legislation. More pertinently, the package should include directives, codes of practice, or circulars from Government departments to different fiefs and the promotion of training and different attitudes within fiefs.

There is only one body that can encourage the development of such a package—the same body that is able to enact its legislative elements—Parliament. But even Parliament cannot put together its own package with no other resources. There is a prior step to be taken: to produce a policy which attempts to address all the needs of victims in the context of a discussion of the balance to be struck between the needs of the various fiefs and of defendants and victims in the criminal justice system. Even the initiation of this policy will be difficult. The medieval solution to a plethora of independent fiefs was a Round Table committed to the pursuit of justice. Such a standing convention of fiefs could discuss relevant policy and likely practicalities before legislation is drafted.

The continued non-development of policy by the 'fiefs' raises another spectre: that of growing unrest by the 'peasants'—the victims—or by those who represent their interests. This unrest may, indeed, lead to the subsequent adoption of the only apparently successful formula for action within the system: in other words, the current stasis may be leading to the birth and growth of another small fief—that of victims, or of associations and people pressing on their behalf. Such a fief will have to distinguish its interests from those of other fiefs. It will become more adversarial in respect to other parties, including offenders, than the current groupings have been. The overall question is whether the English criminal justice system has within itself the ability and determination to discuss, and if necessary legislate, a package of rights, duties, and services in respect of victims before such a fief is created.

Bibliography

Ashworth, A. (1983), *Sentencing and Penal Policy*, London: Weidenfeld and Nicholson.

Baril, M., Durand, S., Cousineau, M. and Gravel, S. (1984), *Victims d'Actes Criminels: Mais Nous, les Temoins*, Canada: Department of Justice.

Bragg, C. (1986), *Meeting the Needs of Victims: Some Research Findings*, Ottawa: Ministry of the Solicitor General of Canada.

Burney, E. (1985), 'All Things to All Men: Justifying Custody under the 1982 Act'. *Criminal Law Review*, pp. 284–93.

Canadian Federal-Provincial Task Force (1983), *Justice for Victims of Crime: Report*, Ottawa: Canadian Government Publishing Centre.

Chambers, G. and Millar, A. (1983), *Investigating Sexual Assault*, Edinburgh: HMSO.

Council of Europe (1983), *European Convention on the Compensation of Victims of Violent Crimes*, Strasbourg: Council of Europe.

—— (1985), *The Position of the Victim in the Framework of Criminal Law and Procedure. Recommendation No. R(85)11*, Strasbourg: Council of Europe.

—— (1987), *Assistance to Victims and the Prevention of Victimization. Recommendation of the Council of Europe*, Strasbourg: Council of Europe.

Crown Prosecution Service (1986), *Code of Conduct for Crown Prosecutors*, London: Crown Prosecution Service.

Elias, R. (1983c), *Victims of the System*, New Brunswick: Transaction Books.

Feeney, F. (1985), 'Interdependence as a Working Concept,' in D. Moxon (ed.), *Managing Criminal Justice*, London: HMSO.

Gostin, L. (1977), *A Human Condition: Volume 2*, London: MIND.

Holmstrom, L. and Burgess, A. (1978), *The Victim of Rape: Institutional Reactions*, Chichester: John Wiley.

Kelly, D. (1982), 'Victims' Reactions to the Criminal Justice Response,' Paper delivered at the 1982 Annual Meeting of the Law and Society Association, Toronto, Canada.

Maguire, M., Vagg, J. and Morgan, R. (1985), *Accountability and Prisons: Opening Up a Closed World*, London: Tavistock.

Maguire, M. and Corbett, C. (1987), *The Effects of Crime and the Work of Victims Support Schemes*, Aldershot: Gower.

Moxon, D. (1985), *Managing Criminal Justice: A Collection of Papers*, London: HMSO.

NOVA (National Organisation for Victim Assistance) (1985), *Victim Rights and Services: A Legislative Directory*, Washington, DC: US Department of Justice.

Rock, P. (1987), 'Government, Victims and Policies in Two Countries,' *British Journal of Criminology*, Vol. 27, Autumn 1987.

Shapland, J. (1981), *Between Conviction and Sentence*, London: Routledge & Kegan Paul.

Shapland, J., Willmore, J. and Duff, P. (1985), *Victims in the Criminal Justice System*, Aldershot: Gower.

Shapland, J. and Cohen, D. (1987), 'Facilities for Victims: The Role of the Police and the Courts,' *Criminal Law Review*, (January), pp. 28–38.

Steenhuis, D. (1986), 'Coherence and Coordination in the Administration of Criminal Justice,' in J. van Dijk, C. Haffmans, F. Ruter, J. Schutte and S. Stolwijk (eds), *Criminal Law in Action*, Arnhem: Gouda Quint.

Waller, I. (1986a), 'Victima vs Regina vs Malefactor: Justice for the next 100 years' in J. Van Dijk, C. Haffmans, F. Ruter, J. Shutte and S. Stolwijk (eds), *Criminal Law in Action*, Arnhem: Gouda Quint.

—— (1986b), 'Crime Victims: Orphans of Social Policy. Needs, Services and Reforms,' in Miyazawa, K. and Minoru, O. (ed.), *Victimology in Comparative Perspective*, Tokyo: Seibundo.

Further Reading

Theoretical approaches to crime and punishment

BRAITHWAITE, JOHN, 'Shame and Modernity' (1993) 33 *British Journal of Criminology*, 1.

—— and PHILIP PETTIT, *Not Just Deserts* (Oxford University Press, 1990), chs. 4–6.

FOUCAULT, MICHEL, *Discipline and Punish: The Birth of the Prison*, tr. Alan Sheridan (Penguin, 1977), pts. II–III.

GARLAND, DAVID, *Punishment and Modern Society* (Oxford University Press, 1990), ch. 12.

HEIDENSOHN, FRANCES, 'Models of Justice: Portia or Persephone? Some Thoughts on Equality, Fairness and Gender in the Field of Criminal Justice' (1986) 14 *International Journal of the Sociology of Law* 287.

HUDSON, BARBARA, *Justice Through Punishment* (Macmillan Education, 1987), chs. 1–3.

—— *Penal Policy and Social Justice* (Macmillan, 1993).

KING, MICHAEL, *The Framework of Criminal Justice* (Croom Helm, 1981), ch. 2.

LACEY, NICOLA, *State Punishment: Political Principles and Community Values* (Routledge, 1988), chs. 1, 2, 7, 8.

MCCONVILLE, MIKE (ed.), *Criminal Justice in Crisis* (Edward Elgar, 1994).

PACKER, HERBERT L., *The Limits of the Criminal Sanction* (Stanford University Press, 1968), pt. II.

SUMNER, COLIN, 'Reflections on a Sociological Theory of Criminal Justice Systems', in Colin Sumner (ed.), *Censure, Politics and Criminal Justice* (Open University Press, 1990), 41.

WORRALL, ANNE, *Offending Women* (Routledge, 1990), ch. 2.

The media and the social construction of crime

COHEN, STANLEY, *Folk Devils and Moral Panics* (St Martin's Press, 1972).

HALL, STUART, CHAS CRITCHER, TONY JEFFERSON, JOHN CLARKE, AND BRIAN ROBERTS, *Policing the Crisis* (Macmillan Education, 1978), ch. 3.

SPARKS, RICHARD, 'Dramatic Power: Television, Images of Crime and Law Enforcement', in Colin Sumner (ed.), *Censure, Politics and Criminal Justice* (Open University Press, 1990), 123.

YOUNG, ALISON, 'Strategies of Censure and the Suffragette Movement', in Colin Sumner (ed.), *Censure, Politics and Political Justice* (Open University Press, 1990), 142.

Policing, pre-trial processes, and diversion

BALDWIN, JOHN, *Pre-trial Justice* (Basil Blackwell, 1985).

—— and MICHAEL MCCONVILLE, *Negotiated Justice* (Martin Robertson, 1977).

BOTTOMLEY, KEITH, and KEN PEASE, *Crime and Punishment: Interpreting the Data* (Open University Press, 1986), chs. 1–3.

CHRISTIAN, LOUISE, 'Restriction without Conviction', in R. Fine and R. Millar (eds.), *Policing the Miners' Strike* (Lawrence & Wishart, 1985).

HARRINGTON, CHRISTINE, 'Popular Justice, Populist Politics' (1992) 1 *Social and Legal Studies* 177.

JEFFERSON, TONY, MONICA WALKER, and MARY SENEVIRATNE, 'Ethnic Minorities, Crime and Criminal Justice: A Study in a Provincial City', in David Downes (ed.), *Unravelling Criminal Justice* (Macmillan, 1992).

JOHNSTON, LES, *The Rebirth of Private Policing* (Routledge, 1992), pts. I and III.

KING, MICHAEL, 'Social Crime Prevention a la Thatcher' (1989) *Howard Journal of Criminal Justice* 291.

LUSTGARTEN, LAURENCE, *The Governance of Police* (Sweet & Maxwell, 1986), ch. 10.

MCBARNET, DOREEN, 'It's Not What You Do but the Way that You Do It: Tax Evasion, Tax Avoidance and the Boundaries of Deviance', in D. Downes (ed.), *Unravelling Criminal Justice* (Macmillan, 1992), 247.

MCCONVILLE, MIKE, and CHESTER MIRSKY, 'Looking Through the Guilty Plea Glass' (1993) 2 *Social and Legal Studies* 173.

—— ANDREW SANDERS, and ROGER LENG, *The Case for the Prosecution* (Routledge, 1991), chs. 2 and 9.

MARSHALL, TONY, 'Out of Court: More or Less Justice?', in R. Matthews (ed.), *Informal Justice?* (Sage, 1988), 25.

PEARSON, GEOFFREY, HARRY BLAGG, DAVID SMITH, ALICE SAMPSON, and PAUL STUBBS, 'Crime, Community and Conflict: The Multi-Agency Approach', in D. Downes (ed.), *Unravelling Criminal Justice* (Macmillan, 1992), 46.

REINER, ROBERT, *The Politics of the Police* (Wheatsheaf, 1985; 2nd edn. 1993).

WEAIT, MATTHEW, 'The Letter of the Law? An Inquiry into Reasoning and Formal Enforcement in the Industrial Air Pollution Inspectorate' (1989) 29 *British Journal of Criminology* 57–70.

The trial and sentencing

ALLEN, HILARY, *Justice Unbalanced* (Open University Press, 1987), ch. 4.

ASHWORTH, ANDREW, *Sentencing and Criminal Justice* (Weidenfeld and Nicolson, 1992).

BANKOWSKI, ZENON, 'The Jury and Reality', in M. Findlay and P. Duff (eds.), *The Jury under Attack* (Butterworths, 1988), 8.

BOTTOMLEY, A. KEITH, 'Sentencing Reform and the Structuring of Pre-trial Discretion', in Ken Pease and Martin Wasik (eds.), *Sentencing Reform* (Manchester University Press, 1987), 139.

CARLEN, PAT, *Magistrates' Justice*, Martin Robertson, 1976.

—— 'Crime, Inequality and Sentencing', in Pat Carlen and Dee Cook (eds.), *Paying for Crime*, (Open University Press, 1989), 8.

EATON, MARY, *Justice for Women?* (Open University Press, 1986), ch. 2.

HOOD, ROGER, *Race and Sentencing* (Oxford University Press, 1992), chs. 1, 6, 11, 12.

KENNEDY, HELENA, *Eve was Framed* (Chatto and Windus, 1992).

LACEY, NICOLA, 'Discretion and Due Process at the Post-conviction Stage', in I. Dennis (ed.), *Criminal Law and Justice* (Sweet & Maxwell, 1987), 221.

ROCK, PAUL, 'Witnesses and Space in a Crown Court' (1991) 31 *British Journal of Criminology* 266.

SMART, CAROL, 'Law's Truth/Women's Experience', in Regina Graycar (ed.), *Dissenting Opinions* (Allen & Unwin, 1990), 1.

VON HIRSCH, ANDREW, and NILS JAREBORG, 'Guaging Criminal Harm: A Living-Standard Analysis' (1991) 11 *Oxford Journal of Legal Studies* 2.

WASIK, MARTIN, and KEN PEASE, 'Discretion and Sentencing Reform: The Alternatives', in Ken Pease and Martin Wasik (eds.), *Sentencing Reform* (Manchester University Press, 1989), 1.

Penal processes

BOTTOMS, ANTHONY E., 'Neglected Features of Contemporary Penal Systems', in D. Garland and P. Young (eds.), *The Power to Punish* (Heinemann Educational, 1983), 166.

BOYLE, JIMMY, *A Sense of Freedom* (Pan, 1977).

DOBASH, RUSSELL, R. EMERSON DOBASH, and SUE GUTTERIDGE, *The Imprisonment of Women* (Blackwell, 1986).

DOWNES, DAVID, *Contrasts in Tolerance* (Clarendon Press, 1988), ch. 7.

JEFFERSON, TONY, and MONICA WALKER, 'Ethnic Minorities in the Criminal Justice System' (1992) *Criminal Law Review* 83.

MATTHEWS, ROGER, 'Privatization in Perspective', in Roger Matthews (ed.), *Privatizing Criminal Justice* (Sage, 1989), 1.

MAWBY, R. I., 'The Voluntary Sector's Role in a Mixed Economy of Criminal Justice', in Roger Matthews (ed.), *Privatizing Criminal Justice* (Sage, 1989), 135.

PECKHAM, AUDREY, *A Woman in Custody* (Fontana, 1985).

RICHARDSON, GENEVRA, 'The Case for Prisoners' Rights', in Mike Maguire, Jon Vagg, and Rod Morgan (eds.), *Accountability and Prisons* (Tavistock, 1985), 19.

SCULL, ANDREW, 'Community Corrections: Panacea, Progress or Pretence?', in D. Garland and P. Young (eds.), *The Power to Punish* (Heinemann Educational, 1983), 146.

SIM, JOE, 'Working for the Clampdown: Prisons and Politics in England and Wales', in Phil Scraton (ed.), *Law, Order and the Authoritarian State* (Open University Press, 1987), 190.

VAGG, JON, ROD MORGAN, and MIKE MAGUIRE, 'Introduction: Accountability and Prisons', in Mike Maguire, Jon Vagg, and Rod Morgan (eds.), *Accountability and Prisons* (Tavistock 1985), 1.

Victims of crime

CHAMBERS, GERRY, and ANN MILLAR, 'Proving Sexual Assault: Prosecuting the Offender or Persecuting the Victim?', in Pat Carlen and Anne Worrall (eds.), *Gender, Crime and Justice* (Open University Press, 1987), 58.

CHRISTIE, NILS, 'Conflicts as Property' (1977) 17 *British Journal of Criminology* 1.

MIERS, DAVID, 'The Responsibilities and the Rights of Victims of Crime' (1992) 55 *Modern Law Review* 482.

MORGAN, JANE, and LUCIA ZEDNER, *Child Victims: Crime, Impact and Criminal Justice* (Oxford University Press, 1992).

SHAPLAND, JOANNA, JON WILLMORE and PETER DUFF, *Victims in the Criminal Justice System* (Gower, 1985), ch. 10.